RISK MANAGEMENT IN BANKING AND INSURANCE

RISK MANAGEMENT IN BANKING AND INSURANCE

Edited by

S.B. VERMA
Faculty of Commerce,
SNS College, Muzaffarpur,
BRA Bihar University, Muzaffarpur
Former Reader
Nagaland (Central) University, Kohima

YOGESH UPADHYAY
Reader
Institute of Commerce and Management
Jiwaji University, Gwalior

R.K. SHRIVASTAWA
Faculty Member
University Department of Commerce
BRA Bihar University, Muzaffarpur

DEEP & DEEP PUBLICATIONS PVT. LTD.
F-159, Rajouri Garden, New Delhi-110027

RISK MANAGEMENT IN BANKING AND INSURANCE

ISBN 978-81-8450-015-8

Typeset by VERONICA GRAFIC ARTS
VP-216A, Pitampura, Maurya Enclave, Delhi - 110 088

Printed in India at MAYUR ENTERPRISES
WZ Plot No. 3, Gujjar Market, Tihar Village, New Delhi - 110 018

Published by DEEP & DEEP PUBLICATIONS PVT. LTD.
F-159, Rajouri Garden, New Delhi - 110 027
Phones : 25435369, 25440916
E-mails : deep98@del3.vsnl.net.in • ddpbooks@yahoo.co.in
Showroom :
2/13, Ansari Road, Daryaganj, New Delhi -110 002 • Telefax : 23245122

Contents

PART IV: RISK IN INSURANCE SECTOR

PART V: RISK IN BANKING SECTOR

Preface

The rapidly changing, increasingly complex global economy, advent of advance electronic technologies, multiplicity of activities and our growing interdependence make larger and larger disasters. Inevitable progress has put more people, more companies at risk than ever before. Traffic multiplies on roads, in the air, and at the sea. The disasters cause death or hardship for many more people and properties than those directly involved. Defective goods can cause injury, mistakes do happen and accidents can kill or maim employees and general public. It is the intelligent assumption of risk, not its avoidance, that create value in a company. Pandit Nehru once wrote, "people avoid action often because they are afraid of the consequences for action means risk and danger." Risk is universal, present in all things, all lives, inherent in being. The concept of a person free from risk is as theoretical as the concept of perfection.

This environment has caused a basic shift in the paradigm of risk management practices, and has placed greater emphasis on the successful indentification, quantification, mitigation, control and financing of risk. Evolving concepts of risk are leading to complex management perspectives requiring an integrated view of the finances and operations of a corporation. Today's risk manager must generate a comprehensive context of risks faced by the enterprises. Risk ensures that revenue generating capacity of the asset is not affected and contributes to shareholder value in two ways on expense side as well as revenue side. It can be made as the possibility of loss arising because of uncertainty of outcome of a particular transaction.

A bank acts as an intermediary between providers of capital and those needing it. Thus, risk in any variation is the outcome. This is useful because it includes both desirable and undesirable outcomes.

Risk management starts from the proposition that risks can be measured by using some measure of variability. It is to identify, measure and more importantly monitor the risk profile of the bank. While Non-Performing Assets (NPA) are the legacy of the past in the present. It is the proactive steps taken at present for the future. It is nothing but managing the change before the risk manages everyone. Its objective is to minimise losses arising from risk exposes. The process of risk management involves the following:

- Recognition and understanding,
- Measurement, and
- Monitoring and control.

In order to effective risk management, a comprehensive risk management policy has to be formulated incorporating a detailed structure of limits and guidelines to be followed, and a strong Management Information System (MIS) build up for continuous monitoring and reporting of risk exposures. Risk faced by financial intermediaries are many and varied, viz., (a) Credit Risk, (b) Liquidity Risk, (c) Interest Rate Risk, (d) Exchange Risk, and (e) Contingency Risk. In this way, risk management is concerned with the planning, arranging and controlling of activities and resources in order to minimise the impact of uncertain events.

No organisation, especially a financial services sector entity can afford to ignore the risk in view of the implicit costs of not managing the same. Appropriate risk management not only instils confidence in the minds of investors/lenders, it also enables comparison of various institutions on a uniform parameter viz. Risk Adjusted Return on Capital (RAROC). Also, while an institution, in a bid to capitalize on the dictum of 'No Risk, No Gain', may follow very aggressive strategies and this have a very high-risk appetite, it should also keep the mitigation aspect in mind in order not to repeat the unfortunate occurences in the past.

Forex market is one of the most volatile markets where banking institutions can incur heavy losses if they do not have a 'risk management policy'. Audit of Forex transactions can establish as to whether regulatory aspects are properly complied with credit facilities at concessional rate of interest are not misused and the forex dealings are conducted in a disciplined manner. This will help the economy to build up healthy forex reserve, prevent illegal money transfers and robust industrial growth.

Insurance is the pooling of fortuitous losses by transfer of such risks to insurers, who agree to provide other pecuniary benefits on their occurance, or to render services connected with the risk. It is the transfer of financial responsibility for the risk at the point of occurence and conventionally involves the insurer in a commitment to pay. The insured is thus exchanging the uncertain cost of losses for certain and known cost of the premium. The insurance services lead to efficient and productive allocation of capital resources, facilitate growth of trade and commerce. Substitute for governments social security programmes and assist individuals and firms in efficient management of risks. The insurance market may tremendously as India represents huge untapped market. However, globalisation will certainly increase insurance penetration and all professionals shall equip themselves to exploit the opportunities offered by this sector.

The insurance sector plays a very vital role in the process of economic development of any country. It acts as mobiliser of savings, as financial intermediary, as promoter of investment activities, as stabilizer of financial markets and as a risk manager. Insurance services lead to efficient and productive allocation of capital resources facilitate growth of trade and commerce, substitute for government's social security programmes, and assist individuals and firms in efficient management of risks. Post 9/11 the Chief Executive Officers (CEOs) of major companies world over have realised the need for adequate insurance in all perceptible areas affecting their firms.

The insurance operations in India are in the phase of getting more structured and increasingly more complex. With this the expectations from the professionals have also increased. The financial statements and audit reports of the insurance companies are also required to be strictly in accordance with the Insurance Regulatory and Development Authority Act, 1999 (IRDA).

Concerted efforts are required to increase the coverage and penetration level through a wide range of actions in the areas of strategic business planning, product innovation, management accountability, efficiency in investment management, technology management, human resource management, service quality management, improvement in disclosures and corporate governance.

Many contributors, writers and people who have helped to shape the venture to whom I (Dr. S.B. Verma) thank immensely. I am highly obliged to my wife late Dr. Hema Verma, Deputy Collector, who encouraged me to do the pursuit.

I would like to articulate my deep sense of gratitude to my father late Baban Pd. Srivastawa, Additional District Magistrate as well as my father-in-law late Harinandan Pd. Verma, Deputy Collector and my mother late Mrs. Lalmuni whose invisible soul inspired me to carry out the project.

The Editors-*cum*-anthologists are thankful to the *Chartered Accountant, Yojana, Kurukshetra, Employment News, IBA Bulletin, Journal of Indian Institute of Bankers*, and other journals for giving their permission to reprint the articles published by them.

The book will undoubtedly be useful for various segments of society as a whole.

Muzaffarpur EDITORS

List of Contributors

A.K. Trivedi: Assistant General Manager, The Vysya Bank Ltd., Mumbai.

Anil Chandra Pathak: University Deptt. of Commerce and Business Administration, T.M. Bhagalpur University, Bhagalpur.

A.S. Rajeev: Consultant, Risk Management.

Barun Kumar Gosh: Member, ICAI, New Delhi.

B. Ratna Ravi Kumar: Member, ICAI, New Delhi.

Chitta Ranjan Sarkar: Member, ICAI, New Delhi.

Gopal Prasad Dokania: Member, ICAI, New Delhi.

Hena Naqvi: Freelance Jounalist.

H. Sadhak: Director, L.I.C. of India, Management Development Centre, Mumbai.

Joseph T. Wells: Professor at the University of Texas, Austin, U.S.A.

Kanchana Khanna: Senior Manager, MIS Cell, MASD, Head Office, PND, New Delhi.

K. Parameswaran: Assistant Professor, S.P. Jain Institute of Management and Research.

K.V. Mallik: Chief Officer, Treasury and Investment Management, UCO Bank, Calcutta.

Manish Kumar Jain: Member, ICAI, New Delhi.

Mrutyunjaya Padhan: Deputy Manager (Risk Management), State Bank of Hyderabad, Hyderabad.

Narendra M. Apte: Member, ICAI, New Delhi.

N.D. Gupta: Chairman, Prefessional Development Committee, ICAI, New Delhi.

Niall S.K. Booker: M.A., M.LL. (Cambridge University), U.K.; Chief Executive Officer, HSBC, Mumbai; Member of RBI Technical Advisory Committee; Vice-chairman, Indian Bankers' Association; Member, Managing Committee, Bombay Chamber of Commerce; Chairman, Indo-British Business Committee and Industry; Chieftain, Bombay Caledonian Society.

N. Jeyaseelan: Project Manager, Indian Bank's Special Unit for Micro Finance.

P.P. Pathrose: Senior Manager, The Federal Bank Ltd., Regional Office, Mumbai.

Prabhat Singhal: Consultant in Risk Management.

P.V. Subba Rao: Consultant, Risk Management.

Ravi Kumar Shrivastawa: Reader, University Department of Commerce, BRA Bihar University, Muzaffarpur.

R.C. Guria: Member, ICAI, New Delhi.

R.S. Raghavan: Member, ICAI, New Delhi, Senior Manager (Risk Management), Vijaya Bank, Head Office, Bangalore.

R.S. Raghavan: Senior Manager, Risk Management Department, Vijaya Bank, H.O., Bangalore.

Sam Ghosh: Chief Executive Officer, Bajaj Allianz Life Insurance Company Ltd.

Sawalia Bihari Verma: Professor, Faculty of Commerce, SNS College, Muzaffarpur, BRA Bihar University, Muzaffarpur, Bihar. Former Reader, Nagaland (Central) University, Kohima.

S.B. Singh: Consultant, Risk and Profitability.

Shiv Kumar Singh: Reader, Institute of Commerce and Management, Jiwaji University, Gwalior.

Shyam Ramadhyani: Member, ICAI, New Delhi.

S.K. Bagchi: Member, ICAI, New Delhi.

Suvendu Bose: Consultant, Risk Management.

Vishnu Kanhere: Member, ICAI, New Delhi.

V. Ramaswamy: Senior Manager, IRMD, Syndicate Bank, Bangalore.

V. Sreeraman: Member, ICAI, New Delhi.

V.V. Kamath: Managing Director, Canbank Venture Capital Fund Ltd., Bangalore.

Yogesh Upadhyay: Reader in Management, Jiwaji University, Gwalior. Ex Faculty Member, Prestige Institute of Management. Ex Chairman Library and Comptroller. Ex Dean, Faculty of Commerce, MGCG University, Chitrakoot. Participant, FDP Programme, IIM Ahmedabad.

Y. Srinivas: Manager, Compliance and Audit Group, ICICI Bank, Mumbai.

PART I

CONCEPT OF RISK MANAGEMENT

1

Risk Management: The Banking Perspective

PRABHAT SINGHAL

Hotmail Guru Sabeer Bhatia says, "The biggest risk in life is to take no risk at all". Thus, to undertake any venture, trade or business, one has to have some risk appetite. However, the risk one actually takes has to be a calculated risk and one must also simultaneously adopt suitable measures for mitigation of the risk so calculated. This is what can be a concise definition of Risk Management.

WHAT IS RISK?

The term 'risk' in literal sense would mean exposure to possible harm, loss or injury. The nature and extent of such harm, loss or injury would, however, depend significantly on the nature of business in question. For instance, when related to an industrial activity, the harm may be physical in nature while in relation to an occupation involving higher degree of mental exercise; the same may be more of psychological in nature. However, one loss, which is omnipresent in all business/activities, irrespective of their nature and size, is the monetary loss. Such pecuniary loss may arise from a multitude of exposures or circumstances that, again, are peculiar to the particular business in question.

WHY RISK MANAGEMENT?

Even after having understood the concept of risk and having

perceived the various risks involved in a particular business, one may tend to argue as to the very need of risk management, especially in view of the cost implications. However, on a close study of the issue, one may eventually find that the cost of not managing the risk can, at times, be larger than that of managing it. The securities scam in India and the high incidence of Non-performing Assets in financial organisations are a few cases in point where ignoring the risk resulted in high cost implications for the economy as a whole. Further, proper risk management while enabling meaningful comparison or risk-adjusted business performance across the entities and industries, also yields higher returns for the investors/ other stakeholders and thus creates value for the shareholders.

RISK MANAGEMENT: THE BANKING PERSPECTIVE

Having understood the definition and genesis of the term, we may like to look at the risk management exercise from a banking perspective, which has been gaining considerable momentum for some time and which has a profound impact on the entire economy as a whole.

The business of banking which, as per the statute, means "acceptance, for the purposes of lending, deposits . . ." is indeed a business built on risk. While the definition of banking as per the statute, which is the narrowest meaning assigned to the term, itself reflects a number of risks inherent in the business, the actually horizon of banking in today's world encompasses much greater and larger risks.

To enumerate a few, the risks in banking business could be credit risk, interest rate risk, foreign exchange risk, liquidity risk, pricing risk, portfolio risk, country risk and risks related to legal and regulatory issues. The globalisation of financial markets further increases the vulnerability of all players. Besides, with the increasing computerization of the banking industry, a new factor to enter the list, last but certainly not the least, is security risk.

It would thus be appreciated that true business of banking, unlike most of the other businesses, require proper and timely identification of risks (not only in a particular transaction but also for the business as a whole), precise calculation/ measurement of such risks and building appropriate systems and internal controls to ensure mitigation of such risks at all times.

It may also be pertinent to note that as banking is a business built on risk, the concept of risk management cannot be said to be a new concept, as such risk management would have existed in some form or the other from the very beginning, without which it would not have been possible for the business to survive. Thus, the greater emphasis being presently laid down is only due to higher degree of sophistication that has been brought into the business.

It is in thought of the so highly pronounced need for risk management in banking that Reserve Bank of India issued a Guidance Note on Credit Risk Management in September 2001. However, the Guidance Note deals with only one of the various risks involved in banking viz. Credit Risk. Though a number of other risks can be said to be indirectly covered in the said Guidance Note (in view of their having a direct or indirect bearing on credit risk), a host of other risks like 'Security Risk' have not been touched upon by the Guidance Note issued by Reserve Bank of India.

Shri N.R. Narayana Murthy, Chairman and Chief Mentor of Infosys Technologies while addressing a FICCI banking conference on "Global Banking – Paradigm Shift" in Bangalore has said, "Only those banks which use **speed, imagination and excellence** in execution will survive. Others will disappear like dew in the morning. . . . The individual banks should adopt a strategy to have uniqueness in market place. . . . There is an urgent need for Indian banks to bring in innovation to have tremendous flexibility, next practices and best practices".[1]

The imagination, excellence, uniqueness and innovation, referred to above, for a banking industry player would appear to include not only innovative products and uniqueness in service but also imagination as to the best possible risk management systems to be built in order to have the competitive advantage which a pro-active rather than a defensive risk management strategy offers.

The financial markets have opened up in recent times in a number of ways. Needless to mention, the same is accompanied by concomitant risks. The developments, which are relatively more important from the viewpoint of risk management, are deregulation (of interest rates as well as the sector as a whole), the consequent volatility in markets, opening up of the banking sector for private players resulting in increased competition and ever changing portfolios. Further, higher reliance on private capital due to dwindling government support and improved corporate governance practices have together led to coming up of a new breed of well-informed and demanding investors. All these factors have brought to the fore a host of new risks which have been, time and again, attracting attention of the institutions.

As said above, the risks in banking (financial services) industry could be multifarious in nature. Of the various such risks, *one of the most important risks, which is common to all constituents of the financial services industry is Credit Risk.*

Credit Risk is basically the risk of default of the counterparty to meet its commitments. The same may arise out of both—the inability as well as unwillingness—of the counterparty (viz. the borrower, in banking parlance) to meet the commitments (obligations). In other words, it encompasses both genuine default as well as wilful default.

There are two broad determinants of credit risk viz. Default Risk (as discussed above) and Portfolio Risk. Portfolio Risk, in turn, comprises Intrinsic Risk and Concentration Risk. While the Intrinsic risk denotes the risk inherent in certain products/areas (like Venture Capital or Foreign Currency denominated exposures, concentration risk refers to the skewness of the portfolio towards certain high risk sectors. The concentration risk also denotes the risk arising at the group level in a financial conglomerate. Thus, we may say:

> Credit Risk = Default Risk + (Intrinsic Risk + Concentration Risk).

Where the last 2 variables in the equation add up to Portfolio Risk, after adjusting for diversification which acts as a mitigant for the said risk.

Besides, another important component of credit risk is the risk of loss of valuation arising due to downgrade of rating and associated losses, which is defined in banking jargon as 'Mark to Market' (MTM) Risk.

Once we have understood the credit risk obtaining in banking/ lending business, the next question which comes to one's mind could be as to the method of management of the credit risk. The risk management process in banking industry on the following lines:

IDENTIFICATION

This is the initial stage of understanding the peculiarities of the business and nuances of the trade and thus deducing the various risks that may arise out at the same. In banking sector, depending upon the coverage at operations of the particular entity, the various risks may be credit risk, interest rate risk, foreign exchange risk, liquidity risk, pricing risk, portfolio risk, country risk, security risk and risks related to legal and regulatory issues. A layman, on looking at the list, may often be misled to conclude that it may neither be feasible nor practical to measure and mitigate these many risks. However, what is important to understand is that while almost all the risks are present in all businesses, the actual measurement or mitigation would relate to the risks that dominate the others and ignoring of which may have material adverse effects. It should, however, not be concluded that the less dominant risks need be absolutely ignored. The only intent behind the exercise is to take up the important ones first and then providing for the remaining ones so that the whole exercise remains manageable.

As mentioned above, the risks obtaining in financial services industry could be multifarious in nature. However, the exact nature and extent of risks would depend on the sub-set in which the particular entity in question operates, i.e. whether it is a bank or a financial institution or an NBFC (Non-Banking Financial Company). For example, a financial institution, unlike a commercial bank, does not accept demand deposits but operates primarily out of resources borrowed from the various national/multilateral investors/lenders and selectively through term deposits (like Suvidha Deposits of IDBI [now IDBI Ltd.]). The resources thus borrowed are on-lent to various entities as per mandate given by the controlling authority—be it Government or the various investors/lenders. Thus, the liabilities of a financial institution are generally medium and long-term in nature. To that extent, risk of Asset-Liability mismatch in a financial institution is not as pronounced as in a commercial bank. However, as the funds borrowed by a financial institution are committed for medium/long-term, it is posed with the risk of not being able to reinvest/recycle the funds at the desired return, which acts as the major mismatch risk for the institution. Similarly, depending upon the profile of liabilities and exposures, foreign exchange risk, country risk, etc. may or may not be relevant for a particular entity. However, since in our present discussion, the most dominating risk, which has far-reaching implications, has already been identified (i.e. Credit Risk), let us confine our discussion to Credit Risk.

MEASUREMENT

Measurement would primarily involve deciding on the critical parameters and development of suitable methodologies for evaluating the risk adjusted performance (Risk Adjusted Return on Capital, i.e. RAROC), effectiveness of risk management systems and judging the desirability of continuing the mitigation measures since adopted. For instance, in a trading business, the critical parameters could be incidence of bad debts, geographical concentration of bad debts, sensitivity analysis with respect to the fluctuations in prices, political and economic stability of the major markets, etc. Suitable methodology for evaluation could, thus, be inter-firm comparisons, y-o-y growth, analyzing the proportion of sales to high-risk markets.

The key parameters, which could be identified for judging the efficacy of the risk management system in a particular bank/ financial institution, could be sufficiency of capital to cover the assets (exposure), rate of recovery/ incidence of devolvement of non-fund-based exposures, non-settlement of securities, non-repatriation of funds in case of cross-border exposures, overall profitability, etc. The same is, however, only an inclusive list and additional factors could be considered depending upon the nature of business.

The aforesaid key parameters could be quantified and reflected in the measurement units and compared/analysed as given below:

MITIGATION

Mitigation covers actually instituting the control systems and establishing trigger points that, in turn, put the immediate action in play. Such systems would consistently ensure that the risk actually being taken by the organization does not cross the desired risk appetite. For instance, a financial institution/ intermediary may like to put in place exposure norms for various industries, set-up an Asset Liability Committee (ALCO) for proper liquidity management, enter into various hedging positions to cover foreign exchange-related risks, decide the areas not to be assisted (negative list) and decide on the maximum extent of off-balance sheet exposures like contingent liabilities. These trigger points may be well related to the overall broad parameters identified at the second stage, i.e. measurement. To illustrate, ignorance of any of the aforesaid trigger points may eventually have a significant bearing on the level of standard assets or capital adequacy.

Parameter	*Measurement Unit (Quantification)*	*Evaluation Methodology*
Sufficiency of capital	Capital Adequacy Ratio	Compliance with RBI guidelines
Rate of Recovery	Percentage of Non-Performing Assets [Further sub-classified as per RBI guidelines]	Comparison with industry averages
Incidence of devolvement of non-fund-based exposures	Delinquency Ratio	Comparison with other players in the industry
Non-settlement of Securities	Delinquency Ratio	Comparison with other players in the industry
Non-Repatriation of funds in case of cross-border exposures	Hedging Positions, Uncovered exposures and Sensitivity Analysis	Analysis with reference to surveys and studies
Overall Profitability	Margins (Average Rate of Return minus Average Cost of Capital)	Year on Year Growth and further analysis with reference to Profit Centre concept

Before discussing in detail this part of risk management from the banking perspective, let us first have a look at 2 important issues, which are pertinent to the subject.

RISK MANAGEMENT/RISK AVERSION

1. Credit-Risk Conflict

In today's world where not only the private sector entities but the public sector institutions are also working in a target-driven environment, there is always a possible but avoidable conflict between the two diverse ends of credit performance (portfolio build up, achievement of targets) and risk management (containment of risk). While the credit targets keep on pushing towards aggressive approach, the risk management aspect compels for being conservative. However, an intensive analysis of the study would reveal that the aforesaid conflict, which is perceived more often than not, is unwarranted.

To ensure proper risk management without compromising on credit performance, one has to ensure that no short cuts could be followed in credit processes. In a bid to achieve the targets laid down for a particular responsibility centre, it cannot afford to circumvent the procedures laid down for risk mitigation (appraisal mechanism). At the same time, overemphasis on risk management should not act as a de-motivator for credit performance. Thus, one has to strike a balance between the said two aspects in line with 'Risk-Return Trade Off'. Credit Risk conflict may be better understood with the following matrix:

High		
	LOW CREDIT HIGH RISK INCOMPETENCE	HIGH CREDIT HIGH RISK AGGRESSION
Risk	LOW CREDIT LOW RISK RISK AVERSION	HIGH CREDIT LOW RISK RISK MANAGEMENT
Low	Credit	High

As would be seen from the above matrix, there can be four possible scenarios for an institution, viz. Risk Aversion (where the institution in order to avoid the risks becomes conservative and thus credit remains on a lower side), Aggression (where the institution is quite bullish, it generally has a high risk appetite and follows very aggressive strategies, often ignoring the aspect of risk mitigation), incompetence (where the credit officers lack suitable training and thus credit, though on a lower side, entails high risk) and Risk Management (where high credit is achieved while sustaining lower levels of risk). *It may also* be *mentioned that the last mentioned scenario could also* be *attained by deploying the funds in very low-risk investment avenues like G-Secs. However, the same could not be considered as Risk Management.*

RISK MANAGEMENT: COMPLIANCE WITH STATUTORY GUIDELINES

1. Risk Management vis-a-vis Compliance with Statutory Guidelines

Risk Management cannot be looked at as a synonym for mere compliance with statutory guidelines laid down by the regulatory authorities like Reserve Bank of India. While the guidelines prescribed by the regulator are also aimed at avoidance of the various industry constituents getting exposed to unwarranted/inordinately high levels of risk, it is not practically feasible to provide for each possible risk as each constituent of the industry has its own peculiarities. The regulator could only provide for the risks inherent in the system (referred to as 'systemic risks').

Therefore, merely by complying with the statutory guidelines, an organization institutes control systems providing only for a part of the risks (viz. systemic risks) and not for other risks (which may often be equally important), which are peculiar to the particular organization (referred to as institutional risks).

An indicative list of the various control systems and trigger points requiring immediate action as also the mitigation measures, which could be followed by a bank/financial institution is given below:

Control Systems	Delegation of Powers, Loan Review Mechanism, ALCO, Negative List, separate Risk Management Committee, Portfolio Behaviour, Review of Loan Policies, monitoring of potential NPAs.
Trigger Points	Exposure Norms, Deposit Mix, Credit Rating, Unexpected loan, loss levels, Expected Loan loss reserve, Classification of Degrees of Risk, Valuation of Loans.
Mitigation Measures	Risk Pricing, Hedging, Income Mix, Fixed Floating Rates, Stress Testing, Sensitivity Analysis.

As would be observed from the above, the institution may establish one or more of the control systems given above to ensure that the risk profile at any given point of time is in line with the desired risk appetite. For example, the document laying down the Delegation of Powers may prescribe the authority at various levels of organizational hierarchy and the Asset Liability Committee may look at the liquidity and asset-liability mismatch aspects. These two systems together partly provide for the credit risk and liquidity risk. Similarly, a separate but single committee may be constituted to look at various risks arising out of the business and laying down suitable mitigation measures to be followed by the credit team. Prescribing a negative list (sectors/regions not to be assisted/assisted only with special approvals) also operates as a control point. The Committee may also study the portfolio behaviour across the industries/geographical regions and thereafter decide exposure levels for each such industry/ sector/ region, which, in turn, can operate as a trigger point.

Other trigger points could be unexpected loan loss levels (risk appetite quantified), expected loan loss reserve/ risk fund (to meet the losses arising out of various sub-sets of portfolio) and periodic valuation of loans (and deciding the benchmark, i.e. the floor limit for valuation of portfolio).

As *additional parameters* for *risk mitigation*, an institution may use the following tools:

1. *Risk Pricing*

This essentially means pricing of products in accordance with the risk entailed/ credit rating/ probability of default, whereby the risk premium or a part thereof could go to the risk fund. The institution may devise suitable models for rating of the account to assess the degree of risk involved and pricing in accordance therewith.

2. *Income Mix*

In order to ensure optimum utilization of resources and appropriate maintenance of risk levels, an institution may decide the desirable income mix. For instance, it may like to earn at least a certain percentage (say 20-25 per cent) of the total income by way of fee-based income.

3. *Hedging*

The institution having foreign currency denominated exposures may opt for suitable hedging to cover the risks (forward/ options contracts) and may, therefore, decide upon the level of unhedged exposures or the extent of forex exposure to units having no natural hedge, which may operate as trigger points.

4. *Stress Testing*

As a tool of financial modelling, the institution may carry out stress testing of a unit applying for a product (loan product) against various adverse scenarios to assess its resilience against such unforeseen contingencies.

The above is, however, again only an indicative list highlighting a few of the various risk mitigation measures, which may be used by a financial sector entity.

Evaluation

Evaluation means not only ascertaining the effectiveness of the various systems instituted at the third stage (viz. control systems and trigger points) in maintaining satisfactory performance as judged on the parameters identified at the second stage but also judging the need for any addition to or deletion from the list of parameters/methodologies decided at the second stage. For example, after carrying on the operations on the above lines for some time, one may find that the Rating Model (*control system*) being used by the institution has not been able to contain the risk to a considerable extent and even the applications entailing high risk are not captured by the system with the result of low recovery in such cases leading to higher NPAs (*identified parameter*). Thus, the rating model would thus need to be fine-tuned in order to capture high-risk cases and ensure that the rating reflects correct degree of risk involved.

Strategizing

Strategizing includes strategizing of both – the systems as well as the organization. Strategizing of the systems at this stage may be, more often than not, confused with the exercise done at the mitigation stage. There is actually a thin line of demarcation between the two. While the strategies decided at the mitigation stage are relatively short-term in nature, which need continuous improvement and time testing at frequent intervals, the same to be done at this stage has a broader canvass and the strategies are relatively long-term in nature. Intervention with the same is considered only when the circumstances warrant urgent action or a material unintended adversity results from such strategies. For instance, strategizing of the systems at this stage may involve modification in the tolerance limit (desired level of risk appetite), drastic changes in the rating models, change in methods of risk pricing, enhancement/reduction in exposure cap on high risk areas like Venture Capital, substantial variations in portfolio mix (investment pattern), re-orientation of approach to internal auditing, etc.

Strategizing of the organization, on the other hand, has a much larger perspective in the sense that it aims at bringing fundamental changes in the organization and imbibing the requisite culture into the very foundation of the organization. It may cover, for instance, re-engineering the Delegation of Powers, training of the personnel for risk management, formation of a separate Risk Management Group with suitable sub-committees to look at various risks, putting in place a Disaster Recovery Team, etc.

The above five stages are, however, unending and enduring in nature, actually forming a *continuous cycle. Risk Management is, therefore, not* a *task to be accomplished but an ongoing and constant exercise.*

Besides the credit risk management, a number of other risks also arise out of the business processes that may also be important to address. However, as mentioned earlier, in order that the entire exercise remains manageable, it is advisable to address the various risks in order of degree of their impact on the operations of the organization.

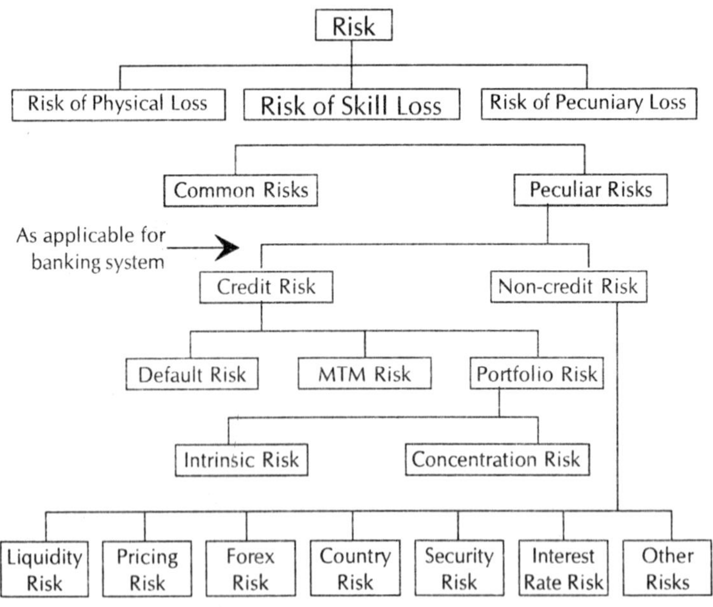

FIG. 1.1

SUMMING UP

It would thus be seen that no organization, especially a financial services sector entity, can afford to ignore the risk in view of the implicit costs of not managing the same. Appropriate risk management not only instils confidence in the minds of investors/ lenders, it also enables comparison of various institutions on a uniform parameter, viz. Risk Adjusted Return on Capital (RAROC). Also, while an institution, in a bid to capitalize on the dictum of 'No Risk, No Gain', may follow very aggressive strategies and thus have a very high-risk appetite, it should also keep the mitigation aspect in mind in order not to repeat the unfortunate occurrences in the past.

The belief expressed by the Hotmail Guru may be correct in the sense of risk-taking ability being a pre-requisite for being a successful entrepreneur, his statement may not be misunderstood to conclude that one may take rash business decisions without providing for the unwarranted results.

NOTE AND REFERENCE

1. Source: *Business Line*, September 17, 2004.

2

Risk Management in Micro Finance

N. JEYASEELAN

INTRODUCTION

In this era of globalization, even though many developments take place from time to time, the problem of poverty remains as an important issue in many parts of the world. Poverty blocks the access of the poor to the productive resources like education, health, nutrition, training, credit, market and technology. In 2000, the United Nations declared the Millennium Development Goals (MDG) and the first goal is to halve the proportion of people below the poverty line from the present level by 2015. Of late, the Micro finance is emerging as a poverty reduction and empowerment tool, which has made a visible impact in the lives of the poor women members of the Self-Help Groups (SHGs) in rural India.

In India, NABARD launched the pilot project of SHG—bank linkage program in 1992 and the RBI evolved a supportive policy framework and created an enabling atmosphere for the growth of the micro-finance sector. In the last few years, the growth of SHGs has been spectacular and the SHG credit off-take from the banks has gained momentum, which is evident from Table 2.1 presented on next page. Up to 31st March, 2005, the banks in India, have credit linked 15,97,804 SHGs, disbursed Rs. 68,666 million as SHG loans through 35,294 bank branches and benefited 119.8 million poor.

The phenomenal growth in the micro-finance sector has thrown

TABLE 2.1

SHG Bank Linkage in India—Cumulative Progress

Sl. No.	*Up to March end*	*No.of SHGs financed*	*Growth over last year (%)*	*Bank loan disbursed (Rs. in Million)*	*Growth over last year (%)*
1.	2000-01	2,63,825	129.86	4,809	149.17
2.	2001-02	4,61,478	74.92	10,263	113.41
3.	2002-03	7,17,360	55.45	20,487	99.62
4.	2003-04	10,79,091	50.43	39,042	90.57
5.	2004-05	15,97,804	48.07	68,666	75.88

Source: MCID, NABARD, Mumbai.

up a lot of challenges to all the stakeholders and these challenges need to be tackled by taking concerted actions at various levels. These challenges of growth expose the banks to varying levels of risks. The banks are preparing themselves for complying with the Basel II norms and every bank is putting in place a risk management system. Under this context, the risk management in Micro-finance assumes significance.

DESIGN OF THE STUDY

Objectives

The study has the following objectives:

- To identify the potential risk factors associated with SHG-Bank linkage.
- To analyze the risk perception of the Branch Managers on SHG lending.
- To classify the risk factors into High, Medium and Low risk categories.
- To offer suggestions for risk mitigation measures.

Methodology

The present study is based on both the primary and secondary data. The primary data has been collected from 68 Branch Managers (35 from Madurai District and 33 from other districts) of commercial

Banks, who implement the SHG Bank linkage program in Madurai, Dindigul, Sivaganga, Ramanathapuram and Theni districts. Focus Group Discussions have been held to elicit the views from the Branch Managers. Non-Government Organizations (NGOs) and NABARD officials on emerging risks at the SHG and NGO level. Ten risk factors have been short-listed and a 5 point likert scale was constructed for collecting the data from the branch managers of commercial banks. The questionnaire was pre-tested and used in the study. The study was carried out during January-July 2005. The secondary data was collected through a review of related literature on the topic and from the Assistant General Manager of NABARD, Madurai, and from MCID, NABARD at Chennai and Mumbai. Statistical tools like frequencies, percentages, mean, standard deviation and a 5 point likert scale has been used to analyze the data collected and conclusions have been drawn.

Risk Management

Risk is inherent in SHG lending, where no collaterals are taken. Risk management aims at identifying the risks, measuring them, evolving strategies for risk mitigation, implementing the strategies and monitoring the risk. Micro-finance portfolio is exposed to the Credit risk and Operational risk. Credit risk is the possibility of losses associated with diminution in the credit quality of the SHGs or NGOs as the case may be. Operational risk is the risk of loss resulting from inadequate or failed internal processes, people and systems or from external events. E.g. SHG leader commits a fraud and uses a SHG Bank loan proceeds of another member for her use. The credit risks and operational risks which are bound to be prominent at the SHG and NGO level, have been looked into in depth from the implementing branch manager's perception.

Analysis

The categorization has been done using the Mean and Standard Deviation for each factor and given in the following Table 2.2.

FINDINGS

From Table 2.2, it is observed that out of ten risk factors identified, 6

TABLE 2.2

Risk Perception on SHG Lending by Branch Managers

Sl. No.	Risk Factors	High risk		Medium risk		Low risk	
		No.	%	No.	%	No.	%
1.	Lack of Monitoring of SHGs by NGOs	–	–	54	79.40	14	20.60
2.	Reduction in grants to NGOs for group promotion	4	5.90	52	76.50	12	17.60
3.	Frequent switch over of NGO Field staff	14	20.60	44	64.70	10	14.70
4.	Quality of Human resources of NGO	–	–	58	85.30	10	14.70
5.	Maintenance of Group A/cs by a few and not transparent	25	36.80	25	36.80	18	26.40
6.	Dual financing as members join more than one SHG	–	–	59	86.80	9	13.20
7.	Dependence on a single SHG leader for a long time	–	–	58	85.30	10	14.70
8.	Loan size not commensurate with the capacity of SHG members	13	19.10	43	63.20	12	17.70
9.	Increasing possibility for loan default with increase in loan size	7	10.30	56	82.40	5	7.30
10.	SHGs shouldering too much Government program responsibilities beyond their capacity	18	26.40	37	54.50	13	19.10

risk factors have emerged as High risk category factors as per the perception of the Branch managers. The risk factors are dealt in detail herein below.

Lack of Monitoring of SHGs by NGOs

NGOs assist the banks in monitoring the credit linked SHGs. In the earlier years of SHG-Bank linkage program implementation, a NGO field staff supervised 15 to 20 SHGs on an average. Hence, the supervision of SHGs was close. But, now each field staff looks after around 50 to 80 SHGs. In most of the cases, the field staff could not attend the group meetings even once in two or three months. As a result, the branch managers who act on the feedback from these field staff could not know the early warning signals and not able to nip the SHG problems in the bud. This has resulted in poor monitoring of the SHGs. Over a period of time, poor monitoring will lead to non-performing SHGs as well as to non-performing assets in the SHG loan portfolio. This factor has not been viewed as a High risk category.

Reduction in Grants to NGOs for Group Promotion

NGOs received the group promotion grants from do not agencies and governments and provided exclusive staff for looking after the SHG program. But, of late, group promotion grants have been reduced substantially which have forced the NGOs to drop their program staff and they manage the SHGs with a small team of their core staff. As a result, the capacity building inputs are not available to the SHGs on an ongoing basis, after bank credit linkage and the growth of SHGs towards sustainability is at stake. Still many of the rural households are under the clutches of the moneylenders and they need to be brought to the bank's fold and unless adequate group promotion grants are available to the NGOs, they can not enlarge their outreach to reach the unreached poor with bank credit. It is found that 5.90 per cent of the Branch Managers consider this as a High risk factor.

Frequent Switch over of NGO Field Staff

Many NGOs face this problem of switch over of field staff from one

NGO to another. Due to this, continuity in the SHG program to implementation is affected. Some branch managers are found hesitant to lend to those SHGs promoted by such NGOs which have the staff turnover problem. This risk factor is deemed as High risk factor by 20.60 per cent of branch managers.

Quality of Human Resources of NGOs

SHG's performance is directly proportional to the level of capacity building inputs received by the SHGs from the dedicated and knowledgeable NGO staff. Normally, the NGO field Staff are well versed in social skills and lack exposure in management concepts. Some NGOs recruit professionals, who may be good at management capability but not aware of participatory processes-based development approaches. Inadequate investment in quality of human resources of NGOs will affect the quality of SHGs promoted and thereby the credit absorption capacity of SHGs will be limited. Branch Managers have not perceived this risk as a High risk factor.

Maintenance of Group A/cs

It is always desirable that the Group Accounts writing is known to at least 4 or 5 members of the group. Generally, the Group Accounts of SHGs are maintained by the SHG leaders. As substantial portion of the members of SHGs are illiterate, in most SHGs, only one person keeps the accounts. Such groups are prone for fraud. After fraud, the SHGs become defunct and the bank credit to such SHGs become sticky. It is observed that 36.80 per cent of the branch managers rate this factor as a High risk factor.

Dual Financing to Members

As more than one NGO operate in villages, where there is more concentration of SHGs, the SHG members have a chance to become members in more than one SHG. There is a possibility for these members to receive two loans from the bank through two different SHGs. As the banks are exposed to face the risk of dual financing, to the same member, the credit risk is more in such cases. It is noted that the Branch Managers have not viewed this risk as a High risk factor.

Dependence on a Single SHG Leader

Even though SHGs have a rule that once in two or three years, their leaders should be changed. In many SHGs, it is a common phenomena that the same leader continues as the SHG leader for years together and no other member of the group is not willing to take the responsibility for succession. As a result, such leaders become autocratic and the members involvement in decision-making is reduced. So, there is a possible risk of misuse of bank loan allocation to a selected few, who are close to the leaders. This risk is not a high risk factor as per the perception of the branch managers.

Loan Size not Commensurate with SHG Capacity

In case of subsidized loans to SHGs like SGSY—Economic assistance, it is found that the SHG loan size is found bigger as Rs. 3 lakhs or Rs. 4 lakhs and not commensurate with the management capacity of the SHGs and as well as with entrepreneurial capacity of the SHG members. It is observed that 19.10 percent of the branch managers consider this risk as High risk category.

Possibility for Loan Default *vs.* Loan Size

In SHG lending, the peer pressure is the collateral. This works well in loans of smaller sizes. In the second, third or fourth time of repeat loans taken by SHGs, only a few members (active borrowers with an entrepreneurial spirit) take a larger pie of the loan and the rest of the group even fear to exert the peer pressure against the few. In such a situation, when the per member loan size is above Rs. 50,000 or more, the possibility of loan default increases. It is inferred that 10.30 per cent of the branch managers rated this risk as a High risk category.

SHGs shouldering too much Government Program Responsibilities beyond their Capacity

As the SHGs have proved themselves that they are very effective delivery units, many Government departments have come forward to route their programs/services through the SHGs (e.g. SHGs running the Fair price-ration shops, SHGs maintaining the sanitary complex). This has added burden to the SHGs and sometimes even led to the collapse of the groups as needed management capacity of SHGs was not built up simultaneously. SHG is not a panacea for all rural problems. It is found that 26.40 per cent of the branch managers viewed this risk as a high risk category.

Risk Mitigation Measures and Suggestions

The following are the risk mitigation measures suggested to manage the risks in a prudent way in SHG lending.

- Banks should ensure that only a part of the group shares the SHG Bank loan (and the loan not shared by all members) at any given point of time so as to maintain the peer pressure.
- Banks should encourage the SHGs to take short-term loans (of 8 months, 10 months and 12 months periods) initially and build a credit history in the bank.
- Banks should give the repeat loans to the SHGs within a short period, which will reinforce the message to others that once the SHG closes the loan, they will get the next higher loan quickly.
- Banks shall ask the SHGs to take up a restructuring exercise after each loan and before the release of the subsequent loan, which will add to the stability of the group (i.e. removing any member if they violated any rules in the previous loan cycle or changing the leader if required).
- After 2 or 3 successful loan repayments, when an individual member of a SHG wants a larger loan of above Rs. 50,000 in a SHG bank loan, such cases may be migrated by the banks separately and considered under the Individual loan schemes.
- Banks should ensure that the SHG loan disbursement reaches the ultimate SHG members in a transparent way.
- Banks shall encourage the SHG members to come to the bank in rotation every month.
- Banks may put in place a MIS, that will supply the required extensive data on SHGs lending for the better risk management.
- For SHG loans of above Rs. 2 lakh categories, Banks shall

rate the groups every year on an ongoing basis and can offer risk-based pricing to such matured SHGs.

- Banks shall offer Micro insurance products to the SHGs in tie up with the insurance companies to protect against the life and non-life risks.
- Federation of SHGs should be formed and trained to take up the monitoring of SHGs at the outset.
- Banks shall enter into strategic alliance with NGOs and share the group promotion costs.
- NGOs shall select active SHG leaders as their field staff to prevent the staff turnover problem.
- SHG records writing should be made known to more than one person in SHGs.
- Banks shall insist that leaders of SHGs should be changed once in 2 or 3 years as per the provisions of the group bye-laws.
- NGO shall take up internal auditing of SHGs account and external audit by Chartered Accountants be taken up once in a year. The contents of the balance sheet and Income and Expenses of the SHG should be explained to all the members of SHG.
- NGOs should arrange for need-based management training to the SHGs before recommending them for larger loans for group activities.
- Government departments should limit the delivery responsibilities of the SHGs for selective programs only matching with its capability.

CONCLUSION

Even though the SHG lending is outside the purview of the individual credit risk rating framework right now and only the portfolio approach is adopted, as the bank's exposure in SHG lending is on the increase day-by-day, all the banks have necessarily to be ready with a road map for managing both the credit risk and the operational risk in Micro finance. The present study will be of immense help to the branch managers and NGOs, who implement the SHG-Bank linkage program and will enable them to manage the risk effectively and upscale their SHG portfolio.

3

Managing Risk: A Challenging Task

CHITTA RANJAN SARKAR

Risk Management is a systematic approach in identifying, analysing, and controlling areas or events with a potential for causing unwanted change. It is through risk management that risks to any specific programme are assessed and systematically managed to reduce risk to an acceptable level. Risk Management signifies the basic ideology to identify, analyse, evaluate and treat the different business and financial risks that are frequently tackled in day-to-day business operations. Risk is an all-pervasive feature. Risk Management is the act or practice of controlling risk. It includes risk planning, assessing risk areas, developing risk-handling options, monitoring risks to determine how risks have changed, and documenting overall risk management programme.

There is no standard approach for risk management. However, there are some common elements of successful risk management efforts:

- Recognition that risk management is a programme management responsibility.
- The risk management process includes:
  - Planning for risk management;
  - Continuously identifying and analyzing programme events;
  - Assessing the likelihood of their occurrence and consequences;

- Incorporating handling actions to control risk events; and
- Monitoring a programme's progress toward meeting programme goals.

RISK AND OPPORTUNITY

Risk is not bad in itself; risk is essential to progress, and failure is often a key part of learning. But we must learn to balance the possible negative consequences of risk against the potential benefits of its associated opportunity. Risk and opportunity go hand in hand. The line of demarcation between the terms 'risk' and 'uncertainty' is very thin.

Types of Risk

Risks are of two types—Market risk and Unique risk. They are also termed as systematic risk and unsystematic risk respectively. Market risk is the general risk prevalent in the economy and is not attached to any specific organisation or its activities like the general market situations, government's attitudes in public spending, taxation policy and structure, fluctuation in interest rates, impact of global and economic liberalization policy, etc. Market risk is a type of risk that cannot be diversified away as it affects all securities in the market and in most of the cases tends to remain uncontrolled and untamed. Unique risk is a specific risk which stems from the particular nature of the security, viz. the development of a new competitive product, labour strike, etc. Events of this nature affect the specific organisational activities of a firm. The unique risk is easily identifiable and can be avoided or diversified while the market risk is very sporadic and relatively less unidentifiable and as such not easily controllable.

Risk Management Process

Risk management process refers to the process of measuring, or assessing risk and then developing strategies to manage the risk. In ideal risk management, a prioritization process is followed whereby the risks with the greatest loss and the greatest probability of occurring are handled first, and risks with lower probability of occurrence and lower loss are handled later. In practice the process is somehow very difficult to achieve, and the balancing between risks with a high probability of occurrence but lower loss *vs*. a risk with high loss but lower probability of occurrence may be misleading too.

Strategies of Risk Management Process

Identification and Assessment

The first step in the process of managing risk is identifying the potential risks involved in the instant case. The risks must then be assessed as to their potential severity of likely losses that might have to be suffered and to the probability of occurrence, time and again. Risk is a measure of the inability to achieve overall programme objectives within the defined cost and time schedule, and technical constraints that may be embedded therein and has two components: (a) the probability of failing to achieve a particular outcome; and (b) the consequences of failing to achieve that outcome.

Possible Alternative Actions

Once risks have been identified and assessed, the next strategy is to devise plans how to deal with the risks so identified and analysed as to their outcomes. There cannot be any ready-made solution that will match every finding. The techniques to manage the risk usually fall into one or more of the four major categories as may be envisaged – **Avoidance, Retention, Transfer, Hedging**.

Ideal use of all these strategies at any particular point of time and in respect of any specific risk problem may not be possible in real life situations for various reasons. These strategies are not mutually exclusive rather they are exhaustive. Some of them may involve trade offs that are not acceptable to the organization or person making the risk management decisions. A judicious combination of these may at best help better risk management.

Risk Avoidance

It includes deliberate attempt on part of the person taking risk decision not to perform an activity or not to accept a proposal, which is risk prone. An example would be not buying a property or business in order to not undertake the liability that comes with it.

Another would be not flying in order to averse the risk that the plane may be hijacked. But avoiding risks also means losing out potential opportunities of gaining something.

Risk Retention

It involves accepting the loss when it occurs by taking risky proposal or risky assignment where there are no other alternatives to avoid risk. Various government proposals or projects are undertaken in national interests despite their high vulnerability to risk and loss making.

Risk Transfer

It means causing another party to accept the risk, typically by contract. It involves a process of shifting risk responsibility on others. The risk, which should have been borne by one, is deliberately shifted on the shoulders of others. Insurance is one type of risk transfer, which is widely used in common parlance. Some ways of managing risk fall into multiple categories. Risk retention pools are technically retaining the risk for the group, but spreading it over the whole group, involves transfer among individual members of the group. This is different from traditional insurance, in that no premium is exchanged between members of the group.

Risk Hedging

Risk hedging is a systematic process of reducing risk associated with an investment proposal or in some other assignments where risk is inevitable, i.e. the risk is of such nature that it cannot be avoided altogether. The business world, the households, the social institutions, etc. are under sheer pressure to deal with risk and its gruelling impact on them by devastating their normal propensity to grow and survive. Risk hedging with the objective to risk reducing is a challenging task and is more a journey than a destination—a promise rather than a list of achievements. To one who has the unflinching aptitude to grow and prosper amid all disappointments and hazards, risk hedging is an oasis in the desert. The evolution of modern risk management tools like Hedging Contracts and Derivative Trading like Forwards, Futures, Options, and Swaps, etc.

have a dominating impact in reducing risks to a considerable extent although not in its entirety.

Derivatives and Derivative Trading

Derivatives are specific financial instruments having high liquidity and flexibility with an intent of contingent claims. Derivatives are those financial instruments which do not have an intrinsic value in themselves but whose value depends on the values of basic underlying variables/assets and are derived from the underlying variables and are so called as 'Derivatives'. The derivatives are usually Forwards, Futures, Options and Swaps. The business financial risk can be reduced or avoided systematically with the help of derivative tradings.

Forwards

Forward or more commonly a forward contract is an agreement to buy or sell an asset at a certain future time for a certain price. This contract is generally entered into between two financial institutions or between a financial institution and one of its corporate clients. It is not normally traded on an exchange.

One of the parties of the forward contract who agrees to buy the underlying asset on a certain specified date for a certain specific price is in the long position and is called long. The other party who agrees to sell the underlying asset on the same date for the same price is *in short position and is called short*. The specific price so mentioned in the forwards is termed as 'delivery price'.

At the time the contract is entered into, the delivery price is so chosen that the value of forward contract to both parties becomes zero. This implies that it costs nothing at the date of contract to take either a long position or a short position.

A forward contract is settled at maturity. The holder of the short position delivers the underlying asset at the delivery price in cash amount to the holder of the long position. Although a forward contract is worth zero at the initiation, later it may become positive or negative depending on the price fluctuations of the underlying asset. The value of the long position will be positive and the short position negative if the market value of the underlying asset rises sharply after initiating contract. The forward buyer (long position holder) is obliged to purchase the underlying asset at the specified contract price or enter into an offsetting transaction. When in future, the spot or market price becomes higher than the contract price, the forward buyer's gain is the difference between the spot price and the contract price and forward seller's loss is the difference between the contract price and spot price.

Thus in the condition of upward price fluctuations, i.e. in the inflationary situations, the forward buyer gets an opportunity to reduce his risk of loss owing to price rise by exercising his right of buying an asset at a price lower than the spot price and ultimately gains. Similarly in conditions of deflation when prices of goods/ assets fall, the forward seller gets the opportunity to reduce his risk of loss owing to falling price by exercising his right of selling an asset at a price higher than the spot price and ultimately gains. This way forward contracts help the parties to the contract to reduce their risk of loss to a great extent.

Futures Contract/Futures

A futures contract or simply futures is an agreement between two parties to buy or sell an asset at a certain time in future for a certain price. Unlike forward contracts, futures contracts are normally traded on an exchange. The futures prices are determined on the floor of the exchange on the simple basic rule of demand and supply. If more investors/traders on a particular day want to go on long position than to go short, the price will go up and if the reverse is true, the price will go down. However, in futures the parties to the contract may settle the contract without buying or selling the asset with the differences of prices and this way they can reduce their risk of loss during price fluctuations, although it is obvious that when the futures buyer gains, the futures seller incurs loss and the *vice-versa.*

Options

An option is a contract conveying the right but not obligation to buy or sell a specified financial instrument at a fixed price before or after a certain future date. An option gives the owner the right to buy or sale an underlying asset on or before a given date at a fixed price. The Option Holder is the buyer of the option who has the right but no obligation to buy or sell a specified quantity of underlying asset at a specified price (exercise price or striking price, i.e. the price at which the option holder agrees to sell or buy the underlying asset) on or before a specific date (expiration date or maturity date, i.e. the date when the option expires or matures) in the future.

Options are of two types: Call Option and Put Option. A call option gives the holder of the option the right to buy an underlying asset. Thus, the buyer of a call option may choose whether or not it will be profitable to him to buy the underlying asset and act accordingly. If the strike price becomes higher than the market price of the underlying asset as on the maturity date of the option, the holder of the call option can simply allow to the option to expire. A put option gives the holder of the option the right to sell an underlying asset. Thus, the buyer of a put option may choose whether or not it will be profitable to sell the underlying asset and act accordingly. This way the option holders can have the opportunity to substantially reduce the risk of loss of buying or selling the underlying asset at a specific date.

Swaps

Swaps are usually specific techniques involving the exchange of one set of financial obligation for payment with another set. Swaps are entered into between two parties to exchange the designated cash flows in future according to a predetermined schedule with the basic objective to reduce the risk of loss due to fluctuations in interest rates or foreign currency payments. Swaps are basically of two types—Interest Rate Swap and Currency Swap.

In Interest Rate Swaps, an agreement is entered involving the exchange of one stream of interest schedule with another set previously arranged in a manner that the parties to the agreement do not suffer much in spite of frequent fluctuations in market interest rates.

Currency Swap is another type of popular swap. In its simplest form, currency swap involves exchanging principal and fixed-rate interest payments on a loan in one currency for principal and fixed-rate interest payments on an approximately equivalent loan in another currency. With this mechanism the parties involved get an opportunity to reduce their risk of loss due to wide fluctuations in currency exchange rates while paying and receiving the agreed instalments in a loan agreement.

Portfolio and Managing Portfolio Risk

A portfolio is simply a combination of different investment proposals having separate risk and return patterns. Portfolio theory demonstrates how an investor can reach his optimal portfolio position such that risk is minimized and return is optimized. It has resemblance to the strategy of the egg sellers not to put all the eggs in a single basket but to put them in different baskets to minimize risk of loss by accident, mishandling, etc. Portfolio management is a systematic and judicious process of tackling risks of a portfolio investment comprising several securities/investment opportunities coupled with individual risk and return schedule in an objective and efficacious manner to optimize return and to minimize risk of the portfolio investment.

Managing Unique Risk of Portfolio

The risk management strategy plays a magnificent role to minimize portfolio risk. Whereas unique risk of a portfolio can be tackled and reduced substantially with the help of diversification of fund, market risk of portfolio cannot be reduced by diversification of fund. For reducing market risk, some other techniques like Beta Estimation, Hedging, etc. may be reasoned to get the optimum results.

The most common statistical measure of portfolio risk is the standard deviation of the expected value of portfolio returns. The variance of a probability distribution (σ^2) is the sum of the squares of the deviations of actual returns from the expected returns, weighted by the associated probabilities and is expressed as—

$$\sigma^2 = \Sigma P_1 (R_1 - R)^2$$

Where P_1 = Probability of the return of the portfolio,
R_1 = Actual return, and
R = Expected return.

Managing Market Risk of Portfolio

It is really difficult and rather a futile attempt to try to reduce market risk of a portfolio because of the inherent distinctiveness of market risks. Market risk is typical in character and is highly sensitive as well as vulnerable to respond to market ups and downs, economic conditions, global threats and many other factors most of which are imperceptible in common parlance and are not to be easily estimated.

The sensitivity of a portfolio security to market movements or market volatility is called beta (β) of the security. Practically beta of a security gives an idea how the security return tends to be affected by the fluctuations in market rate of return. Considering the wide and sharp responsiveness of individual security to market return of portfolio, the beta estimation (β) of a security is usually done applying the simple linear regression equation model by the OLS (Ordinary Least Square) method to highlight the degree of inter-relationship between the return of security and the market return of portfolio. The line of best fit of the regression equation is:

$$R = \alpha_S + \beta_S P + U$$

where, R (Dependent Variable) = Rate of Return of Security
P (Explanatory Variable) = Market Rate of Return of Portfolio
U (Random Variable) = Stochastic Disturbance or Error Term
d_S (Regression Parameter) = Intercept Term
β_S (Regression Parameter) = Regression Co-efficient, i.e. the beta estimate of the Security

The regression parameters can be estimated as below:

(i) $$\beta_S = ?(r_j\, P_i)/Sp_i^2$$

where, $r_i = (Ri - R^*)$; $Pi = (Pi - P^*)$; $R^* = \Sigma R/n$, and
$P^* = \Sigma P/n$;
n = No. of observations

(ii) $$\alpha_S = R^* - \beta_S\, P^*$$

Hedging Market Risk

The most sophisticated and effective way of controlling market risk is hedging scheme. Hedging is a systematic and procedural attempt to reduce risk. Through hedging an investor can have the opportunity to augment better rate of return than the market rate of return in a less risky manner.

Hedging using Futures

A company or an investor who is currently assigned to sell a particular asset at a future point of time can hedge the risk by taking a short futures position. This is known a *short hedge*. If the price of the asset goes down, the seller's loss on sale is offset by the gain for occupying the short futures position. Alternatively, if the price of the asset goes up, the seller's gain due to higher sale price is matched by the loss on the futures position. In the same fashion, a buyer of an asset at a future point of time can hedge his risk by taking a long futures position. This is termed as a *long hedge*. However, this philosophy of controlling risk through hedging does not always become really fruitful in real life situations because of various reasons viz. the asset whose price is to be hedged may not be exactly the same as the asset underlying the futures contract; the hedger may be uncertain as to the exact date when the asset will have to be sold or bought; the hedge may require the futures contract to be closed out well before the expiration date.

Hedging using Options

Another important refinement in the effective attainment of hedging risk through options is delta (∇) hedging. The delta of a stock option is the ratio of change in the price of a stock option to the change in the price of the underlying stock. It is the number of units of the stock that one should hold for each option desired to be a riskless hedge. The idea of achieving a riskless hedge is referred to as *delta hedging*.

CONCLUSION

Risk is all-pervasive. The philosophy of treating risk has gained wide popularity because risk is not just a threat but also a powerful device to combat fierce competitions and ultimately to learn how to grow and survive amid all adversities of risk. There is always a trade-off between return and risk. The trite phrase "Higher is the risk higher is the return" also signifies the true inter-relationship between the return and the risk. In the present era of globalization and abstract technological advancements, risks abound and as such a conscious and deliberate attempt is highly needed towards risk synchronization; risk reduction; risk transfer and above all risk diversification and risk hedging. A number of sophisticated and deliberate mechanisms, have been evolved like Derivative Trading, Hedging by Futures, Hedging by Options, Diversification of Fund for Portfolio Investment, various estimates like *beta, delta, gamma, vega,* etc. to reduce or to hedge risk as far as practicable or at best to achieve risk immunization since amid all attempts risk cannot be avoided in its entirety.

4

Operational Risk Management in Banks

S.K. BAGCHI

For almost 200 years since the advent of Commercial Banking, the business of Banking was being primarily driven by Credit Risks on Counter parties. Then, the lendable resources were at the disposal for remunerative deployment. Not much attention was either needed or relevant in the area of operational risks. Such risks in their hidden form were taken for granted as an inseparable part of the business.

But then came the big change. June 2004 proved to be a watershed in the world of Banking business as Basel Accord II were published. Although the pronouncements in the Accord II were not mandatory in nature, it had a great impact. Operational Risk Management was born out of the Accord as the heir-apparent of Credit Risk and Market Risk Management in Banking.

WHAT IS OPERATIONAL RISK MANAGEMENT

Any Banking risk other than Credit Risk and Market Risk is the plain vanilla expression of operational Risk. Basel Accord II has, however, provided clear and concise definition as under:

"Operational Risk is defined as the risk of loss resulting from inadequate or failed internal processes people and systems or from external events. This definition includes Legal Risk but excludes Strategies and Reputation Risk."

SEGMENTAL APPROACH

Operational Risk in Banking is, therefore, considered to be having three albeit inter-linked segments:

1. People, Process and System-related risks including Legal Risk.
2. External Events-related Risk, and
3. Strategic and Reputational Risk.

People, Process and System-related risks in Banking issues generally cover:

- Payment/settlement risk due to breakdown in process/ reconciliation system.
- Incorrect processing of service charges/cost (other than interest matter)
- Inappropriate product selection/product complexity especially in related segments.
- Lack of integration of various processes, e.g. Deposit of cash by a customer of demand draft (D/D) and subsequent issue of D/D.
- Inadequate infrastructure for control of process/systems.
- Inadequate data information execution.
- Fraud by staff or by others.
- Mistakes/Errors not with any fraudulent motive.
- Workforce disruption, e.g. strike/lockout.
- Loss of high skilled people, e.g. head of Technology Services Department.
- Health and safety issues of staff.

External Event-related risks are generally the following (which are not only applicable to Banking but to their lending areas as well).

- Act of God such as Flood, Earthquake, Volcano or any other natural calamities affecting business.
- Act of Miscreants such as Terrorist attacks or disruption or law and order problem.

Strategic and Reputational Risks may be broadly the following ones (which again are not restricted to Banking business only):

Adverse business decisions by the Top Management arising out of inadequate/inappropriate appreciation of market/industry changes, etc. and/or ineffective implementation of Top Management decisions may be treated as Strategic Risk areas, which may affect a Bank's profit/capital.

Shrinkage of market share is, however, a symptom of Reputational Risk, which has the effect on Goodwill of a Bank (Converting Goodwill into Bad will?) and in turn may affect Bank's profit/capital. This category of risk may be the following:

- Negative public opinion about product/service or health and safety standards.
- It is often said that an Internet Bank is exposed to greater Reputational Risk than a traditional Bank as the customer may quickly quit a Bank if a negative opinion is formed.
- Adverse opinion by Regulatory Authority in regard to working of a Bank.
- Basel II Accord has not prescribed any special treatment for Strategic and Reputational Risk probably because of difficulties that may be associated in proper identification, measurement and monitoring such risk. Hence, such risks in banking would for the time being (till a probable Basel III comes up) continue to be managed as hitherto.

Ten Basic Principles of Management of Operational Risk

Basel Committee has identified following ten principles for successful management of Operational Risk:

- Board of Directors should be aware of major aspects of Operational Risk of the organisation as distinct risk category.
- The Board of Directors should ensure that operational management framework of the organisation provides for effective and comprehensive internal audit.
- Senior Management of the organisation should consistently implement approved operational management framework of the organisation.
- In all material products, activities, processes and systems, operational risk contract should be identified and assessed.
- Regular Monitoring System of Operational Risk profiles and material exposures to losses should be in place.
- Policies, processes and procedures to control/mitigate Operational Risk should be evolved.
- Contingency business plans should be evolved.

- Regulatory Authorities should review periodically about organisation's approach to identify, assess, monitor and control/mitigate Operational Risk.
- Regulatory Authorities may ensure that appropriate mechanisms are put in place to allow them to remain apprised of position of Operational Risk Management of the supervised organisations.
- Adequate Public Disclosures to be made to enable market participants to assess organisation's approach to Operational Risk.

CONVERGENCE

The convergence of capital measurement and standards in operational banking is out of the focus areas these days.

One of the main purposes of covering Operational Risk as a separate risk category is to provide added focus to such risk areas in Banking in order that any abrupt incident does not disturb the well being of a Bank.

Basel Accord II provides that to take care of Operational Risk Banks should maintain separate Capital base in addition to Capital requirement for Credit Risk and Market Risk (no separate capital requirement for Strategic and Reputational Risk). Such capital requirement may be measured and standards set in the following manner:

(1) Basic Indicator Approach

Under the system, capital required will be worked out as under:

(a) A fixed Percentage of Gross Annual Income will be the requirement.
(b) Gross Annual Income will be worked out on the basis of average of previous three years.
(c) Minimum 15 per cent of such average annual income must be maintained.

'Gross Income' for the above purpose consists of Net Interest Income plus Non-Interest Income. Extraordinary Income/Expenses is to be ignored.

OR

(2) Standardised Approach (SA)

Under the system capital requirement will be arrived at in the following manner:

(a) Bank's activities are to be divided into 8 Business Lines e.g. Corporate Finance, Trading and Sales, Retail Banking, Commercial Banking, Payment and Settlement, Agency Services, Asset Management and Broking.
(b) Capital Charge for each business line is calculated by multiplying Gross Income by a factor assigned to a business line.
(c) Total Capital charge is calculated as 3-year average of simple summation across each business line in each year.

OR

(3) Advanced Measurement Approach

Subject to approval of Regulatory Authorities of each country the capital required will be worked out taking into account the risk measure generated by Bank's integrated Operational Risk measurement system using qualitative and quantitative criteria as laid down in the Accord.

As per RBI Press Reports, RBI is likely to ask Banks in India to adopt Basic Indicator Approach for the time being.

It is therefore clear that Banks will have to embrace the new requirement of Operational Risk management and thereby provide for regulatory capital adopting any of these options stated above.

CONSTRAINTS IN IMPLEMENTATION

India is blessed with around 100 Commercial Banks (except Cooperative Banks and Foreign Bank branches operating in India). But implementing aforesaid wide-ranging but quite valuable guidelines in such a massive network may pose following constraints:

- Wide variance in size and area of operation of Banks,
- Degree of varying sophistication of products and services, and
- Risk Philosophy and Risk Appetite of banks is not always professionally conceived.

Availabilities of skilled manpower and usage of up-to-date technology are also not uniform.

Operating Instructing/Manual of Banks is not in all cases structural/updated.

ROLE OF RBI

Under Pillar 2 of Basel Accord II, the Reserve Bank of India has to undertake periodical Review Process of Banks in India so as to ascertain in respect of Operational Risk Management:

- That the Bank has in place appropriate Operational Risk Management System.
- That appropriate Capital Charge Computed under any method of computation as above is maintained.

Need for External Annual Audit

- Operational Risks in Banking are of wide ranging area and often are mixed up with Credit Risk. Hence audit of Operational Risk may partly serve the purpose of audit of Credit Risk.
- What risk mitigants are in place, i.e. fidelity insurance for staff if available, Bank's Property Insurance, etc.
- How frequently Bank's Manual Instructions are updated and whether guidelines are clear and disseminated to all levels in the Bank.
- What specific arrangements of staff skilling/re-skilling are made.
- What reward/punishment measures for intentional/deliberate mistakes/frauds are in place and how effective they are.

While RBI may undertake periodical on-site/off-site review process an External Audit System on an annual basis may well supplement their efforts. The functional role of such an external audit mechanism is expected to cover:

- Assessment of Top Management involvement in managing operational risk matters.
- Evaluation of intensity of each component in Operational Risk in a Bank.

- Whether technology for managing Operational Risk to be outsourced and if so to what extent.
- On the top of all whether Operational Risk Capital Change of any point of time is properly computed as per the guideline.

CONCLUSION

Basel II Accord on Operational Risk Management is a welcome move. This will surely strengthen the business orientation and focus of Indian Banking. Furthermore, since each Bank is likely to have a specific Operational Risk Policy it will provide a clear direction to operating staff and simultaneously enable Top Management to monitor and control the risk on an ongoing basis.

'Control' is one of the basics of any Risk Management architecture, an external audit, preferably on annual basis, should be put in place by each bank.

5

Operational Risk Management—Systems and Process

V. RAMASWAMY

One of the important features of the New Basel Accord is the introduction of Operational Risk as one of the three important risks that banks have to assess and provide for Basel literatures describe the capital computation processes and the sound principles governing the operational risk and the methodologies of establishing the operational risk management. Reserve Bank of India has also recently come out with a guidance note for operational risk like the ones released for credit and market risks. The relative complexities associated with the operational risk and its management and the high cost involved makes it comparatively difficult for the banks to lay down the systems and procedures to manage operational risk.

BACKGROUND

With deregulation, many of the barriers to globalisation have vanished and the banking operations are no more restricted to domestic market but have become more global and carried out through twenty-four hours of the three hundred and sixty-five days of a year. More complex products and services, higher integration of the process with technology lead to increased range and magnitude of operational risk. Operational risk is not just internal; it can result from any component of the value chain. Careless applied automation and integration of systems can increase the operational risk by decreasing organisation's ability to perceive, detect and comprehend fully the risk and its magnitude. For e.g. while automation decreases the likelihood of simple human errors, it actually increases the likelihood of major losses that otherwise would have been caught by a human operator. Like any other risk, operational risk also is associated with loss for the organisation and organisation has to assess this loss and factor the same in the pricing models.

Implementation of Operational Risk Management in Banks

Banks to implement the operational risk management have to first of all understand the different components of ORM and then decide the methodology to be followed in implementing them and finally put the methodology into practice. The components of a best practice ORM are:

* Developing operational risk management policy,
* Identifying the risk,
* Measuring the risk,
* Mitigating the risk,
* Transferring/Financing the risk,
* Monitoring the risk, and
* Providing capital to cover the risk.

Developing ORM Policy

A well-defined policy is a pre-requisite for any management area, and an effective ORM policy should include the following:

Scope and Objectives

The scope and objectives describe the areas and the degree of depth and sophistication desired by the top management for ORM at this point of time. It also outlines the purposes for which ORM is going to be used as a tool and the other objectives that are to be linked to ORM.

Risk Appetite

Risk appetite may be defined as "the risks that an organisation in business is willing to take, given the context of its corporate goals

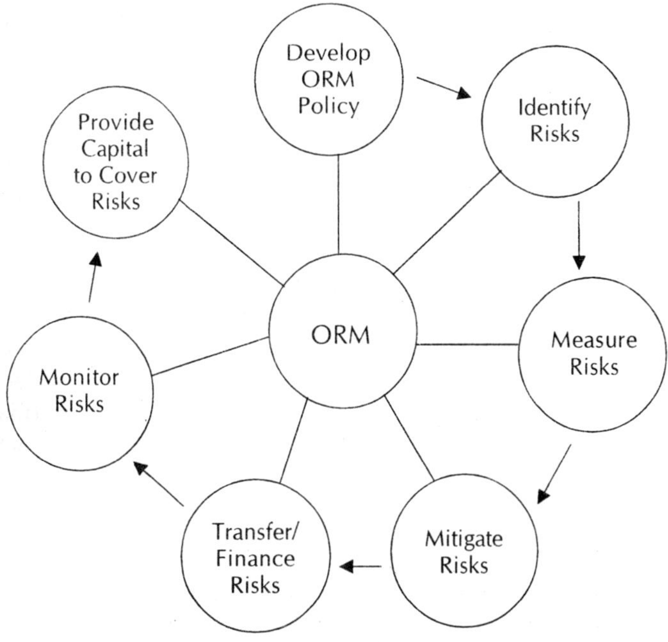

FIG. 5.1
Steps in Operational Risk Management

and its strategic imperatives." Risk appetite represented in terms of threshold or measurement limit is Risk Tolerance. Risk appetite of the management has to be clearly explained, which reveals the management's policy and strategies as to what level of risk is acceptable to the management and what level of risk it is willing to take for fulfilling the broad objectives of the organisation.

Risk Management Strategies

The strategies indicate and aid the operational staff to decide on the risks and its level to be taken in the products and processes.

Risk Management Architecture

The policy has to describe the ORM organisational framework and the responsibilities and the powers of the different committees and the functionaries associated with the ORM.

Setting Risk Limits and Targets

The different limits and targets connected with operational risk have to be explained and fixed, process/product-wise for each functionary/group/department. Procedure to be followed in respect of breach of limits should also be laid down.

Establishing Methodology

The systems and procedures for identifying, measuring mitigating, transferring/financing and monitoring the risks and to provide capital to cover the risks have to be clearly laid down.

Risk Identification (Risk Mapping)

This is the most difficult but important step in ORM. For proper identification of risks, answers for the following questions have to be found out:

What can go wrong in the organisation?
In which process, which product, which level in the organisation, which geographical area, which operational unit, or by whom—an event can happen resulting in present or future, direct/indirect loss?

Risk mapping is an overview of the organisation's processes, business units and functions outlining the source of the various risks. They are an effective way to allocate responsibility and accountability for risks down the line and are useful for defining weak points in the chain, where risk should be managed and more attention to be given. Risk mapping involves the following dimensions:

Identification of the Different Processes and Risk Areas

The different processes (including the support processes rendered by the systems) undertaken in the various functions, products and services and business units in the organisation have to be identified.

Once this is done, the various sub-processes that constitute the major process have to be looked into. After identifying the sub-processes, the events that can result in loss for the organisation have to be listed out. The event may be action or inaction or a bottle neck in the process flow.

Identification of Risk Indicators

The risk indicators are those factors that signal the presence of risk and indicate the extent to which the organisation is exposed to a particular risk. Risk indicators are also used to track and monitor the indicated risk.

Identification of Risk Drivers

Once the risk areas, loss events and risk indicators are identified, the next step is identification of the risk drivers. Risk driver is the cause of the risk and risk is the effect of it. Analysis and identification of risk drivers form significant basis in establishing control mechanisms for risk mitigation.

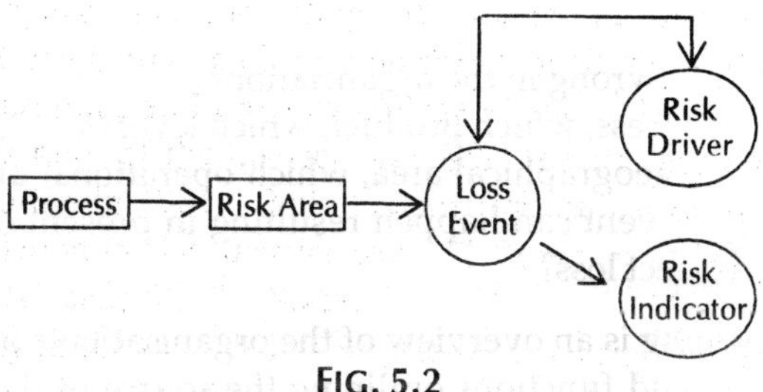

FIG. 5.2

Assigning the risk drivers and risk indicators to risks: Each of the risk driver and risk indicator has to be assigned to one or more risk areas/events. There can also be more than one risk indicator and risk driver for a particular risk. Similarly, a single risk driver or risk indicator may be assigned to more than one risk.

Approaches to Risk Mapping

Anyone or combination of the following approaches may be chosen for risk mapping:

Self-Assessment by the Expert Group

The risk management group experts may make an assessment of the different areas of risks in the organisation.

Brain Storming Exercise

Ideas and opinions may be invited through questionnaires by the risk management group from the different functional and operational units and the raw information received are analysed and evaluated.

Risk Workshop

Workshops focused at risk mapping may be conducted participating people from operational and functional units and the risk inventory received by the discussions, deliberations and consensus of the participants of the workshop are evaluated by the risk management team.

RISK MEASUREMENT

This process involves assessment of the risk and evaluates it based on its criticality. Acceptance of core risks that are inherent to the business, as a necessary part of being in business, is an important preamble to managing risk. Risk management does not mean risk elimination. Though a large number of events or risks could potentially affect a business, no analysis could ever consider all of them. Event models invariably assume the Pareto principle, which holds that most of the risk comes from a very small number of events. The Pareto principle suggests that 80 per cent of the risk comes from 20 per cent of the identified loss events. The cost benefit principle also does not drive for analysing and monitoring and treatment of all the risk of the business. Hence, identification of the critical events assumes significance. The criticality is assessed by analysing the following:

Impact of the Loss Events

The severity of the loss caused by the event is analysed. The impact of the loss event is the product of the loss and the time structure of the event. A risk that resides for long in the process or system may cause devastating or catastrophic loss.

Likelihood of the Loss Event

The likelihood of the event occurring over a period of time is analysed. The likelihood or the probability of the occurring of the event indicates how often the risk manifests or appears resulting in loss.

Criticality of the Loss Event

The simplest measure of an event's risk is its criticality. It is the product of the likelihood of occurrence of the event in a particular time period and its impact on the firm should the event occur in that time period. The most critical events are those that occur frequently with high impact.

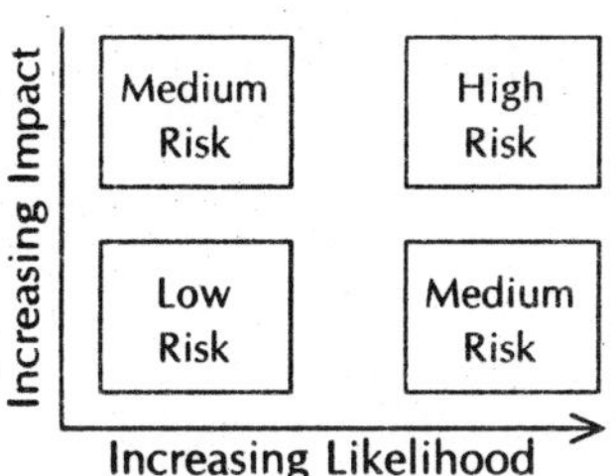

FIG. 5.3

Likelihood *vs.* Impact

Events depending upon their likelihood and impact fall under high risk, medium risk and low risk categories.

Risk Mitigation

The risk may be mitigated by establishing control mechanisms, which decreases the likelihood of occurring of the risk, thereby reducing the criticality of it. The nature of control system to be established or the number of control systems to be introduced depends on the nature of the risk, its risk driver and the effectiveness of the control system to mitigate the risk.

Risk Transfer

Risk transfer is the process of transferring the risk to external parties thereby shifting the loss on occurrence of the loss event out of the business of the organisation. Risk transfer can take the form of Insurance, Hedging, etc.

Risk Financing

The organisation accepts the risk in its full criticality or severity and decides to financing of the loss, if it occurs. Risk transfer or risk financing do not change the event or the risk factor, rather they transfer or offset the risk to limit the effect of the event on the organisation as and when it occurs.

Risk Monitoring

Risks have to be continuously monitored. Ongoing monitoring is an important aspect of risk management process, because the nature of the activities is likely to change rapidly due to change in product, process, systems (including technology) and market. Risk monitoring is done through the Risk MIS. Typical Risk MIS can be as one shown below:

Operational Risk Report

Process	*Risk Area*	*Risk Event*	*Likelihood of the Event*	*Impact of the Event*
(1)	*(2)*	*(3)*	*(4)*	*(5)*
Documentation for Credit	Faulty documentation	Cases decided against bank	1*	4*

Criticality of the Risk	*Control System Available*	*Risk Driver*	*Risk Indicator*	*Remarks*
(6)	*(7)*	*(8)*	*(9)*	*(10)*
Medium	Audit	Lack of Knowledge of the Staff	No. of Faulty documents Reported in audit	Priority Risk – GM's Attention

Loss Event Report

Description	Particulars
Risk category	Human Resources
Business line	Retail Banking
Event Type	Execution, Delivery and Process Management
Event	Cases decided against bank
Gross Loss event	Rs. 15 lakhs
Insurance/Recovery	Nil
Net Loss	Rs. 15 Lakhs
Remarks	Control mechanism to be toned up—workshops to credit staff in loan documentations.

Capital to Cover Risk

For those risks that cannot be transferred or eliminated, Management has to provide adequate capital to absorb the risk loss. The pro-active provision of loss has to be made for not only expected loss but also to cover any unexpected loss and to some extent for catastrophic losses. Loss Distribution Method under Advanced Measurement Approach (Pillar-1 of Basel-II Capital Accord) calculates capital for operational risk based on the distribution of loss events.

Management Action

Prudent management of operational risk calls for prompt and continuous pro-active action to be taken by the management and deal with each of the risks in the most effective manner as possible.

The category to which the risk falls decides the degree of attention to be imparted and the action to be taken by the management. Risks categorised as high and medium attract more attention and low category risks draw lesser attention of the management.

Depending on the categorisation of the risk, action taken can be in the following lines:

High Risks

Banks may either avoid taking high risks, by changing the business process/ sub-process which carry the risk or exit from such business that carry these high risks. Rarely risk transfer is also resorted as management action to handle these risks.

Medium Risk

These risks are to be handled by the bank and the bank is prepared to carry the same. But based on the considerations of cost benefit analysis, residual risk intensity and the root cause of the risk, bank may chose to adopt any of the following risk treatment measures:

Risk Control

Control systems are introduced and the risk is controlled/mitigated. While implementing control systems, thoughts are given to the cost involved for the control mechanism to be built in and the loss that may be caused by the residual risk and the effectiveness of the control system to mitigate the risk.

Risk Transfer

In case of certain risks, the control mechanisms are either not feasible or economical, and in such cases management decides to go in for risk transfer.

Risk Financing

In case of Risks that are not desirable to be controlled or transferred, risk financing is done.

Low Risk

Risks categorised as low, do not pose danger by virtue of low impact and least likelihood. Such risks prove to be uneconomical to be addressed. Hence such risks are allowed to remain as such in the system.

References

1. Measuring and Managing Operational Risks in Financial Institutions— Dr. Christopher Lee Marshall.

2. Risk Management by Michel Crouhy, Dan Galai, and Robert Mark.
3. Operational Risk and Resilience by Chris Frost, David Allen, James Porter, Philip Bloodworth of Pricewaterhouse Coopers.
4. Sound Practices for the Management and Supervision of Operational Risk, February 2003—BCBS Paper.

6

Operational Risk—A Real Nightmare?

A.S. RAJEEV

Deregulation, globalization and disintermediation have changed the definition of the markets and altered the economics of operating within these markets. The Basel Committee on Banking Supervision has developed a new, more comprehensive framework for capital regulation based on three pillars—minimum capital requirements, supervisory review and market discipline. An improved Capital Accord is intended to foster a strong emphasis on risk management and to encourage ongoing improvements in banks' risk assessment capabilities. The Committee believes that minimum capital requirements can and should be closely aligned with prevailing strong risk management practices. On the basis of risk sensitive minimum capital requirements, bank capital can be more efficiently used to protect against risk.

In a survey conducted by Pricewaterhouse Coopers in UK, approximately 70 per cent of UK banks considered their operational risks as important as their market and credit risks. Historical loss data from operational risk suggests that the financial services might have lost as much as $ 200 bn. from operational disasters over the past 20 years.

INTRODUCTION

Banks face risks other than credit and market and these risks may

Reprinted with permission from *The Journal of Indian Institute of Banking & Finance.*

be substantial. Under existing Basel accord, these other risks are covered implicitly under credit and charged the required capital. These other risks shall be called as operational risks and the measurement of the same is still in a nascent stage in India. Of the three types of risks, viz. credit, market and operational risks, the management of operational risk is the least advanced, and hence it demands the most general approach. Operational risks in banks are increasing due to various reasons and this is one of the reasons for several large bank failures in recent years. In view of this, increased supervisory attention is being focused on the importance of sound operational risks management and Basel-II has included a proposal for a separate capital charge for operational risks in its proposed new accord.

The Committee believes that operational risk is an important risk facing banks and that banks need to hold capital to protect against potential losses from it. This view is shared by a number of globally active financial institutions, which have been at the forefront of analyzing and assessing operational risk. The Committee defines operational risk as the risk of loss resulting from inadequate or failed internal processes, people and systems, or external events.

This definition includes legal risk, but strategic and reputational risks are not included for purpose of minimum regulatory risk capital charge. Some of the examples of operational risk are:

- Clients bring a litigation suit charging the bank with negligence.
- A major earthquake disrupts part of bank's data centre.
- Incorrect historical data used to price a new product.
- Head of investment desk unexpectedly resigns.
- Wrong credits to account, conversion, etc.

While the finance sector has led the way in developing sophisticated quantitative and qualitative techniques for identification, measurement and management of credit and market risk, it can still learn from the ongoing operational issues that are being faced by industries.

Though the number of operational losses and bank failures are comparatively less in India as compared to global business, security scam of year 1992 and the consequent losses to banks, large-scale diversion and siphoning of bank funds by outsiders during recent times, etc. are examples of operational losses.

WHAT IS OPERATIONAL RISK MANAGEMENT?

Operational risk management comprises a host of activities:

(i) Identifying the risk,
(ii) Measuring the risk,
(iii) Predicting operational losses,
(iv) Preventing operational losses,
(v) Operational risk management process – Risk financing – Mitigating the loss impact after it has occurred by reducing the firms sensitivity to the event or transferring the risk to external parties like insurance. Changing the form of risk to another type of risk and dealing with that risk. Example, transforming credit risk to operational risk by the use of margin/ collateral, and
(vi) Allocating capital to cover operational risk.

(i) Identifying the Risk

The bank can prepare an indicative list of areas relating to operational risks based on checklist as referred by Basel-II and the broad areas of events that may happen in operational areas like:

(i) Internal Fraud,
(ii) External Fraud,
(iii) Employment Practices and Workplace Safety,
(iv) Clients, Products and Business Practices,
(v) Damage to Physical Assets,
(vi) Business Disruption and System Failures, and
(vii) Execution, Delivery, and Process Management.

(ii) Measuring the Risk

Basel Committee Recommendations

"We cannot manage what we cannot measure." Effective risk assessment always precedes effective management.

The Basel committee has put forward a framework consisting of three methods for calculating capital charge viz.:

(i) the Basic Indicator Approach,
(ii) the Standardized Approach, and
(iii) Advanced Measurement Approaches (AMA).

Banks are expected to move along the range towards more sophisticated approaches as they develop more sophisticated ORM systems and practices meeting the prescribed qualifying criteria. The bank will be permitted to use a combination of approaches standardized for some business lines and an advanced measurement approach for others, subject to a materiality requirement that at least a minimum percentage of the banks business should be in AMA. A bank will not be allowed to choose to revert to a simpler approach once it has been approved for a more advanced approach without supervisory approval. In addition, if a supervisor determines that a bank using a more advanced approach no longer meets the qualifying criteria for this approach, it may require the bank to revert to a simpler approach for some or all of its operations, until it meets the conditions specified by the supervisor for returning to a more advanced approach.

Approaches to the measurement of operational risk continue to evolve rapidly, but are unlikely to attain the precision with which market and credit risk can be quantified in short-term. This poses obvious challenges to the incorporation of a measure of operational risk within the minimum capital requirement. Nevertheless, the Committee believes that such inclusion is essential to ensure that strong incentives exist for the continued development of approaches to operational risk measurement and management and to ensure that banks are holding sufficient capital buffers for operational risk. It is clear that a failure of operational risk within the minimum capital requirement (pillar one) would reduce these incentives and result in a reduction of industry resources devoted to operational risk issues.

However, the recommendations are yet to be finalized by the committee and the same is expected to be finalized during 2004 and to be implemented from 2006.

BASIC INDICATOR APPROACH (BIA)

Banks using the Basic Indicator Approach must hold capital for operational risk equal to a fixed percentage (denoted alpha) of average annual gross income over the previous three years. The charge may be expressed as:

$$KBIA = GI \times \alpha$$

where, KBIA = the capital charge under the Basic Indicator Approach.

GI = average annual gross income over the previous three years.

α = 15 per cent which is set by the Committee, relating to the industry wide level of required capital to the industry wide level of the indicator.

Gross income is defined as net interest income plus net non-interest income excluding realized profits/losses from the sale of securities in the banking book and extraordinary or irregular items. It is intended that this measure should reflect income before deduction of operational losses.

THE STANDARDISED APPROACH

Under this approach, bank activities are divided into eight business lines, against each of which a broad indicator (gross income) is specified to reflect the size or volume of bank activities in that area. The proposed business lines are Corporate Finance, Trading and Sales, Retail banking, Commercial banking, Payment and settlement, Agency services and custody, Asset management and Retail brokerage. Within each business line, the capital charge is calculated by multiplying the indicator by a factor (beta-β) assigned to that business line. Beta will be set by the committee and serves as a rough, proxy for the industry-wide relationship between the operational risk loss experience for a given business line. If a bank is unable to allocate an activity to a particular business line, the committee has proposed that the income relating to that activity should be subject to the highest beta factor. The total capital charge is calculated as the simple summation of the regulatory capital charges across each of the business lines. Banks using the standardized approach should comply with operational risk sound practices paper.

$$KTSA = \Sigma(GI\ 1\text{–}8 \times \beta\ 1\text{–}8)$$

where, KTSA = the capital charge under the Standardised Approach,

GI 1-8 = the average annual level of gross income over the past three years, as defined above in the Basic Indicator Approach, for each of the eight business lines, and

β1-8 = a fixed percentage, set by the Committee, relating

the level of required capital to the level of the gross income for each of the eight business lines. The values of the betas are detailed below.

Business Line	*Beta*
Corporate Finance	18
Trading and Sales	18
Retail Banking	12
Commercial Banking	15
Payment and Settlement	18
Agency Services	15
Asset Management	12
Retail Brokerage	12

The Committee has proposed that at national discretion, banks can use Alternative Standardised Approach (ASA) for calculating operational risk capital charges and hence RBI has suggested to the Committee that the level of performing advances with reduced alpha/beta factor shall substitute gross income.

A HYPOTHETICAL EXAMPLE OF STANDARDISED APPROACH

Operational risk capital and the risk weighted assets of ABC Bank with two business lines under standardised approach.

Year	*Business Line*	*Gross Income*	*Average Income for three years*	*Beta*	*Capital Charge for Operational Risk*
2001	Commercial	1000.00	1200.00	15	180.00
	Others*	300.00	350.00	18	63.00
	Total Gross Income	1300.00			
2002	Commercial	1200.00			
	Others*	350.00			
	Total Gross Income	1550.00	Total Capital Charge		243.00
2003	Commercial	1400.00			
	Others*	400.00			
	Total Gross Income	1800.00			

*Highest Beta factor.

As per *standardised approach, the operational risk capital requirement for the year 2003-04 is Rs.243.00 crore and hence the risk weighted assets is Rs.2700 Cr @ 9% CRAR.

ADVANCED MEASUREMENT APPROACHES (AMA)

Under the AMA, regulatory capital requirement will equal the risk measure generated by the bank's internal operational risk measurement system using the quantitative and qualitative criteria for the AMA. Use of AMA is subject to supervisory approval. Banks adopting the AMA will be required to calculate their capital requirement using this approach as well as the existing Accord for a year prior to implementation of the New Accord at year-end 2006.

In advanced measurement approach, the bank can use any of the methods viz. (i) Internal measurement approach (IMA), (ii) Loss Distribution Approach (LDA), or (iii) Scorecard Approaches.

Internal Measurement Approach

The approach assumes a fixed and stable relationship between expected losses and unexpected losses. This relationship may be linear, i.e. the capital charge would be a simple multiple of expected losses or non-linear, i.e. the capital charge would be a more complex function of expected losses.

The calculations are generally based on

- PE: The probability that an operational risk event occurs over some future horizon, generally one year,
- LGE: The average loss given that an event occurs, and
- EI: An exposure indicator that is intended to capture the scale of bank activities in a particular business line.

Combining these parameters, the IMA capital charge for each business line as:

$$K = \gamma *.EI * PE * LGE$$

Where the parameter γ (to be specified by banks and subject to acceptance by supervisors) translates the estimate of expected losses (EL) for business line in to capital charge. The overall capital charge is generally calculated as sum of the capital charges for individual business line.

On the other hand, the Committee is prepared to allow an unprecedented amount of flexibility to banks in choosing how to measure operational risk and the resulting capital requirement.

Under the advanced measurement approaches (AMA), banks will be permitted to choose their own methodology for assessing operational risk, so long as it is sufficiently comprehensive and systematic. The extent of detailed standards and criteria for use of the AMA are minimal in an effort to spur the development of innovative approaches. The Committee intends to review progress in regard to operational risk approaches on an ongoing basis. In order to qualify for use of the Standardized or AMA, a bank must satisfy its Supervisor that the minimum qualifying general and specific standards are attained and maintained.

A HYPOTHETICAL EXAMPLE OF INTERNAL MEASUREMENT APPROACH

[The working methodology/concept has been conceived from consultative document on operational risk of Basel Committee issued on 31.05.01 (Para VI)].

Assumptions

(i) ABC Bank is projecting a business, say Rs. 50000 crore for the year 2003-04 and considering the EI as total business of the bank.
(ii) Total business the same is assumed as segment.
Historical data computed from previous three-year actual.

PE = 0.55, average for three years. (Probability distribution).

The average loss occurred during the past three years—Rs. 10 crore and average EI for last three years be Rs. 45000 crore and hence LGE is 0.0222 per cent.

$\gamma = 3$, which Management expects (Three times of expected losses) as the supervisory validation is not in force.

If we consider the relationship as linear, and the resultant IMA capital charge for Rs. 50000 crore business is

K = 3 *50000 * 0.55 * 0.0222 per cent
= 18.32 crore or operational risk assets @ 9 per cent CRAR is Rs. 203.55 crore.

A HYPOTHETICAL EXAMPLE OF LOSS DISTRIBUTION APPROACH (BOTTOM-UP APPROACH)

As referred in areas of identification of risk, the average incidents occurred and the amount involved in past three years is shown below in case of ABC Bank.

Years	No. of cases	Gross loss (in cr.)	Net loss (in cr.)	3 year Average Gross loss (in cr.)	3 year Average Net loss (in cr.)
2000-01	130	15.00	8.00	17.67	10.00
2001-02	140	18.00	10.00		
2002-03	150	20.00	12.00		

Expected losses tell us about the range of possible losses or the unexpected losses. This range is always measured by standard deviation (SD) of the distribution (some times a multiple of SD is used and assuming a particular distribution, converted into an estimate of VaR). For infrequent events, we shall use the following formula to estimate the unexpected loss over a number of possible outcomes.

$$\text{Unexpected loss} = \frac{\sqrt{\begin{array}{c}\Sigma \text{ likelihood of loss} \times \\ (\text{Loss} - \text{Expected loss})^2\end{array}}}{\text{Event i}} \qquad (1)$$

Or its continuous equivalent.

Likelihood of future events or probability of an event occurring in the future is very difficult to estimate through either subjective or objective methods. Not only is the future unknowable *ex ante*, but also humans have systematic biases that impede accurate estimations of event likelihood, even when the data is present (in the form of historical event frequencies). Risk factors with values that change over time can be said to follow a stochastic process. The most commonly used proxy for the likelihood of an event is the number of events during some time period. Hence, it may consider the number of events per year as the proxy. This assumes that the future will be more or less like the past.

In order to find out the probability of occurrence, by Poisson distribution, we shall fit the probability distribution as the conditions of Bernoulli process hold good. In general, many event frequencies are reasonably well fitted to the Poisson distribution, although there is a tendency for the distribution to over estimate the low-frequency days relative to high frequency days. This is because events in most real world applications are not independent—when an event occurs, other events tend to occur in tandem.

From the table, it shows that the total number of cases is 130 in 2000-01, 140 during 2001-02 and 150 during 2002-03. Hence, the mean number of cases is 140.

The cumulative probability of continuance of 140 cases per year in future years by using the Poisson distribution works out to be 0.5225.

Hence the unexpected loss with probability of 0.5225 as given in equation (1) is:

$$\text{Unexpected loss} = \sqrt{0.5225 \times (17.67 - 10.00)^2}$$
$$= 5.54 \text{ crore at 68 per cent confidence level}$$

In order to get more comfort requirement of economic capital allocation say, 99.87 per cent c.f. the required σ (sigma) is 3.00 (three SDs of normal distribution) and correspondingly the estimated economic capital requirement for unexpected loss is Rs. 16.62 crore for one-year duration. Hence if the capital charge would be a more complex function of expected losses, the economic capital requirement is Rs. 16.62 crore or operational risk assets @ 9 per cent CRAR is Rs. 184.66 crore.

(iii) Predicting Operational Losses with Loss Events

There are a large number of events that could potentially affect a business. No analysis could ever consider all of them. A loss event has several important aspects that should affect how operations managers try to deal with them. These include:

- The likelihood of event occurring in a particular time period. The most commonly used proxy for likelihood of a frequent event is the number of occurrences of the event during some period—its frequency. This assumes that the future will be like the past.

  Event likelihood in a future period

= No. of event occurrences during representative historical time period length of the historical time period.

For less frequent events, historical frequencies are less helpful and hence we must rely on different approaches, which are either subjective or the likelihood based upon our knowledge. The Stochastic models like Poisson process shall also be used in frequent events as above.

- The impact on the firm should the event occur—
  Operational loss events may have three general types of financial impact on the firm viz., Direct (either through a reduction in income or a loss in value of firm's assets and liabilities), Indirect (as a result of damage to the firm's reputation or downstream effects on other loss events) and Opportunity costs (potential earnings foregone because of occurrence of loss events).
- Event criticality—an approximate measure of the event's risk
  The simplest measure of event criticality—the product of the likelihood of events in a particular time period and its impact on the firm should occur in that time period.
  Event criticality = Event likelihood × Event impact.
- The time structure—how the event unfolds over time
  The incidents involving extensive human mismanagement can be analyzed with detailed structure of the event i.e., how the events unfold over time. Making this event structure helps us to answer the modalities, prevention and minimization of length of impact as well as the mitigation strategy.
- Event uncertainty—how well can we predict the various aspects of the event's risk.
  The probability of distributions of both frequency and impacts are subject to uncertainty. For more frequent events we can generally estimate more accurate risk figures.

(iv) Preventing Operational Losses

Some of the losses could have been prevented and some could have been less likely through the redesign of systems and process, some could have been passed to outside parties by insurance, hedging or outsourcing.

Carelessly applied automation and integration of systems can increase operational risk. Automation decreases the likelihood of simple human errors but increases the likelihood of major losses that otherwise would have been caught by human operator.

Pareto Principle

Vilfredo Pareto, an Italian economist argued that approximately 80 per cent of the wealth of society would always be held by approximately 20 per cent of the population. A similar principle can be applied to risk and cost analysis i.e., 80 per cent of the risk comes from 20 per cent of the identified loss events. On the cost side, handling 20 per cent of all transactions that are exceptions in any process will require 80 per cent of the total process cost. Thus, the Pareto principle implies that decreasing loss events by just 5 per cent can decrease cost by as much as 20 per cent. Hence, Pareto diagrams can help us focus on the subset of identified events that cause the bulk of the risk. However, unknown events are not considered in this principle.

Efficiency is a prerequisite for operational excellence in business. Inexperienced staffing is the important risk factor that leads to unexpected losses.

Internal Control aims to safeguard the firm's assets from external and internal threats. Internally the risk comes from breakdowns in internal controls and corporate governance that can lead to financial losses through fraud, error or failure to perform in a timely manner.

(v) Operational Risk Management—Actions and Process

The range of possible management interventions to predict, reduce and finance a risk is enormous. Some of the areas are discussed hereunder.

- Financial risk management.
- Total quality management (Comprises techniques such as inspection, statistical quality control, quality assurance and strategic quality management. Other analytical tools such as Pareto analysis, fault tree analysis, fish bone diagrams and process maps have been used to facilitate quality management).
- Insurance.

- Personnel selection (Effective personal selection, training and promotion is critical for the management of risks).
- Culture Management (It is a shared system of beliefs, values and norms).
- Organizational design (The formal reporting structure has important implications for its ability to handle risks).
- Relationship Management (Manage good relationship with external parties like shareholders, creditors, customers, counter-parties, clients, competitors, regulators, media groups, etc.).
- Audit and internal control.
- Operations management Reliability Engineering.
- Facility management and Contingency planning.
- Risk financing (Which involves either transferring the loss to some external party for a fixed premium or restructuring the organization to be more able to handle the risk).
- At micro level, insurance, hedging vehicles like forwards and futures/swaps/options/hybrids, collaterals, third party guarantees covenants and direct loan sales mitigate the losses including catastrophic losses.
- Firms can also choose to avoid potential exposures to loss by reducing the levels of risky assets or abandoning the business lines or high-risk activities. At macro level, by and large, external insurance, contingency planning, public relations, etc. mitigate the catastrophic losses.
- Other systems like Boundary systems (limits and sanctions), Contractual risk transfers, Effective compliance programmes, Computer security management, Physical security management and Internal and External audit are effectively managing the operational risk.

(vi) Allocation of Economic Risk Capital and Treatment of Losses

There are two forms of risk penalty. The first form of risk penalty uses the loss provision to cover the expected losses. The second, risk capital, is a cushion provided by equity holders against the unexpected losses. By definition, management expects the expected losses to occur and accepts them as a part of business loss. Consequently expected losses are covered by the firm's ongoing revenues and theoretically should not require additional risk

Capital. The economic risk capital is the capital required to cover the risk of potential losses or a cushion against unexpected capital losses up to some level of insolvency risk.

The real nightmares facing banks is not the expected or unexpected losses for which risk management provides some level of protection. Their concern is for **catastrophic losses** that threaten the viability of the organization. These typically involve rogue trading, insider fraud, bad lending, poorly understood derivatives, inadequate controls, natural disasters or snowballing of reputational losses.

Some of the issues relevant in the context of the emerging markets and developing countries

(I) The explicit capital charge for operational risk of ABC Bank under different approaches is shown below
   (i) Standardised Approach – Rs. 243.00 cr.
   (ii) Advance Measurement Approach
      (a) Internal Measurement – Rs. 18.32 cr.
      (b) Loss Distribution – Rs. 16.62 cr.

   From the above, we see that standardized approach expects much higher (13 times) capital than the internal measurement approach. Though the catastrophic losses (which cannot be estimated) also needs capital, the quantum of capital by Standardised approach is very high.

(II) As economic capital is to be computed by internal risk measurement basis, there will be a huge variance between Standardised and AMA approach.

(III) The nominal benefit accruing from credit risk, due to less capital requirement for very few external rated accounts/ retail portfolio/ residential property is to be shifted to unrated claims on banks, lower rated borrowers, past due loans and high risk exposures.

(IV) The long duration of investments of Indian Banks needs more capital for market risk. As the capital is expected on one-year duration basis, market risk may be allowed to compute for one-year duration basis and thereby the quantum shall be reduced.

(V) The QIS 3 results (CP 3) for the Standardised Approach show a significant increase in capital requirements of at least 3-4 per cent CRAR to keep the same level of assets for most of the Indian banks.

In view of the above, it may be desirable to review the relevant provisions of CP 3 with respect to the Standardised Approach.

REFERENCES

1. Papers/documents on 'operational risk' in web site of BIS (www.bis.org).
2. *Measuring and Managing Operational Risks in FIs—Tools, Techniques and Other Resources* by Dr. Christopher Lee Marshal.

7

Credit as well as Credit Risk Management in Banks

R.S. RAGHAVAN

Bank optimizes utilization of deposits by deploying funds for developmental activities and productive purposes through credit creation process. Deposit mobilization and Credit deployment constitute the core of banking activities and substantial portion of expenditure and income are associated with them. In the case of deposits, barring few stray instances of operational risks linked to the system and human failure culminating in fraud, forgeries and loss, there may not be anything very alarming. But credit portfolio is the real dynamic activity that requires close monitoring and continuous management. This article attempts to focus on not only credit management but also credit risk management.

Till recently, all the activities of banks were regulated and hence operational issues were not conducive to risk taking. The financial sector, now, wears a relaxed and liberated look. Banks have grown from being a financial intermediary, in the past, to a risk intermediary, at present. In credit, risks are co-related and exposure to one risk may lead to another having deeper ramification and hence, the real mantra for prudent banking lies in successfully managing the risks in an integrated and pro-active manner to optimize the exposure already taken or to be assumed by the bank. Adherence to standards of quick decision and providing adequate and need-based financial assistance on attractive but safe terms, without losing the sight of the associated risks involved therein, appears to be a difficult proposition. There is an implicit understanding on the part of the planners that in the post nationalization era, banks will meet what is called social obligations through directed lending. Early stage of nationalization belonged to security oriented approach; in the nineties it was the spread-oriented era and in the early 21st century the focus is shifted to risk. When the security oriented approach was followed, economic activities and banking products were simple and "instances of frauds and forgeries were few and far in between."

It is very much essential to conduct credit investigation before taking up a proposal for consideration. This preliminary study should lead to valuable information on borrower's integrity, honesty, reliability, credit worthiness, management competency, expertise, associate concern, guarantor, etc. A due diligence report shall invariably accompany the credit proposal evaluation. Banks have to strictly adhere to the KYC (Know Your Customer) norms to ensure *bona fide* identification of borrows and should also follow the prescribed Fair Practice Code on Lenders' Liability, by evolving their own best practices to be followed by the field functionaries, so as to avoid complaints from customer at a later date.

LENDING METHODS

Even though Tandon Committee norms have been dumped to dustbins, alternative methods being practiced by the banks are yet to pass the test of time. While some banks adopt the method of justifying the sanction of loan, others follow a combination of Turnover method, Cash Flow Method, Cash Budget Method, Projected Balance Sheet Method, Net Owned Fund Method and the popular one-size fits all Second Method of lending. Proper logistics should be built into the method of assessment—be it fund-based or non-fund-based requirement. What may be lacking is assessment of credit with risk perception.

Banks have to structure the assessed limits in the form of various credit facilities, having regard to the nature of activity, process/ business cycle, trade terms, availability of security, operational convenience, etc. Loan System of Credit Delivery is one such system, developed a few years ago. This discipline in cash flow management, on mutual understanding between the bank and the borrower, should be observed in respect of credit exposures beyond a cut-off level of say Rs. 10 crore or so. In view of the growing competition in the banking, take over of borrowal account is considered to be one of the major routes to accelerate credit expansion. It is just a shift of the lender, though there is no additional credit or asset creation activity. However, bankers should exercise due diligence and caution while entertaining a proposal for take over of an account from another lender.

When cash flow method is followed, repayment capacity of the borrower is well established and the return to the bank by way of interest is examined. But the question is how to rely on the projected cash flows. This can be overcome by building up industry-wise data and the financials of the borrower. Information such as credit exposure in terms of sector, industry, security and region-wise to all the credit appraisers in the institution should be uniformly made available with reasonable up-date so as to enable them to price, dispense, manage and monitor.

It is observed that extent of credit dispensation power is not related to the credit skill acquired by the authority, but linked to the position in the hierarchical ladder and, delegation has been based on the credit size and not the credit risk perceived in a proposal. For this, discretionary powers should be linked to the risk rating of the borrower. Banks are yet to fully move from credit rating to the risk rating of a borrower. When a borrower secures 95 per cent marks and rated AAA, what is implied is credit rating is 95 (AAA) and the risk rating is 5. The mind set should change from credit rating to risk rating and proper system should be put in place in this regard. Proposals of non fund-based limits should also be subjected to the same level of appraisal standards as adopted for appraising fund-based limit so that the asset quality of the bank do not suffer any undue setback. Multiple analytical ratios are to be worked out in the credit appraisal duly discussing about the implications of these ratios. Detailed discussion on cash generation should compulsorily form part of credit appraisal.

Based on the risk rating, the type of security to be obtained and cash margin to be insisted can be decided. Care should be taken that non-fund-based limit in exclusion of fund-based limit is not considered by a bank and proportionate fund and non-fund-based limits are only considered. Banks should put in place their own Security Standards, Guarantee Standards, Documentation Standards and Renewal/ Review Standards to suit their appetite and quality standards.

In big-ticket credit, analytical tools will have to be used in various aspects of credit dispensation such as appraisal, delivery, monitoring, reporting, re-scheduling, restructuring, etc. As lenders feel that most of exposure ceiling/setting up limits, etc. are regulator driven, it is better to be pro-active in these areas. Banks themselves should compile separate list of sectors to guide the field functionaries in the matter of credit deployment and some of these are given below:

- Indicative sectors where additional/fresh exposures can be considered without any prior reference to higher authorities,
- List of activities where selective approach is to be adopted and fresh/additional exposures can be considered only with the prior approval of appropriate authorities, and
- Sectors/business segments where additional/fresh exposure is prohibited for the time being.

CREDIT MONITORING

Credit Monitoring is an important function of credit management and some of these aspects are discussed in brief: Credit decisions do not get better, all because more people review the proposal. It can be improved only when those who review it are knowledgeable and carry with them requisite experience in credit portfolio. Credit Department should be expertise-oriented rather than going by the scale and grade in the organization, as there are many who climbed the organization ladder without being exposed to the requisite credit management. This anomaly should be properly understood by one and all. Typically, in PSU banks, branch head has a three-year tenure in a particular branch. They are geared for asset-based lending, disregard of lending-based on the forecast of cash flows. Even in Asset-Based Lending, appraiser is bogged down in the paper financial ratios rather than cash flows which are vital in certain type of industries like, hospitality, construction, transport, hotel, etc. where there are significant fluctuations in the cash flows. It requires totally different mind-set. Though some banks, in line with the express RBI guidelines on credit risk management, follow the committee approach for credit sanction, in reality the committee hardly meets to share the broader range of skills, expertise and knowledge. Getting passed the proposal through circulation is more often the rule than an exception and one person's decision gets the sanctity of committee. The committee approach is helping the bank in diffusing individual responsibility from the angle of CVC.

At present, due to lack of credit appraisal skill at the field level, manned by many generalist officials spread across the branch network, there is greater duplication of work at the sanctioning level at HO causing enormous and avoidable delay as the papers pass through more than a dozen senior officials, before it is placed before the sanctioning authority. Business Process Re-engineering and Core Banking Project may come to the rescue of banks.

Exposure to sensitive sectors such as Real Estate, Capital Market and Commodities sector need to be kept under constant watch and adequately disclosed in the balance sheet of banks; Monitoring of unsecured exposures, both fund-based and non-fund-based, through internal ceilings prescribed by the Bank; Rating-wise exposure ceilings, i.e. achieving not more than 30 per cent of gross exposures in anyone grade; Stipulation of exposure levels under some of the following headings:

(a) Sub-PLR lending.
(b) Fixed Interest rate.
(c) Geographical region-wise ceiling.
(d) Maturity-wise exposures.
(e) Precious Metals like gold, diamond.
(f) Retail Lending.
(g) Small and Medium Enterprise.
(h) Large Borrowers beyond cut-off level.

CREDIT RISK

As observed by RBI, Credit Risk is the major component of risk management system and this should receive special attention of the Top Management of a bank. Credit risk is the important dimension of various risks inherent in a credit proposal, as it involves default of the principal itself. Credit risk may arise due to internal-meaning faulty appraisal, inadequate monitoring, unwillingness on the part of borrower to honour commitments despite being capable or external factors such as government policies, industry-related changes.

Credit Risk is the potential that a bank borrower/counter party fails to meet the obligations on agreed terms. There is always a scope for the borrower to default from commitments for one or the other reason resulting in crystalisation of credit risk to the bank. These losses could take the form of outright default or alternatively, losses from changes in portfolio value arising from actual or perceived deterioration in credit quality that is short of default. Credit risk is inherent to the business of lending funds to the operations linked closely to market risk variables. The objective of credit risk management is to minimize the risk and maximize bank's risk adjusted return by assuming and maintaining credit exposure within the acceptable parameters. Measurement of credit risk is crucial if the banks have to appropriately price their loan products, set suitable limits on amount of credit to be extended as well as the loss exposure it accepts from any particular counter party.

Credit risk consists of primarily two components, viz. Quantity of risk, which is nothing but the outstanding loan balance as on the date of default and the Quality of risk, which is the severity of loss defined by Probability of Default as reduced by the recoveries that could be made in the event of default.

Thus credit risk, is a combined outcome of Default Risk and Exposure Risk. The elements of Credit Risk is Portfolio risk comprising Concentration Risk as well as Intrinsic Risk and Transaction Risk comprising migration/ down gradation risk as well as Default Risk. At the transaction level, credit ratings are useful measures of evaluating credit risk that is prevalent across the entire organization where treasury and credit functions are handled. Portfolio analysis help in identifying concentration of credit risk, default/ migration statistics, recovery data, etc.

In general, Default is not an abrupt process to happen suddenly and past experience indicates that, more often than not, borrower's credit worthiness and asset quality declines gradually, which is otherwise known as migration. Default is an extreme event of credit migration. Managing default risk through efficient risk management system helps bank in building healthy credit portfolio besides maximizing returns. Risk Management System would help in providing unity of direction in accomplishment of the corporate goals.

Off-balance sheet exposures such as foreign exchange forward contracts, swaps, options, etc. are classified into three broad categories such as Full Risk, Medium Risk and Low Risk and then translated into risk weighted assets through a conversion factor and summed up.

Thus the management of credit risk includes:

(a) measurement through credit rating/ scoring,
(b) quantification through estimate of expected loan losses,

(c) Pricing on a scientific basis, and
(d) Controlling through effective Loan Review Mechanism and Portfolio Management.

TOOLS OF CREDIT RISK MANAGEMENT

The instruments and tools, through which credit risk management is carried out, are detailed below:

(a) Exposure Ceilings

Prudential Limit is linked to Capital Funds—say 20 per cent for individual borrower entity, 45 per cent for a group with additional 5 per cent/10 per cent for infrastructure projects, subject to approval of the Board of Directors. Threshold limit is fixed at a level lower than Prudential Exposure; Substantial Exposure, which is the sum total of the exposures beyond threshold limit should not exceed 600 per cent to 800 per cent of the Capital Funds of the bank (i.e. 6 to 8 times).

(b) Review/Renewal

Multi-tier Credit Approving Authority, constitution-wise delegation of powers, sanctioning authority's higher delegation of powers for better-rated customers; discriminatory time schedule for review/renewal, Hurdle rates and Benchmarks for fresh exposures and periodicity for renewal based on risk rating, etc.

(c) Risk Rating Model

Set-up comprehensive risk scoring system on a six to nine point scale. Clearly define rating thresholds and review the ratings periodically preferably at half yearly intervals, to be graduated to quarterly so as to capture risk without delay. Rating migration is to be mapped to estimate the expected loss.

(d) Risk-based Scientific Pricing

Link loan pricing to expected loss. High-risk category borrowers are to be priced high. Build historical data on default losses. Allocate capital to absorb the unexpected loss. Adopt the RAROC framework.

(e) Portfolio Management

The need for credit portfolio management emanates from the necessity to optimize the benefits associated with diversification and to reduce the potential adverse impact of concentration of exposures to a particular borrower, sector or industry. Portfolio management shall cover bank-wide exposures on account of lending, investment, other financial services activities spread over a wide spectrum of region, industry, size of operation, technology adoption, etc. There should be a quantitative ceiling on aggregate exposure on specific rating categories, distribution of borrowers in various industries and business group. Rapid portfolio reviews are to be carried on with proper and regular on-going system for identification of credit weaknesses well in advance. Steps are to be initiated to preserve the desired portfolio quality and portfolio reviews should be integrated with credit decision-making process.

(f) Credit Audit/Loan Review Mechanism

This should be done independent of credit operations, covering review of sanction process, compliance status, review of risk rating, pick up of warning signals and recommendation for corrective action with the objective of improving credit quality. It should target all loans above certain cut-off limit ensuring that at least 30 per cent to 40 per cent of the portfolio is subjected to LRM in a year so as to ensure that all major credit risks embedded in the balance sheet have been tracked and to bring about qualitative improvement in credit administration as well as Identify loans with credit weakness. Determine adequacy of loan loss provisions. Ensure adherence to lending policies and procedures. The focus of the credit audit needs to be broadened from account level to overall portfolio level. Regular, proper and prompt reporting to Top Management should be ensured. Credit Audit is conducted on site, i.e. at the branch that has appraised the advance and where the main operative limits are made available.

RISK RATING MODELS

The need for the adoption of the credit risk-rating model is on account of the following aspects:

- Disciplined way of looking at Credit Risk.
- Reasonable estimation of the overall health status of an account captured under Portfolio approach as contrasted to stand-alone or asset-based credit management.
- Impact of a new loan asset on the portfolio can be assessed. Taking a fresh exposure to the sector in which there already exists sizable exposure may simply increase the portfolio risk although specific unit level risk is negligible/minimal.
- The Co-relation or co-variance between different sectors of portfolio measures the inter-relationship between assets.
- Concentration risks are measured in terms of additional portfolio risk arising on account of increased exposure to a borrower/group or co-related borrowers.
- Need for Relationship Manager to capture, monitor and control the overall exposure to high value customers on real time basis to focus attention on vital few so that trivial may do not take much of valuable time and efforts.
- Instead of passive approach of originating the loan and holding it till maturity, active approach of credit portfolio management is adopted through securitisation/credit derivatives.
- Pricing of credit risk on a scientific basis linking the loan price to the risk involved therein, though the factor of business compulsion and competition is always there.
- Rating can be used for the anticipatory provisioning, certain level of reasonable over-provisioning as best practice.

Given the past experience and assumptions about the future, the credit risk model seeks to determine the present value of a given loan or fixed income security. It also seeks to determine the quantifiable risk that the promised cash flows will not be forthcoming. Thus, credit risk models are intended to aid banks in quantifying, aggregating and managing risk across geographical and product lines. Credit models are used to flag potential problems in the portfolio to facilitate early corrective action.

COUNTRY RISK AND INTER-BANK EXPOSURE

During the course of their business operations, banks invariably assume inter-bank exposures of varying degree arising from customer's trade transactions, placement of money as bank's liquidity management, hedging, trading in securities, transactional banking services such as clearing, custodial and depository services, etc. As these transactions involve credit risk proper evaluation of credit risk is essential wherever an exposure on other banks is assumed in any form.

In this regard, the bank shall put in place proper credit rating models to evaluate the credit risk and rate the counter party so as to fix suitable exposure limits and mechanism for the off-balance sheet exposure, maximum tenor of exposure, etc. in inter-bank transactions. The rating model shall take into account both financial (capital adequacy, asset quality, profitability, liquidity) and non-financial (country, ownership, management, market perception) parameters. Depending on the past exposure and dealings, in respect of various rating categories of the counter party banks, the maximum exposure ceiling may be suitably fixed in relation to the Capital Funds position of the bank so as to assume and absorb the credit risk.

When a bank undertakes cross border lending and investment activities and finance is extended to its constituents under foreign trade transactions, it encounters country risk, comprising of Settlement Risk, Transfer Risk, Sovereign Risk, Non-Sovereign Risks, Cross Border Risk, Currency Risk, etc. Country risk management involves aggregation of country exposures and monitoring thereof against pre-defined limits on the basis of rating framework. Till such time banks evolve their own internal rating mechanism, the country risk classification adopted by ECGC Ltd.—the seven categories classification of countries ranging from Insignificant risk to off-credit rating, may have to be adopted. Currency risk is the possibility that exchange rate changes will alter the expected amount of principal and return of lending or investment. At times, banks may try to cope with this specific risk on the lending side by shifting the risk associated with exchange rate fluctuations to the borrowers.

BASEL II REQUIREMENTS

Basel II, released by Basel Committee on Banking Supervision in June 2004, has proposed the adoption of a better risk sensitive and balanced portfolio framework for the calculation of capital to risk weight on credit exposure. It is intended to bring the regulatory capital requirement more in line with the economic capital allocation approach.

The expected loss/unexpected loss methodology forces banks

to adopt new Internal Ratings Based approach to credit risk management as proposed in the Capital Accord II. Under the IRB approach (both Foundation and Advanced) banks will be allowed to use their own internal estimates to determine the borrower's credit worthiness to assess the credit risk.

In todays parlance, default arises when a scheduled payment obligation is not met within 90 days from the due date. Exposure risk is the loss of amount outstanding at the time of default as reduced by the recoverable amount. The loss in case of default is D * X* (1-R), where D is Default percentage, X is the Exposure Value and R is the recovery rate. The extent of provisioning required could be estimated from the Expected Loss Given Default (which is the product of Probability of Default, Loss Given Default and Exposure at Default). That is ELGD is equal to PD X LGD X EaD. After knowing the PD, it is necessary to calculate the proportion of loan loss on default. A historical data of 5 to 10 years may be considered enough for estimating the proportion of loan loss on default and the average may be tabulated in respect of all the rating grades, as under:

Rating of a/c	*AAA*	*AA*	*A*	*BBB*	*BB*	*B*	*C*	*D*
PD								
LGD								

Under the New Basel II Accord, assessment of Credit Risk can be carried out in any of the three approaches, viz. Standardised Approach, Foundation Internal Rating Based Approach and Advanced Internal Rating Based Approach. At present, banks in India in general and PSU banks in particular, are ready to migrate to Basel II only at a conceptual and academic level and they have to travel a long distance when it comes to organizational and technological readiness to go ahead with it to adopt the international practice.

In Standardised Approach, bank allocates risk weight to each of the assets and off-balance sheet items and produces a sum of Risk Weighted Asset Values (RW of 100 per cent may entail capital charge of 8 per cent and RW of 20 per cent may entail capital charge of 1.6 per cent). The risk weights are to be refined by reference to a rating provided by an approved External Credit Assessment Institution that meets certain strict standards. Under the Foundation Internal Rating Based Approach, Bank rates the borrower and results are translated into estimates of a potential future loss amount that forms the basis of minimum capital requirement. Under Advanced Internal Rating Based approach, the range of risk weights will be well diverse.

CONCLUSION

Growth in the economy during the last decade or so has been facilitated the Non-Banking Financial Sectors and hence there is an urgent need to focus on the need to integrate the financial market by leveraging on the strengths of NBFS. Banks are risk averse to lending, owing to lack of proper credit information mechanism, high transaction cost, weak enforcement of collateral, bankruptcy framework, high NPA, directed credit issues, staff accountability concept, etc. Laid back banking approach and related structural problems in the banks needs to be addressed. The explosive growth in the markets for securitised assets and for credit derivatives has offered bank new ways and means in managing as well as transferring credit risk.

In many banks in India, particularly in the PSU sector, it is believed that loans are akin to Indian marriages, where divorce is not feasible even when it is clear that the relationship is incompatible. Despite detailed technical analysis that supports a credit decision, it is the credit officer who decides on a proposal based on his own judgment. However, when it comes to rating of a borrower, the system and model in place should be such that who ever in the bank rates the borrower, the result should be same in at least 90 per cent of the cases. Banks need both the information and system to rate the level of risk in a credit proposal. In order to achieve this, credit officers should work as a team and share learning with an institutional commitment to develop capabilities through ongoing and well-designed credit training. Bank should lend according to its appetite within the need-based assessment of the credit requirement of the borrower.

The ideal credit risk management system should throw a single number as to how much a bank stands to lose on credit portfolio and therefore how much capital they ought to hold.

8

Enterprise Risk Management—An Eye Opener

V. SREERAMAN

Business is all about returns for the risks undertaken. However, every commercial enterprise has to cope with uncertainty. Uncertainty adds to risk but also provides an opportunity that, if properly exploited, could enhance the value of the firm and, if not addressed at the right time, could also result in erosion of value. A risk-centric business management approach advocates responding to risk and exploiting the opportunities as they arise. Such a strategy can help the business think tank identify and grow business that offer optimal risk-adjusted returns and hence maximize shareholder value.

Thus, CROs (Chief Risk Officers) seem to be on the rise advocating Enterprise Risk Management (ERM) as a solution to the increasing complexity witnessed in the global business environment; in other words, enterprise risk management is all about determining what level of risk an organization is prepared to accept as it seeks to build shareholder value.

In simple terms, the essence of ERM is to answer the question—"Am I taking the right risks as well as the right amount of risk?" ERM is characterized by a more integrated and forward-looking approach that applies a common risk language in aligning strategy, processes, people, technology and knowledge to the evaluation and management of risks. An important aspect of ERM is the strong linkage between measures of risk and measures of overall organizational performance.

CHANGING SCOPE

Traditionally, risk management in organization was limited in scope to evaluation of pure loss exposures, such as property risks, liability risks and personnel risks. This was addressed by way of entering into relevant contracts with insurers. In the 1990s, as many businesses began to expand, the scope of risk management had to widen to look into speculative financial risks. This led to the birth of Financial Risk Management that began to address commodity price risk, interest rate risk and currency exchange rate risk.

Encouraged by the success of financial risk management, some organizations are taking the next logical step, to address comprehensively organization's pure risks, speculative risks, strategic and operational risks.

This approach has come to be regarded as Enterprise risk management. At the heart of this approach is the desire to increase shareholder value.

WHY ERM?

Traditionally, organizations used to adopt "managing risks by silos" approach. This was based on the belief that different types of risks are the responsibility of various corporate rate and business units. However, the last decade has witnessed financial disasters of severe levels occurring on a regular basis resulting in collapse of organizations once considered as "well managed".

The collapse of Barings Bank was an eye opener in revisiting the belief aforementioned. Also, with factors such as globalization, technology, regulation, restructurings, changing markets, and competition (both within the local markets as well as from across the borders) creating uncertainty, there scans to be a paradigm shift in the way the organizations think about management of risks. Organizations have come to accept that in an extremely competitive environment, crisis management or contingency planning would never help; it is embarrassing, time consuming and expensive. Crisis management can at the most protect oneself against the down-side but could not guide towards improvement of the business performance. Contingency planning might help one to be flexible enough to follow an alternate plan to counter the unforeseen surprises in the chosen plan, primarily with a view to curtail the negative implications. To put it in layman's words, both these might help us avoid pitfalls and surprises on the way but may not enable us to reach the destination targeted. Rather, given that uncertainties have to be accepted, preparing oneself to understand them and prepare accordingly seems to be key to success.

Mark Haynes Daniell, in his book, *World of Risk – Next Generation Strategy for a Volatile Era*, lists down "ten sets of recurring patters". He suggests that an understanding of these elements is a fundamental requisite for meeting the strategic challenges of contemporary business environments. These are:

1. Globalisation which redefines many of the major sources of risk and opportunity that we face today.
2. Complexity of the dynamic global system that is increasingly rapidly every day.
3. Turbulence creating or reflecting greater than average discontinuity in a system.
4. Dynamism forcing the organization to understand, anticipates, influence and take advantage of the inevitable movements and changes.
5. Acceleration in the pace of change in virtually every global system.
6. Continuous Obsolescence and Re-invention driving horse the point that traditional models of business management are no more useful.
7. Connectivity leading to a new state of business dependence on technology.
8. Convergence by way of two non-identical systems moving towards a common end point or pattern without merging or fully consolidating into one entity.
9. Consolidation of sub-systems and formerly independent entities into a larger unified block.
10. Rationalization whereby over time, systems tend towards a more efficient relation of means to ends.

Considering the emerging phenomenon listed above, it is imperative that organizations have in place a process that continuously monitors the impact of various risk factors influencing the organizational performance. This is where ERM is considered to be a significant contributor.

ERM analyzes and measures the integrated effects of risks on strategic objectives, including finances and cash flows. By aggregating risks, an organization can identify risk concentrations as well as offsetting risk patterns. This approach leads to superior resource allocation decisions because they are based on the risk-return characteristics of the organization's entire risk portfolio as opposed to those of its individual risk "silos".

EMERGENCE OF ERC

The collapse of mega companies, accounting scandals, market volatility, litigation and terrorism present a vast range of threats and risks. In this scenario, the top managements have come to clearly understand that earnings can no more be managed only by the accountants but more by identifying the earnings drivers and pro-actively managing them. Study of literature clearly reveals that ERM as a concept has emerged as a result of internal demand and external developments. Advances in risk management tools and methodologies have also aided the growth of this body of knowledge. ERM differs from TQM in that the latter tolerates no failures.

ERM preaches that a defined number of failures can be tolerated if the organization is convinced that the cost of guarding against them is more expensive than the risks they impose.

Internal Demand

With increase in accounting irregularities coming to limelight, resulting in sudden death of large organizations, the shareholders across the world have started demanding more transparency in the way the business is managed.

The frequency of reporting has increased as well as the details provided. Post Enron, the role of people managing strategic issues have come under extensive scrutiny. "Corporate Governance" is one of the latest buzz words doing the rounds in major corporate entities.

Consequently, the people who manage the business would like to carry out a scientific analysis of all risk factors that would influence the results both in the short and in the long run before committing anything to the stakeholders.

External Development

Development in e-business, Changes in regulations, say, reporting of quarterly earnings/segment reports, availability of risk transfer products like credit derivatives, catastrophe bonds allowing the option to retain the risk as well as to hedge are all pointers to the fact that risks have come to be accepted but require careful analysis. Derivatives, insurance and hybrid products are available at the disposal of management to reduce undesirable risks, but these carry a cost. Therefore, an integrated approach to perceiving the impact of different risks at an organizational level is essential before a decision to challenge the risk is taken.

ERM addresses following queries –

- What risks am I facing, and how do they compare to those of my peers?
- Do I understand inter-relationship of different risks?
- How are these risks changing based on changes in my business environment?
- What level of risk should I take?
- How should I manage those risks?
- Do I know who our risk owners are? Do they have systems in place for measuring and monitoring risk?

Traditional Approach and Enterprise Risk Management

Traditionally, functional, divisional or departmental barriers guided the approach to managing risks. In a multi-product corporation, independent business units addressed the business risks associated with their overall strategy and profitability, such as those related to products, pricing and relationship management. Collection of overdue debt and handling of bad debts was considered the responsibility of the marketing executives while abnormal increase in interest cost much more than the budgeted levels was taken to be the effect of treasurer's action. The quality department had to bother about the defectives and finance department had to look into the optimal level of insurance covers as if it just involved the principle of minimizing the costs. Such a strategy did not work, simply because, risks are highly interdependent and cannot be segmented and managed solely by independent units. For instance, by outsourcing a non-core function to mitigate performance risk, an organization assumes credit and supply-chain risks. Moreover, such an approach would not provide the strategic management team with a consolidated report that displays the "total risk" the enterprise is subject to. The objective is to move from "Risk is not my responsibility" mind-set to "Risk is everyone's responsibility".

Traditional focus was on risk mitigation (using controls to limit exposures to problems) while the trend is towards risk portfolio optimization (finding a fit between the risk appetite and opportunities with a view to capitalize on the rewards that would arise).

TYPES OF RISK

Several bases of classification of risk are reported in literature. Based on these, we could classify the types of risk as follows:

1. *Credit risks* – Lending and counter-party exposures.
2. *Market risks*—Interest rate, foreign exchange, equity and commodity exposures.
3. *Business risks*—Volatility in volumes, margins or costs.
4. *Operational risks* – Day-to-day processing errors to fraud.
5. *Strategic risks*—Environmental influences that prevent the organizations from meeting the business objectives.
6. *Reputation risks* – Damage to brand and corporate image.
7. *Regulatory or contractual risk.*
8. *Financial risks*—Unreasonable liabilities to support day-to-day operating activities.
9. *Information risks* – Unreliable, irrelevant information and also untimely in addition to inadequate security systems, and
10. *New risks* – New competitors or emerging business models, recession risks, outsourcing risks, political risks and the like.

ERM looks at all these risks in the light of inter-dependencies amongst them as well as the probability of occurrence against the implications on performance.

ERM Process

As a process, ERM is composed of eight inter-related components:

1. **Internal environment**—defined in terms of ethical values, personnel (competencies and capabilities, in addition to

attitudes and beliefs), management's operating style and culture, apart from the most significant of all—risk appetite.

2. **Objective setting**—with reference to four major perspectives, viz., strategic, operations, reporting and compliance, after finalizing the views on risk appetite and risk tolerance.
3. **Event Identification**—for the purposes of assessing risk through an understanding of the inter-relationships between events, by aggregating them horizontally across an entity and vertically within operating units.
4. **Risk assessment**—involving evaluation of both the likelihood and impact of potential events and their effects on the objectives using qualitative and quantitative methods.
5. **Risk response**—dealing with selection of a strategy that consider both the risk appetite and costs *vs.* benefits and normally falls under one of the four categories, viz., avoidance, sharing, reduction and acceptance.
6. **Control activities**—concerned with laying down policies and procedures to ensure that risk responses are carried out efficiently and encompass IT infrastructure and management, security management and software (general controls) as well as ensuring completeness, accuracy and validity of data capture and processing (application controls).
7. **Information and Communication**—suggesting the significance of capturing and sharing relevant information from both internal and external sources in a form and time-frame that would enable timely, efficient and effective reaction in addition to exchange of relevant data with external parties such as customers, vendors, regulators and shareholders.
8. **Monitoring**—both on an ongoing basis and via one-time evaluation to see to it that the process is applied at all levels.

ERM AND PORTFOLIO EFFECT

The concept of active portfolio management can be applied to all the risks within an organization. If the different risks the organization is subject to can be viewed as a portfolio, then diversification effects from natural hedges could be fully exploited. For this, the strategic management should consider themselves as fund managers, setting portfolio targets and risk limits to ensure appropriate diversification and optimal portfolio returns.

There is another issue worth considering. The bad things do not occur in concert. The different devastating effects, say, earthquake, serious power failure, competitive threats, supply chain disruptions, financial market volatility, management malfeasance, etc. do not tend to affect the earnings potential and hence the performance in the same fiscal period. In other words, these events are not perfectly correlated. There might be an element of negative correlation in built into the relationship amongst these elements. For instance, when rupee value falls against major foreign currencies, raw material imports may prove costlier but sales revenue registers growth due to surge in export business. Therefore, there is the need to have a holistic view of the risks influencing the organization, thereby focusing one's attention on the independence and interdependence of the risks to unravel the "natural hedge" among some of their effects. This is where there is a lesson drawn from the Modern Portfolio Theory. This theory clearly advocates that what matters is not the risk of the individual investment but the risk of the entire portfolio. Therefore, by diversifying the effects of risks that are not perfectly correlated, the organization can achieve optimal results.

The first step in implementing an Enterprise Risk Management process would involve detailed discussions with various heads of the departments. This is done to get an insight into different risks as perceived at a departmental level.

After sharing information on the different strategic, financial, operations and hazard risks facing the company, the next step is to pick those risks that would benefit from a portfolio approach.

The key is to select those risks that are lease correlated. All the risks are mathematically reduced to a common denominator, called a unit of risk, which permits comparison with each other. The exercise helps determine the most advantageous portfolio of risk to take to market.

ERM PRACTICES AT ROLLS-ROYCE

At Rolls Royce, it was found that the finance manual that explains their financial policies and authorization requirements for obtaining project funding needed amendment. A project could be anything from launching a new aero-engine or installing an industrial engine in a power project to relocating a business from one country to another. The finance manual explained how to compile a business case for a project, explaining the forms to be submitted for authorization and asking for extensive information about financial variables.

However, it was noticed that nowhere it asked for a qualitative or quantitative assessment of potential risks and what effect they might have on outcomes. The consequence was that resources were not allocated to areas based on marketing data and similar analyses but not based on risk data leading to sub-optimal returns and substantial time and money was wasted on activities like drafting agreements that is not significant when analyzed from a risk perspective. It was therefore decided that when someone proposes a project, they must attach a "risk register" that analyzes the key risks and their potential consequences.

CONCLUSION

No business entity in a risk free environment. ERM does not attempt to create one such environment. Rather, it empowers the management to operate more effectively in environments filled with risks. It provides enhanced capability to—

1. Align risk appetite and strategy.
2. Link growth, risk and return.
3. Enhance risk response decisions.
4. Minimize operational surprises and losses.
5. Identify and Manage cross-enterprise risks.
6. Provide integrated responses to multiple risks.
7. Seize the opportunities.
8. Rationalize the capital.

ERM is a process that is not limited to one event or circumstance. It is a dynamic process that unfolds over time and permeates every aspect of an organization's resources and operations.

9

Strategic Risk Management

VISHNU KANHERE

Risk is a word of many meanings. It means different things to different people. It is an issue, which touches our lives every day, every moment. It transcends from small risks like whether your will be caught in the rain without an umbrella to a major risk like a car crash where you are not using seat belts.

"Risk is an issue that could impact (may be impair) your ability to meet your objectives." Risk occurs when there is an event with more than one possible outcome with consequences in either direction—desirable/undesirable. Each outcome has an associated frequency or probability of occurring depending on the circumstances. Though the occurrence of risk is probabilistic, it is a fact of life, which we have to live with.

We have been told—The smart fish gets the worm. But here again, the worm could be fixed to bait and the so-called smart fish that catches the worm would end up on someone's dinner plate.

WHY IS RISK BECOMING SO IMPORTANT TODAY?

Risk has been with us since the beginning of the human race. Why is it that addressing, comprehending, analyzing and managing it has become so important today. The most important reason for the increased importance of risk in our lives is that we have now started appreciating the fact that uncertainty and the resultant negative impact of risk are growing with globalization. Risk is becoming more important than ever before because changes are so rapid and a all pervasive that it requires preparedness and quick reflexes to launch pre-emptive moves to counter emerging, altered, scenarios. Let us look at some of the major factors that have made risk so important today.

Legislation is becoming tougher

- Legislation is now more extensive – from compensation to environmental laws, third party liability to PIL's. Public laws granting compensation for corporate wrongs are becoming stricter.
- Legislation is more stringent – Corporate Governance – Naresh Chandra Committee – Sarbannes Oxley Act, the list is growing everyday.
- Risk assessment is necessary to avert legal liability – esp. in areas of health and safety.

Insurance is more Expensive and Difficult to Obtain

- Insurance is no longer the cheap option.
- Open-ended cover is not widely available.
- Insurance Companies expect and require clients to manage risks on their own and do not offer a blanket cover any longer.
- Insurance does not recoup full loss even if the claim is accepted by the insurer.
- Insurance payouts are slow and difficult to obtain.
- Many risks are not covered more specifically intangibles like loss of goodwill reputation.
- Insurance ultimately is reactive and not a pro-active way of mitigating risk.

Customer—Attitudes

- Corporate clients want to pass on risks to suppliers and service providers and want to de-risk their own business.
- Consumers are more aware and this has led to greater litigation and claims.
- Stockholders are more aware of risks-affecting business value and therefore increased risk reflects in lower stock values and *vice-versa*.

Public Awareness

- People/society at large expects higher standards of probity in corporate behaviour, which means that companies have to manage risk in a better way than in the past.

Management Attitudes

- Management is wiser, from past incidents and wants risk management practices in place.
- Professional and pro-active managements promote risk management.
- With the advent of Global Corporations, Risk has become internationalized. Corporations face, global worries and short fuse wire of decisions have a greater impact on corporate bottom lines.
- Privatization—High-risk infrastructure sectors are now in the business domain leading to greater understanding and provisioning for business risks.

TYPES OF RISK

Risk is contingent on a number of factors. An event, action, happening or outcome, which in one situation is perfectly normal or insignificant, can in a different setting be a cause of grave risk. It comes in different shapes and sizes and is different for different people in different situations. Typically, risks have been classified in many ways and are of different types. The list is seemingly endless and takes on that shade of meaning and colour as the objective in looking at it.

Risk Appreciation

Human beings appreciate and understand in two ways and respond to it also in two basic ways. We appreciate risk logically, systematically and analytically or by instinct and gut feel.

Both approaches used individually have their shortcomings and flaws. But used in combination work best. Tempering logic with gut feel and reasoned hunches work better.

Before we will look at strategic risk management in the management's perspective it is worthnoting the two types of responses to risk. There are two basic types—Risk averters and Risk takers.

Those avenue to risk tend to try and minimize it to maximize value.

Those who are Risk takers don't mind taking risks to make gains (and of course bear losses).

At lower levels of stakes the difference between the two approaches and options does not seem very significant but this difference in approach makes a considerable difference when the stakes are high. You are offered a lottery ticket where you pay Rs. 10 with a 10 per cent chance of winning Rs. 100. You will probably be indifferent to buying it. What if the investment is Rs. 1,000,000 and the pay-off 10,000,000 with a 10 per cent chance of success? It will surely not be the same.

The decision will depend on your attitude to risk as well as your "Risk appetite". How much risk can you stomach?

GENESIS OF RISK

Risk originates from vulnerabilities and threats and results in an adverse impact when it occurs. It is a function of threats, vulnerabilities and their impact. Vulnerabilities produce weaknesses that increase risk. Threats are external adverse factors that have a chance of occurrence. Greater the threat, greater the risk. The impact is the adverse consequences and damages that can flow from the materializing of the threat. The greater the impact, the higher the risk. Thus minimizing the chance of threat materializing, reducing vulnerabilities and minimizing the damage of impact helps to mitigate risks.

Though in looking at all these, one cannot lose sight of selecting the right approach and the correct perspective and if one addresses risk with preconceived notions about its probable causes it can lead to disastrous results as the real threat often lies elsewhere.

A Bank which builds a strong security system and spends substantial money on protecting itself from on external threat of robbery or dacoity often ignores that it could eventually turn out to be on insider job and by not paying enough attention in screening and monitoring its employees it exposes itself to avoidable risk, losing a substantial money in the bargain. It ends up spending on security, which goes waste and also loses money over and above due to insider abuse, which it is unable to prevent.

SRM: THE DEBATE

- Risk management is the process by which executive management, under board supervision, identifies the risk arising from the business . . . and establishes the priorities for control and particular objectives. . . . The Cadbury Report, 1992.
- There is still no general agreement on where the boundaries of the subject lie, and a satisfactory definition of Risk Management is notoriously difficult to formulate. . . . For practical purposes, therefore, the emphasis of risk management tends to be on risk awareness, assessment and mitigation.
- Risk Management consists, basically, in altering in a desirable manner the states a system may reach and their probabilities or manage their consequences.

The Road Map to risk management can be summed up below:

- Risk Analysis and Assessment.
- Awareness.
- Assessment—Monitor threats, Assess Vulnerabilities, Estimate impact.
- Prioritization—Analysis into acceptable, un-acceptable and middle of the road risks.
- Prevention.
- Planning for the future.
- Risk Mitigation.
- Prevention of occurrence of Threats.
- Strengthening the system against Vulnerabilities.
- Minimizing the Impact of damage.

What then are the Requirements for Successful Risk Management?

- Management must be aware of the hazards and their impact on the business, and how they could be avoided, prevented and reduced.
- There must be appropriate facilities and equipment.
- There must be appropriate systems and procedures, including monitoring and auditing performance.
- There must be an appropriate organization, sufficient level of competence, with suitable communication and training arrangements.

- There must he appropriate arrangements for detecting and handling emergency situations.
- Risk Management must be actively and continuously promoted throughout the organization.

The Tools, which can be used for effective risk management, are – Control, Insurance, Loss Prevention, Technological Innovation, Learning, Information, Distribution and Robustness.

The Mantra for success thus seems to be to Bear, Share and Insure. Bear what you can yourself, given your risk appetite. Share risk within the industry by creating risk sharing and averting mechanisms and finally insure what cannot be controlled and pass on the risk to insurers.

Monitoring and Planning for the future involves a continuous process to adopt a Plan, Do, Check and Act cycle, in order to de-risk your business to the extent possible.

MANAGING RISKS THE PRO-ACTIVE WAY

The Right Corporate Strategy

This involves creating and putting in place proper Ownership structure, carrying on your business on sound premises based on de-risking the processes and following Risk policies which minimize exposure to uncertainties.

Managing People

Managing people is another way of managing business risks. This involves –

- Setting standards from the top.
- Quick adaptation to change.
- Balance and experience – multi-tasking employees.
- Allocate responsibility for risk Management.

Manage Processes

This is the nuts and bolts of risk management and involves developing and putting in place Sound Policies, Best Practices. Adequate Procedures, Easy to implement Guidelines, Sufficient

Documentation, Drills, Safer Solutions, Isolation of threats and Active protection of assets.

Spread the Risk

The next step in managing risk in a pro-active way is to spread it by, Outsourced processes, shared risks, spreading risks using hedging option, swaps and derivatives.

Insure against Risks

What cannot be controlled or shared is protected by taking intelligent insurance cover.

Disaster Recovery Planning—Business Continuity Planning

Finally, DRP-BCP is the last resort to minimize the effects of the damage caused due to the adverse impact of threats materializing into reality.

What then is effective Risk Management?

- Continuous Risk Management (CRM) is a structured management practice with processes, methods, and tools for managing risks in support of project or program's goals.
- CRM provides a disciplined environment for pro-active decision making to:
  - assess continually what could go wrong (risks),
  - determine which risks are most important to deal with,
  - implement strategies to deal with those risks,
  - measure and assure effectiveness of the implemented strategies, and
  - The Risk Management Framework used in CRM and be summarized below:

Formulation

- Develop Risk Management Plan.
- Perform risk assessment during systems analysis sub-process.
- Establish an initial set of risks (simplest technique is brain-storming).

- RM plan and risk profile evaluated and base-lined in evaluation sub-process.

Implementation

- Implement risk management process defined in the plan.
- Implement risk tracking system.
- Use risk management continuously to control and mitigate risks.
- Use risk assessment to identify and analyze risks.

The effective use and implementation of CRM results in a paradigm shift in the way businesses plan, implement and operate.

Key Issues

What then are the key issues in strategic risk management today?

1. Risk management at what cost?
2. Risk *vs.* Returns.
3. Risk-Stability-Change (Change as a risk management tool).
4. Environmental issues – Union Carbide is a classic example of what can go wrong.
5. Health and Safety – Pepsi/Coke episode of unacceptable levels of pesticides and its impact on their sales is a case in point.
6. Maintaining Security – 9/11 is the most glaring example, which comes to mind.
7. Pre-empting Fraud – ENRON sums it up all.
8. Staying financially healthy – PSUs, dotcoms and once again Enron gives us food for thought.
9. Special Risks: IT Risks, Financial Risks, Business Risks, People Risks pose special risks which need specialist advice and action, and
10. Contingency Planning and Crisis Management.

CRISIS MANAGEMENT

Management error or external changes lead to crisis. In the event of a crisis, inaction leads to failure. Recognizing the crisis, taking prompt action and effecting change leads to survival and improvement.

In fact in today's competitive world one can say that corporations gain market leadership through risk management.

A final word of caution! We come across a number of quantitative models including sophisticated software tools for managing risks. Essentially they attempt to forecast uncertainties and extrapolate likely cash flows and losses. Simulation techniques are also used to understand how individual risk sources contribute to a company's consolidated risk and also judge the Company's appetite for risk. The competing insurance options are also evaluated using statistical techniques and present value analysis.

But what one has to clearly bear in mind is that the apparent sophistication of quantitative risk assessment can conceal critical and dubious assumptions and seriously impair and invalidate the assessed magnitude of risk. Any quantitative assessment of risk should be accompanied by a non-quantitative descriptive assessment also. "Decision-making starts where Formulae end". As a wag has remarked, "There was only a 5 per cent chance of the bank failing, but when it did fail I didn't lose just 5 per cent of my money, I lost all of it."

The Need of the hour then is to convert Vulnerabilities and Weaknesses into Strengths and use Threats as opportunities for change.

10

Corporate Governance, Risk Management and Internal Audit

NARENDRA M. APTE

To begin with it would be appropriate to note definitions of the two terms, 'Corporate governance' and 'Risk management'. Organization for Economic Co-operation and Development defines 'Corporate Governance' as a 'set of relationship between company's management, its Board, its shareholders and other stakeholders. Corporate governance also provides the structure through which the objectives of the company are determined. Good corporate governance should provide proper incentives for the Board and management to pursue objectives that are in the interest of the company and its shareholders/ stakeholders and should facilitate effective monitoring, thereby encouraging firms to use resources more effectively. 'Risk management', on the other hand, is defined as the identification, analysis and economic control of all such risks that may threaten assets, resources, or earning capacity or a firm/company.

Risk management is in reality 'an all business activities embracing' tool and with a high standard of risk management, it would naturally be possible to ensure high standard of corporate governance. The close relationship between corporate governance and risk management can thus be easily understood.

Two broad categories of risks that the professional risk management deals with are:

(a) Business Risks, and
(b) Pure or Insurable risks.

Ordinarily, internal auditor does not get involved in any decision-making process. It is felt that in case of risk management it would be prudent for the internal auditor to have a say. The internal audit should ensure that risk management practices adopted by the concerned departments are adequate, considering the nature of various risks and their likely impact on the business operations of the company.

In a large company, different departments, depending on the nature of risk involved, may handle the risk management function. It would, therefore, be necessary for the Internal auditor to first get a fair idea of various categories of risks and action to be taken to confirm that enough safeguards are in place for managing different risks.

FINANCIAL RISKS

If the internal auditor has to report on how the financial risks are being managed, he would consider the impact of following sub-categories of financial risks:

- Market risks: Under this sub-category foreign exchange risk, interest risk, commodity risk and equity risks are considered.
- Liquidity risk.
- Credit risk.
- Economic risk arising out of changes in economic structure.
- Sovereign risk: failure of a government company/corporation or a State government to honour its loan obligations or other commitments.

While examining the financial risks, the internal auditor has to pay special attention to the following points:

- *Receivables and bad/doubtful debts:* This is one significant item, which has to form part of the internal auditor's report, as in many companies financial crisis starts with a poor control on this item. It has a direct bearing on the financial health of many companies, particularly those companies with a very large number of customers, like telecom companies, electricity companies.
- *Inventories:* Optimum Inventory levels are decided by the Production and other concerned departments but it is the

internal auditor who can ensure that the inventory carrying cost is properly controlled and is optimum.

- *Investments:* The risk arising out of changes in interest rate policies of the Central Government/Reserve Bank of India can be quite substantial and has to be assessed at regular intervals because such changes result in substantial erosion of investments as in Debt schemes of Mutual Funds, etc.
- *Foreign exchange transactions:* The risk of financial loss on account of depreciation of foreign exchange bank balances or receivables has to be critically examined for reporting to the Board.

STRATEGIC RISK

This risk arises out of wider aspects of a company's activities, e.g., risk arising due to poor marketing strategy/acquisitions, strategy, changes in consumer, behaviour, poor product launches. From the point of corporate governance, management of strategic risks may be considered to be responsibility of the senior management/Board of Directors. In such a scenario, the internal auditor may not be entrusted with the responsibility of any critical examination of the risk management process.

OTHER RISKS

In case of other risks like environmental, technological and operational risks the internal auditor may not have an expert knowledge of the severity of the risks and he would have to take help of the concerned Departmental heads to critically examine the process of the risk management.

INSURABLE OR PURE RISKS

In this case, one major issue that the internal auditor may be required to examine could be adequacy of the insurance cover and the cost of such cover. For this purpose he would have to examine the past experience about insurance claims, loss prevention and safety measures, and, of course, the risk profile of various assets. In view of the increased competition between the general insurance companies, both in the public and private sectors, it has become possible to obtain a mega policy cover and the internal auditor may be the right authority to critically examine all aspects regarding the insurance cover obtained for all risks of a company.

It would be necessary for the internal auditor to weigh impact of all these risks on the financial performance of the company and make a suitable quarterly report to the Board of Directors/CEO/MD of the company. This report could be submitted when the Board considers the Quarterly performance of the company.

Mr. Prakash A. Shimpi, in a book edited by him, gives a very useful and illustrative list of various risks faced by companies operating in different industries like: Telecommunication, drug manufacturing/pharmaceutical and airlines. Obviously the same risk management techniques will not work in all situations and to that extent it makes the job of corporate governance *vis-a-vis* risk management more complex and challenging.

In large companies, very often, different departments manage different type of risks. It, therefore, becomes essential to ensure proper co-ordination between the various departments managing risks. An integrated approach to risk management is hence recommended to ensure better management and better results.

Audit Committees have a significant role to play in ensuring proper co-ordination between different departments managing different risks.

Many big companies have already recognized the role of the Audit Committee in regard to risk management and there is a growing realization that integration of all risk management functions can deliver better results if the audit committee can provide the necessary guidance.

DISCLOSURE PRACTICES

As per the Listing Agreement, the Audit Committee of a listed company has to review risk management policies of the company.

It is reasonable to expect that the corporate governance report covers the areas of existing or potential risks to the business of the company and briefly outlines the Board's perception of such risks and action taken by the company.

When we examined Annual reports of leading companies for the year 2003-04 we observed that although a growing number of companies have started disclosing their risks, the level of disclosure differs as also the content.

In the following paragraphs we look at disclosure in annual reports of companies operating in different sectors of our economy.

- In the Corporate Governance Report (CGR) of Raymond Ltd., for the year ended 2003-04, there is only a passing reference to terms of the Audit Committee of the company which included, *inter-alia,* 'reviewing the adequacy of internal control systems, and internal audit function, ensuring compliance of internal control systems and reviewing the Company's financial and risk management policies'.
- In the CGR of Tata Steel Ltd., also for the year 2003-04, it is recognized that "Risk is inherent in business activity, particularly in the steel industry. The report says that the Company has processes in place to identify warning signals at an early stage to hedge itself against potential threats. On the other hand, it explains, these processes enable early recognition of opportunities emerging in the business environment.' The Tata Steel CGR also highlights certain important facts, e.g., "the Steel industry displays strong commodity characteristics and is subject to cyclical price movements in business cycles. The Company has sought to mitigate the impact of this commodity characteristic of the steel industry in its focus markets and it has achieved some measure of success in its endeavour." 'On the production front, the report says, "development of value added products has significantly enriched the product mix, which is less susceptible to price cycles. The Company follows prudent financial practices. It is considered opinion of Management that it has taken all possible steps to maintain and enhance the competitive position of the Company."

In the Annual Report of Infosys Technologies Ltd. for the year 2003-04, there is a separate, comprehensive 'Risk Management Report' (RMR). The RMR provides details of all key risks faced by the Company and steps taken by the Company to manage those risks. In a way this RMR is a model for all companies to follow. It will not be out of place to note here the External and Internal Risk factors, *vis-a-vis* the Business objectives of the Company, enumerated in the RMR of Infosys Technologies:

Business Objectives	*External Risk Factors*	*Internal Risk Factors*
Financial performance	Macro economic factors	Financial reporting
Achieve revenue growth	Exchange rate fluctuations	risks Liquidity and
Sustain profitability	Political environment	leverage Contractual
Increase revenue productivity	Competitive environment	compliance,
Client and market focus	Concentration of revenues	Compliance with
Grow client relationships	inflation and cost structure	local laws
Differentiate client offerings	Immigration regulations	intellectual property
Broaden geographical footprint	Security and business	management
Execution excellence	Continuity Technology	Engagement
Leverage Global Delivery Model	obsolescence	execution
Control operational costs		Integration of
Improve quality and productivity		subsidiaries, Human
Organizational development		resource
Develop and retain competencies		management
Develop global workforce		Culture, values and
Develop 3 tiers of leadership		leadership.

In the annual report of Tata Motors Ltd., risks and concerns of the Company have been classified under four heads: (a) risk arising out of increase in input costs, (b) risk arising out of increase in fuel prices, (c) risk arising due to exchange fluctuations, and (d) risk arising out of acquisition of a car company in South Korea. Impact of the above risks on the profitability of the Company has been mentioned in the report.

In the annual report of Tata Power Ltd., risk management has been dealt with separately. Major risks faced by the Company have been mentioned as (a) risk on account of electricity tariff regime changes, (b) risk on account of reducing availability of gas for Trombay Thermal Power Station of the Company, (c) risk on account of increase in price of feed material, (d) risk of financial liability on account of major legal case with a competitor, (e) risk to proposed power projects on account of adverse changes in Government policies/regulations in the power sector and risks associated with development/construction, and (f) a risk associated with the telecom business wherein the Company has significant investments.

SUGGESTIONS FOR BETTER DISCLOSURE

Since standard of risk management practices has a direct influence on the financial health of the company, it is felt that the level of disclosure in the Annual report in this regard should be specified in the Listing Agreement itself. Obviously, it would require a change in the Listing Agreement but time has come for making appropriate reforms in this important governance indicator. It is felt that standard of disclosure of the level of Infosys Technologies Ltd., though ideal, may not be immediately achievable. However, even if companies are given time of say three years to achieve, it would mean a new beginning, something to be happy about.

11

Managing Exchange Risks

YOGESH UPADHYAY AND S.K. SINGH

A new economic era has arrived. The world is quickly becoming economically integrated, forcing unprecedented changes at every level of industry. Companies, small and large, are facing record levels of foreign competition for domestic and international market share. And the proliferation of trade agreements and trade blocs among countries is not only increasing the complexity of international trade but also heightening the level of competition.

Nearly a decade after the phrase "global marketing" came into vogue, the world's largest consumer companies are coming to terms with what it really means. Marketing guru Theodore Levitt first coined the phrase in 1983, arguing that consumers around the world were beginning to have more and more alike.[1] As their tastes converged, the argument went, brands, products, and campaigns would become increasingly uniform, allowing global companies to benefit from cost efficiencies as they sold the same product the same way all over the world. He wrote:

> "The world is becoming a common marketplace in which people— no matter where they live—desire the same products and lifestyles. Global companies must forget the idiosyncratic differences between countries and cultures and instead concentrate on satisfying universal drives."

In an effort to gain secure and preferential access to foreign markets and in turn achieve a higher degree of economic security while manoeuvring into the twenty-first century, effectively managing international financial risk has become essential for export-oriented firms and a mainstream need in the market place. Accelerating international receivable and managing international credit risk are increasingly viewed as a variation on domestic collections and credit management. On the sale side, more and more firms now use trade finance as just another tool to sell their goods, often providing an increasingly important advantage over competitors.

As the international trade increases, the economic importance of exports grow and competition increases, customers are requiring more sophisticated and competitive trade finance solutions. To defend market share and customer base, and more importantly, to be pro-active in meeting these needs, it is essential to—

1. understand how international trade agreements, emerging trade blocs, and global trends will impact customer base;
2. identify and assess target market's international opportunities, risks and finance needs in this environment;
3. target the international niche that matches the firm's competitive strengths and appetite for international risk; and
4. deliver timely, cost-effective solutions.

In an effort to increase the competitiveness, many countries have entered into trade agreements with one another. From 1947 through 1994, a total of 108 regional trade agreements were notified to the General Agreement on Tariff and Trade (GATT), the international body that governs approximately 90 per cent of world trade. Some of these agreements are between two countries; others are among many, creating trade blocs.

As growth in exports accelerates and global competition intensifies, the focus should be on the markets best for firms. The markets can be identified in a number of firms. The markets can be identified in a number of ways. Companies, for example, can be classified by their size (small, medium or large) or by their geography (e.g., those located in different regions). They can be identified by their industry, by their needs. They can even be categorised by their target export or import markets or developing countries. Another approach is to evaluate the revenue potential of the different market categories sorting by a variety of criteria. After analysing the firm's market, find the best match between the firm's international risk appetite, resources and target market. Whatever markets the firm chooses to target, delivering timely, cost-effective need-based solutions is the key.

The demand for new and more creative financing by companies of all sizes will continue to increase. Offering trade finance solutions to meet these needs can be a defensive strategy to prevent competitors from making inroads in a firm's customer base and market place. To compete in this increasingly demanding environment, banks must first identify and focus on their preferred international market niche. Identifying the right niche may require more than one method of analysis.

Understanding trade finance needs is vital if many of the firm's customers export to developing countries, for example, and the firm wishes to keep the competition at bay and increase its value to these companies. It is important to understand the obstacles they face. For example, a real impediment to selling to companies in developing countries is the buyer's difficulty and expense in obtaining financing to pay for imports. By assisting developing country importers with liberal payment terms. Exporters can often export more of their products.

This strategy is becoming more important because of the exponential increase in global competition. Exporters that can manage risks and move quickly to arrange financing at attractive rates will win the business. Increasing competitive pressures, changing market environments, and new information processing technologies are allowing bankers to offer new financial products and services. In order to effectively provide additional, value-added services, commercial banks must better understand the needs of the customers they serve and develop products to meet these needs. In developing these services, it is important to remember that banks are shifting emphasis from activities related to deposit intermediation to the business of managing risks. Unfortunately, the values of today's currencies oscillate widely, to the despair of international companies that want to plan ahead.[2]

THE ECONOMIC CONSEQUENCES OF EXCHANGE RATE CHANGES

The general concept of exposure refers to be degree to which a company is affected by exchange rate changes. Growth in international business has made more firms susceptible to exchange rate risk. Foreign exchange rate risk is a result of unexpected currency fluctuations that affect the value of the firm (i.e., the net present value of its cash flow streams). This risk arises whenever firms transact business in more than one currency. Thus, exposure to exchange risk can occur when settlement for a transaction is in a foreign currency.

Transaction Exposure

Transaction exposure arises out of the various types of transactions that require settlement in a foreign currency. Unexpected variability in cash flows caused by fluctuating currency exchange rates is a result of the firm's transaction exposure.

Operating Exposure

A real exchange rate affects a number of aspects of the firm's operations. An important factor is its pricing strategy. In international market that a firm tries to ensure that:

1. Its margins remain intact in home and abroad in all currencies;
2. Successfully save its margins as competition with foreign low-priced-goods intensify, and
3. Pricing strategy of the firm which can provide a cushion to adjust exchange risk.

Accounting Exposure

Accounting exposure is the result of translation of foreign operations form local currencies involved to home currencies. It arises whenever a company is committed to a foreign currency-denominated transaction. Here the assets and liabilities of foreign subsidiaries are converted from the foreign currency to the domestic currency, by way of an accounting translation process that reflects one of several exchange rate adjustments. As a result, the values of assets and liabilities can change, thus affecting the consolidated financial settlements of the parent corporation. In short, both transaction exposure and translation exposure contribute to foreign exchange risk.

Here, attempt has been made to analyse the tools available and application thereof, to manage transaction exposure.

Tools to Manage Transaction Exposure

This process of risk reduction is called *hedging*. Essentially, hedging involves assuming risks that counterbalance on the risks that one is attempting to avoid. Hedging a particular currency exposure means establishing an offsetting currency position such that whatever is lost or gained on the original currency exposure is exactly offset by a corresponding foreign exchange gain or loss on the currency hedge.[3] Regardless of what happens to the future exchange rate, therefore, hedging locks in a home currency value for the currency exposure. In this way, hedging can protect a firm from unforeseen currency movements. There are costs to hedging. Businesses must determine their risk tolerance levels and the amount they are willing to spend to hedge a unit or risk. Once the amount they are willing to spend to hedge a unit of risk. Once the amount of risk that a business wants to hedge has been determined, the next step is to identify the instrument to be used to reduce the unwanted risk. These instruments are commonly referred to as derivatives.

A derivative is a financial contract whose value is derived from an underlying asset or index. There are several types of derivatives, including forward contracts, futures, equity swaps, interest rate swaps, and options. While each of these instruments can play a role in minimising risk, forward contracts, currency futures, currency options and currency swaps are most often used in mitigating foreign exchange rate risks. Table 11.1 gives an account of the most common derivative instruments used to hedge against foreign exchange risk.

In a complex and rapidly evolving financial environment the banker can develop new relationships and strengthen existing ones by becoming familiar with these instruments and how they work to reduce foreign exchange rate risk. To conclude, growing recognition of the economic benefits of derivatives markets, a better understanding of such instruments and more prudent use of them means closer competition and greater management responsibility against actual or potential risks.

Forward Market Hedge

In a forward market hedge, a company that has sufficient foreign currency will sell foreign currency forward, whereas a company that is in short of foreign currency will buy the currency forward. In this way, the company can fix the selected currency value of foreign currency cash flow.

TABLE 11.1

Market for Selected Financial Derivative Instruments

(in billions of US dollars)

Instruments	*Notional amounts outstanding*					
	1990	*1991*	*1992*	*1993*	*1994*	*1995*
Exchange-traded instruments	2290.4	3519.3	4634.4	7771.1	8862.5	9185.3
Interest rate futures	1454.5	2156.7	2913.0	4958.7	5777.6	5863.4
Interest rate options	599.5	1072.6	13850.4	2362.4	2623.6	2741.7
Currency futures	17.0	18.3	26.5	34.7	40.1	37.9
Currency options	56.5	62.9	71.1	75.6	55.6	43.2
Stock market index futures	69.1	76.0	79.8	110.0	127.3	172.2
Stock market index options	93.7	132.8	158.6	229.7	238.3	326.9
Over-the-counter instruments	3450.3	4449.4	5345.7	8474.6	11303.2	17990.0
Interest rate swaps	2311.5	3065.1	3850.8	6117.3	8815.6	–
Currency swaps	577.5	807.2	860.4	899.6	914.8	–
Other swap-related derivatives	561.3	577.2	634.5	1397.6	1572.8	–

1. Calls and puts. 2. Data collected by the International Swaps and Derivatives Association (ISDA) only; the two sides of contracts between ISDA members are reported once only. 3. Adjusted for reporting of both currencies; including cross-currency interest rate swaps. 4. Caps, collars, floors and swaptions.

Source: Futures Industry Association, various Futures and Options Exchanges, ISDA and BIS calculation adapted from V.K. Bhalla, "Global Trade Financing and Use of Derivatives in Volatile Forex Market", *Chartered Secretary*, July, 1997, p. 779.

Currency Futures

In 1972, the Chicago Mercantile Exchange opened its International Monetary Market (IMM) division. The IMM provides an outlet for currency speculators and for those looking to reduce their currency risks. Trade takes place in currency futures, which are contracts for specific quantities of given currencies; the exchange rate is fixed at the time the contract is entered into, and the delivery date is set by the board of directors of the IMM. These contracts, which represented the first step in the development of financial futures, are pattered after those for grain and commodity futures contracts, which have been traded on Chicago's exchanges for over 100 years.

Currency futures is just like any other future deal, where an agreement is entered to buy or sell a standard object of value on a future day at a rate (price) agreed between parties through a transaction in an organised market. The unique feature is that it is a future deal in a specific currency. Such currency futures (CF) are transacted on the floor of an organised Future Exchange. Though forward exchange and CFs contract look similar. Some differences could be enlisted below:

- Forward exchange enjoys a global market where banks and financial institutions form the basic players. CFs, however, are traded only on certain floors of specified exchanges. Chicago, New York, London, Tokyo and Singapore happens to be some of the important floors where currency futures are traded.
- Forward Exchange uses sophisticated trading system using electronic and satellite media GLOBEX, an electronic Mercantile Exchange System (introduced in 1992), whereas in currency futures, open outcry in the pit of the aforesaid Exchange is still practiced.
- Forward exchange contracts have tailor made contract size for customers. But in currency contracts, contract sizes are standardised. The Chicago currency futures exchange (the largest amongst the CF exchanges) are mentioned in Table 11.2.

TABLE 11.2

Contract Size for Currency Futures in Chicago Financial Future Exchange[4]

Exchange	*Contract size*	
Pound Sterling	£	25,000
Canadian Dollar	C$	1,000,000
Deutsche Mark	DM	1,25,000
Dutch Guilder	DG	1,25,000
Franc (France)	FF	12,50,000
Yen (Japan)	V	1,25,000
Franc (Swiss)	SFr	1,25,000
Mexican Peso	Peso	10,00,000

- Forward contracts are very flexible in terms of their maturity or delivery time or date. But, in case of CF, maturity and delivery has been standardised. They fall on 10th March, June, September and December, i.e., every quarter of a calendar year.
- Forward contracts are settled through contracts with banks, whereas CFs are settled through a clearing house especially set-up, for the purpose.
- Leverages tend to be high in CFs. However, in case of forward there are no such leverages and such contracts are based on client-bank relationship.
- CFs are extremely liquid because of standardised contracts in comparison to future context.
- Last but not the least, is the question of credit risk. In case of CFs, the credit risk is borne by the clearing house where the contract is executed. This is not the case of forward exchange contract. Under forward contract, the counterpart entering the agreement generally bears the risk.

Money Market Hedge

An alternative to a forward market hedge is to use a money market hedge. A money market hedge involves simultaneous borrowing and lending activities in tow different currencies to lock in a specific currency value of a future foreign currency flow.

The equality of the net cash flows from the forward market and money market hedges is not coincidental. The interest rates and forward and spot rates were selected so that interest rate parity holds. In effect, the simultaneous borrowing and lending transactions associated with a money market hedge enable a concern to create *homemade* forward contract. The effective rate on this forward contract will equal forward rate if interest rate parity holds. Otherwise, a covered interest arbitrage opportunity would exist.

Risk Shifting

Selling companies tries to avoid the risk of transaction exposure altogether by asking the counterpart to price the order in the home currency of the selling company. Despite the fact that this form of risk shifting is *zero-sum game,* it is common in international business.

Firms typically attempt to invoice exports in strong currencies and import in weak currencies. Though, it not possible to gain form risk shifting if one is dealing with informed customers or suppliers.

Pricing Decisions

In case of credit sales made overseas, the general rule is to convert the home currency and the importers country's currency by using the forward rate, not the spot rate. If the exporter's currency price is high enough, the exporter should follow through with the sale. Similarly, if the dollar price on a foreign-currency-denominated import is low enough, the importer should follow through on the purchase. This is keeping in view that the price of currency is volatile.

Exposure Netting

Exposure netting involves offsetting exposures in one currency with exposures in the same or another currency, where exchange rates are expected to move in such a way that losses (gains) on the first exposed position should be offset by gains (losses) on the second currency exposures.[5] The assumption underlying the exposure netting is that the net gain or loss on the entire currency exposure portfolio is what matters, rather than the gain or loss on any individual monetary unit.

Companies practice multi-currency exposure netting all the time.

In practice, exposure netting involves one of three possibilities:

1. A firm can offset a long position in a currency with a short position in that same currency.
2. If the exchange rate movements of two currencies are positively correlated (for example, the Swiss franc and Deutsche Mark), then the firm can offset a long position in one currency with a short position in the other.
3. If the currency movements are negatively correlated, then short (or long) positions can be used to offset each other.

Currency Risk Sharing

In addition to, or instead of, a traditional hedge, the currency risks associated with the contract can be shared by the companies involved. Currency risk sharing can be implemented by developing a customized hedge contract imbedded in the underlying trade transaction. This hedge contract typically takes the form of a price adjustment clause, whereby a base price is adjusted to reflect certain exchange rate changes. Here, as the base price crosses a limit, then only the parties would share the currency risk. The *neutral zone* represents the currency range in which risk is not shared.

Currency Options

Whatever advantages the forward or the futures contract might hold for their purchaser, they have a common disadvantage: While they protect the holder against the risk of adverse movements in exchange rates, they eliminate the possibility of gaining a windfall profit from favourable movements. This was apparently one of the considerations that led some commercial banks to offer *currency options* to their customers. Exchange-traded currency options were first offered in 1983 by *Philadelphia Stock Exchange* (PGLX).

Currency Options (COs) are the rights given to the buyers of foreign currency to buy (call) or sell (put) a specific amount of foreign currency at a specific exchange rate (the strike price) till a specific date when the contract expires. The seller of the put option or call option must fulfil the contract if the buyer so desires it. Because the options not to buy or sell has value, the buyer must pay the seller of the options some premium for this privilege. An *American options* can be exercised at any time up to the expiration date; a *European option* can only be exercised at maturity.

Options are purchased and traded either on an organized exchange (such as the PHLX) or in the over-the-counter (OTC) market. Exchange-traded options or listed options are standardised contracts with predetermined exercise prices, standard maturities (one, three, six, nine and twelve months), and fixed maturities (March, June, September, and December). Options on the PHLX are available in the ECU and seven currencies – Deutsche Mark, Pound Sterling, French Franc, Swiss Franc, Japanese Yen, Canadian Dollar, and Australian Dollar – and are traded in standard contracts half the size of the IMM futures contracts. Other organized option exchanges are located in Amsterdam (European Stock Exchange).

Table 11.3 enlists the standardized currency options in Philadelphia Exchange.

In many circumstances, the firm is not sure whether the hedged

TABLE 11.3

Currency Options Contract Size for Various Currencies Provided by Philadelphia Exchange[6]

Exchange	*Contract size*	
Australian Dollar	A$	50,000
Pound Sterling	£	31,250
Canadian Dollar	C$	50,000
Deutsche Mark	DM	6,200
Franc (France)	FF	2,50,000
Yen (Japan)	V	62,50,000
Franc (Swiss)	SFr	62,500
European Currency Units	ECU	62500

foreign currency cash inflow or outflow will materialize. For example, a company X GE learned on January 1 that it had won a contract to supply boilers to Y. But suppose that although X's bid on the contract was submitted on January 1, the announcement of the winning bid would not be until April 1. During the three-month period from January 1 to April 1, X does not know whether it will receive a payment of DM 25 million on December 31 or not. This uncertainty has important consequences for the appropriate hedging strategy.

Company X would like to guarantee that the exchange rate doesn't move against it between the time it bids and the time it gets paid, should it win the contract. Until recently, X or any company that bid on a foreign contract in a foreign currency and was not assured of success would be unable to resolve its foreign exchange risk dilemma. The advent of currency options has changed all that. Specifically, the solution to managing its currency risk in this case is for X, at the time of its bid, to purchase an option to sell DM 25 million on December 31. For example, suppose that on January 1, X can buy for $ 1,00,000 the right to sell Citibank DM 25 million on December 31st a price of $ 0.3828 per Deutsche mark. If it enters into this option contract with Citibank, X will guarantee itself a minimum price ($ 9.57 million) should its bid be selected, while simultaneously ensuring that if it lost the bid, its loss would be limited to the price paid for the option contract (the premium of $ 1,00,000). Should the spot price of the Deutsche mark on December 31 exceed $ 0.3828, X would let its option contract expire unexercised and convert the DM 25 million at the prevailing spot rate.

Two types of options are available to manage exchange risk. A *put* option, such as the one appropriate to X's situation, gives the buyer the right, but not the obligation, to sell a specified number of foreign currency units to the option seller at a fixed dollar price, up to the option's expiration date. Alternatively, a *call* option is the right but not the obligation, to buy the foreign currency at a specified dollar price, up to the event its bid is rejected. A put option is required when the party requires foreign exchange. By buying a put option the party sells the domestic exchange to procure the right amount of foreign exchange at a specified rate. The reverse is done, when payment is needed to be done by the party. A call option is entered so that foreign exchange can be bought by exchanging the domestic currency.

RELEVANCE TO INDIA

Many exporters lack a complete understanding of the foreign exchange risk associated with this new global era. In India, the bankers provide additional, value-added services to these exporters by helping them understand the nature of their foreign exchange rate risk and assisting them in developing and implementing appropriate strategies to minimise these risks.

Use of derivatives or hedging instruments does not seem to be very attractive in India. This may be due to lack of flexibility in such future contracts, especially in terms of settlement date and contract size.

Besides, the commercial banks in India provide for forward contracts quotations for up to a year and also provide hedge against the currency rate fluctuations. This makes the future contract laclustre to Indian firms. The fact remains that, over the counter forward contracts covered by the banks are more convenient to the firms.

Sooner or later, as the rupee is made fully convertible at current as well as capital account, the use of derivatives to manage exchange risk shall become inevitable.

CONCLUSION

Derivatives are not available to Indian firms. This is because they come within the ambit of the foreign exchange regulation and require governments approval. The other side of the picture remains that, such instruments are lack-lustre before the ever competing commercial banks who provide over the counter facilities with better forward contracts. However, as the country is moving towards globalisation and the foreign banks entering into every sphere, the business sooner or later shall join the global current.

NOTES AND REFERENCES

1. "Global Marketing with a Pinch of Local Salt", *Economic Times, Ibid.*, p. 6.
2. *The Economist*, May 28, 1988, p. 81.
3. Alan C. Shapiro, *Multinational Financial Management*, Prentice-Hall of India Pvt. Ltd., New Delhi, 1996, p. 201.
4. Abhijit Dutta, "Currency Futures and Currency Options: Innovations in International Money Market", *Chartered Secretary*, May, 1996, p. 483.
5. Alan C. Shapiro, *Ibid.*, p. 201.
6. Abhijit Dutta, *Ibid.*, p. 484.

REFERENCES

1. Cornell, Bradford, and Alan C. Shapiro, "Managing Foreign Exchange Risks", *Midland Corporate Finance Journal*, Fall 1983.
2. Dufey, Gunter and S.L. Srinivasulu, "The Case for Corporate Management of Foreign Exchange Risk", *Financial Management*, Summer, 1984.
3. Giddy, Ian H., "The Foreign Exchange Option as a Hedging Tool", *Midland Corporate Finance Journal*, Fall 1983.
4. Srinivasulu, Sam and Edward Massura, "Sharing Currency Risks in Long-Term Contracts", *Business International Money Reports*, February 23, 1987.
5. *Using Currency Futures and Options*, Chicago: Chicago Mercantile Exchange, 1987.
6. Garman, Mark B. and Steven W. Kohlhagen, "Foreign Currency Option Values", *Journal of International Money and Finance*, December, 1983.

12

Role of Logistics in Supply Chain Management

ANIL CHANDRA PATHAK

Logistics and purchasing are relatively tactical. During the years, both of them have progressed and are recognized as critical functions. Today, logistics spends approximately 10 percent of a manufacturer's income. Purchasing (supply management) spends some 60 percent.

Logistics is concerned with the movement of goods. In many cases, logistics is responsible for both incoming goods and the distribution of goods to the next member of the supply chain and frequently to the end customer itself. In virtually all cases, logistics professionals design and manage the firm's distribution system, consisting of warehouses, distribution points, and freight carriers.[1]

The relationship between supply management and logistics tends to vary from firm to firm. In some cases, supply management plays a dominant role in sourcing and pricing logistics services. In other cases, the logistics department performs these services with little or no supply management involvement. The critical issue should not be one or jurisdiction. Rather, it should be one of professionalism and excellence. It should not matter whether supply management or logistics plays the key (or dominant) role. What does matter is that professional supply management practices are employed.

WORLD CLASS LOGISTICS MANAGEMENT (WCLM)

World Class Logistics Management (WCLM) forms the third side of the WCSCM triangle. Logistics professionals play an important role in the success of supply chain management in the management of transportation, storage and warehousing activities. Unfortunately, many companies define logistics as synonymous with the term SCM, thus ignoring the contributions and roles of supply management and demand management. A model for WCLM is presented in Figure 12.1.

Logistics management deals with the handling, movement, and storage activities within the supply chain, beginning with suppliers and ending with the customer. One of the best selling books in logistics states: "Logistics is the part of the supply chain process that plans, implements, and controls the efficient, effective flow and storage of goods, services, and related information from point of origin to point of consumption for the purpose of conforming to customer requirements."[2] Typical logistics roles include the management of many or all of the following activities:

- Traffic and transportation.
- Warehousing and storage.
- Industrial packaging.
- Materials handling.
- Inventory control.
- Order fulfilment.
- Demand forecasting.
- Site location analysis.
- Returned goods handling.
- Parts and service support.
- Field service and maintenance.
- Value-added services.
- Salvage and scrap disposal.

The list above is not exhaustive. In some organizations, supply management reports to logistics. If that is the case, then logistics is also responsible for all activities in the supply management discipline.

Storage points for goods and information, such as outside warehouses and stocking points within a firm's distribution network, are critical in meeting customer satisfaction goals. For example,

Clerical

- Process paperwork.
- Confirms actions of others.
- Emphasis is on expediency.
- Reactive focus is on current planning and replenishment period.
- In-bound and out-bound transportation are organizationally separate.
- Lack of collaboration between supply chain members.
- Reporting is at a very low level with virtually no organizational power.
- Data are historical.

Mechanical

- Historical demand and stock-outs drive replenishment.
- Functional discrimination between warehousing/ stores transportation, material handling and field service still operate relatively independently in a decentralized manner.
- Historical demand and stock-outs drive replenishment decisions.
- High transaction levels exist with associated costs.
- Logistic contributes little to firm's bottom line.
- Report to logistics/ warehouse/transportation manager.

Pro-active

- Cross-functional team orientation.
- Aligns distribution resource plan with master planning process
- Involved with Marketing and Sales to reconcile forecast errors.
- Inbound and outbound logistics are integrated Reports at an enough level that it can influence upper management strategy, but in a "hit and miss" manner.
- Improved customer satisfaction through pro-active storage and distribution.
- Balance schedule attainment, customer satisfaction, inventory risk, and investment.
- Real-time data are now available and used, but not across entire chain.

World Class

- Manage logistics requirements of the "extended enterprise".
- Actively involved in developing corporate strategy.
- Enable customization at the product level to better meet diverse customer needs.
- Increased value added activities and process employed in-transit of products and materials as well as the point of sale.
- Logistics specifications are integrated with product specifications.
- Real-time traceability or materials and product exists throughout the supply chain and the information is utilized.
- Comprehensive performance measurement is realized.
- Works in collaborative cross functional teams that include suppliers and/or customers when appropriate.
- Logistics chain competencies are enhanced via a consultancy role within the supply chain as a "logistics process improvement education".

1 2 3 4 6 7 8 9 10

FIG. 1

Four-Stage Model of World Class Logistics Management Logistics Defined

transportation costs represent about 40-50 percent of the total cost of logistics and perhaps 4-10 percent of product selling prices. Thus, from a total systems viewpoint, logistics becomes the means whereby the needs of customers are satisfied through the coordination of materials and information flows that extend from the marketplace, through the firm and its operations, and beyond that to suppliers.

INTEGRATION OF LOGISTICS PLANNING

The imperative to integrate logistics planning with material and capacity planning throughout the supply chains is very real. Noted logistics scholar Martin Christopher has observed: "The concept of integration within the business and between businesses is not new, but the acceptance of its validity by managers is." The integration of logistics, multi-level planning, and supply management objectives makes sense when one considers the highly customer-centric business strategies that have emerged in recent years. Customer needs vary, and firms can tailor logistic systems to serve them better and more profitably.

Indeed, whether they know it or not, senior managers of every retail store and diversified manufacturing company compete in businesses that are distinguished by their logistics, in effect "logistically distinct businesses", organized, or potentially organized, around the delivery characteristics of logistic pipelines: the channels of transport, warehousing, handling, and control through which manufactured goods flow.

As the competitive context of business continues to change, logistics activities and processes must be integrated into strategic-level thinking and planning. In addition to organizational integration, much of the focus on logistics has been on reduction of cycle times in logistic activities. Cycle-time reduction and the elimination of waste in logistics processes have had a direct correlation to the enhancement of customer satisfaction.

EVOLUTION TO WCLM

In completing the third side of the WCSCM triangle, WCLM includes the following:

- *Increased Value-Added Activities.* WCLM "tailors" products to meet customer needs. The logistics characteristics for each type of customer are incorporated into each product's specifications. This includes such features not traditionally considered as part of a product "form, fit, and function." For example, product testing prior to delivery, applying special customer features and options prior to delivery, using packaging for a unique method of storage and/or marketing, applying special marking or labelling, employing technology to track materials throughout the supply chain, etc. The notion of "Tailored Logistics" implies that the product characteristics of how a product is packaged, handled, shipped, stored and supplied becomes every bit as much a part of a product's "specifications" as its material and operating attributes.[3]

- *Real-Time Traceability of Materials and Product throughout the Supply Chain.* WCLM organizations employ the use of paperless information technology to track inventory status and movement in real time.
- *Logistics Competencies Enhanced via Consultancy Role as "Logistics Process Improvement" Advocates.* WCLM experts are "on the road" a significant part of the time surveying supply chain member's logistics competencies. They educate supply chain members on "best practices" in a spirit of continuous improvement and the elimination of waste. The focus of logistics is "outward" toward the "extended enterprise".
- *Collaborative Cross-Functional Teams.* WCLM teams involve both customers and suppliers. The complexities of logistics environments and the ever-changing technology and world economic and political events necessitate a team-based, collaborative approach to logistics planning and execution. Teams typically are organized around product families as well as commodities.

IMPLICATIONS FOR SUPPLY MANAGEMENT

The fact that supply management is the key to SCM does not imply that other functional areas are not important. On the contrary, each functional area serves an important role in achieving WCSCM. The difference is that professionals in logistics, operations, information technology, engineering, accounting, marketing, legal, finance, and other functional areas commonly do not have the skills and experience required to manage the interrelationships on which successful supply chains are built. The integration of these interrelationships is what separated excellent supply chains from lesser ones.

Lead- and cycle-time reduction initiatives, the elimination of waste, and the implementation of advanced, integrated information systems that have characterized supply management in recent years also are well under way in the field of logistics. Unfortunately, supply management and logistics frequently do not collaborate in many companies. The time has come for collaboration to occur. Logistics and supply management will realize their greatest gains in efficiency and effectiveness through such collaboration. Only then can both traditionally separate disciplines achieve world-class status.

CONCLUDING REMARKS

For many in the field of SCM, the future holds substantive and far-reaching changes. These changes are largely driven by the following trends:

- Institutionalization of the SCM perspective.
- Increasing emphasis on supply chain relationships.
- Increasing emphasis on the long-term view.
- Use of information technology to enhance supply chain communications.
- Use of information technology to foster rapid decision making.
- An increasing focus which looks "outward" toward the intricacies of supplier and customer relations.
- The emergence of the supply management professional as a "manager and facilitator of relationships," versus and information broker whose attention is defined by commodity knowledge.

Increasingly, supply management professionals spend a majority of their time outside the boundaries of the employer's facilities. They will often "be on the road", adding value to their enterprise by helping suppliers achieve World Class Supply Management status.

A thorough grasp of the continually evolving perspectives of SCM is a necessary component of the skill set of any pro-active supply management professional. Such perspectives recognize the continuing need to integrate many competencies traditionally resident in other functional disciplines, in particular, demand management and logistics. Further, successful supply chain optimization depends on the coordination of cross-functional competencies in cross-enterprise teams. The supply management professional is the logical "team-leader" for such initiatives.

NOTES AND REFERENCES

1. D.M. Lambert and J.R. Stock, *Strategic Logistics Management*, 3rd edn. (Homewood, IL: Irwin, 1993.
2. D.J. Bowersox and D.J. Closs, *Logistical Management: The Integrated Supply Chain Process* (New York: McGraw Hill, 1996).
3. Joseph B. Fulier, James O'Connor and Richard Rawlinson, "Tailored Logistics: The Next Advantage", *Harvard Business Review*, May-June 1993, p. 87.

PART II

FINANCE AND RISK

13

Risk Finance

B. Ratna Ravikumar

Venture Capital is finance given to entrepreneurs with novel ideas for untried and emerging technologies. VC funding is not the normal tangible security-based financing with expectation of regular income flows like interest or dividend. It is risk capital, invested with an expectation of capital appreciation over 3 to 5 years. The points of distinction between Venture Capital and conventional financing by a banker/lender are given in Table 13.1.

VENTURE CAPITAL AND PRIVATE EQUITY FINANCE

Venture Capital refers to early stage financing given to young or fledgling companies. It bridges the gap between an idea and the first trickle of revenues. This includes the following:

(a) Seed Capital

This is the finance provided to companies when the business is still in the conceptual stage. It includes R&D financing for product development and for testing the technical feasibility of the product.

(b) Start-up Capital

This is the finance provided for manufacturing and commercializing the product including initial marketing expenses.

Private Equity Financing is a broader term. Besides Venture

TABLE 13.1

Points of Difference between Venture Capital and Conventional Financing

Sl. No.	*Points of Difference*	*Conventional Financing*	*Venture Capital*
1.	Primary Focus	Debt Servicing capacity of the investee Co.	Growth Potential of the Project.
2.	Collaterals	Secured against movable/immovable property	No Security/Guarantee; relies on the project and its promoters.
3.	Risk	Very Less	Very high
4.	Target Return	15%-16% p.a.	30%-40% (50% to 100% in some cases).
5.	Exit	Only through retirement of debt	Disinvestment options.
6.	Period of Investment	Can be short-term or long-term	3-5 years.
7.	Bureaucracy bottlenecks	More	Less.
8.	Participation Level	Does not take active interest in the project	Extends support at all the stages of the project.

Capital, it includes later stage financing given for expansion of companies that have already demonstrated their business potential but do not have access to the public securities market or to credit-oriented institutional funding sources. It includes finance given in buy-out and turnaround situations. Thus while venture capitalists invest in the early stages of business growth, private equity funds invest in the entire life cycle of the investee company.

TABLE 13.2

Some of the Top Deals Recently Made

	Name of the VCF	*Amount of Investment (Rs. in crores)*
1.	Newbridge capital and Temasek Holdings (direct investment Co. of Singapore Govt., the second largest foreign private equity investor in India) in MATRIX LAB, Hyderabad-based pharmaceutical Co. for 14 per cent stake @ Rs. 1500 per share. P/E ratio 15	607
2.	ICICI Ventures 50 per cent stake in Tata Infomedia	115
3.	Warburg Pincus, India's largest private equity investor in Radhakrishna Food Land, Mumbai-based fast food chain	230
4.	CDC (Now called Actis) in Punjab Tractors, a state government owned Co.	262
5.	ICICI Ventures 15 per cent stake in Samtel Colour, India's top colour picture tube maker (for future capacity expansion programme)	50
6.	ICICI Ventures Subhiksha Trading (Retail Sector)	38
7.	ICICI Ventures Glaxo Real Estate (Real Estate Sector)	30
8.	ICICI Ventures in Welspun India (Textile Sector)	75

GENESIS OF VENTURE CAPITAL

Venture Capital originated in United States of America in the mid-fifties. General George Doroit, a French born military man, who founded American Research and Development Corporation (ARD) in 1946, is considered to be the 'Father of Venture Capital'. In U.S., Apple Computers, Federal Express, Compaq, Intel, Sun Microsystems, Genetic and Microsoft are famous examples of companies, which received Venture Capital in the early stage of their development. In India, Venture Capital industry had its formal introduction in the budget speech of Dr. Manmohan Singh, the then Finance Minister and the present Prime Minister, in 1988. A cess of 5 per cent was levied on all technology import payments to create a pool of funds.

The Venture Fund that was created out of this cess was to be administered by the Industrial Development Bank of India. In November 1988, guidelines were issued for setting up of Venture Capital Funds/Companies (VCFs/VCCs) for investing in unlisted companies. India's first private sector Venture Capital Fund was set-up by ANZ Grindlays Bank.

HOW VENTURE CAPITAL WORKS

Venture Capitalist is a financial intermediary, that raises funds from several investors (called primary investors) and then invests it in growth-oriented new companies (called the venture capital undertakings or the investee companies).

(A)		(B)		(C)
Primary Investors	Investors' ⇒ Provide funds	Venture Capitalist (VCC/ VCF)	Invest funds in VCU ⇒	Investee Co./ Venture Capital Undertaking (VCU)

From the point of view of fund raising, funds are of the following three types:

(a) ***Captive Fund:*** This is an in-house private equity arm funded by a company and/or its clients.

(b) ***Semi-Captive Fund:*** This fund is similar to a captive fund but a portion of the money is raised from third party sources.

(c) ***Independent Fund:*** This is a VCF which raises money wholly from outside investors.

(A) Primary Investors are the following:

- Financial Institutions (All India Level/State Level).
- Commercial Banks.
- Insurance Companies.
- Corporate Sector.
- Mutual Funds.
- Multilateral Development Agencies such as World Bank.
- Foreign Institutional Investors.
- Non-Resident Indians.
- Public and others.

The primary investors have a large risk appetite as they contribute to venture capital companies/funds, which invest in companies that have no major collateral security to offer as security. Since they assume great risk, their return expectation from investment in venture capital companies/funds is also high.

(B) Structure of the Venture Capital Industry

There are broadly four categories of venture capital companies –

1. Venture Capital Funds sponsored by All India Development Financial Institutions, e.g.:
   (i) ICICI Ventures (sponsored by ICICI).
   (ii) Risk Capital Fund (sponsored by IDBI).
   (iii) Risk Capital and Technology Finance Corporation Ltd. (sponsored by IFCI).
2. Venture Capital Funds promoted by the State-Level Development Financial Institutions, e.g.:
   (i) Kitven Fund (Karnataka Information Technology Venture Capital Fund) promoted by KSIIDC, KSFC and SIDBI.
   (ii) Andhra Pradesh Venture Capital Limited promoted by APSFC.
3. Venture Capital Funds sponsored by public sector banks or their subsidiaries such as Canbank Ventures and SBI Caps.
4. Venture Capital funds set-up by Indian or foreign private sector institutions.

Private Funds have expectations of higher returns than funds promoted by banks or financial institutions. According to a survey, the return expected by foreign and private investors from information technology businesses is a minimum IRR of 43 per cent as against 30 per cent expected by public financial institutions. However, the bottom line is that if the deal succeeds a VCF gets a very high return on its investments. If the financed venture fails, the investment has to be written off. Some instances of such doomed investments are:

(i) e-ventures wrote off its $10 million investment in Chaitime.
(ii) Citibank Private Equity and Edelweiss Capital shut down Icleo, a portal for women and wrote off Rs. 1 crore.
(iii) Chryscapital wrote off $ 2 mn. invested in Avigna,— $1 mn. each invested in Broadcast India and Cheecoo. Like mutual fund, a Venture Capital Company may develop a portfolio of funds. Each fund may have a focus on different sector. Some funds finance early stage deals and some funds finance later stage deals. Funds, which invest in various industry sectors, across various geographical locations and in various stages of a company's life, are called generalist investors. Specialist venture capital companies invest in only a particular geographical area and in one or two sectors

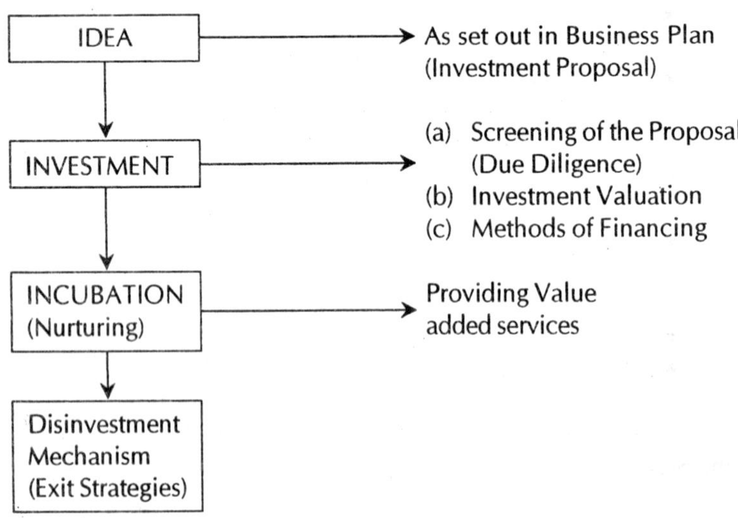

FIG. 13.1

Typical Stages in an Investment Cycle

only. The size of the deals considered for investment by different funds may also vary.

The Indian Venture Capitalist Association (IVCA) is the association of premier venture capital companies in India. The association was founded in 1992 to coordinate the activities of its members and has been building up a database on the venture activity in the country. It publishes an annual report every year.

(a) *Business Plan*

The first step in procuring Venture Capital is the preparation of Business Plan. A business plan should normally cover the following points:

- Full details of the project concentrating on the four basic elements – people, product, market and competition.
- Detailed Bio-data of the promoters and the key personnel.
- Cost of the project and means of finance, duly supported by the related plans, detailed estimates, proforma invoices, quotations, etc.
- Details of market studies, projected demand and supply.
- Projected Financial Statements for 5 years with assumptions underlying the figures.
- In case of an existing company audited financial statements relating to the preceding 3 years and estimates for the current year.
- Competitors in the field and competitive edge of the applicant-company in terms of product features, pricing, quality, etc.
- Details of all Government and statutory clearances/approval required for the project and copies of approvals/clearances already obtained from the authorities.
- Schedule of implementation of the project.
- The exit route and the year in which such exit is proposed to be offered.

(b) *Screening of the Proposal*

The Venture Capitalists do not finance all the ventures for which proposals are received. They invest only in a small percentage of business proposals, which they review. It is said that it is as hard to convince a VC that a business is sound as to get a first novel published. Proposals are subjected to due diligence process. The venture capitalist assesses whether the applicant has the passion, commitment and ethical values to turn his idea into a business.

What one should look for in a Venture Capitalist if he/she has the luxury of selecting a Venture Capitalist:

- Make sure that the VC approached has domain knowledge of the space you hope to be in.
- Find out if his existing portfolio of investments matches the type of business you hope to build.
- Match the stage of your project with the funding pattern of the VC.
- Choose between a domestic fund and an overseas fund based on what your business demands – dollar or rupee inputs.
- Track the VC's network of contacts and affiliations and judge if they can add value to your business.
- Find a fit between the returns your VC expects and what you see as the potential scalability of your business.
- Listen to your instincts – if the chemistry is right, sign with the VC.

(c) *Valuation Methods*

After having decided to finance a project, the next questions addressed by a venture capitalist would be how much to finance and how to finance.

How much to invest?

To determine the percentage of ownership to be acquired in a VCU, the VCI normally adopt the following valuation methods:

(a) Conventional Venture Capitalist Valuation method.
(b) The First Chicago method.
(c) The Revenue multiplier method.

Conventional Valuation Method

E.g. B Ltd. has developed a prototype that needs to be commercialized. B needs Rs. 4 million to establish production facilities and set-up a marketing programme. The company is expected to go public in 5 years and is expected to have revenues of Rs. 100 million and a PAT margin of 10 per cent on sales. Assume for the sake of convenience that there would be no further addition to the equity capital of the company.

The VC has a hurdle rate of return of 75 per cent (discounted) over a 5 years period. Firms with comparable sales and profitability and risk profile trade at 15 times earnings on the stock exchange.

What is the valuation of the company at the time of raising capital? Determine the percentage stake required by VC in B Ltd.

In order to get a 75 per cent return p.a., the initial investment of Rs. 4 mn. must grow to $4 \times (1.75)\ 5 = 4 \times 16.4 = 65.6$ mn. on disinvestments in year 5.

B's market capitalization in five years is likely to be $100 \times 0.1 \times 15$ mn. = Rs. 150 mn.

Percentage ownership that is required to yield the desired accumulation will be $(65.6/150) = 44$ per cent approximately.

The valuation of B at the time of raising capital

$$= \frac{100 \times 4}{44} = 9.09 \text{ mn.}$$

Pre-money valuation = Post-money valuation.
Less Cash being brought in by the venture capital investor.
Pre-money valuation = 9.09 – 4 mn. = 5.09 mn.

Steps to be followed for valuation of the investee company:

1. Evaluate future revenue and profitability at the time of exit.
2. Forecast likely future value of the firm based on expected capitalization or expected acquisition proceeds depending upon the anticipated exit from the investment.
3. Obtain the present value of the investee company using a suitable discount factor.
4. Target an ownership position in the investee firm so as to achieve desired appreciation on the proposed investment. The appreciation desired should yield a hurdle rate of return on a discounted cash flow basis.

The weakness of this method is that it over-emphasizes the stream of earnings for the year of exit only.

The First Chicago Method

This method considers the entire earnings stream between the starting point and the exit point of the investment. The sequence of steps in valuation and the determination of the percentage share ownership of the VC are:

(i) Three alternative scenarios namely SUCCESS, SIDEWAYS SURVIVAL and FAILURE are considered.
(ii) Each one of these is assigned a probability rating.
(iii) Using a discount rate, the discounted present value of the VCU is computed.
(iv) The discounted present value is multiplied by the respective probabilities.
(v) The expected present value of the VCU is equal to the total of these in the three alternative scenarios.

E.g.: If the expected present value of the VCU is Rs. 5 crore and the fund requirement from the VC is 2.5 crore, the minimum ownership required is 50 per cent.

Daksh-e-services, taken over by IBM, was estimated to have revenues of about USD 50 million and net profits of USD 10 million for financial year 2004. The value of the deal estimated to be between USD 130 to 170 million works out to a sales multiple of 3 and earnings multiple of 15.

Revenue Multiplier Method

This method can be used in the case of early stage/start-up venture capital investments when after-tax profits may be low/negative. Value is estimated by multiplying the revenue with a revenue multiplier. A revenue multiplier is calculated as follows:

$$M = \frac{V}{R} = \frac{(1 + r)^n \times a \times p}{(1 + d)^n}$$

where a = expected after tax profit margin percentage at the time of exit,

p = expected price/earnings ratio at exit time,

r = expected annual rate of growth of revenue,

d = appropriate discount rate for a venture investment at this stage, risk and other relevant factors,

R = annual revenue level, and
V = present value of the VCU.

It may be difficult to estimate the revenue multiplier as it requires a lot of data like expected growth rate in the revenue stream.

(d) *Structuring of the Deal/Methods of Financing*

The structuring of the deal refers to the financial instruments through which venture capital investment is made.

These could be anyone or a combination of the following:

(i) ***Equity Instruments:*** Normally not more than 49 per cent of the total equity is issued to private equity investors as the promoters like to retain control over the company.
(ii) Cumulative Convertible Preference shares.
(iii) ***Conditional Loan:*** No interest is paid on these loans. A royalty or (a very high interest rate) of 2 per cent to 15 per cent on sales is paid after the VCU is able to generate sales. In some cases, instead of royalty, certain share of post-tax profits may be paid.
(iv) ***Income Notes:*** These are hybrid instruments where VCU pays both interest and royalty at low rates, and
(v) Partially Convertible Debentures.

(e) *Value Addition and Nurturing*

A private equity investor adds value to the investee company at every stage. Suppose the promoters of a company raise Rs. 10 lakhs from savings and personal bank loans and invest it in 10 lakh equity shares of Re. 1 each in their company. Further suppose the entire amount was fully spent on design and testing of the product. The Balance Sheet at this stage would be as follows:

Balance Sheet

(Market value, Rs. in lakhs)

Original Equity held by entrepreneurs	10	Intangible assets	10

As there are no tangible fixed assets at this stage, a traditional banker/lender would not touch the proposal even with a barge pole. But, suppose, the promoters are able to convince a venture capitalist that the business is a good investment opportunity which has a potential to generate capital appreciation and the VC invests 10 lakhs in the company for a 50 per cent stake. By making such investment, the VC has implicitly valued the company at Rs. 20 lakhs. The Balance Sheet after this first stage financing would look like this:

First Stage Balance Sheet

(Market value, Rs. in lakhs)

Original Equity held by entrepreneurs	10	Intangible assets	10
New Equity from Venture Capitalist	10	Cash	10
Total	20	Total	20

This cash is again fully utilized and the company asks for more money from the VC for pilot production and test marketing of the product. The VC agrees for a second round of financing for 40 lakhs. It revises upward the value of the intangible assets by 10 lakhs marks up its investment in the company to 15 lakhs. The promoters also note an additional paper gain of Rs. 5 lakhs in their original investment. The Balance Sheet would now look like this:

Second Stage Balance Sheet

(Market value, Rs. in lakhs)

New equity	40	Cash	40
Original equity held by entrepreneurs	15	Intangible Assets, as revalued by the VC	30
First stage VC funding	15		
Total	70	Total	70

This value addition goes on with every stage of investment. The paper gains made by the VC and the promoters will turn into fungible wealth once the company goes public.

The Venture Capitalist does not stop at providing finance. It is not a passive investor—there is a substantial degree, of active involvement in the investee company by way of providing managerial support, technical know-how, marketing expertise, customer contacts, financial structuring. VCI tries to create synergies between the various companies they have invested in—a company that has a great product but does not have a distribution network may be paired with another company in the venture portfolio that has a better distribution technology.

Exit Strategies

The following are the disinvestments mechanisms open to a VC:

(1) Mergers and Acquisition: Ex: IBM's 100 per cent acquisition of Daksh-e-services, a leading BPO services provider gave an exit opportunity—to private equity investors—Citigroup Venture Partners, Actis and General Atlantic Partners.
(2) Sale to other Venture Fund: Ex: Actis brought another VC viz., Baring's stake in Mumbai-based Jyothy Laboratories.
(3) Initial Public Offer: Biocon's IPO gave an exit route to ICICI Ventures, AIG and GW Capital.
(4) Buyback of VC's stake by the promoters.
(5) Sale on the OTC market.
(6) Management buyout of the VC's stake.

Legal and Regulatory Framework

(1) Salient Elements of SEBI (Venture Capital Funds) Regulations, 1996

According to these regulations, a VCF means a fund established in the form of a trust or a company and registered with SEBI. A VCU means a domestic company whose shares are not listed on a recognized stock exchange in India and which is engaged in providing services/production/manufacture of any article/thing/activities/sectors except those mentioned in the Third Schedule of the Regulations.

(1) Registration:
   (a) All VCFs must be registered with SEBI and pay Rs. 25,000 as application fee and Rs. 5,00,000 as registration fee for grant of certificate.
   (b) The applicant should be a company or a registered trust. In case of a company, the MIA should prohibit invitation to public to subscribe to its securities.

(2) Investment Conditions and Restrictions:
   (a) Each scheme launched/fund set-up by a VCF should have a firm commitment from the investors for contribution of at least 5 crore before the start of its operation.
   (b) The minimum investment in a VCF by an investor must be Rs. 5 lakh.

(3) Restriction on Investment by VCFs:
   (a) The VCF should disclose the investment strategy at the time of their registration.
   (b) They cannot invest more than 25 per cent corpus of the fund in one VCU.
   (c) At least 66.67 per cent of the investable funds of the VCF should be invested in unlisted equity shares, equity linked instruments.
   (d) Not more than 33.33 per cent may be invested by way of:
      (i) Subscription to IPO of a VCU whose shares are proposed to be listed.
      (ii) Debt instruments of a VCU in which the VCF has already made an investment by way of equity.
      (iii) Preferential allotment of equity shares of a listed company subject to a lock-in period of one-year, the equity shares or equity linked instruments of a financially weak company or a sick industrial company whose shares are listed.
      (iv) Special Purpose Vehicle, which are created by a VCF for the purpose of facilitating or promoting investment according to these Regulations.

(4) Prohibition on Listing

No VCF shall be entitled to get its units listed on any recognized stock exchange till the expiry of three years from the date of issuance of units by it.

Third Schedule (Negative List) of the SEBI Regulations which prohibit a Venture Capital Fund from giving finance.

To an NBFC (excluding those NBFC which are registered with RBI and have been categorized as Equipment Leasing or Hire Purchase Companies.)

For Gold Financing (excluding those companies which are engaged in gold financing for jewellery).

Relevant Income Tax Provisions

I. Any income of a Venture Capital Company or VCF set-up to raise funds for investment in a VCU is totally exempt u/s. 10(23FB) provided it is registered under SEBI and has satisfied the conditions specified by SEBI.

II. Chapter XII F: Special Provisions relating to tax on income received by the primary investors from VCC or VCF: (Section 115 U).

(1) Such income shall be chargeable to Income Tax in the same manner as if it were the income received by such person had he made investments directly in the VCU.

(2) It is deemed to be of the same nature and the same proportion in the hands of the person receiving such income as if it had been received by or had been accrued to the VCC or the VCF as the case may be during the previous year.

A statement of distributed income, details of the nature of such income (Capital gain, dividend, interest, etc.) in Form 64 duly verified by a Chartered Accountant shall be furnished to the investor and the Income Tax Department by 30th of November of the year following the previous year.

CONCLUSION

Kiran Mazumdar, the Chairperson and Managing Director of Biocon and Padmashree awardee, in an interview published in the *Economic Times* discussed the financial and other problems she faced initially in setting up her business in 1978 when biotechnology sector was still in its infancy.

She had stated that at that time the bankers demanded all sorts of guarantees from her father and others. She had to wait for over a quarter century to reach the position in which she is today. With the coming of age of private equity capital in India, the technocrat-entrepreneurs may not have to wait for such a long period to taste success. In fact, in the current scenario of bull run on the stock markets, the target company promoters have turned greedy and their expectations are becoming tough to meet by the private equity investors.

Due to stretched valuations, fresh round of funding have been kept in abeyance and the venture capitalists are waiting for more realistic ask prices as per ET report (dated 01.10.2004). And, since Venture Capitalist are beginning to evince interest in small and medium scale enterprises across diverse sectors, fresh opportunities have been thrown open to more and more chartered accountants. They can advise and assist prospective entrepreneurs in areas like the preparation of business plans, short-listing of suitable VCs, negotiating with the VC, etc.

14

Venture Capital: The Need of the Hour

K.V. MALLIK

The concept of Venture Capital Fund (VCF), which had originated in USA, came much later to India. The Government was keen for entrepreneurial development to boost the pace of industrial development of the country. The first generation new entrepreneurs were facing immense difficulty to raise funds from the capital market. The general public, shy and selective in their investments for the risk involved as well as for better returns available elsewhere, was more interested in other types of financial assets. The financing institutions like banks, term-lending institutions, etc. were also guided by and large by the profitability of a project while taking decision on its funding. Considering the problems faced by the new entrepreneurs in raising funds to finance their projects, the Government decided to promote VCF in the country as a part of its industrial development programme. R.S. Bhatt Committee, Technology Policy Implementation Committee, United Nations Development Plan, R&D Cess Act, etc. were all steps in this direction. Venture Capital guidelines were issued by the erstwhile Controller of Capital Issues (CCI) in 1988. The first Venture Capital Fund was, however, established in 1986 by the Government under the management of IDBI with an initial corpus of Rs. 10 crore. Under the R&D Cess Act, 1986, 5 per cent cess was provided on all payments made for import of technology and crediting the cess realised to the VCF of IDBI. Earlier, the VCF in India was development-oriented. The concept has since spread and commercial orientation began with the establishment of TDICI, a joint venture of UTI and ICICI, as well as entry of private companies. Today, there are about 11 such funds in India.

VCF has often been perceived as a source of finance for greenfield ventures based on sun-rise technologies. It will be unfair to brand this source of finance for greenfield projects only. The projects financed by a VCF may be classified under following categories:

(a) ***Greenfield Projects:*** Projects for developing new concepts or technology.
(b) ***Early Stage Development Projects:*** Projects having full management team but not the completed product.
(c) ***Expansion Projects:*** Projects approaching BEP after commencement of commercial production.
(d) ***Late Stage Development Projects:*** Established units requiring finance for expansion to enable it to quicken the pace to completion.
(e) ***Import of Technology:*** Project with technology being imported from abroad and which is not available in the country.

Venture capital is thus a source of long-term finance for projects with high risk reward ratio, that is, projects which could generate substantial return but also carry high degree of risk.

FORMS OF ASSISTANCE

The assistance is generally provided in the form of equity support. However, finances by way of conditional loan or conventional loan are also common in the Indian context.

Equity Support

In case of equity support, the shares are generally retained till such time the assisted project starts making profit. Once the unit starts generating profits, the shares are sold: (a) to the public in the secondary market at a profit, or (b) to the promoter under buyback arrangement at a negotiated price. Till the shares are sold, the VCF follows 'Eyes on but hands off' policy and does not take part in the day-to-day management, contrary to popular belief. They lend management support to units that are in need of it, especially those of greenfield projects.

Conditional Loan

In case of conditional loans, the assisted unit is provided with loan support. While the project is being implemented, no interest is generally payable but once it starts commercial operation, it has to pay royalty on sales and has to repay the loan according to a predetermined schedule.

Conventional Loan

In case of conventional loan type of assistance, the loan generally carries a lower fixed rate of interest till the unit becomes commercially operational. Thereafter, the loan carries higher/normal rate of interest. The loan has to be repaid in terms of a predetermined schedule.

DISINVESTMENT OR EXIT

The assistance under VCF is generally provided by way of equity. As the VCF carry a high degree of risk, the reward should also be substantial. In the event of assisted units being successful, the VCF will receive dividend as a shareholder. Receiving periodical dividend after waiting through a barren implementation period, and that too without the idea of having management control of the unit, is not the objective of VCF. It will have to off-load its holding and yet earn a profit higher than the average return on capital employed.

One way of getting out of the investment is to sell the shares to the promoters under buyback arrangement at a negotiated price after the assisted unit has grown sufficiently to attract investment from the general public. This form of disinvestment by the VCF finds more acceptability in India. The recognition of partnership role of capital is absent in India. Unlike in developed countries where the proprietors are willing to accept outsiders and share the management, Indian promoters wish to retain control over management and also to pass it onto the next generation in the family in due course. However, it becomes difficult for the promoters, the kind of promoters who obtain VCF assistance, to become cash rich to buy-back the shares held by the VCF. The other way out is to sell the shares to the public in the secondary market, but there are certain difficulties/obstacles in taking this road. In case of smaller companies (and generally the VCF companies are not big corporates), the share capital will not be large, but stock exchanges do not list companies with aggregate share capital of less than Rs. 3 crore. Thus, the course open for disinvestment through this path in such cases is to off-load the shares through OTCEI. The functional OTCEI is yet to gather momentum. The other difficulty is, as stated above, resistance from the promoters. Till now, buy-back of own share by the company is not permissible under the laws of the country. The VCFs are also in a disadvantageous position in tax treatment compared to mutual funds. VCFs have to pay tax on dividend and capital gain tax at normal rates, while in case of mutual funds the tax is nil. However, the Finance Bill, 1995 proposes to exempt dividend and long-term capital gain of VCF in certain circumstances. Since the portfolio of VCFs consists of high risk investments – while in some cases it can make super profits, it can lose the entire investments in other cases.

- The bank should promote the underlying goals of financial sector reforms to provide competitive, efficient and low cost financial intermediation services to society at large.
- The banks should be financially viable.
- The banks should result in upgradation of technology in the banking sector.
- The banks should avoid the malpractices, such as unfair pre-emption and concentration of credit, monopolisation of economic power, cross holdings with industrial groups, etc. which perplex the private sector banks prior to nationalisation.
- The free entry in the banking sector may have to be managed carefully and judiciously.

RBI GUIDELINES

On the basis of the considerations stated above, the RBI has formulated the following guidelines for establishment of new banks in the private sector:

(1) The new private sector banks shall be registered as public limited companies under the prevision of Companies Act, 1956 and the RBI shall grant a licence under Banking Regulation Act, 1949 to such a bank. At an appropriate

TABLE 14.1

Present Position and Performance of Private Sector Banks

Bank	*Total Deposits*	*Total Advances*	*Net Profit*	*Net Profit to total income*	*Net Profit to net worth*
Vysya Bank	2538.57	1425.85	20.24	7.65	28.13
Federal Bank	1717.82	865.88	8.27	4.14	33.74
Bank of Rajasthan	1206.16	571.69	5.86	3.74	16.02
South Indian Bank	1000.33	493.30	2.41	1.97	12.62
Karnataka Bank	843.56	474.27	6.63	5.70	31.71
Bank of Madura	570.95	281.58	3.48	4.13	19.12
Karur Vysya Bank	549.41	233.78	5.12	6.98	24.23
T.N. Marcantile Bank	547.70	288.38	6.65	9.28	26.62
Sangli Bank	536.72	243.33	0.73	1.08	2.48
Bharat Overseas Bank	446.59	241.38	0.60	1.07	4.97
Lakshmi Vilas Bank	405.78	188.60	3.30	5.94	27.16
Banaras State Bank	309.52	111.63	−15.40	−50.21	770.00
City Union Bank	264.28	141.98	2.00	5.69	22.75
Nedungadi Bank	263.40	121.93	0.11	0.31	1.54
Dhanlakshmi Bank	214.12	110.06	0.51	1.86	10.92
Bareilly Corporation Bank	174.95	65.27	0.09	0.44	1.42
Ratnakar Bank	101.33	55.66	0.06	0.47	2.60
Lord Krishna	87.66	57.46	2.03	16.33	16.12

Figure (in Rs. crore) are with reference to March 1993.
Source: Economic Times, March 22, 1994.

time, the bank may also be included in the second schedule of the Reserve Bank of India Act, 1934. The RBI decision shall be final in the matter.

(2) The authorised, subscribed and paid up capital of banks shall be governed by the provisions of Banking Regulation Act, 1949. The banks must have at least Rs. 100 crore as paid-up capital. The contribution of promoters of the banks shall be determined by RBI and will also be subject to other applicable regulations. The shares of such banks shall be listed on stock-exchanges..

The RBI prescribed that new private sector banks should have at least 100 crore as paid-up capital so that they may have broader capital base. The argument in favour of this requirement is that RBI does not want to allow the repetition of the events which occurred to many under-capitalised banks. It would allow only serious, organised and competent players to whom the entry barrier appeared reasonably necessary.

However, the entry barrier of paid-up capital could keep away smaller companies who might have the desired expertise and experience. Indeed, no arithmetic can be offered to explain the reason of fixing paid-up capital at a minimum level of Rs. 100 crore. Experts point out that smaller banks do not have to cater to corporate clients so that they would not need to buy very sophisticated equipment. Moreover, smaller banks will not be needed to provide a very large range of services and so they will also not require too large and upfront investment. The deputy governor RBI asserts that the central bank would not like to see a mushroom growth of non-viable banks. It has therefore insisted on an internationally accepted norms of 8 per cent of risk-weighted assets capital adequacy.

The promoter's minimum contribution for a manufacturing company is 20 per cent and for others it is 40 per cent. It is likely for a bank promoter to contribute about 25-30 per cent. In order to avoid any partiality in lending operations of the bank, the RBI specified that no more than 25 per cent of the total capital and reserve can be lent to a single company and no more than 50 per cent can be lent to a group. Since industrial groups which owned banks are known to have appropriated funds for their business, there are good chances that RBI will also come up with norms preventing them from lending to their own firms.

(3) Presently, the headquarters of banks are concentrated in a very few metropolitan cities. In order to avoid such concentration of headquarters, the RBI prefers granting licence to those banks which have proposed to locate their headquarters in cities, other than metropolitan cities or centres, which do not have headquarters of other banks.

The issue of banks' headquarters being located in places where none exists had added another problem. If this condition is followed, it will be difficult to get professionals. Moreover, exercise of operational and management control would be comparatively difficult and may involve higher costs. However, the problem can be solved by locating registered office in smaller towns but head offices in the metros.

(4) Section 12(2) of the Banking Regulation Act shall govern the voting right of an individual shareholder. According to this section, the individual voting right shall be restricted to 1 per cent of the total voting right. However, public financial institutions shall be excepted from this ceiling under Section 53 of the said Act.

(5) Permission shall not be granted to new banks to appoint a person as a director who is director of any other banking company or companies which among themselves are authorised to exercise voting rights in excess of 20 per cent of the total voting rights of all the shareholders of the banking company, as laid down in the Banking Regulation Act, 1949. This provision indicates that even non-working director of a company will not find a place on its bank's board.

(6) The management set-up liquidity requirements and scope of operations of banks shall be governed by the provisions of Reserve Bank of India Act, 1934, the Banking Regulation Act, 1949 and other relevant statutes. All the directives, instructions, guidelines and advice given by the RBI shall be applicable to such banks as in the case with other banks. The provisions have been made with the object to provide level-playing field to the private sector banks along with the public sector banks.

(7) The prudential norms with respect to banking operations, accounting policies and other policies as laid down by the RBI shall also be observed by the new banks. From the very beginning, the new banks shall acquire the norm of 8 per cent capital adequacy ratio. The new banks shall also be required to observe norms for income for recognition, asset classification and provisioning from the very beginning. These norms will provide sound capital base to the banks and protect them from becoming sick or financially unviable.

(8) The priority sector lending targets shall also be applicable to new banks as are applicable on other domestic banks. The RBI, in order to provide some relaxations with respect

to priority sector lending, has included advances to retail traders and advances to service-oriented businesses in the list of priority lending. Further, the RBI has also qualified housing loans made by banks as priority sector lending. The limit for schedule caste/scheduled tribe borrowers qualified as priority sector advances had been hiked to Rs. 2 lakh. The housing loans made to all categories of borrowers will now qualify as priority sector lending.

(9) The directives issued by RBI with respect to export credit shall also be applicable on such banks as applicable to existing bank. The banks may also act as authorised dealer to deal in foreign exchange.

(10) After the establishment of new banks for at least three years, they will not be allowed to set-up subsidiaries or mutual funds. The investment of such banks in the equity of other companies shall be subject to the following provisions:

   (i) 30 per cent of bank's or the investee company's capital funds, whichever is less, as set out under the Banking Regulation Act, 1949.

   (ii) 1.5 per cent of the bank's incremental deposits during a year as per RBI guidelines.

   The maximum permissible investment in the subsidiaries and mutual fund (if and when set-up) and portfolio investment in other companies is 20 per cent of the banks own paid-up capital and reserves.

   (iii) The new banks are free to open branches at various centres including urban/metropolitan centres without the prior approval of RBI. However, they have to comply with capital adequacy and prudential accounting norms. In order to avoid over crowding of bank branches at metropolitan areas and cities, a new bank will be required to open rural and semi urban branches also as may be laid down by the RBI.

NEW INDIAN PRIVATE SECTOR BANKS

Taking advantage of the new liberalised measure in the banking sector, the UTI Bank, the Industrial Bank, ICICI Bank and Global Trust Bank have already started their banking operations. The Gujarat Fertilizer Corporation, IDBI, HDFC, Jayanta Madras, Times of India Group, Reliance Industries, Sahara India Group, 20th Century Finance Corporation, ITC are some of the examples of groups which have finalised their proposals to set-up banks in private sector.

The UTI Bank has been promoted with the equity capital of Rs. 100 crore and it is expected that it will be increased to the level of Rs. 200 crore. The bank has started its banking operations at its first branch located at Ahmedabad. The bank is planning to open seven branches at different places.

The ICICI Bank, promoted by both ICICI and SCICI, has paid up capital of Rs. 105 crore. The subscribed capital is Rs. 150 crore and authorised capital Rs. 300 crore. The bank started its banking operations from its first branch located at Madras, it has opened its second branch a Bangalore. The bank is planning to open 60 branches all over the country in the next four years.

The Global Trust Bank has been promoted by Mr. Jayant Madhab along with Mr. Gelli and Mr. Sridhar Subasri. The promoters and their friends and associates have contributed 41.6 per cent to the Global Trust Bank capital and the two international institutions – The International Finance Corporation and the Asian Development Bank will hold 9.6 per cent of the total equity of the bank. The bank has issued 2.6 crore shares of Rs. 10 each to raise Rs. 26 crore. This will take the bank's paid-up capital to Rs. 104 crore. The bank is planning to open to branches during the first year of its operation and the number will increase to 50 in five years of operations.

The Centurian Bank is promoted by 20th Century Finance Corporation. The KEPPEL Corporation limited will acquire an equity stake of 26 per cent in the Centurian Bank by an investment of Rs. 27 crore. Through its wholly owned subsidiary – Kephinance Investment Pvt. Ltd. The International Finance Corporation and the Asian Development Bank will also participate in the equity of the bank. The total equity capital, after the public listing will be Rs. 13.5 crore. The bank's first two branches in Bombay and Madras were set-up before the end of 1994.

The HDFC Bank Ltd. has been floated by the Housing Development Finance Corporation (HDFC). Recently, the RBI approve the equity structure of the bank. Sat Pal Khattar, a NRI and owner of Singapore's largest solicitor firm, is picking up 4.54 per cent in the bank. Mr. Khattar is acquiring the stake through an overseas corporate body, Jarrington Private Limited in which he has 60 per cent stake. The HDFC Bank Ltd. will initially have a paid-up capital of Rs. 200 crore. HDFC will contribute 25 per cent in the equity, shareholders of HDFC 15.46 per cent, employees of HDFC, 5 per cent, employees of HDFC bank, 5 per cent, Jarrington, 4.54 per cent and public, 25 per cent. The National Westminster Bank Plc will hold 20 per cent stake in the bank.

STRENGTHS AND WEAKNESSES

The new private sector banks are more enthusiastic to provide a whole range of services, such as, tele banking, desk-top banking, relationship banking, any time money services and electronic transfer of funds, etc. All this require heavy investments in the development of basic infrastructure to provide fully automated services to the customers. Under these circumstances, the staff needed would require to be highly motivated and trained. It will also entail comparatively high cost of operations.

Computerie and Automated Services

For better and qualitative services to the customer, the new private sector banks have concentrated on modern techniques of banking. Almost all of the banks are planning to use state-of-the-art technologies, such as automatic teller machines, note counting machines, cheque book dispensers which expedite and improve the quality of services. Thus, the banks have much better operational infrastructure than public sector banks.

Specialised Services

The banks are developing their basic infrastructure in such a way as to provide better and effective specialised and need-based services to the customers. Thus, the customer would be in a position to avail even specialised services of banks, not otherwise available.

Thinner Staff Structure

Modern and technically innovated system of banking operations would need a thin staff structure. The bank should take all care to see that their staff structure remains thin and superlately trained and skilled. They make it possible by exercising emphasis on inducting leader staff and eliminating clerical staff. Thus, the new private sector banks have got an edge over the others in terms of productivity and profitability.

Human Resource

The new private sector banks have the advantage of the large pool of trained manpower already available in the country. They can easily hire professionals and specialists of the field. Moreover, they are not required to the trained initially and in this way the banks have to expand comparatively very small amount for the training of the staff.

Smaller Network

The bank's limited resources restrict their spending on the development of basic infrastructure for qualitative and effective services to the customers. To overcome the limitations, the new banks have signed Memorandum of Understanding with one or more banks, especially public sector banks, which have very wide network of bank branches, to establish correspondent relationships with them.

High Operations Cost

The new private bank having all the automatic system of banking operations are faced with high cost of operations of the system. These costs are eventually borne by the customers.

Higher Servicing Cost

With the operation cost being higher than elsewhere, the servicing cost charged by the banks shall be exorbitantly very high. Moreover, cost free services provided by the public sector banks shall be provided by the private sector banks at some cost. Hence, ordinary investors and general public would not be able to afford and enjoy the quality services offered by the new banks.

BANKING STRATEGIES

Most of the new private sector banks are aiming to provide their customers everything from retail banking to merchant banking. However, there are differences with respect to their strategies. Some banks are planning to concentrate on retail banking, while others are developing strategies to tap NRIs and wholesale deposits. They have different strategies to mobilise funds from saving account, current account and time deposits. In order to cover more geographical area under their banking operations, almost all of the new private sector banks have signed their Memorandum of Understanding, with different public sector banks which have a very wide network of bank branches, to establish correspondent banking relationships. The banking strategies of different new private sector banks have been discussed hereunder:

(i) *Deposit Target:* The UTI Bank, ICICI Bank and HDFC Bank have finalised their projections for deposit mobilisation. The UTI Bank has struck to its initial target of Rs. 750 crore which was increased to Rs. 5,000 crore in the fifth year. The ICICI Bank has scaled up its target from Rs. 250 crore to Rs. 500 crore at the end of first year which was increased to Rs. 4,500 crore at the end of fifth year. Similarly, the HDFC Bank has projected a deposit mobilisation of Rs. 400 crore at the end of first year of its operations which is expected to touch to the level of Rs. 1,100 crore at the end of third year, this has been shown in Table 14.2.

The above projections indicate that UTI Bank and ICICI Bank are rather optimistic and have very ambitious plans, in view of their annual average growth of bank deposits

TABLE 14.2

Deposit Target

(*Rs. in crore*)

	At the end of the year				
	one	*two*	*three*	*four*	*five*
UTI Bank	750	1500	2500	3100	5000
ICICI Bank	500	1200	2000	3500	4500
HDFC Bank	400	750	1100	–	–

Figures of HDFC are not final.
Source: Economic Times, Dec. 23, 1993.

being around 16.5 to 17.5 per cent primarily in rural areas. The projections also indicate that UTI Bank would collect an average deposit of over Rs. 100 crore per branch. It is planning seven branches. Same is the case with ICICI which is planning to open six branches in the first year of its operation. However, these projections are not difficult to achieve, considering the fact that aggregate deposit of private sector banks have grown by about 26 per cent for the year ended March 1993. Virtually, the growth rate of Lord Krishna Bank was a whopping 78.64 per cent and that of Vysya Bank it was 65.25 per cent.

(ii) *Profit Projections:* The UTI Bank has projected profits that it is expected to be earned from its banking operations during the first five years of operations. Similarly, ICICI Bank and HDFC Bank have also estimated their profits expected to be earned by them during first year of their banking operations.

The UTI Bank is expected to earn a profit after tax of Rs. 23.2 crore which is supposed to touch the level of Rs. 157.62 crore at the end of fifth year. The earning per share is projected at 2.32 at the end of first year and 7.88 at the end of fifth year. The details of the projections have been shown in Table 14.3.

TABLE 14.3

UTI's Five-Year Projections

(Rs. in crore)

	At the end of the year				
	one	*two*	*three*	*four*	*five*
Priority Sector advances	163.14	318.27	601.54	868.71	1168.68
Total advances	543.81	1060.89	2005.14	2895.70	3895.32
Equity	100.00	200.00	200.00	200.00	200.00
C/D	72.51	70.73	80.21	78.26	71.91
Reserve and Surplus	8.20	76.61	135.20	328.70	200.00
Profit after tax	23.20	42.42	82.59	117.50	157.62
Capital Adequacy	19.90	26.07	16.72	14.80	14.44
EPS (in Rs)	2.32	2.12	4.13	5.88	7.88

These are rough estimates.
Source: Economic Times, Dec. 23, 1993.

The HDFC Bank has projected a profit after tax of Rs. 11 crore and ICICI Bank is expecting to earn a profit after tax of Rs. 8 crore at the end of first year. The details of the projections have been shown in Table 14.4.

TABLE 14.4
Projected Profits

(*Rs. in crores*)

	HDFC	*ICICI*
Income		
Interest Income	60	23
Non-interest income	7	3
	67	26
Expenditure		
Interest Expenditure	17	6.0
Overheads and Depreciation	30	5.5
Other expenses	–	3.5
	47	15.0
Profit Before Tax	20	11.0
Net Profit	11	8.0
Return on equity	3.66%	8%

These are rough estimates.
Source: Economic Times, Dec. 23, 1995.

The banks have made the above projections after careful consideration of factors affecting the banking operations and conditions under which banking operations shall be performed. Under the given circumstances, these targets are difficult to achieve.

(iii) *Deposit and Advances Strategies:* The UTI Bank has developed a strategy to mobilise total deposit in proportion of 3 : 2 : 5 in saving account, current account and time deposit respectively. It is planning to focus on retail banking both for its advances and deposits taking advantage of 3.6 lakh unit holders. Besides, the UTI Bank will also attract its corporate clients who are expected to keep their deposit with the bank. It may be pointed out that the loan portfolio of the UTI is about Rs. 1 0,000 crore. Even if a very small portion of it is kept with the bank in current account, the bank would be able to easily achieve its deposit targets. The bank will target retail investors to mobilise interest-bearing deposits. For this purpose, the bank is planning to open bank branches near UTI centres so that unit holders may be mobilised to keep their deposits with the bank. As far as loaning of funds is concerned, the bank is planning to serve the needs of the small investors and medium-size companies. In order to serve the small investors, the bank is planning to set-up private investment clubs and investment centres.

The ICICI Bank aims to provide 'total service' to customers through developing strategies and leveraging its existing relationships between its existing businesses. It is making a start of all businesses. It will however settle down to a thrust area only after about three years. The bank will not only target the corporates but will also spread its wings far in to the rural segment.

The ICICI Bank is planning to concentrate on cash-rich corporates, trusts and institutions for its wholesale deposits. It has estimated that it will grab the deposits of the firms and about 10 per cent of the total deposits of foreign airlines and shipping companies, which usually park their float funds with foreign banks. The estimates are based on the ICICI's expanding client base. As the bank will be a one stop shop for long-term loans, cash credit, merchant banking, corporate and foreign exchange advisory services, it may assume to tap float funds of these firms. Besides wholesale deposits from corporates, it will also pay enough attention on retail deposits from specific target groups. The total deposit composition will consist of 20 per cent current account deposit and 80 per cent interest-bearing deposits. The bank is also expected to meet the funding requirements of the agriculture sector. In this context, the bank has already drawn up a strategy for advancing funds to agro-business.

The HDFC Bank has been promoted with the objective to provide multi-services catering to a wide range of banking services primarily for the corporate sector. The bank is planning to offer the full gamut of commercial banking as well as select areas of investment banking.

15

Venture Capital

SAWALIA BIHARI VERMA AND
RAVI KUMAR SHRIVASTAWA

The concept of Venture Capital (VC) was originated in USA, came much later to India. The first generation new entrepreneurs were facing immense difficulty to raise funds from the capital market. Keeping in view this problem, the government took keen interest for entrepreneurial development to boost the pace of industrial development in the country. The government decided to promote venture capital as a part of its industrial development programme. Venture capital guidelines were issued by the erstwhile Controller of Capital Issues (CCI) in 1988. The first venture capital fund was established in 1986 by the government under the management of IDBI with an initial corpus of Rs. 10 crore. The government introduced a cess of 5 per cent on all know-how import payment to create a pool of funds for VC activities of IDBI. In this way, venture capital came into existence to develop entrepreneurship and exploit technological potential in India.

The term 'Venture Capital' comprises of two words, viz. 'venture' and 'capital'. Venture means a course of proceedings associated with risk, the outcome of which is uncertain and 'capital' means resources to start the enterprise. Ordinary venture capital is understood as the capital which is available for financing new business venture. Technically, it can be interpreted as the investment of long-term equity finance where the venture capitalist earns his returns from capital gain.

As per Dr. Neil Cross of Britain, "Venture capital as the provision of risk bearing capital usually in the form of participation in equity, to companies with high growth potential. Relatively high risks are compensated by the possibility of high returns, usually through substantial capital gain in the medium-term." As per Bank of England, "Venture capital is an activity by which investors support entrepreneurial talent with finance and business skills to exploit capital gain."

As per Richard B. Robinson, "Venture capital is an alternative form of equity financing for small businesses, and a venture capitalist is similar to a mutual fund manager who finds equity investments for the pool of the investors. Unlike mutual fund managers and most other security specialists, venture capitalists focus on high-risk entrepreneurial businesses. They provide start up (Seed Mind) capital to new ventures, development funds to business in their early growth stage and expansion funds to rapidly growing ventures that have the potential to "go public" or that need capital for acquisitions." (David H. Holt in *Entrepreneurship: New Venture Capital*, p. 435.)

We may define it, "Venture capital as the long-term equity investments in business which display potential for significant growth and financial return. The investor bears the risk of venture but would earn a return commensurate with its success. Thus, the return for the investor is not through a steady dividend or interest yield but through capital gain.

This definition incorporates the three main features that distinguish venture capital investment from other forms of capital investment. They are –

- supporting entrepreneurial talent by providing finance,
- providing business management skills, and
- a return in the form of capital gains.

Venture capital is generally regarded as a risk capital. The venture capital investor thus looks for markets with tremendous growth potential to be exploited with entrepreneur towards a highly rewarding relationship. To foster the growth of better technology new risky lines of business need support in the form of venture capital and VC is emerging to fill the particular need.

Venture capital is thus a source of long-term finance on a high-risk project related which could generate substantial return but also carry high degree of risk to some innovations or new technological developments contemplated by a company. VC also means a combination of capital and management expertise provided for the initial risks of a new and emerging company, which has a good growth prospect in terms of products, technologies, business concepts or services with the objective of retrieving the investment with a handsome reward at a future date.

The main purpose of VC is thus to exploit new and untried or advanced technologies and turn them into commercially viable proportions naturally with an expectation of spectacular returns later. In nutshell, the success of VC rests largely with—

- The venture capitalist who comes forward with a flexible financing arrangement and also tends support or provides inputs specially in managerial and marketing areas.
- The promoters-people with ideas in new and high technology areas, and
- Macro-level initiative and policy support.

FEATURES/CHARACTERISTICS OF VC

Conventional financiers employ in proven technologies and low risk units, whereas venture capitalists employ in new technologies with high risk. The following characteristics are given below—

1. Equity-debt

Venture capitalists manage for both equity and debt finances. They employ in shares to get high returns. They earn capital gains by selling the shares once the enterprise provides profitable. The debt financing may be on the form of debentures. They provide finance for starting up stage, for expansion or for development stage. Debt financing may be straight without any condition or some terms and conditions may be fixed. But venture capitalists stress 'equity' as their preferred form of investment.

2. Stages of Investment

Early stage investments are made either at the seed or the start-up stage. At the start-up stage or the commercial inception of a new project, the risks are quite high for the venture capitalists. The middle stage involves investment by venture capitalists in projects at the development stage. Last stage investments are those where the capitalists invest more than half of their funds. These include expansion and addition projects, management buy-outs, buying and turnaround investments.

3. Professional Entrepreneurs

Venture capital is provided to those entrepreneurs who are professionally or technically qualified but lack adequate funds to start a new venture. The entrepreneur should have the capability to make an intense effort to do the business. He should also have proper knowledge of his markets, along with risk management quality.

4. Participation in Management

Venture capitalists not only supply funds but also participate in management of the enterprise in which they invest. They use their managerial skills. They provide support in the operations of the new enterprise without interfering in its day-to-day activities.

5. Serve as an Intermediary

A venture capital firm serves as an intermediary between investors looking for high return on their money and entrepreneurs in search of needed capital for their start-ups. The venture capitalist joins the entrepreneur at a co-promoter in projects and shares the risks and rewards of enterprise, with the object of long-term capital appreciation.

6. Harbinger of Entrepreneurship

Venture capital is the harbinger of entrepreneurship. It enjoys a great deal of flexibility. It has given birth to what are today mega corporations. It helps translate project ideas into a raising operations.

7. Encouraged New Ideas

Venture in most cases came in at the idea stage. It propelled new ideas to major commercial successes. It helps entrepreneurs to launch enterprises with a specific promise. It is ideal for promoters who have good projects but lack margin money. It provides the necessary help to convert your business idea to commercial venture.

8. Kinds of Ventre Capital Firms

Among the principal kinds of venture capital firms are—

(a) ***Traditional Partnerships,*** which are often established by wealthy families to manage a portion of their money.
(b) ***Professionally Managed Pools,*** which are formed by such institution as pension funds and foundations.
(c) ***Investment Banking Firms,*** and
(d) ***Insurance Companies.***

9. Long-term Investment

Venture financing is a long-term investment of funds. Funds are provided for 5 to 10 years. Venture capital is not repayable on demand. The investor has to wait for a long time to earn profit.

10. Importance of Exit Route

The main objective of the venture capitalist is to exit from the investment at a good profit to himself usually by way of a capital gain.

11. Facilities of Growth

In addition, financing high technology venture capital facilitates the growth of industries. It is closely linked with innovation, high growth and profit.

12. Global Concept

The concept of venture capital has now become a global concept in the field of funding technology-based industrial projects.

13. Creative Capital

Venture capital is thought of as a creative capital which is expected to perform economic functions different from other investment vehicles which primarily serve as expansion capital.

14. High Risk

Venture capitalist provides finance to high risk units which also have high reward potentials. These risks may be such as technology risks, product market risk, liquidity risk and other physical ones. The concept of risk and reward sharing is an integral part of venture capital.

15. Expectations

The venture capitalists expect—

(a) to invest in ventures which have exceptional growth prospects, and
(b) to get superior returns for high risk over a period of five years.

16. New Technology

Venture capitalists provide finance usually to those entrepreneurs who try to employ new technology which may produce uncertain results.

17. Equity Pool

Equity pool is more accurate to view venture capital broadly as a professionally managed pool of equity capital. Frequently, the equity pool is formed from the resources of wealthy limited partners.

David H. Colt has advocated the following criteria as investment decision guidelines—

- Entrepreneur capable of sustained efforts.
- Entrepreneur familiar with market.
- Entrepreneur able to evaluate and react well to risk.
- Market or industry attractive to venture capitalist.
- Product fits well with investor's long-term strategy.
- Target market enjoys significant growth rate.
- Product or innovation can be legally protected.
- Entrepreneur has demonstrated leadership ability.
- Potential to return 10 times investment in 5-10 years.

FORM OF ASSISTANCE

The assistance is generally provided in the form of equity support.

However, finances by way of conditional loan or conventional loan are also common in the Indian context.

1. Equity Support

In the case of equity support the shares are generally retained till such time the assisted project start making profit. Once the unit starts generating profits, the shares are sold –

(a) to the public in the Secondary Market at a profit, or
(b) to the promoter under buy-back arrangement at a negatively price.

Till the shares are sold, the venture capital financing follows 'Eyes on but hands off' policy and does not take part in the day-to-day management, contrary to popular belief. They lend management support to units that are in need of it, especially those of greenfield projects.

2. Conditional Loan

In case of conditional loans, the assisted unit is provided with loan support. While the project is being implemented, no interest is generally payable but once it starts commercial operation, it has to pay royalty on sales and has to repay the loan according to a predetermined schedule.

3. Conventional Loan

In case of conventional loan type of assistance the loan generally carries a lower fixed rate of interest till the unit becomes commercially operational. Thereafter, the loan carries higher/normal rate of interest. The loan has to be repaid in terms of a predetermined schedule.

4. Structure of the Deal

After a careful and thorough analysis of various risk factors involved in the project, a structural deal is finalised in the form of an MOU between the venture capitalist and the entrepreneur. This deal will include the method of financing, total outlay of funds, nature of business, payment of royalty on the sales effected, payment of charges for value-added services the option for further financing, exit conditions, appointment of the Board of Directors, restriction on lease, sale or transfer of technology, control of operations of the company and so on.

Further the timing of disinvestment and the method of valuation of shares in the case of management buy-outs are also decided in the MOU signed between the venture capitalist and the entrepreneur.

STAGES OF VENTURE CAPITAL

As the risk involves in financing a new venture is high, professional investors would always like to go through the draft of the business plan carefully and study it thoroughly before making up their mind. The prospect of the new business will be explored through the draft plan and the amount of risk involves therein will be carefully assessed. Such an exercise will help the venture capitalist to eliminate the chances of adverse selection.

An entrepreneur needs venture capital at different stages of his firm from start up to growth, from expansion to acquisitions. Hence, there are stages of financing in the life of an enterprise. This has promoted various types of venture capital finances. There are following stages in venture capital financing—

1. *Early Stage*

This involves very high risk as funds are made available for a period ranging between 3 to 10 years.

Seed—Relatively small amount of capital is provided to the entrepreneur to prove the concept.

Start-up—Funds are provided to entrepreneurs/companies for use in product development and initial marketing.

Early Stage—Funds are provided to entrepreneurs that have expended their capital and require funds for sales and manufacturing. This financing is provided for the following activities—

- Idea and concept studies (Seed Capital).
- Financial feasibility studies.
- Research and product development.

- Initiating operations and developing prototypes. This will require Start-up Capital.
- Producing few units of product for testing.
- Changing designs of the product before commercial product.
- Starting full-scale commercial production and marketing.

2. *Expansion/Development Stage*

It involves medium-level risk as funds are provided for a period ranging between 1 and 3 years. Such financing is required for the following activities:

(a) *Second Stage*—To fulfil the needs of working capital and initial expansion.
(b) *Third Stage*—To make expansion when venture is having rapidly growing sales and profits.
(c) *Bridge Stage*—To prepare the venture for public offering that is issue of shares and debentures and so on. Within six to twelve months, often bridge finance is structured so that it can be represented from the proceeds of an IPO.

3. *Acquisition and Leveraged Buy-out*

This financing involves medium risk. At this stage, funds are made available for a period ranging between 1 and 3 years. This financing is used and required for the following activities—

(a) Acquiring a firm for further growth,
(b) Enabling a manager or a group of managers from outside the venture to but the venture or a part of its business, and
(c) Turning around a sick unit to revitalize and revive it with this intention, funds are provided to a company at a time of operational or financial difficulty.

SOURCES OF SUPPLY/RAISING VENTURE CAPITAL

Prior independence, managing agents acted as venture capitalists. They provided risk finance to meet the working capital as well as fixed capital needs. They also provided funds for expansion and modernisation of ventures/firms. They were also providing management skills for new ventures. By investing they build goodwill for the firms and created confidence among the industrialists or investors to invest in firms. The concept of venture capital gained popularity only during post-independence period. In the last five decades, several public and private sector firms have entered the venture capital industry. The sources of raising venture capital in India are given below –

1. State Governments

The State governments have realized the significance and role of venture capital in industrial development. There are some venture capital funds which have been promoted by State governments. Some among them are as under –

(a) Gujarat Venture Finance Ltd. (GVFL), and
(b) Andhra Pradesh Venture Capital Ltd.

Other States are also setting up their own venture capital finds with the assistance of All India Financial Institutions. GVFL was promoted with a fund of Rs. 24 crores, contributed by IDBI, SFLS, Gujarat Industrial Investment Corporation in July 1990. It provides venture financial assistance in form of equity and quasi-equity investment. The extent of financing ranges from Rs. 2.5 lakhs to Rs. 2 crores.

2. Semi-government Institutions

As per venture capital guidelines 1988, Government of India authorised all Indian financial institutions, commercial banks and their subsidiaries to launch venture capital companies ICICI in 1988 formed Technology Development and Investment Corporation in India. This corporation managed various schemes of venture capital financing on commercial lines. Venture capital activities were also started by Canbank Financial Services Ltd., which is a subsidiary of Canara Bank. It finances through equity as well as conditional loan.

3. Financial Institutions

At very outset, the all India financial institutions stated their venture capital funds by diverting a small part of their available funds for investment in venture capital activities. Later on, they created their asset management subsidiaries to promote venture capital funds. These are IFC's, Risk Capital and Technology Finance Corporation, SIDBI's Small Venture Capital Ltd., ICICI's Technology Development and Information Company of India Ltd., IDBI's Risk Capital Fund, and UTI's Venture Capital Fund. At present, 9 State financial institutions have got their venture funds registered with Securities Exchange Board of India (SEBI).

However, two types of problem arose—

(a) Where equity support was required by small and medium projects, the SFCs and SIDCs as well as all India institutions could mainly give loan (secured) support, and
(b) Innovative projects required a different kind of support.

4. Commercial Banks

In order to operate on small scale, Canara Bank has sponsored Canbank Venture Capital Fund. Another capital fund was sponsored by a foreign commercial bank. It is named as 'Investment Funds of ANZ Grindlays Bank Plc. Canfina VCF is the only bank which has registered its venture fund with SEBI.

5. SEBI Registered Venture Capital Funds

As per amendment on 25th January, 1995 in SEBI Act, SEBI acquired a power to register and regulate the working of venture capital funds. Thus, 39 venture capital funds were registered with SEBI on June, 2004. These have been promoted by different organisations.

6. Private Sector Firms

About 18 private sector funds have been registered with SEBI. The venture capital guidelines, issued by the Government of India in November 1988, have allowed private firms to raise venture capital funds. Several funds have been established which are as below—

(a) *Credit Capital Venture Funds*

It was set-up in April 1989 with subscribed capital of Rs. 10 crores of which Rs. 6.5 crores was subscribed by International Financial Agencies and rest through public subscriptions.

(b) *Indus Venture Capital Fund*

It was established with a capital of Rs. 2 crores contributed by several Indian (NRI), international institutions like Bank of Tokyo, FMO, Holland, Deutsche Bank and companies. The company is owned to the extent of 35 per cent by private sector, 35 per cent by internationals and rest 35 per cent by the Government of India.

7. Overseas Venture Capital Funds

India has attracted overseas venture capital funds for investment, which have started their operations in India. Some of them are as under—

(a) Grindlays Bank Venture Capital Fund—It was set-up with a fund of Rs. 12 crores. It mainly finances through equity.
(b) Baring Private Equity.
(c) HSBC Private Equity.
(d) Indocean Chase Capital Advisors.
(e) Draper International.

These are registered with SEBI. Their true name is of 'private equity funds' not venture capital. However, they act like venture capital funds.

8. Risk Capital Technology Finance Corporation Ltd. (RCTC)

RCTC was set-up in January 1988 as a subsidiary of IFCI with a fund of Rs. 25 crores. It provides assistance in the form of conventional loans and interest-free conditional loans on a profit and risk sharing basis. The extent of financing is decided on need-base depending on interest.

9. Venture Capital Fund

It was set-up under long-term fiscal policy of Government of India with an initial fund of Rs. 10 crores. This fund was raised by imposing levy and collection tax of 5 per cent on all payments made for import technology through research and development. Under this scheme, equity fund is provided without any interest or voting rights. The minimum and maximum projects assistance ranges between Rs. 5 to Rs. 250 lakhs.

ELIGIBILITY CRITERIA

Venture capital does not finance to enterprises which are engaged in trading investment brokerage or financial services, agency or liaison work. The scheme offered by most of the venture capital institutions focus on projects with technological risk and provide support to indigenous efforts in technological development. The IDBI encourages projects involving commercial application of indigenously developed technology to wider domestic application. Proposal could range from setting up of pilot plant based on process developed in-house in national/other laboratories, technological innovations of various firms, substitute of imported raw material components and so on.

Basically, professional and technical qualified entrepreneurs venturing into hightech areas are eligible for venture capital support. A few of them criteria are below –

(a) Project should be of innovative nature.
(b) It should offer potential for substantial return.
(c) It should have a sustainable competitive advantage.
(d) It should have a strong management team with high degree of commitment and integrity.
(e) It should lay emphasis on new technology to suit Indian conditions.
(f) It should also have a potential for long-term capital gain.
(g) It should have high growth prospects and potential for capital appreciation.

Along with the riskiness of the project, greater attention is focused on individual proposal even if the volume of investment is small. Most of the venture companies provide both equity and loan financing. Some companies focus on unlisted small-scale units established as private or public limited companies in information technology and software industry. Some venture funds promote enterprises based on new technology, innovative products and process with potential for high growth rate, high risk and high returns. Not only this, biotechnology, chemical polymers, drugs and pharmaceuticals, environmental engineering, non-conventional energy and so on come under venture capital scheme.

DOCUMENTATION REQUIRED

Tylebjee and Bruno have analysed a process model of venture capital investment. We shall describe this along with the documents and papers required at different stages. It has the following steps –

1. Deal Orientation

How can the venture capitalist learn about potential entrepreneurs for financing? For this purpose, three sources can be used –

(a) *Referral System*

Deals or cases can be referred to venture capital companies by their parent organisations (like IDBI, IFC and so on) trade association, consultants, industry partners and other clients.

(b) *Active Search*

Search for potential enterprises for financing can be made through trade fairs, conferences, seminars, network and so on.

(c) *Intermediaries*

They make effort to match a venture capital company and the potential entrepreneurs.

At this stage a letter of introduction is necessary from the referring party sent to the venture capital company. It should present details about the potential venture, its technical viability and good image of the entrepreneur.

2. Screening

Screening of proposals is necessary to save the time and money cost. Only the proposals which clear screening test considered for evaluation. Thus, the venture capital company carries out initial screening of all projects on the basis of some broad criteria. These criteria differ from one venture capitalist to another. These may be the industry, technology, product, market scope, size of investment, geographical location, size of venture or the management team.

At this stage, the venture capital company may ask for technology and product profiles as well as venture or investment profile depending on the criteria used in the screening process.

3. Evaluation or Due Diligence

This is the process of detailed analysis. Here the screened proposals must pass through a detailed evaluation process. Most of the enterprises are new which have no track record, and entrepreneurs have no kind of operating experience. In such cases, the venture capital company uses a subjective but comprehensive evaluation. This process of evaluation depends on the stage of financing. Generally, the venture capitalists evaluate the managerial and entrepreneurial qualities of entrepreneur along with his management team. Besides, the product features and market potential are also evaluated.

At this stage, business plan of the entrepreneur is required to evaluate the possible risk and return on the venture because business plan is the best introduction of the venture and the entrepreneur. Business plan is the good way to gain attention of the venture capitalist and to obtain the needed finance. It is a 'single most important document' which contains detailed information about the proposed venture. It gives information about entrepreneur's ideas and intentions of doing the business seriously. In sum, it presents the information about the following–

(a) Business background and its future.
(b) Production plan–production process, technology, raw material details, requirement of utilities, production programme and so on.
(c) Organisational structure.
(d) Management personnel.
(e) Market plan and strategy.
(f) Financial plan–risk factors and return on investment.
(g) Exit strategy available to the venture capitalist.

4. Deal Structuring

During evaluation process, if the proposed venture and its business plan are found as viable, the venture capitalist accepts this proposal. Thereafter, the terms of the deal are negotiated. In deal structuring, various terms and conditions are decided which may be about the amount of money to be invested, the form of investment (that is equity or debt), the price of investment, exit period and so on. This agreement also includes the terms and policies regarding—

(a) the venture capitalists' right to control the investor's venture;
(b) the representatives of the venture capitalist on the venture's management board;
(c) the right to change its management if needed;
(d) buy-back agreement;
(e) acquisition and initial public offering, and
(f) earn-out policy that specifies the entrepreneur's equity share.

The negotiation is done to protect the interests of venture capitalists. On the other hand, the entrepreneur also tries to protect his interest. Hence, he considers to earn reasonable return, to minimise taxes, to have enough liquidity to operate his business and not to lose too much management powers to the venture capitalist. But there are a number of areas of common interest. Hence, they both try to agree to protect their mutual concerns and interests.

At this stage, a written agreement is prepared between the entrepreneur and the venture capitalist. This contains all the terms and conditions agreed between them. This agreement is written on a stamp paper, signed by both and is registered with the government agency. It is treated as a valid evidence before a court of law in case of a dispute.

5. Post-Investment Activities and Exit

When the agreement is finalised, the venture capitalist acquires the position of a partner. He assumes the role of a collaborator. He participates in venture's decisions for better management. In fact, the venture is benefited with venture capitalist's managerial and business experience especially in finance area. However, the venture capitalist does not interfere in day-to-day affairs of the venture. He intervenes only when some managerial or financial doubts arises. To exit, a venture capitalist has three choices—

(a) initial public offering,
(b) buy-back of his shares by the entrepreneur himself, and
(c) acquisition or purchase of the venture by a third party.

The exit process is performed by preparing proper documents and by implying with terms and conditions decided earlier.

REGULATION AND GUIDELINES

Venture Capital Association is a self-regulatory body and it decides professional standards and practices in venture capital industry. SEBI Act, 1992 empowers SEBI to register and regulate the venture capital institutions. Central Board of Direct Taxes through Income Tax Act also regulates the activities of the venture capital firms.

The Government of India issued guidelines on November 18, 1988 to promote a broad framework for the operations of the venture capital companies. The features of guidelines are as given below –

1. Establishment

Companies wishing to undertake venture capital activities may be established using the term 'venture capital'. Approval will be given by the Department of Economic Affairs, Ministry of Finance. Application for the issue of capital should be made under the Capital Issue (Control) Act.

All India financial institutions, State Bank of India and other scheduled banks including foreign banks operating in India, and the subsidiaries of the aforesaid would be eligible to start venture capital funds/companies.

2. Management

It is required that the venture capital funds are managed by professionals such as banks, managers and administrators and persons with adequate experience of industry, finance, accounts and so on.

No person would be permitted to be the full time chairman/ president, Chief Executive, Managing Director or Executive Director or a whole-time Director of a venture in any other company.

3. Assistance

Venture capital assistance should go mainly to enterprises where the risk element is comparatively high due to new or untried technology. Assistance should be given to relatively new, professionally or technically qualified promoters or entrepreneurs who have inadequate resources. Total investment should not exceed Rs. 10 crores (Rs. 100 million).

4. Size

The minimum size of venture capital fund would be Rs. 10 crores. If it desires to raise funds from the public the promoters' share shall not be less than 40 per cent.

5. Capital Issues

Capital issues may be made in following manners—

(a) Funds may be raised through public issues and/or private placement to finance venture capital funds.
(b) Foreign equity up to 25 per cent multilateral/international financial organisation, development finance institutes, reputed mutual funds, and so on would be permitted.
(c) NRI investment would be permitted up to 74 per cent on a non-repatriable basis and up to 25-40 per cent on a repatriable basis.
(d) An application should be addressed to Ministry of Finance, Investment Division, North Block, New Delhi.

6. Debt-Equity Ratio

The debt-equity ratio may be a maximum of 15:1.

7. Underwriting Listing

The Venture Capital Fund may be listed as per the prescribed norms. Its issue may be under-written at the discretion of the promoters.

8. Exit

Pricing of the shares at the time of disinvestment by a public issue of general offer of sale by the venture capital fund may be done by team subject to this being calculated on objective criteria like book value, profit earning capacity, and so on and the basis being adequately disclosed to the public.

9. Eligibility for Tax Concession

The preferential tax treatment would be available to the approved venture capital fund only in respect of financing of such assisted units as are eligible to be treated as venture capital units as defined aforesaid.

Application for registration and grant of certificate are to be made along with an application fee of Rs. 25,000 in a prescribed form. A venture capital fund should have Rs. 5 crores before it can start venture capital activities.

PROSPECTS OF VCF IN INDIA

In developed countries like the UK, the USA, VCFs have been catalysts in developing new entrepreneurs and have played an important role in the development of the country's industry and economy. VCFs can be an important source of finance in India also for developing projects which the country needs. The conventional sources of finance are shy due to high risk context in such projects, e.g. the extent of use of high technology for sustainable development. The risk inherent in such projects, beside the risk of continuous technological upgradation, is the limited market for high technology products in India. However, if such technologies, which are new in India but have been successfully tested abroad, are imported the risk could be minimised and with the liberalisation of the Economy coupled with the coffer of foreign exchange overflowing, the potentiality has increased manifold. Moreover, India has the advantage of low-wage structure and thus labour-intensive projects with new technology could also be profitably promoted.

In view of the difficulty for the new breed entrepreneurs obtaining finance for their projects the Government of India has pioneered venture capital culture in India through VCFs. Till now, the institutional investors have dominated the field. In countries like the UK, the USA the VCF came mainly from pension funds, insurance companies, industrial houses, etc. In the USA, VCFs were initially sponsored by affluent individuals and families. In India, VCFs have been viewed as development-oriented institutions and not as commercial ventures.

Pragmatism is not required to bring forth private capital into its fold and make the VCFs successful in India. Private capital will be attracted if there is considerable freedom to manoeuvre and make good profits. Certain fundamental changes are required both in the legislation of the country and in the perception of venture capital concept. The constraints of unfavourable tax treatment for VCFs and narrowness of the exit route (e.g. limited capital market, absence of buy-back of own shares by companies, etc.) have already been discussed. The constraints of promoters' attitude in keeping control and passing of the legacy to the next generation has also been discussed. This attitude of the promoters is, in fact, a big constraint and the same ought to be changed, despite difficulty, for real growth of venture capital culture in the country.

Several other legislative changes are also required, e.g. no notice of trust can be recognised under the Companies Act, restriction on inter-corporate investment, free investment by VCFs in different available avenues to get a reasonable return to investors, etc. The Government is not unaware of the problems. It is understood that the Government is examining the issues with SEBI to pave the way for development of venture capital in the country and to make it more attractive and competitive. The proposed amendments to the Companies Act should also include buy-back provision of own shares by the companies. A favourable tax treatment for VCFs is needed.

16

Taxation of Banks and Financial Institutions

BARUN KUMAR GHOSH

TAXATION OF INTEREST ON NON-PERFORMING ASSETS

The banks and financial institutions (FIs) in India had to bear with the controversy regarding the taxability of interest on sticky loans, which are doubtful of recovery which are better known as non-performing assets. The issue was whether they were liable to income tax on interest on sticky loans under the mercantile system of accounting. It is the common practice to account for interest on sticky loans by debiting the customer's account and crediting interest suspense account. Thus without recognizing revenue, interest on doubtful loans and advances can be accounted for by banks to keep control on accrual of interest. The Central Board of Direct Taxes (CBDT) had clarified through a beneficent circular No. 201/21 of 1984 ITA-II dated 9th October 1984 that interest credited to suspense account in respect of sticky/doubtful accounts should be excluded in computation of total income of the banks.

The problem arose for the first time when the Supreme Court dealt with the issue in the case of State Bank of Travancore *vs.* CIT, 158 ITR 102 (SC). While dealing with the issue of interest on sticky loans and advances, the Supreme Court took the view that circulars of CBDT would be binding on all officers and persons employed in execution of the Income Tax Act, 1961 (the Act), but no instruction or circular could go against the Act. The appellant bank, while computing the total income for the relevant year, excluded interest on sticky loans and advances. The Supreme Court held that interest on sticky loans and advances, whether credited to interest suspense account or not, was liable to income tax, as the assessee followed accrual system of accounting. The Board also withdrew the circular. Later a two-judge bench of the Supreme Court in the case of Kerala Financial Corporation *vs.* CIT, 210 ITR 29 (SC) on identical fact also took the same view.

Earlier the Supreme Court considered the beneficent circulars issued under section 119 to be binding on the revenue authorities, even if circulars deviated from the provisions of the Act. Some landmark judgements are Navnit Lal C. Javeri *vs.* K.K. Sen, 56 ITR 198 (SC); Ellerman Lines *vs.* CIT, 82 ITR 913 (SC); K.P. Varghese *vs.* ITO, 131 ITR 597 (SC); Keshavji Ravji & Co. *vs.* CIT 183 ITR 1 (SC) and CB Gautam *vs.* Union of India, 199 ITR 530 (SC).

In May 1999, the Supreme Court once again had the occasion to deal with the identical issue in the case of UCO Bank *vs.* CIT, 237 ITR 889 (SC).

In this case, the Supreme Court has overruled its own judgement in the Kerala Financial Corporation's case (*Supra*) and has brought back the interpretation regarding beneficent circulars as per the earlier decision of the Supreme Court. The fact was that the UCO Bank in respect of assessment year 1981-82 credited certain amount by way of interest to a suspense account, because recovery of the said amount was considered doubtful and there was no recovery in those accounts in the preceding three years. The amount credited to interest suspense account was excluded by bank in computation of its total income.

The assessing officer completed the assessment on the basis of the beneficent circulars of the CBDT. But the commissioner invoked the revisionary power under section 263 and included the said amount in the income of the assessee. A three-member bench of the Apex court analysed the accounting practice followed by the bank in respect of interest on loans and advances. The court concluded that the accounting policy of crediting interest on doubtful debts to interest suspense account and not recognising this as income before actual realisation conformed to the generally accepted accounting practice. The court felt that this particular issue might arise before several assessing officers exercising jurisdiction over different banks and the CBDT's circular was, therefore, within its powers under section 119.

The Supreme Court, in UCO Bank's case, analysed the history of decisions, as stated earlier and also the impact of the beneficent circulars. The court observed that in State Bank of Travancore's case (*supra*), the decision of the constitution bench of the court in Navnit Lal C. Jhaveri *vs.* K.K. Sen (AAC), 56 ITR 198 (SC) and the decision in K.P. Varghese *vs.* ITO, 131 ITR 597 (SC) were not pointed out to the court. Even the CBDT circular dated 9th October 1984 (*supra*) had not been brought to the notice of the court. There was a mere submission that the interest on sticky loans was allowed to be exempted for considerable long time, the practice followed by the State Bank of Travancore had transformed itself into a law and this could not have been deviated from law. It was in this background that the court had opined that the circulars being executive in nature do not alter the decision of the law and these are in the nature of concessions, which could be withdrawn prospectively.

Their Lordships, while dealing with the case of UCO Bank, respectfully disagreed with the judgement in the case of Kerala Financial Corporation. Rather, The court in UCO Bank's case said "the question is not whether a circular can override or detract from the provisions of the Act, but the question is whether the circular seeks to mitigate the rigor of a particular section for the benefit of the assessee in certain specified circumstances". The court went on to say "so long as such a circular is in force, it would be binding on the departmental authorities in view of the provisions of section 119 to ensure a uniform and proper administration and application of the Income-tax Act."

Thus, in the UCO Bank's case (*supra*), the Supreme Court restored the binding nature of the beneficent circulars on the departmental authorities. Therefore, interest on sticky loans and advances need not be taxed if they fall within the purview of the beneficent circulars issued by the Board.

The same problem came up in the case of some State Industrial Investment Corporations that are incorporated under the Companies Act, 1956. The amendment in section 209 of that Act made accrual basis of accounting mandatory. However, the amendment was followed by the Notification No. GSR 550(E) dated 16th May, 1989 issued by the Central Government under section 610 of the Companies Act, which requires a Government Company engaged in providing finance for industrial projects and approved under section 36(1)(viii) to account for income from interest on loans and advances on cash basis disclose such accrued income, which is not accounted for by way of a note in the annual accounts.

Therefore, the financial institutions, which are companies and engaged in providing long-term finance cannot account for interest on loans and advances on accrual basis. They have to follow cash basis of accounting as far as interest on loans and advances is concerned. But a disclosure is required to be made in the accounts of the institution.

The Government's concern regarding the difficulties of the banks and financial Institutions arising out of the Supreme Court's decision in the case of State Bank of India *vs.* CIT (*supra*) is evidenced by insertion of section 43D to override all other provisions of the Act so that in the case of public financial institutions or a schedule bank or a state financial corporation or a state industrial investment corporation, the income by way of interest in relation to such categories of bad and doubtful debts as may be prescribed by the Reserve Bank of India in relation to such debts, shall be taxed in the previous year in which it is credited to profit and loss account or in which it is actually received, whichever is earlier. In view of section 43D, interest on sticky loans or advances (non-performing assets) shall not be taxed on accrual basis.

One may appreciate that the provision of section 43D recognises the real income concept and also the prudential norms for income recognition followed in India and abroad. The provision is also in keeping with Accounting Standard-9 (Revenue Recognition) issued by the Institute of Chartered Accountants of India.

Despite section 43D, in assessment of state industrial investments corporations following cash basis of accounting in respect of interest income on loans and advances, the department has raised the issue whether it is correct for the assessee to offer for tax interest income on cash basis when the assessee follows accrual system in respect of interest expenditure and other expenditure. In the case of West Bengal Industrial Investments Corporation Limited *vs.* JCIT (ITA Nos. 1368/Cal/2000; 987/Cal/2001; 1295/Kol/2001; 757/Kol/2002) in respect of assessment years 1995-96 to 1998-99 the Tribunal decided the matter in favour of the assessee. However, the department has preferred appeal to the High Court under section 260A.

Though a company engaged in providing long-term finance to industries is required to follow cash system of accounting in respect of interest income on loans and advances, whether good loan or doubtful loan, as per the Government of India's Notification No. GSR 550(E) dated 16th May, 1989, for tax purpose such companies should consider that section 43D permits offering for tax on cash basis in respect of interest on bad and doubtful loans only. Interest on loans, which are not sub-standard or doubtful or loss asset, shall be taxed in the year of receipt. Therefore, even if interest on loans including good loans is not accounted for on accrual basis following the aforesaid notification of the Government, the company should include interest on good loans, i.e. standard assets in the computation of total income in the return.

Another interesting point is that banks and FIs account for interest on standard assets on accrual basis, while interest on non-performing assets is recorded on realisation. Thus, they follow hybrid system of accounting as per RBI's prudential norms, which is definitely contrary to the provision of section 145 of the Act, which deals with method of accounting for computation of business income and income from other sources. Section 145 permits assessee to follow either cash system or mercantile system of accounting with effect from assessment year 1997-98. The section rules out hybrid system. If the assessee's method of accounting is not in conformity with section 145, the assessing officer can make a best judgement assessment. However, the conflict between RBI's guidelines and the provision of section 145 hardly affects the banks or FIs.

THE PROVISIONING

Banks and financial institutions provide for non-performing assets on objective criteria laid down by RBI in its prudential guidelines. Unfortunately, the banks and financial institutions suffer an artificial disallowance by virtue of the provision of section 36(1)(viia), (viib) and (viic).

The clause (viia) was inserted by the Finance Act, 1979 with effect from 1st April, 1980 and the said clause was amended from time too time. Presently section 36(1)(viia) contemplates deduction at 7.5 per cent of total income (before allowing deduction under the said clause and Chapter VI-A) as increased by 10 per cent of aggregate average advances made by rural branches. The provision is in two parts—one limits the deduction to 7.5 per cent of the aggregate average advances made by the rural branches and the other allows a further deduction for provision for doubtful debts made by all banks limited to 10 per cent of the total income.

A bank can, at its option, claim deduction for provision made for doubtful assets or loss assets as per RBIs directive up to an amount calculated at 5 per cent (10 per cent for assessment years 2003-04 and 2004-05) of the year-end amount of such assets as per books from assessment year 2000-01 to 2004-05.

Foreign banks and financial institutions can also claim such provision only up to 5 per cent of its total income. A financial institution can, at its option, claim deduction for provision made for doubtful assets or loss assets as per RBI's norms up to 10 per cent of the year-end amount of such assets as per books for assessment years 2003-04 and 2004-05 only. However, the section is not happily worded. The limit is 10 per cent of total income. 'Total income' has not been defined for this purpose. Section 2(45) defines total income as the total amount of income referred to in section 5 computed in the manner laid down in the Act. As the expression 'total income' is used, it appears that the limit should be applied to the total of income under all the heads of income. Further, doubt arises as to whether limit of 5 per cent is to be applied on total income before setting off carried forward losses or after such set off. The ITAT, Kolkata Bench, while dealing with this matter in the case of West Bengal Industrial Development Corporation Ltd. *vs.* Jt. CIT (ITA No. 987/CAL/2001-unreported), took the view that the amount admissible under section 36(1)(viia) was to be computed before setting off brought forward business losses as the set off was the matter of chapter VI consisting of sections 70 to 80 and not falling within chapter IV-D in the manner of computation of business income as per sections 30 to 44D. The ITAT relied on the Madras High Court's decision in CIT *vs.* L.M. Van Moppes Diamond Tool (India) Ltd., 107 ITR 386 in connection with the erstwhile section 80E.

There seems to be no logic to limit the allowance as indicated above while RBI desires that provision is made as per its prudential guidelines to reflect real income. This results in payment of tax on what is not real income. The Kelkar Committee has recommended that provision made as per RBI's guidelines should qualify for full deduction.

Investment Valuation

The distinctive features of investments of banks are that RBI guides it and a significant portion of investments is made to maintain minimum level of liquid assets. Investments consist of Government securities, other approved securities, shares, debentures, bonds, commercial paper, the units of mutual fund and venture capital funds.

The Banking Regulation Act, 1949 has prescribed the disclosure requirement of investments in a particular manner in the Balance Sheet. For the purpose of valuation, a bank classifies its entire investment portfolio under three district categories, viz. held-to-maturity (HTM), held-for-trading (HFT) and available-for-sale (AFS). HTM consists of securities acquired with the intention to hold them till maturity; HFT comprises securities acquired with the intention of trading and AFS consists of securities acquired neither for trading purpose nor for being held till maturity. HTM securities are shown at cost unless it is more than face value, in which case premium is amortised over the period till maturity. However, provision is required for any permanent diminution in the value of investments in subsidiaries or joint ventures. The AFS scrips are marked to market at year-end or at more frequent intervals. Net depreciation is recognized and fully provided for. Net appreciation is ignored. Depreciation is AFS category is debited to profit and loss account and equivalent amount (net of tax benefit, if any) is transferred from investment fluctuation reserve account to profit and loss account. AFT scrips are revalued at monthly or at more frequent intervals and the net appreciation/depreciation is recognized in the profit and loss account. The issue is whether depreciation provided on investments held by banks as per RBI guidelines is deductible for tax purpose. In fact, the Act does not specifically provide for the same.

It may be noted that the classification of investments into HTM, AFS and HFT as per RBI guidelines is only for the purpose of compliance. For tax purpose, investments constitute stock in trade. Hence, investments can be valued at lower of cost or market value. The decision of Supreme Court in United Commercial Bank *vs.* CIT 106 Taxman 601 (SC) for assessment year 1982-83 is relevant here. The Bank valued stock (investments) at cost for the purpose of the balance sheet in terms of section 29 of the Banking Regulation Act, but for income tax purpose valuation was made at cost or market price whichever is lower. It was contended by the bank that the revenue had accepted the method for over last 30 years. The Apex Court made it clear that preparation of balance sheet as per statutory provision would not disentitle the bank in submitting return of income on real taxable income as per the method of accounting adopted by it consistently and regularly. For income tax purpose, what is to be taxed is the real income, which is to be deduced on the basis of accounting system regularly maintained by the assessee.

Thus, the decision of the Supreme Court sets at rest any controversy regarding depreciation on investments.

Broken Period Interest

A bank purchases securities of the face value of Rs. 10 lakhs at a price of Rs. 11 lakhs, which includes interest, accrued on the securities till the date of purchase. The bank bifurcates the purchase price into investment in securities valued at cost Rs. 10 lakhs and interest of Rs. 1 lakh, which is debited to interest paid account as per accepted practice. The issue obviously is whether interest of Rs. 1 lakh is allowable as deduction. The Supreme Court addressed the issue in Vijaya Bank Ltd. *vs.* CIT 187 ITR 541. The view of the Apex court is that the fact that securities have the face value of Rs. 10 lakhs and the accrued interest as on the date of purchase is Rs. 1 lakh is not relevant. The entire sum of Rs. 11 lakhs is capital expenditure and portion attributable to interest for broken period is not deductible from income from securities (now assessable as income from other sources). This decision seems to be applicable to securities under HTM categories, which are intended to be held till maturity by the banks. Such securities are likely to be classified as capital assets under section 2(14) of the Act. One possible view is that interest being part of the cost of acquisition of securities is not deductible from business income of the banks but would be available for deduction for computation of capital gain on maturity. The ratio is not applicable to investments under HFT and AFS categories.

Application of Sec. 14A

Banks and FIs face problems in assessment with regard to allocation of expenditure relating to exempted income after introduction of section 14A. The section provides that expenditure incurred in relation of income, which does not form part of the total income under the Act. If there is no expenditure, which is directly attributable to earning the exempted income, the question of allocation of any expenditure does not arise. Banks and FIs have several sources of income, some of which may be exempt (e.g. dividend). The common expenditure should not be apportioned to exempt income and taxable income for the sake of disallowance. It is felt that the Supreme Court's decisions in CIT *vs.* Rajasthan State Warehousing Corporation 250 ITR 218, CIT *vs.* Indian Bank Ltd. 56 ITR 77 and Maharashtra Sugar Mills Ltd. *vs.* CIT 82 ITR 452 are good law even after introduction of section 14A. Banks have started reporting segment results as per AS-17 (Segment Reporting) showing two distinct business segments – treasury operations and other banking operations. Therefore, it is possible for the department to examine the expenses allocated to treasury operations (which includes dealing in Government and other securities) in the segment reporting. It would be most appropriate to prepare a cash flow showing increase in non-interest bearing deposits, i.e. balances in current account as the source for making investments generating tax free income. It is now apprehended that the section is likely to be a source of protracted litigation.

Special Reserve of FIs

Financial corporations engaged in providing long-term finance for industrial or agricultural development or development of infrastructure facility in India or by a public company engaged in providing long-term housing finance are allowed to claim deduction under section 36(1)(viii) for an amount up to 40 per cent the profits derived from such business before making this deduction, provided such amount is carried to a special reserve. The most important aspect is that with effect from assessment year 1998-99 the assessee is required to create and maintain such special reserve. Therefore, where any amount out of special reserve is withdrawn, the assessee shall suffer taxation in the year of withdrawal in view of the provision of section of section 41(4A) of the Act. A question arises as to whether section 41(5) applies where special reserve created before assessment year 1998-99 is withdrawn. The matter is not free from doubt. However, reasonable interpretation seems to be that amount withdrawn from special reserve created in or after assessment year 1998-99 should suffer tax. Secondly, where a financial institution provides both long-term finance and short-term finance, the amount of business income derived from the business of providing long-term finance is to be ascertained for computing the eligible amount of deduction.

MERGER OF BANKS

Section 72A provides for carry forward and set off of accumulated loss and unabsorbed depreciation in amalgamation. The Finance Act, 2003 amended section 72A from assessment year 2004-05. As a result of the amendment where there is an amalgamation of a banking company referred to in section 5(c) of the Banking Regulation Act with a specified bank, then the accumulated loss and the unabsorbed depreciation of the amalgamating banking company shall be deemed to be the accumulated loss and allowance for depreciation of the amalgamated banking company for the previous year in which the amalgamation is effected. Thus, the carried forward loss and unabsorbed depreciation of amalgamating bank immediately before amalgamation can be claimed by the amalgamated bank.

However, only SBI or its subsidiaries or banks constituted under Banking Companies (Acquisition and Transfer of Undertakings) Act, 1970 or under the Banking Companies (Acquisition and Transfer of Undertakings) Act, 1980 are specified banks for this purpose. Therefore, the amended law does not consider the cases of merger of two banks in private sector or merger of any financial institution with a bank or merger of two financial institutions. The law requires suitable amendment in view of the possibility of such mergers in India.

Foreign Banks and DTAA

The rate of tax applicable to a foreign company on business income is 40 per cent plus surcharge as per the Finance Act. As per section 90(2) where there is a double tax avoidance agreement ('treaty') between India and a foreign country, the provisions of the Income-tax Act applies in relation to the assessee to the extent they are more beneficial to the assessee. The branch of a foreign bank in India is a permanent establishment (PE) within the meaning of Article 5 of a model treaty. Article 7 (Business Profits) provide that the profits of an enterprise of one of the States shall be taxable only in that State unless the enterprise carries on business in the other State through a PE situated therein. If the enterprise carries on business in the other State, the profits of the enterprise may be taxed in the other State but only so much of them as is attributable to that PE. Article

24 (Non-discrimination) provides that the taxation on a PE, which an enterprise of one of the States has in other State, shall not be less favourably levied in that other State than the taxation levied on enterprises of that other State carrying on the same activities.

The law, finally, is that if a foreign company having Indian operation makes prescribed arrangement for declaration and payment within India of dividends out of its income in India, then the tax rate applicable to a domestic company shall apply to such foreign company. Although the word used is "prescribed", the Income-tax Rules have not prescribed any such arrangements. Further, it is not possible for a foreign company to declare dividend in India, as it does not hold annual general meeting in India. Therefore, the condition laid down in the Explanation to section 90 is not capable of being fulfilled and therefore, it would be declared as obscure and useless if the issue is taken to the Court or tribunal. Realising this impossibility an amendment has been made in the Explanation to section 90 by the Finance (No. 2) Act, 2004 which has deleted the words "where such foreign company has not made the prescribed arrangement for declaration and payment within India, of the dividends (including dividends on preference shares) payable out of its income in India" once again with retrospective effect from 1st April, 2004.

It is doubtful whether Indian Government can change the terms of treaty unilaterally through amendment in domestic law, when it is one party to the treaty. The Article 51C Constitution of India that lays down directive principle states that the State shall promote respect for international law and treaty obligations. If Indian law is changed for superseding treaty rule, the foreign country may also bring in similar amendment in its law rendering it difficult for Indian resident doing business in that country.

17

Audit Risk: Its Relevance, Assessment and Minimization

BARUN KUMAR GHOSH

As the time available to the auditors is limited, it is necessary to assess the risk in carrying out the audit. Therefore, interim audit may be taken up before close of the accounting year when the auditor can devote some time to assess the associated risk. Proper risk assessment definitely improves the audit quality, because having assessed the risk element, the auditor can decide the areas requiring focused attention, thereby enabling him to reduce cost. Thus, more time can be devoted to important areas of audit concern. Assessment of risk results in effective audit plan, setting appropriate materiality level, determining appropriate sample size for compliance testing and determination of the timing and extent of substantive procedures. It may be noted that an auditor can minimize audit risk only when he assesses the audit risk objectively and properly.

EVALUATION OF RISK AND INTERNAL CONTROL

The Auditing and Assurance Standard (AAS)-6 Risk Assessments and Internal Control issued by the Institute of Chartered Accountants of India (ICAI) has prescribed standards on the procedures to be followed by the auditor for understanding the client's accounting and internal control systems and on audit risks and its components. The corresponding International Standard of Auditing 400 has prescribed similar procedures. Understanding the client's accounting and internal control systems is essential for making an effective audit plan and developing an effective audit approach. Broadly, audit risk is the risk of a material misstatement of a financial statement item that is or should be included in the audited financial statements of an entity. In this regard, a financial statement item includes any related notes to the financial statements.

Theoretically, audit risk ranges anywhere from zero (complete certainty of no material misstatement) to one (complete certainty of a material misstatement). In practice, however, audit risk is always greater than zero. There is always some risk of material misstatement, as it is not possible, (except for the audit of the simplest of financial statements), due to the limitations inherent in both accounting and auditing, to be absolutely certain that a material misstatement will not exist. Audit risk (AR) can be divided into two components:

1. Risk of material misstatement of a material financial statement item in the unaudited financial statements (RMM).
2. Risk that the misstatement will not be detected by the auditor [i.e. 1 minus the probability of detection by the auditor, 1 - Pr (Da)].

Assuming that there is 40 per cent risk of material misstatement in a financial statement item in the unaudited financial statements and a probability of 70 per cent that the misstatement would be detected by the auditor, audit risk would be calculated as follows:

$$AR = RMM - (1 - Pr\ (Da)) = 0.4 \times (1 - 0.7) = 0.4 \times 0.3 = 0.12$$

The risk of material misstatement in the unaudited financial statement (RMM) may be divided into two parts as follows:

1. Inherent risk of material misstatement occurring (RMMi).
2. Risk that will not be detected by the client [i.e. 1 minus the probability of the client detecting the misstatement 1 - Pr (De)].

Thus substituting the two components of RMM, audit risk can be mathematically expressed as follows:

$$AR = RMMi \times (1 - Pr\ (De)) \times (1 - Pr\ (Da))$$

Hence, if there is 80 per cent inherent risk of a material misstatement in a financial statement item, 30 per cent probability of such a misstatement being detected by the client and a probability of 40 per cent that in case the misstatement is not detected by the client, it will be detected by the auditor, the audit risk is:

$$AR = RMMi \times (1 - Pr (De)) \times (1 - Pr (Da)) = 0.8 \times (1 - 0.3) \times (1 - 0.4) = 0.336$$

The three components of audit risk viz. RMMi, 1 - Pr (De), (1 - Pr (Da)) are referred to as inherent risk (IR), control risk (CR) and detection risk (DR). This gives rise to the following audit risk model:

$$AR = IR \times CR \times DR$$

However, in practice the auditors evaluate risk components using terms such as low, moderate and high rather than using the probabilities. The model has certain limitations like aggregation problem, the lack of independence between variables and the fact that the model focuses on only one decision, i.e. audit approach. Therefore, those limitations are to be kept in mind while applying the model in practical situations. Assessment of audit risk is essentially a professional judgment of the auditor. Therefore, he should use his professional judgment to design audit procedures in such manner that the audit risk is reduced to an acceptable low level.

As stated three components of audit risk are inherent risk, control risk and detection risk.

- **Inherent risk** is the susceptibility of an account balance or class of transactions to material misstatement, individually or when aggregated with misstatements in other balances or classes, assuming there were no related internal controls. Inherent risk is a measure of the auditor's assessment of the likelihood that there are material misstatements in any account balance or class of transactions before considering the effectiveness of internal control system of the client. Inherent risk is the perceived level of risk that a material misstatement may occur in the client's unaudited financial statements, or underlying levels of aggregation, in the absence of internal control procedures. For example, there may be a change in technology that may render number of plant and machineries useless and idle requiring write-down of such plant and machineries. Another example may be when the company is exposed to uncertainty of realisation of dues from its overseas customers due to restriction imposed by the law of the country or when the company is passing through a global recession.

- **Control risk** is the risk that a misstatement will not be prevented or detected and corrected on timely basis by the client's accounting and internal control systems. Such misstatement may occur in an account balance or class of transactions that could be material individually or when aggregated with misstatements in other balances or classes. Thus, control risk is the perceived level of risk that a material misstatement in the client's unaudited financial statements, or underlying levels of aggregation, will not be detected and corrected by the management's internal control procedures. For example, a stores material is directly delivered to the shop floor of the enterprise without entering its central stores and as a result though the consumption might be recorded, the liability might be omitted or the client has not established procedures for physical verification of inventories constituting a material portion of total assets or the client has not established proper cutoff procedures, etc.
- **Detection risk** is the risk that even though the auditors might have performed substantive audit procedures, such procedures may fail to detect a misstatement that can exist in any account balance or class of transactions that may be material on individual basis or when combined with misstatements in other balances or class. Therefore, detection risk is the perceived level of risk that a material misstatement in the client's unaudited financial statements, or underlying levels of aggregation, will not be detected by the auditor. For example, where a bill for a substantial repair job is received by the enterprise's user department, but information about the same is not passed on to the accounts department before the cutoff date for providing the liability or even before finalisation of the accounts. In my opinion the detection risk should be perceived to be more where the prior period items of income and expenses are on the higher side.

It should be noted that audit risk is a function of three types of sub-risk. Inherent risk and control risk are beyond the control of the auditors and therefore, both must simply be assessed by the auditors. If control risk is to be taken as anything other than high, the auditor must undertake specific procedures to confirm the assessment of control risk. Given an acceptable level of audit risk and assessed levels of inherent and control risk, it is ultimately the detection risk that determines the extent of the auditor's work.

While developing the audit approach the auditor should consider the preliminary assessment of inherent risk and control risk for determining the nature, timing and extent of substantive audit procedures.

ASSESSMENT OF INHERENT RISK

There is no straight jacket formula for assessment of inherent risk. In developing the overall audit plan, the auditor should assess inherent risk at the financial statement level. In developing the audit programme, the auditor should relate such assessment to material account balances and classes of transactions at the assertion level or assume that inherent risk is high for the assertion. The assumption of high inherent risk can be made after considering the factors relevant to the financial statements as a whole and to the specific assertions. In order to assess inherent risk the auditor should use his professional judgement to evaluate many factors considering his previous experience with the client, any controls established by the clients to compensate for high risk and his own knowledge of any significant changes that might have taken place since his last assessment.

Factors indicative of high inherent risk at the financial statement level are usually as follows:

(a) Lack of Management Integrity

For evaluation of management integrity the following criteria may be used:

- Is management dominated by a single person or is it a small group? For example, the chairman of the company may be its chief executive or percentage of independent directors in the board is low.
- A high rate of turnover of key accounting or finance people may indicate dispute between management and finance people on reporting standards.

- Extent of significant and prolonged under-staffing may indicate that the management has very little interest in quality financial reporting.
- Absence of significant number of independent directors.
- Extent of related party transactions. Extensive transactions with related parties may affect the interest of owners and the client.
- A continuing failure to correct any major weakness of internal control system that indicates anything from lack of management's interest in internal control to aversion to internal control.
- Past events indicating lack of integrity.
- Recent change in auditors or frequent change in legal counsel.

(b) Lack of Management Competence

It refers to competence of the directors and the senior management personnel. It includes the matters such as industry experience, knowledge of entity's business, commercial skills, knowledge of good corporate governance, etc. The auditor can assess management competence by considering the factors like number of years of experience of each director in the industry, the number of years of experience of each director of the client, the extent of change to management in last several years, etc.

(c) Unusual Pressures on Management

Sometimes there are pressures that may predispose management to misstate the financial statement intentionally or unintentionally. Following are some examples—

- Lack of adequate capital to continue operations or there is downward trend in current ratio.
- Unexpected loss or downturn in profit.
- Client's inexperience.
- Potential going concern problems.
- Client's need to fulfil budgeted result that is communicated to the government or other agency.
- The industry itself is subject to stiff competition.
- The client has unresolved disagreements with the auditors.

- The client is contemplating issue of equity shares.
- Capital market's expectation of improved performance.

(d) Presence of Certain Factors Relating to the Nature of the Client's Business

The following factors are indicative of high inherent risk:

- Senior level management personnel are remunerated based on results.
- Existence of significant equity holding or option over equity holding by senior management.
- Client has some features different from the others in industry, e.g. different ROI, growth, accounting policies, etc.
- Complex corporate structure.
- Client faces increased business risk. This increases inherent risk, because there is risk of concealment of loss through use of inappropriate accounting practices.

(e) Presence of Certain Industry Specific Factors

The nature of industry may be such that it has reduced performance or growth. There is risk that losses may be attempted to be concealed by inappropriate accounting practices. Thus if the client's business is sensitive to economic conditions or fast change in technology or design or the industry is experiencing high rate of failure or depression, the assessment of inherent risk would be comparatively high.

(f) Application of Information Technology to the Data Processing Environment

Most of the businesses today have some level of IT applications. In IT environment organizational independence is more important because of greater concentration of knowledge, but it is more difficult to achieve because there is less personnel. This increases the risk of material misstatement in the unaudited financial statements. In an IT environment there is greater concentration of data compared to a manual environment and both data and software are more vulnerable to unauthorized access, loss or destruction (both accidental or deliberate) as the data are more in machine readable form. The other factors that increase inherent risk include systems with invisible audit trail, absence of invisible audit trail, absence of input document, absence of visible output, possibility of data loss (through broken transmissions) and data and software corruption (through tapping and hacking) and the increased risk of unauthorized data corruption owing to data sharing in a data base system.

Inherent risk is considered as low, when few inherent risk factors are present. It is considered as moderate or high, when a significant number of inherent risk factors are present. For existing clients, much of the information referred to above will be available from prior year's working papers or from knowledge held by the auditor and his/her staff employed on previous engagements. However, changes in, for example, the management, directors, legal advisers, financial and litigation status, market conditions, products sold, and even operating procedures usually indicate a need to reassess the level of inherent risk compared to the previous year.

Factors indicative of high inherent risk at level of assertion of account balance or transaction group are as follows:

(a) Management Discretion over the Value of the Account Balance

Sometime account balance involves high degree of management's estimation or judgement. In that case the inherent risk is assessed as high. Certain balances or transaction groups may be susceptible to misstatement due to high degree of estimation. For example, provision for warranty claims and free service in case of automobile industry, provision for quality complaints in coal industry, accounting for dredging subsidy on the basis of claims made by riverine port, etc. For example, trade debtors are normally subject to a provision for bad debts. This may involve a high degree of management discretion. In such instances, the inherent risk is evaluated as high. The risk factors relating to an account balance assertion are evaluated net of any related provision.

(b) A High Susceptibility of the Asset to Obsolescence

The susceptibility of an asset to obsolescence or change in consumer demand or technological change that can affect its value raises the risk of accuracy of valuation of account balance compared to those account balances that are not susceptible to changes. For instance, the inherent risk relating to the accuracy of the valuation of inventory finished goods inventory of a computer retailer should be assessed as moderate or high, as the value of such inventory is susceptible to technological change.

(c) Susceptibility of Asset to Asset to Misappropriation

The susceptibility of an asset to loss or misappropriation affects the inherent risk relating to completeness of the account balance. For example, multi-product retail store.

(d) Presence of Unusual Transactions

If an account balance contains unusual transactions, inherent risk is assessed high. For example, purchase account of a company may contain significant transactions with related parties. Transactions with related parties require disclosure. There is an increased risk that reportable transactions will not be disclosed. Thus, there is risk of accuracy of description of account balance.

(e) Susceptibility of the Account Balance to Adjustment

If an account balance is susceptible to adjustment, the inherent risk for particular assertion is increased. For example, in the earlier year the account balance was found to be misstated and required adjustment.

All the above factors increase inherent risk for a particular account balance assertion. Inherent risk is rated low when few of the above risk factors are present and it is rated moderate or high when significant numbers of inherent risk factors are present.

It should be borne in mind that inherent risk assumes absence of internal control procedures. If control risk of the client is assessed as less than high, obviously there will be some amelioration of the overall risk of misstatement of account balance assertion.

Inherent risk may be set for segments rather than for the overall audit because misstatements occur in segments. By identifying expectations of misstatements in segments, the auditor is thereby able to modify audit evidence by searching for misstatements in those segments. Extensive misstatements in the prior year's audit would cause inherent risk to be set at a high level (may be even 100 per cent).

Level of Aggregation	Audit Stages				
	Client Acceptance/ Retention	Audit Planning	Control Testing	Substantive Testing	Opinion Formulation
Financial Statement Level	IR_1	NA	NA	NA	IR_5

When inherent risk is increased from medium to high, the auditor should increase the audit evidence to determine whether the expected misstatement actually occurs.

Assessment of inherent risk depends on the auditors having a high level of knowledge of the business of the client. In the first year of audit the auditor may assess many of the inherent risks as high. This can be reduced in subsequent years as the auditor gains more experiences of the client organisation.

AAS 6 Requires Documentation of Assessment of Inherent Risk, when such Risk Assessed is not High

The auditor may assign maximum score to each of the factors considered by him in assessing inherent risk and also assign actual score to each such factor using his professional judgement. At this stage he is in a position to find out percentage of actual scores to the maximum score. He can classify risk score obtained as high, medium or low depending upon his own perception of risk. For example, he may decide to consider risk score over 80 per cent as indicator of high risk, risk score between 50 per cent and 80 per cent as indicator of medium risk and risk score below 50 per cent as indicator of low risk.

Evaluation of Inherent Risk at the Financial Statement Level

Inherent risk at the financial statement level is assessed in the first and last stages of audit. In the client acceptance stage, the evaluation of IR_1 is essentially based on the auditor's preliminary knowledge of the client's business. IR_5 is assessed when the auditor obtains a detailed knowledge of the client's business. Inherent risk is assessed as low, moderate or high.

ASSESSMENT OF CONTROL RISK

Like inherent risk, this risk may be assessed at various levels of aggregation (for example, at financial statement level, account balance level) and at various stages in course of audit (client acceptance or client retention stage or at the stage of planning for audit).

Evidence in relation to evaluation of control risk at the financial statement level is the evidence of the nature of control environment that influences the client's accounting information system. The control environment of client reflects the various control policies established by the client. Certain control environment, i.e. client with extensive control policies is conducive to the minimization of inherent risk. This is called positive control environment. Existence of few or no control policies does not reduce the inherent risk. This is called negative control environment.

Factors indicative of control risk at the financial statement level are as follows:

(a) Risk Averse Management Philosophy and Operating Cycle

Management that is risk averse opts for establishing controls even though establishing and maintaining controls may involve cost.

(b) Established Organizational Policies

A client having a well-structured organisation with defined authority and responsibility pattern can be considered as having more positive control environment.

(c) Well-defined Authorisation Policies

Establishment of policies relating to assignment of authority to management and their employees is an evidence of positive control environment.

(d) Presence of a Structured Internal Audit Function

Existence of a full-fledged internal audit system in an organisation strengthens the control environment. This is more when the internal auditors monitor whether the employees adhere to the established control procedures.

(e) Good Information Technology Policy

Where the policies exist for design, operation and control of the client's information system, the control environment is strengthened.

(f) Well-defined Human Resource Policy

Where the human resource policy aims to enhance the competence of management and other staff, the control environment of the organisation is likely to be positive.

(g) Existence of Independent Audit Committee

Existence of audit committee with majority independent directors is a sign of positive control environment.

For existing clients most of the information should be available from the last year's audit working paper file. However, the auditor should consider any significant change in policies or philosophy since last year.

Control risk at the financial statement level is the risk that a material misstatement in the unaudited financial statements will not be detected and rectified on timely basis. This assessment is a far broader assessment of control risk than the assessment of control risk at specific account balances assertion level. Control risk at the financial statement level is assessed in the first stage and last stage of audit, i.e. at the client acceptance/retention stage. It may be referred to as CR_1 at the client acceptance stage and CR_5 at the audit opinion formulation stage.

Assessment of Control Risk at Financial Statement Level

Level of Aggregation	*Audit Stages*				
	Client Acceptance/ Retention	*Audit Planning*	*Test of Control*	*Substantive Testing*	*Opinion Formulation*
Financial Statement Level	NA	CR_2	CR_3	CR_4	NA

In the client acceptance stage CR_1 is initially evaluated on the basis of the auditor's preliminary understanding of the client's business as opposed to a detailed understanding of the business. A preliminary knowledge of business is necessary to determine whether to accept the audit or not or to continue with the audit.

Control risk at the financial statement level is assessed as low where control environment is fully positive. It is assessed as moderate where control environment is partly positive. Control environment is assessed as high where the control environment is found to be negative or not known to be positive.

Control risk at the account balance assertion level is the risk that a material misstatement of an account balance assertion (including misstatement of an underlying class of transaction) will not be detected and rectified by the client's internal control system on timely basis. The auditor makes assessment of control risk at the account balance assertion level on the basis of the following:

(a) General Understanding of the Accounting Information System and Related Internal Control

Irrespective of audit approach the auditors form an idea of accounting systems and related internal control procedures. Such understanding is obtained through enquiries, inspection of records, review of the systems and systems documentation, observation of the client's activities and operations, review of permanent working paper files. The understanding of accounting information systems and related controls should be documented by the auditor.

(b) Identification of Control Procedures

After obtaining general understanding of the control procedures the auditor should identify specific control procedures that address the risks identified. These are the procedures upon which he wishes to place reliance.

(c) Evaluation of Effectiveness of Design of Internal Control Procedures

The auditor makes an evaluation of effectiveness of the internal controls. The auditor gathers evidence of the effectiveness of the control procedures or evidence as to the theoretical ability of the control procedures to detect or prevent misstatement. Control risk is low if the design and effectiveness of the control procedures relating to particular account balance assertion is more. The auditor should obtain evidence as to the effectiveness of internal control procedures through enquiry, compliance testing or through proper computer assisted audit techniques (these are collectively known as "tests of control"). If the auditor evaluates the control risk less than high, he is expected to document the basis of such evaluation in his work paper. That means the auditor should obtain audit evidence by performing tests of control to support assessment of control risk, which is less than high. Lower the control risk, more evidence as to designing and effective operation of the internal control systems is required to be obtained.

The risk may be assessed at the stages of audit planning, testing of control and substantive audit procedures and may be referred to as CR_2 CR_3 and CR_4 respectively.

Level of Aggregation	*Audit Stages*				
	Client Acceptance/ Retention	*Audit Planning*	*Test of Control*	*Substantive Testing*	*Audit Opinion Formulation*
Account Balance Assertion Level	NA	CR_2	CR_3	CR_4	NA

Evaluation of CR_2 is based on general understanding of the accounting systems and related control procedures, the identification of the control procedures upon which reliance may be placed and the effectiveness of design of internal control procedures upon which reliance is intended to be placed.

CR_3 is evaluated on the basis of the auditor's understanding how effective is the operation of internal control procedures of the client, deviations from control procedures acceptable level of control deviations. CR_3 seeks to provide guide to the auditor as to whether he should continue to rely on the controls as planned.

CR_4 is nothing but a revaluation of CR_3. CR_4 is based on the additional knowledge of effectiveness of internal controls that is obtained through substantive procedures performed by the auditor.

Control risk at account balance assertion level is asse^sed as high, moderate or low.

AAS 6 requires that before concluding the audit, the auditor should make a final assessment of control risk. He should satisfy himself that the assessment of control risk is confirmed through substantive procedures performed and other audit evidences obtained in course of audit. In case deviations from the accounting control systems are noticed, he should make necessary enquiries to consider implications of such deviations. If the deviations are noticed, he should try to obtain evidence from other tests of control to see whether such evidence supports his initial assessment. Otherwise, he should amend his assessment. If the auditor feels that his assessment of control risk requires revision, he should modify the nature, timing and extent of his planned substantive procedures.

ASSESSMENT OF DETECTION RISK

The auditor considers his assessment of inherent risk and control risk to determine the nature, timing and extent of substantive procedures to be performed by him to reduce the audit risk. Audit risk cannot be reduced to zero even if he examines cent percent of the account balances, because the most of the audit evidences are persuasive rather than conclusive in nature. However, the auditor is required to reduce the audit risk to an acceptably low level. He should decide the nature of such test, e.g. whether he should test the debtors' balances by examining the bills and other internal evidences or by examining customer's statement of accounts or balance confirmation. The timing of substantive procedures, i.e. before period end interim audit or after the period end. The extent of substantive procedures, actually refers to the size of samples to be checked.

Whatever the assessment of inherent risk and control risk may be, the auditor should always perform some substantive procedures for account balances and classes of transactions that are material.

Where the inherent and control risks are assessed to be high, the auditor should obtain more audit evidence by performing substantive procedures. The auditor should consider whether substantive procedures would provide sufficient audit evidence to reduce detection risk, thereby reducing the audit risk to an acceptably low level. If the auditor finds that detection risk regarding financial statement assertion for a material account balance or a class of transactions cannot be reduced to an acceptable level, the auditor has no option other than expressing a qualified opinion or a disclaimer, whichever is appropriate.

Like other risks, detection risk may be assessed at various levels of aggregation e.g. at financial statement level and at account balance level and also at various audit stages, e.g. client acceptance/retention stage, planning stage, etc.

Level of Aggregation	*Audit Stages*				
	Client Acceptance/ Retention	*Audit Planning*	*Control Testing*	*Substantive Testing*	*Opinion Formulation*
Financial Statement Level	DR_1	NA	NA	NA	DR_5
Account Balance Assertion Level	NA	DR_2	DR_3	DR_4	NA

The achievable level of detection risk at the financial statement level is the risk that a material misstatement in the unaudited financial statements will not be detected by the auditor. The achievable level of detection risk at the financial statement level can be assessed in the first and last audit stages. The achievable level of detection risk at the account balance assertion level is the risk that a material misstatement of an account balance assertion will not be detected by the audit procedures. Detection risk at the account balance assertion level may be assessed in the three stages, viz. audit planning, test of control and substantive procedures.

CONCLUSION

Assessment of audit risk enables the auditor to reduce the risk of material misstatement through appropriate test of controls and substantive procedures. Risk assessment improves audit efficiency and it helps the auditor to provide value added service to the client through constructive management letter indicating material weaknesses in the accounting and internal control systems and suggesting improvements thereto.

18

Product Costing and Pricing in Banks

MRUTYUNJAYA PADHAN

Product costing and pricing is a host of comprehensive management tools that augment strategic planning to achieve the desired level of goal in an organization. These equip with the management with the information they need about product costs and adopt suitable planning to deploy the available resources in an orderly way. Pricing is a post-costing phenomenon, where every bank's goal should be cost minimization and price maximization.

PRODUCT COSTING

In simple accounting terms, product costing is the process of arriving at the total expenditure incurred for production of an output. Costing is important at different levels for a banking company in a market economy. It is necessary to measure the profit that can be made on its different products or activities, but this is only one of its many applications. Costing is a powerful tool to influence most management decisions, such as allocation of overheads, choice of a product portfolio or the most economic way of using expensive assets. Costing is also a planning and control tool providing relevant information for taking appropriate management decisions in a bank whatever its size. Costing is a complex and "integral part of management accounting practices."

Objectives

Broadly the objectives of costing can be summarized as:

1. Profit maximization,
2. Optimum allocation/utilization of available resources,
3. Management decisions,
4. Planning and control, and
5. Communicating business to other management levels.

COSTING METHODS

It is necessary to gather information relating to the following points before going for product costing:

(a) Bank products information (services, transactions, etc.),
(b) Product sales channels, and
(c) Client segment.

A costing method prescribes how costs are to be defined, collected and prescribed. In purely economic terms, sales prices are defined by the market competition and the product's competitiveness where the product are sold in the market. The simplest product costing method uses only direct costs like, labour cost, raw materials, etc. In the standard costing method, the concept of product costing module utilizes the standard and current material costs of all items purchased to determine the cost of the finished products. Standard costing is a simple and suitable method for actual cost follow-up but may mislead to inappropriate decisions when used in future planning. The main drawback behind is that standard product costing does not provide enough information to enable user to control the overheads and other indirect costs related to the product.

However, there remains a significant difference between the general market products and banking products in terms of its tradeability/visibility and marketability. So far market is concerned, bank products are confined to a limited section in the society unlike other goods and commodities, which have a wider market. As bank services are much more complex than the products of a manufacturing company, the costing approach in banking products is different. Banks must evaluate their operating complexity, capacity considerations, and the nature of competition before deciding which costing system to use. They should also make sure to adopt a system that will reckon all useful information within their decision models. For example, in relation to operation complexity, a bank that produces one product would not need to use a complex cost system since all the overhead incurred to support that one product, whereas, when they produce multiple products would have more complicated cost system decisions to make regarding the need for variable or full cost information and which costing system to use to determine this information. Capacity considerations include whether or not to include fixed cost allocations in product costs when capacity is constrained or whether or not to include excess capacity costs within product costs. Costing influence product margins, decisions regarding whether or not to produce a product and services and the quality of the products, all of which will affect the way the bank competes in both the price and non-price with the counterparts. Several factors, like complexity of the production process, frequency of operation at capacity, market segment or the nature of competition, must be taken into account when deciding what cost system a banking company will adopt. "With a set of given internal and external pressures that bank faces, one cost system may be better suited to serve its needs than another."

COSTING ISSUES

(i) Information is one of the key elements in a competitive market. A reliable information system is first and foremost requirement of a bank to put in place a proper costing system. It should be enabling management to evaluate and communicate what is best for the bank. Crucial information (such as product cost, accurate profit calculation, depreciation assessment, relevant overheads allocation) cannot be obtained without a well-developed and modern management accounting system. Deciding how to allocate resources and other management decisions, for example, to products and processes, communicating business goals to the bank and controlling results must be based on accurate and timely information.

(ii) Reckoning various costs involved in products and services for costing process is another crucial issue. In banking products, apart from fixed and variable costs other costs like tangible, intangible cost, etc. are also incurred. Quantification of all these costs in an absolute term is quite tedious task which may lead to improper costing. The product sales channel is also wide and large. Costs incurred at these various stages are to be encompassed in costing process.

(iii) Capturing sequence of costs incurred at various stages are necessary for an effective costing system. It would be very artificial to allocate general management costs, administrative, general IT, human resources costs, etc. on products. In practice, many organizations create mountains of cost data, but provide management with little or no useful information on cost and performance. This leads to misleading decisions in the organization.

In conventional product costing methodologies only costs measured in the production process are applied to products to determine cost of production. Ideally, so far banks products are concerned, costing should include all cost objects (e.g. process, product, customer, etc.) with the following targets:

- Providing a sound, fundamental cost accounting framework.
- Improving the understanding of the organizational structure and behaviour by products, business processes and business activities.
- Improving product costing to enhance product and customer profitability.
- Highlighting opportunities to reduce/avoid costs.
- Improving cost planning and simulation capabilities.
- Supporting the cost management information needs of financial and non-financial functions, including product design, engineering, purchasing and marketing, etc.
- Better utilization administrative resources.
- Improving performance reporting.
- Increasing the timeliness, efficiency, reliability and accessibility of financial information.

It is important to understand and manage profitability from all of these angles like, knowing what services have been used, what were their costs, what fees have been earned and how changes to costs and pricing arrangements will affect profitability. Calculating costs only at an aggregate level make it impossible to measure the true cost, and hence profitability of individual transactions, accounts and customers. It is essential to apply costs and fees at all these levels.

The ability to manage fee arrangements and special deals based on profitable outcomes can become an essential part of competitive advantage. Fee arrangements will change over time both in value and structure in response to competitive situations there are many examples of banks chasing increasing market share by unwittingly discounting fees to below true cost.

PRICING

In a changing banking scenario, significant changes in banking activities are witnessed in modern day banking. Today, most banking products are commodities. As a result, there is increased pressure on internal costs and on the pricing arrangements used for each customer, transaction, market, product, department and service. While pricing very enormously across countries, most banking institutions in a country adopt a broadly consistent pricing model; so pricing differences in a given country are smaller. This pressure can dominate management time and attention even in the most successful banks. The importance of pricing is necessary due to the factors as mentioned below:

- Profit is the sole criteria for any banking institution. For reaping continuous profit, pricing of the products and services must be rationalized.
- Pricing is a major factor in the decision-making process for the customer and in protecting long-term customer loyalty.
- To be a market leader in the field, pricing should be competitive always and it should be susceptible to the changing competitive environment. If a bank is charging too much for advances and too little for deposits, its share of the market will shrink.
- There is a significant and global shift towards greater reliance on bank fees and charges in place of higher interest margins and cross-subsidies between products.
- To comply with the supervisory and regulatory stipulations.
- For survival of an organization appropriate pricing is a must. A flexible pricing system can only endure in the stiff competitive market conditions.

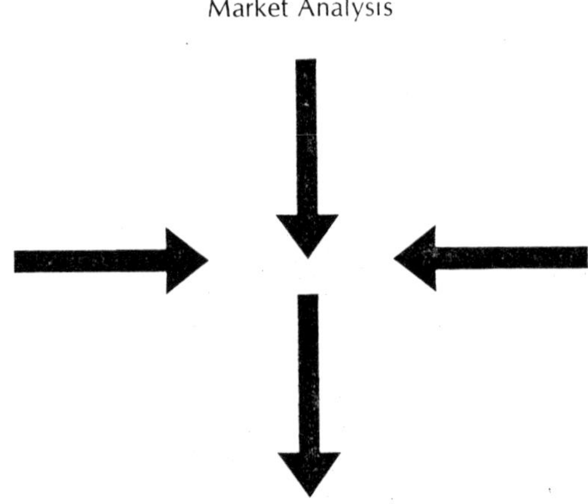

Decision on Pricing Strategy

Pricing can be attributed as an outcome of the centrifugal force arising from financial objectives, costs analysis and market analysis. Diagrammatically, it can be illustrated as above.

Steps Involved for Pricing

- Measure how individual services are being used.
- Measure internal economics of each product.
- Measure costs of providing services and their profitability.
- Measure the value of product and service portfolios.
- Measure value internally and to the market.
- Measure the value of each customer relationship.
- Calculate interest on account balances.
- Calculate earnings allowance.
- Calculate financial service taxes, complex pricing at point of sale (PPOS).
- Analyze operational transactions price by market, customer, account, service, by customer account analysis.
- Segment the customer base.
- Formulate customer friendly services.
- Generate customer, product and operational information.
- Ascertain service details of other finance control systems.
- Evaluate customer statements.

Pricing is a decision, market driven by number of factors (both internal and external) in a bank. Asset-liability composition effects the pricing. A bank cannot sustain growth with a long-term mismatch in asset and liability. Effective management of asset and liability enable the bank in deploying its fund in a productive way to avoid keeping fund ideal. The traditional method of 'supply-side' pricing, where rates are set according to what the competitors are charging and what the bank estimates it can afford will no longer suffice in the present day banking. Rather, presently, it is more of 'demand-side', the demand elasticity must be analyzed and quantified in terms of products, geographical locations, and competitor in the field and client segments. In some products, pricing controlled by some external forces like, the instances of Government sponsored schemes. Social obligation is another factor where the banks may not keep profit as the sole criteria for pricing, e.g. pension accounts and other deposit schemes for senior citizens, etc. where social obligation is considered.

RISK MANAGEMENT AND PRICING

Most of the banks are now preparing themselves for introduction of Basel II norms. Basel II is set to fundamentally change the banking market place. It is understood that the accord will have a major impact on the ways banks manage capital, pricing and margins. It is important for the banks in understanding the strategic impact of Basel II, the implementation costs and benefits, and the route map to compliance. By having a more risk-sensitive approach to capital adequacy, banks will be able to allocate less capital to the strongest credits, while more capital will be required for weaker credits. This will affect the bank's return individual relationships, etc. and can be expected to lead to a change in their behaviour to some clients and products. To ensure safety of their depositors, creditors and shareholders, banks must carefully prepare themselves to manage the risks inherent in their products and services in relation to the impact of implementing Basel II accord.

With the shrinking interest spread and more regulator stipulations ahead, banks may shift their attention more to relationship pricing or individual product pricing, preferential pricing, innovative pricing etc. Credit card business once seem to be a risky business is seen as a lucrative business even today to most of the players in the field. Bundling of products and services and selling them at an attractive

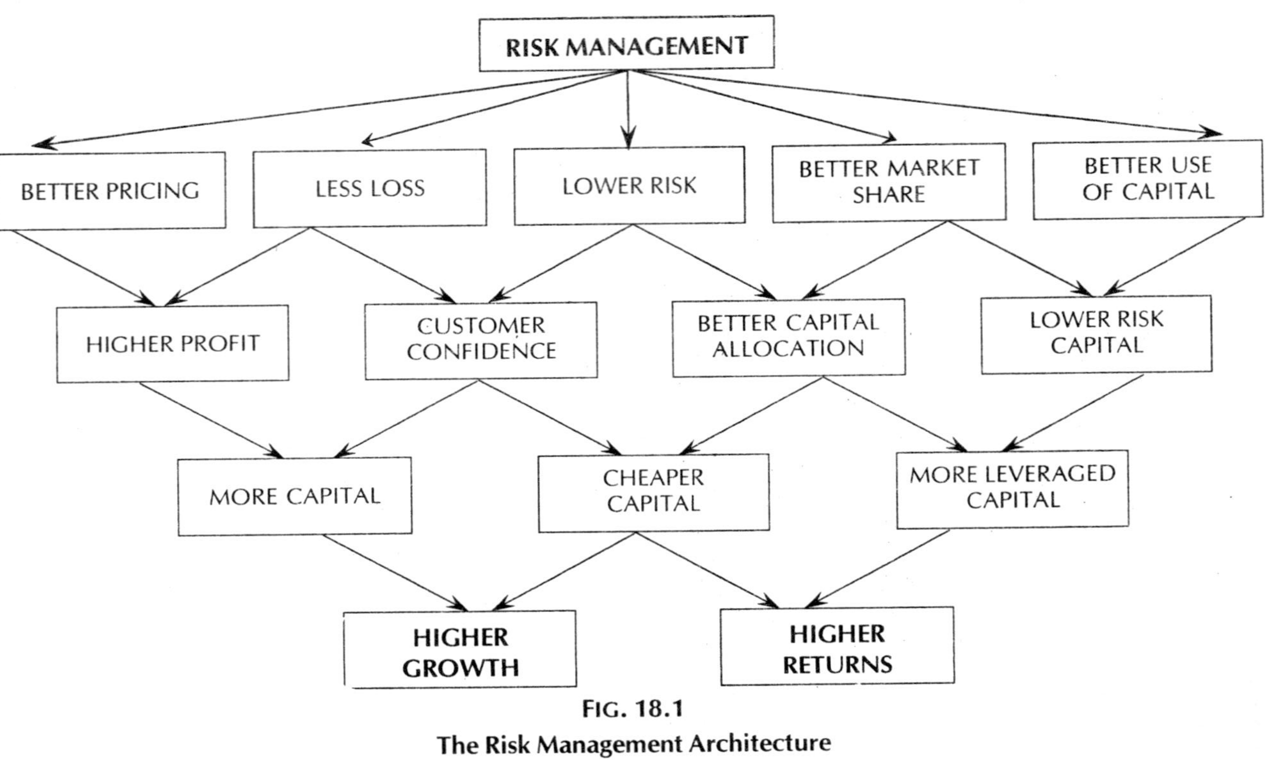

FIG. 18.1
The Risk Management Architecture

discounted pricing is still to take a large shape in India. This will enable banks to offer bundled financial services to enhance market share. It is high time for banks to shift to more scientific approach of pricing of the products and services.

The risk management architecture can be diagrammatically represented as shown on facing page.

PART III

AUDIT AND RISK

19

Financial Crimes and IS Audit

Y. SRINIVAS

The IT-enabled financial crime is a major threat that is taking newer dimensions with newer developments in IT. One important way of addressing the risk of such crime is to adopt a risk-based Information Technology Systems (IS) audit. Several variants of IS audits can form very effective part of overall internal audit programme of a bank.

Financial crimes or financial frauds can be classified as white-collar crimes, which represent the illegal acts that are characterised by deceit, concealment, or violation of trust. Financial crimes are not dependent upon the application or threat of physical force or violence but can result in a substantial financial loss to the customers or to a bank.

The concept of financial crime, as such, is not new. However, the ways in which financial crime is being committed are changing. Criminals are increasingly using Information Technology (IT) to commit financial crimes. This is largely due to the anonymity that the IT systems and the technology banking often offer to the customers.

Proper assessment, evaluation and management of financial crime risk in the light of IT vulnerabilities helps the bank in avoiding loss of reputation in the market that may arise on account of incidents of financial crimes hitting its customers.

THE GROWING THREAT

Banks are increasingly facing the threat of financial crimes on account of both internal and external factors. Internally, the fraudulent bank employees who often deal with the systems and security aspects and externally the IT hackers and fraudsters can pose a significant threat of a financial crime.

There are several adverse consequences of financial crimes. According to an estimate, a financial fraud in case of a credit card can cause the individual great inconvenience taking up to 300 hours to rebuild his credit history. It can bring institutions down to closure and can cause employees loss of their livelihood and investors their life savings. These crimes threaten the stability of a nation's banking system and challenge the law enforcement authorities to unravel their complex schemes.

TYPES OF FINANCIAL CRIMES

Different types of financial crimes presently being detected internationally are as follows:

(a) Phishing or Identity Theft

'Phishing' attacks are those where criminals send spoof e-mails misrepresenting bank identity to trick individuals to disclose personal financial data such as account numbers and Personal Identification Numbers (PINs). The stolen identities through this process are used by the criminals to gain an unauthorised access to the accounts and the debit/credit cards resulting in a financial loss to genuine customers.

(b) Phishing Trojans

'Phishing' Trojans are often auto-downloaded from bogus web pages and secretly log keystrokes when a customer visits an online banking site. The Trojan captures account details and e-mails them to the criminals, which can be used for fraudulent purposes.

(c) Denial of Service Attacks

Denial of Service (DoS) attacks are where a system receives many simultaneous instructions and either cannot cope with the volume of requests and fails or slows its processing down so that a user cannot get a timely response when loading a web page.

(d) Counterfeit Cheques

Fraudsters make use of the latest technology to counterfeit a complete cheque by using scanners, photocopiers, printers, etc. This means that they can reproduce cheques that bear remarkable resemblance to the originals, with only slight differences with regard to paper and printing quality. In many instances even experienced bank personnel mistake these counterfeit cheques for originals.

HOW TO COMBAT IT-ENABLED FINANCIAL CRIMES

As Information security issues can pose significant financial crime threat to a bank, certain techniques to be adopted by the banks to combat them are provided below:

(a) Customer Education

Banks should ensure that the customers are kept aware about the precautions they should take while dealing with cards and PINs and electronic communications representing messages from a Bank. They may also enable their customers to check whether or not the web site they have accessed is a dummy or look-alike site. One way in which customers can check the authenticity of the site is where a bank has its website certified by a reputable certifying agency. By clicking on the certifying agency's logo on the bank's web site, the consumer is able to confirm the validity of the certificate on the agency's site.

(b) Incident Management

Banks need to have incident management procedures commensurate with the size of their operations that define the roles and responsibilities for the staff involved and provide the escalation route to senior management. Internationally the Banks that have been subject to 'phishing' attacks have designed well-developed incident management procedures. These have been repeatedly tested, reviewed and enhanced with each attack experienced to produce an effective incident management response and escalation procedure.

(c) Intrusion Detection Software

Intrusion Detection Software works by identifying patterns of network traffic that look suspicious and may represent an attempt to gain access to a bank's network. Intrusion Detection Software monitors for exceptions to a pre-defined set of rules and will issue an alert to the administrator when it identifies an unexpected pattern.

(d) User Administration

User administration restricts access to functions, applications or networks and can enforce the proper separation of roles and responsibilities. Banks need to ensure that only current employees have access to systems and that these employees have the correct account privileges. Unless user account reviews are regularly conducted there is a risk that staff will leave or move and that user accounts will be used for unauthorised activities.

(e) Employee Education

Employee education is important because no matter how good the policies and procedures are, they are not successful without the co-operation of employees. Employee education in areas such as identification of security features of cheques, currency can prove to be extremely useful in detection of counterfeit cheques/currency. Giving news bulletins to staff about the importance of Information Security, particularly when Information Security makes the news can keep them watchful to protect the bank from being victims of financial crimes.

FINANCIAL CRIMES AND ROLE OF IS AUDIT

The increased reliance on technology in banking operations and the growing threat of IT-enabled financial crimes make the inclusion of IS audit coverage essential to an effective overall internal audit (IA) programme of a bank. Banks need to ensure that their IA function has the relevant IT skills to cover adequately the financial crime risks posed by their IT environment. Banks can consider the use of external resources for audit work where in-house expertise is lacking. Banks' involvement of their IS IA function in internal projects may prove beneficial in terms of monitoring progress, identifying financial crime risks and ensuring requisite Information Security controls are built into the design.

IS IA procedures are most effective when designed into each system during the system development phase. When coupled with a strong financial crime risk management programme, a comprehensive, ongoing IS IA programme allows the institution to protect its interests as well as those of its customers and other participants.

VARIANTS OF IS INTERNAL AUDIT

The different types of IS Internal Audit that can be undertaken by the IS Auditor while examining the bank's Information security framework and the extent to which it is exposed to financial crime risk are as follows:

(a) IT Framework Audit

This part of IS IA procedures cover framework of organisation structure of IT function of a bank comprising of in-house and service provider arrangements. The audit procedures evaluate physical security, risk monitoring and controls, electronic asset protection, intrusion, external threats, and customer confidentiality. The audit focuses on the financial crime risk that may arise out of the outsourcing arrangements of information security aspects.

(b) Audit of Information Security Program

The primary goal of this audit is to ensure the adequacy of written programs aiming at information security appropriate to the size and complexity of the bank and the nature and scope of its activities. The audit also assesses risks that may threaten customer information and expose him to a financial crime risk and review written policies and procedures to manage and control these risks.

(c) Network Computer System Audit

This audit evaluates the bank's internal network systems and end-user microcomputer systems and the extent to which they are exposed to financial crime risk. The audit covers evaluation of the steps towards risk management such as management's technology plan, network administration, security controls, user access, user capabilities, password protection, internet connections, network insurance coverage and management oversight of the network technology.

(d) Electronic Banking Audit

The Electronic Banking audit reviews all the electronic banking services of a Bank. Internal Audit procedures include security issues, risk monitoring controls, intrusion/ penetration testing, contingency planning, emergency disaster recovery and business continuity plans.

Internationally Banking Industry experience suggests that penetration tests forming part of Electronic Banking Audit always lead to findings such as the discovery of old, un-patched software or dangerous services running on web servers that would permit a hacker to enter a system.

(e) Website Audit

The key vulnerable component of a Bank's IT organisational set-up that is exposed to financial crime risk is its website. Hence, website audit examines the bank's website for compliance with regulations and laws established by the banking regulators aimed at protecting the bank from being exposed to financial crime risk. The audit reviews the bank's policies, procedures, and contractual arrangements for website hosting, website maintenance, and website activity. Additionally, the audit program reviews website administration, e-mail procedures, online privacy statements and links to other websites.

RISK-BASED APPROACH

IS Internal audit in the context of a large bank should be more risk-based. The sophistication and formality of risk-based IS internal audits may vary depending on the institution's size and complexity. To determine the appropriate level of internal audit coverage for the organisation's IS environment, management should define an effective risk assessment methodology. This assessment methodology should provide the auditor and the board with objective information to prioritise the allocation of audit resources properly.

A successful risk-based IS internal audit programme can be based on an effective scoring system of different components of IS environment in which the Bank operates in terms of financial crime risk. In establishing a scoring system, the board of directors and management should ensure the system is understandable, considers all relevant risk factors, and, to the extent possible, avoids subjectivity. Some of the examples of risk factors to be considered include adequacy of internal controls, nature of transactions, previous audit results and physical and logical security of the information involved in a process all of them to be examined from the angle of financial crime risk.

The use of the Internet and other web-enabled technologies to provide financial services moves consumers' security vulnerabilities from the purely physical to the IS environment. Because financial crime threats expand as access to a network expands, the system becomes more vulnerable. However, this vulnerability can be reduced by employing a range of controls, including adoption of sophisticated risk-based IS Internal audits, to identify, monitor, control, and prevent potential financial crime risks.

20

Concentrate on Personal Financial Management—It's High Time

SUVENDU BOSE

Financial Life Cycle Planning is the heart of personal financial management. Therefore, prior to having discussions on personal financial management we should understand the Personal Life Cycle Planning.

WHAT IS FINANCIAL LIFE CYCLE PLANNING?

Financial Life Cycle Planning is based on the premises that we all need to think about our financial lives over a long time horizon. Individual financial needs keep changing with time. While typical financial lifecycle pattern is seen to emerge in most cases, yet there are certain contingencies and risk to which most families are subject. These contingencies, which are difficult to predict cannot be foreseen and hence cannot be planned for the financial life cycle.

There are certain commonalities in a typical 'financial life cycle such as the need to protect our family against risk, accumulate wealth; and distribute our wealth and provide for an orderly transition of our assets. Lifestyle situations will affect our financial situation and requirements at different stages in life. The lifestyle situations include but are not limited to Marital Status, Employment Status, Age, and Number of Dependents, Economic Outlook, Education, and Health Status.

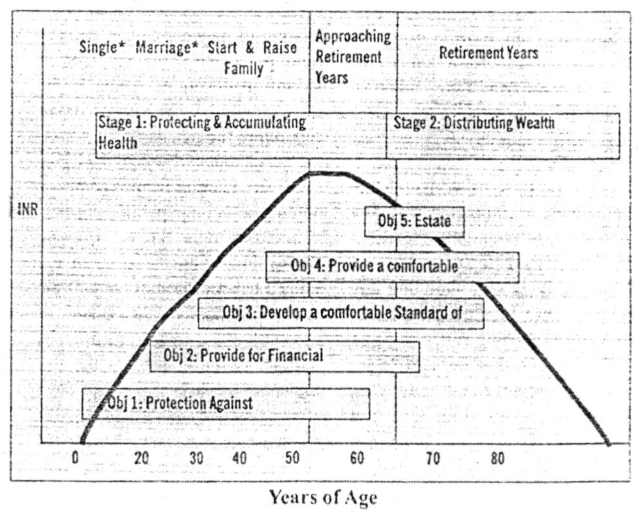

FIG. 20.1

The Personal Financial Objectives

Although each person sets specific financial goals throughout one's life cycle, five basic financial objectives apply to most people.

Objective—1

The first financial objective is to protect ourselves against risk by adopting two basic strategies. The first strategy relates to protection against risk of the unexpected by setting up emergency funds. The second one is to hedge risk by purchasing an adequate mix of insurance that will cover life, disability, health, property and casualty, etc.

Objective—2

The second financial objective is to provide for the financial security of our family and ourselves. This may include providing financial security for extended family members, providing partial or full financial needs for education of family members, purchase of home, cars, and other basic needs. The objective is to provide adequate financial security without placing undue stress on our resources to cause financial crisis.

Objective—3

The third objective is to have a comfortable standard of living that goes beyond the financial security provided for in Objective 2. We might want to have some of the added benefits of life such as vacations, memberships in clubs, entertainment and relaxation, a second home, additional cars, and time from work to pursue other interests.

Objective—4

The next objective is to provide for a financially independency, comfortable retirement during our later years that will provide the same standard of living that we enjoyed during our working years.

Objective—5

The final objective is to provide for an orderly transition and distribution of our assets and wealth. This objective is usually called "estate planning" and should be an important objective irrespective of whether we have accumulated a large estate or not.

PERSONAL FINANCIAL PLANNING OF INDIANS

These days, though Indians are trying hard to save money, however the balance may still be smaller than it was a few years ago. At the same time, their personal goals are getting closer – hence there is a need for financial life cycle planning. Out of all the components of Financial Life Cycle shown below, there are certain items, which are specifically applicable for Indians. These items have been discussed below:

Fixing of Retirement Plan

Saving for retirement is probably Indian's biggest financial goal. However, due to continuous downward trend of interest rates *vis-a-vis* increasing trend of inflation creating little amount of saving for future.

Meanwhile it is important to recalculate how much money we

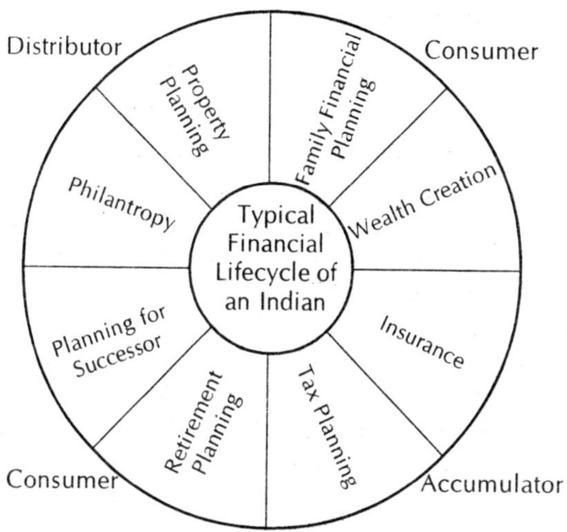

FIG. 20.2

Typical Financial Lifecycle of an Indian

need to save. If our investments have not performed as expected – we cannot continue on the same savings path we plotted in the 1990s. We will probably need to boost our contribution to get back to where we hoped to be. Reassessment of our saving goals and generating new retirement Planning Programs (if required) do a much better job of pinpointing our retirement saving needs and explaining the risk associated with it. It helps in determining the probable mitigative measures for any future economic downturn in India.

The earlier we make adjustments, the less money we will need to add to get back on track. And we won't have to come up with nearly as much if we make the most of the tax benefits created specifically for retirement savers, which have improved significantly over the past few years.

Therefore, we can conclude that, we should not give up. We cannot reach our retirement goals if we stop investing now. We should continue to contribute as much as possible to our retirement plan, invest aggressively as we have more than a decade until we need the money, and make the most of the tax advantages – which save our money, no matter what happens to our investments.

Organising Education Expenditure

Now-a-days education has become one of the costliest livelihoods in India. Based on the current fees charged by Indian School, one has to pay near about Rs. 1 lakh (Rs. 1,00,000) per year per child for any standard private schooling, which reduced to half in case of public schools. For private Engineering Colleges the cost of education will be around Rs. 5 lakhs (Rs. 500,000) in 4 years, which goes down marginally in case of graduation in other subjects and goes up substantially in case of medical graduates. In public colleges however the cost is lower (though not as low as it was 10-15 years back). In this context it is worth to mention that, all the above mentioned cost are exclusive of other associated costs like school bus fees, hostel charges, cost of books, etc.

The best strategy for reaching our educational goal is to save early and often. The more money we can set aside when our child is young, the less we will have to invest to reach the same goal. If we will start saving at a rate of Rs. 2000 per month from the baby's birth, and the saving earns 8 per cent per annum (monthly compounding), we will have around Rs. 10 lakh (1 million) before taxes, when the child will grow up to 18 years, the age of completing high school and starting college.

Another most popular source of fund for higher education (mainly at post-graduation level) is loan from different commercial banks operating in India. It is available at softer terms and can be considered as a deferred liability. Since, in case of educational loan, the loan is being issued to the student concerned with initial moratorium period of 2 to 3 years depending on the length of course and with a condition that, after completion of the course, the student concern will repay it from his/her salary. Here, the parents/guardians will act as guarantor only. This system not only protects the parents/guardians from a huge expenditure, the candidates himself/herself can enjoy the tax shield on the loan repayment.

Because of these new tools, every one should review their saving strategies. The approaches we have been using may be outdated compared to powerful new option. It could be a good time to switch out of them.

Arranging for Home

While stocks have been in the gutter, bank interest rates are falling, housing values have been booming (though in some of the cities of India the real estate values are falling). This is relieving news if we already own a house, but a tough situation if we have been saving for one.

But we can still buy a new house, even during tough times. There is one big thing working in our favour: the housing loan interest rates are fluctuating on a regular basis (at a comparatively lower level), easy availability of home loans, etc. Now-a-days in India, it is less expensive to borrow money and easier to get a loan. Lenders are becoming more lenient – letting us slide with lower down payments, higher loan limits and offering options that let us maximise our cash flow. Therefore, instead of saving for home, it's much easier to shop around for loans, making use of low interest rates and get the best deal so that we can buy a home soon.

Expenditure on Health

In India one of the largest personal expenditure is in health protection. The medical expenditures specifically after retirement becomes a difficult affair for Indians, due to extremely low level of governmental support (lowest in the world, under the comparable situation) in the public health expenditure/health infrastructure creation and lack of social safety net.

Making contingency plan for medical expenditure is also a difficult task for the middle and low-income group Indians. The probable solution may be to take up medical insurance plan and opting for non-money transaction schemes. Otherwise realization of medical expenses from insurance companies (subsequent to incurring it) is a really difficult job in India.

Lowering of Cost as a Source of Fund

Actually, there may be plenty of extra money that we could easily access without making any sacrifices. We just need to know how to get it. The following section of this article will discuss some of the ways to create extra fund under Indian situation –

(i) By eliminating expensive debt,
(ii) Making the most of our tax deductions, and
(iii) Cutting our insurance cost.

Elimination of Expensive Debt

No matter what our goals are, our very first priority should be to eliminate high-interest debt, which can sabotage our other plans. If our funds are limited, we can't afford to waste money on interest when we are struggling to save for more important goals.

Fortunately it's a great time to get out of debt. Since interest rates are near their 20 years low, we have many opportunities to trade in our high interest debt for less expensive versions. Even if we can't afford to increase our payments, lowering our interest rates will stretch our money further and help us to get out of debt faster. And as soon as debt disappears, we will have much more money available to get our long-term savings and investing plans back on track.

It is a good time to look at all types of debt—whether it's credit cards, student loans, car loans or personal loans and see what we can do to lower our rates. Start by attacking the loans with the highest rates first, especially if the interest is not tax deductable (For example, housing loan interest payment is tax deductable item). That usually makes credit cards our first assignment to eliminate.

Lowering of Tax Bill

Many people accidentally overpay the government because they do not realise how much tax write-offs they can take. Tax credits are even more valuable not only because they shrink our tax bill, but also it is easy money, it is our own money. We do not need to cut down on our spending we just need to know the Indian Income Tax Rules.

Reduce Insurance Cost

In India no body likes to think about insurance. One of the major reason may be, we are overpaying our premium. Opening up of Indian Insurance to private sector has given us opportunities to choose. A healthy competition has developed amongst Insurance Companies to provide better benefits at a lower cost to the insurers. It is not unusual for one company to charge us more money (as premium) than another for the exact same coverage. And some people pay those high prices because they do not know about their alternatives.

Taking the time to review our coverage is one of the easiest ways to free-up more cash without having to make any sacrifice. Hence, we can save thousands of rupees on our insurance premiums—just by shopping around, streamlining our coverage and eliminating insurance we do not need.

The Consequences

Fulfilling financial requirements through loans is easier to fund, however, it creates increasing amount of liability on individuals, which in turn sometimes leads to negative net-worth of Indian individuals. Hence, when we reassessed our goals, we may have discovered that we need to boost our savings significantly. But that's tough to do during these difficult economic times—or so it seems, especially, if suddenly our earning stops (mainly in case of closing down of business and VRS/ERS/ESS) or have an emergency that could eat up big chunk of our funds.

Therefore, at this juncture of time not only we have to figure out how to live with our income, but also we need to make important decisions that can affect our financial situation for years. If we are not prepared, we could commit major mistakes—like raiding our retirement plans or racking up high interest debt—that could derail our long-term plan.

The Contingency Plans

The more we do now to prepare; the better our finances will survive. The following strategies may help us by protecting our savings, lowering our bills when our regular flow of income is interrupted or there is a sudden threat of huge personal expenditure—

(i) Building of Emergency Fund.
(ii) Strategy for becoming self-employed/starting of Freelance work.
(iii) Lowering of Health and Life Insurance Premium.
(iv) Make the most use of tax benefits.

These defensive strategies should help us to reach our goals no matter what ends up happening and help us to avoid the troubles further.

Indian Social Structure and Financial Needs

As far as Indian social structure is concerned the life cycle began with a young single, working person living independently, subsequently moving through the various stages of marriage and child rearing and ending as a retired couple (most of the cases no adult children at home). The following table indicates the several stages in the family life cycle and the banking needs are most likely to be experienced at each stage.

Stage	*Financial Situation*	*Banking Needs*
Young, Single People	Few financial burdens; recreation-oriented	Low cost checking, auto loan, credit card
Newly married with child under 6	Home purchasing peak; liquid asset low	Home loans, car loans, credit cards, revolving credit card loan, bill consolidation loan
Matured couples with dependent children	Good financial position: most of the cases husband wife both earning	Home loans, personal loans, equity credit lines, certificates of deposits, money market deposits account, other investment services
Empty Nest: Old couples, no adult children at home, one or both retired	Significantly reduced income	Rollover, Monthly income cheques on CDS and retirement benefits, estate planning and other social security measures.

Note: Not all possible life cycle stages are included.

Our ultimate aim is to draw a suitable and well balanced financial strategy for Indian individual finance. The best way for deriving strategy is developing financial management pyramid. The pyramid follows the typical individual's life cycle, starting with the basic financial requirements at the bottom of the pyramid to establish strength and stability for a healthy financial foundation, and moving up the pyramid to the top where distribution of wealth to one's chosen beneficiaries is the final financial strategy.

Each lower step gradually leads to its upper level. The success of every level is depending on the efficiency of managing its immediate lower level. Decisions about one level have a strong impact on what is done at each higher level of the pyramid. For example, if we have not established a realistic spending plan, we may have a difficult time when it comes to using credit wisely and

Conclusion: Personal Financial Management Pyramid for Indians

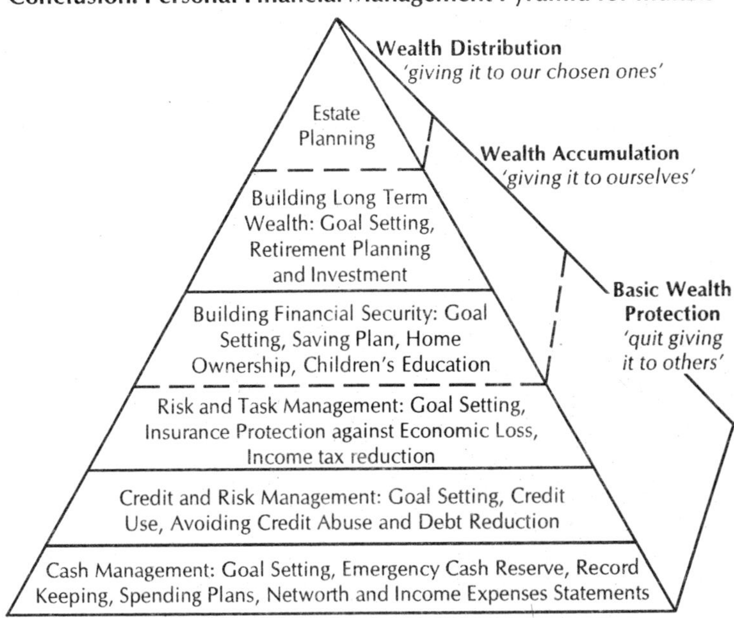

FIG. 20.3

Personal Financial Management by Pyramid for Indian

Based on the Model Prepared by Gail M. Gordon, University of Wyoming, Corporate Extension Service, 2001.

not spending more than we earn, which subsequently will have an impact on our saving. Our financial life becomes more complex as we move up the pyramid. The financial complexities and the changes in our life may require re-evaluating our strategies and setting new financial goals periodically.

Therefore, the time has come to think about our personal Financial Life Cycle Planning seriously. Directly or indirectly we are engaged in financial life cycle planning, however, now we have to focus more professionally. Any wrong decision can have disastrous effect on our life which will influence our dependent also. Therefore, to avoid any such kind of catastrophic circumstances to develop sound financial conditions this is the high time to have our personal financial life cycle planning in place.

21

Risk-based Supervision and Risk

R.S. RAGHAVAN

Risk is inherent in any walk of life and more so in the business of banking as the fundamental economic function of a banking organization is to assume and manage risk.

The Reserve Bank of India (RBI) has been mandated with the task of overseeing the banks in the performance of its duties enshrined u/s 22 of Banking Regulations Act, 1949. When it comes to exercising control and supervision of banks, the RBI has its supervisory mechanism by way of on-site inspection and off-site monitoring (OSMOS) on the basis of the audited balance sheet of a bank, year after year and under CAMELS approach (Capital adequacy, Asset quality, Management aspects, Earnings, Liquidity and System controls), it primarily covers scrutiny of systems and procedures in the indicated areas.

In order to enhance the supervisory mechanism, the RBI decided to put in place a system of Risk Based Supervision (RBS). The RBS may be defined as a process by which the risk facing each supervised entity is analysed and an appropriate supervisory strategy is developed. Under the RBS, which is gaining ground now, supervisors are expected to concentrate their efforts and optimize their resources to ensure that Financial Institutions, more particularly banks, use the process necessarily to identify, measure and control risk exposure. The system is formulated to ensure continuous monitoring and evaluation of risk profile of banks, in relation to business strategy and exposure through self-assessment process by means of risk matrix, followed by final assessment by RBI. The supervisory cycle would vary depending on the risk profile of each bank under the broad view of higher the risk, more the frequency for supervisory exercise. Reduced supervisory scrutiny may include infrequent examination and minimal or no transaction testing. Thus, RBI would customize their supervisory programmes.

In the post-Basel II environment, the Risk-Focused Audit (RFA) would be an additional tool of assessment, as it would be the basic mechanism to judge performance in risk management area and to convince RBI that the bank has a risk management system that functions effectively. The onus would be on the banks' part to convince that RFA system is sound and the off-site data is quite reliable.

The RBS is expected to focus supervisory attention in accordance with the Risk Profile of the bank. The RBI has already structured the Risk Profile Templates to enable the bank to make a self-assessment of their risk. It is designed to ensure continuous monitoring and evaluation of risk profile of the institution through risk matrix. This, apart from optimizing the utilization of the supervisory resources of the RBI, may also minimize the impact of a crises situation in the financial system.

The transaction-based audit and supervision is slated to, slowly and steadily, graduate to risk focused audit. The institutional mechanism set-up to attend to the requirements of RBS should be kept separate and distinct from the institutional mechanism attending to risk management functions.

The supervisory programme would be tailored to banks focusing on high-risk areas and specifying the need for further scrutiny in the identified problem areas. It would comprise off-site surveillance, structured meeting with the banks, commissioning of external audits and issuance of supervisory directions through Monitorable Action Points (MAP). The Risk Profile would highlight the strengths and weakness or vulnerabilities of the Bank so as to provide proper foundation to determine the procedures to be adopted during the inspection. The quarterly up-dated Risk Profile document of the Bank would be a subject matter for deliberations and discussions at the Board of Directors or suitable sub-committee of the Board, as the case may be.

RISK PROFILE TEMPLATE

It is mandatory for the banks to set-up robust risk management architecture to take care of various risks that run through the functional activities. This would obviously necessitate the banks to carry out a fresh review of their current status of risk management architecture, by an expert team and initiate measures to bridge or fill up the gaps, steadily.

As part of moving towards switching over to RBS, the RBI has advised banks to carry-out self-assessment of risk profiling exercise in a structured and comprehensive manner. In order to facilitate smooth transition to RBS as well as ensuring uniformity in the approach among banks, the RBI has come out with a set of standardized Risk Profile Template (RPT). Compilation of risk profile in respect of each bank is the central plank of RBS. Banks are required to document their Risk Profile, containing various kinds of financial and non-financial risks faced by the Bank. These are grouped under Business Risk, containing 4 risk parameters and Control Risk containing 4 risk parameters, in all comprising 12 areas for capturing entire gamut of the banking activities. Business Risks are those risks that are considered inherent in the activities undertaken by a bank irrespective of whether controls are in place, whereas Control Risks enables to arrive at proper judgement as to whether adequate controls are in place. The RPT comprises detailed components of various parameters that are to be examined while carrying out the exercise.

As RBI would structure their inspection programme based on the risk profile document, it is imperative that both the qualitative and quantitative details are correctly drawn as input to the RPT. This Risk Profile document is required to be scrutinized by the Quality Assurance Team, consisting of Top and Senior Management executives representing major business as well as control areas of the Bank, constituted for the specific purpose for an independent evaluation of risk assessment of the bank.

The Risk Profile Template consists of three parts, viz. Overview of the Bank, Summary Risk Profile and Risk Assessment areas. In respect of the identified 12 risk assessment areas, the RPT should conclude with assessment indicating the level of risk in which the bank is in and the direction of movement of risk. The level of risk is indicated as Low, Moderate and High and the direction as Decreasing, Stable and Increasing. The assessment areas to be covered in the RPT are as follows:

(A) Assessment of Business Risks

- Capital.
- Credit Risk.
- Market Risk other than Liquidity Risk.
- Earnings.
- Liquidity Risk.
- Business Strategy and Environment Risk.
- Operational Risk.
- Group Risk.

(B) Assessment of Control Risks

- Internal Control Risk.
- Organisation Risk.
- Management Risk.
- Compliance Risk.

On summarizing the Risk Assessment Templates, under the umbrella of the Business Risks and Control Risks, encompassing all the 12 critical assessment areas, the issues requiring immediate corrective action with medium-term objective are identified. This self-assessment exercise is perused by the RBI to enable them to chalk out plan for their supervisory action under the concept of Risk Based Supervision.

As the risk profile document is intended to be a dynamic one, all changes and developments within and outside the bank that may have an impact on the risk profile, are to be tracked on an on-going and continuous basis. On the happening of certain significant developments in between two exercises, revision/update is also undertaken, when the situation warrants. It may be pertinent to note that while improvement in risk profile normally occur over a period of time, deterioration in the risk profile could occur suddenly or for that matter, in short span of time. Hence, it is desirable that review and updation of the risk profile will have to be carried out, at least, on a quarterly basis.

RISK-BASED INTERNAL AUDIT

In tune with the objectives of RBS, banks should put in place a system of Risk Based Internal Audit (RBIA) so that inspecting officials would focus their attention accordingly. Internal Inspection/Audit Department in banks will have to be made independent from the internal control process and be given an appropriate standing within the bank so as to carry out its assignments with objectivity and impartiality. The internal audit is expected to capture the application and effectiveness of risk management procedures as well as risk assessment methodology, in a larger way, covering critical evaluation of the adequacy and effectiveness of the internal control systems. Banks should move gradually from transaction-based auditing to risk focused auditing by placing greater emphasis on the role of internal auditors and concurrent auditors.

Though transaction testing has served the system well till recently, it cannot keep pace with the continuous changes occurring in banks' risk profiles. It also imposes unnecessary regulatory burden on banks and forces them to devote precious resources to unproductive areas. In addition to the selective and random transaction-based auditing, banks should move gradually towards risk focused auditing. The one-size fits all approach or transaction testing has increasingly been found to be insufficient and untenable in a world where banks dramatically vary in terms of size, business mix and risk appetite.

The Internal Audit, focusing on operational risk areas, is important in view of the following:

- Failures of many banks were the result of internal control problems.
- Operational risk is not generally measurable and is often pervading all through an entity on 24 × 7 basis, implying all the time.
- It reduces unexpected losses to improve profits.
- Unlike credit risk and market risk, which follows typical Risk-Return relationship, operational risk results only in loss.
- Internal control is to accomplish Transaction testing, accuracy and reliability of accounting records, integrity of control reports and checking compliance to regulations.
- Operational risk arises from human or technological error and therefore has innumerable points to emanate.

Whereas, the purpose and utility of Risk Based Internal Audit is to ultimately enable banks to allocate capital for operational risk.

Risk Based Internal Audit should ensure that policies and procedures of the bank are complied with besides looking into the adequacy of these policies and procedures to ensure risk-optimisation.

By prioritizing risk areas, RBIA should capture the application and effectiveness of risk management procedure and risk assessment system.

While ensuring Risk Based Internal Audit at the branches, it may be appropriate to keep the following in mind:

Branch Profile, covering volume of business, inspection rating, issues of serious concern covered in the synopsis, etc. should be complied and branches are to be grouped into different categories. The risk profile of a branch should be complied after taking into account credit risk, market risk and operational risk covering the following aspects.

Credit Risk

- Extent of excess outstanding beyond 30 days in the account over and above limit/DP, on account of arrears in the interest/ principal, TOD, devolved liability; 'Operative borrowal account' not put into active operation.
- Expired credit limit in the case of operative credit limits that are neither renewed nor extended by the competent authority. This is to be classified into three categories such as: (a) expired within three months age, (b) expired beyond three months ago. The period is of importance, as expired limits of more than 90 days require different treatment of classification. Reference date is the risk-based audit date.
- Exercise of Delegated powers at the branch for sanction and fixation of interest rate.
- Quality of credit appraisal for the sanction at the branch and the proposals recommended to higher authorities.
- Increase in the Non-Performing Assets.
- Industry/business sector-wise distribution of loan assets.
- Assessment of risk rating of borrowal accounts and its application.
- Violation of RBI guidelines on credit matters and Lending Policy as well as the Risk Management policies of the Bank.

Market Risk

- Composition of Deposits to be studied to find out whether

there is any bulk deposits that are likely to expose the bank to liquidity risk.

- Deposit mix to be examined to ascertain substantial imbalance between long-term and short-term deposits; presence of low cost deposits, etc.
- Adherence to the ALCO, Market Risk Management and Country Risk Management policies of the Bank.

Operational Risk

- List out pending comments of RBI inspection/LFAR audit/internal inspection/concurrent audit/stock audit.
- Serious defects in documentation regarding legal enforce-ability as pointed out in the Legal Audit/inspection.
- Occurrence of Fraud and similar events.
- Odd/special features observed in certain sensitive accounts.
- Violation observed in the procedures while entertaining a new customer—Deposit/Advance.
- Quantification of income leakage during the last three years.
- Compliance level of Operational Risk Management policy guidelines of the Bank by the field functionaries.

The above aspects can be covered under the following broad parameters in respect of the operations carried out during the risk-based audit.

Credit Management	Forex Risk
Credit Risk Management	Liquidity Risk
Operational Risk	Earnings Risk
Information Technology Risk	Control Risk
Business Strategy Risk	

Based on the above and other similar features, the Risk Profile of the branch is required to be structured to assess the Risk Level of the Branch (Minimal Risk, Low Risk, Moderate Risk, Average Risk and High Risk), and in which direction (increase/stable/decrease) it is likely to move within a foreseeable time frame of maximum of six months, unless corrective measures are initiated.

Banks are required to evolve a policy document for the Risk Based Internal Audit, duly approved by the banks Board and formulate Branch Risk Profile Template for risk profiling and risk assessment of branches. Apart from the branches, the exercise should cover certain sensitive and functional departments like Treasury, Funds Transfer, International Banking, Inter-Branch Accounting, etc. There should be an Audit Plan for carrying out RBIA drawn in such a manner that over a specified period of time even Minimal Risk category branches will be subjected to RBIA.

To begin with, the concept of Risk Based Internal Audit may be introduced on pilot basis in select branches, where there is heterogeneous composition of business. Thereafter, banks only capture a large portion of the business of the Bank through a small number of branches. Under the RBIA approach, banks are expected to re-orient their prevailing system of inspection so as to evaluate adequacy and effectiveness of risk management systems and internal control procedures in the Bank. Till the RBIA is fully implemented across the banks, the existing system of internal inspection or internal audit may co-exist along RBIA. The RBIA would provide quality counsel to management on effectiveness of risk management and internal controls, including regulatory compliance. The focus is to mitigate various risks, instead of inspection/audit serving as a full-scale transaction testing at the branches/offices of Bank.

MONITORING MECHANISM

Hitherto, RBI was monitoring their supervisory exercise annually after the closure of year-end financials of the bank under OSMOS. While the on-site examination is done through the Annual Financial Inspection (AFI), off-site examination is done through the system of DSB returns. As the risk profile of each bank is different, now the monitoring needs would also differ based on the Risk Profile of each bank. Moving over to risk-based supervision necessitates devising a policy for back up and storage of various databases at regular intervals. This should specify details like frequency of backups, media to be used, off-site storage areas, departments and officials responsible for these actions. In respect of specific databases, Data Managers should be made responsible. As accuracy and timeliness of data are very important, banks would have to ensure the same through up-gradation of Management Information System and Information Technology System.

22

Risk-based Supervision

V.V. KAMATH

I. BACKGROUND

1. International scene has witnessed strong trends towards globalisation and consolidation of the financial system and ensuring stability of the financial system has become the major challenge for Bank regulators and supervisors the world over.
2. The Indian banking scene has witnessed progressive deregulation, institution of prudential norms and emulation of international supervisory best practices. The adoption of CAMELS (Capital adequacy, Asset quality, Management, Earnings, Liquidity, Systems and Controls)/CALCS (Capital adequacy, Asset quality, Liquidity, Compliance and Systems) approach to supervisory risk assessments and ratings, tightening of exposure and prudential norms and enhancement in disclosure standards are all introduced by RBI to align the Indian banking system to the International best practices.
3. RBI Governor announced as a part of monetary and credit policy statement for 2000-01 that an overall plan for moving to Risk-based Supervision would be developed by them with the assistance of Price Waterhouse Coopers (PWC), an international consultant.

II. CURRENT APPROACH

The current approach adopted by Department of Banking Supervision (DBS) of RBI involves:

- Onsite inspection conducted to a large extent with reference to audited Balance sheet dates.
- The off site and market intelligence plays a supplemental role.
- Supervisory follow-up commences with the detailed findings of Annual Financial Inspection (API). The process is based on CAMELS/CALCS approach.

III. RISK BASED SUPERVISION (RBS)—A NEW APPROACH

- It entails allocation of supervisory resources and paying supervisory attention by the regulators in accordance with the risk profile of the institution.
- The objective of RBS is to optimize utilization of supervisory resources and minimise the impact of crisis situation in the financial system.
- RBS involves continuous monitoring and evaluation of risk profiles of the supervised institutions in relation to their business strategy and exposures.
- The assessment of the institutions under RBS will be through the construction of Risk Matrix for each institution.
- The effectiveness of RBS will depend upon Bank's preparedness in critical areas such as:
  (a) Quality and reliability of data,
  (b) Soundness of systems and technology,
  (c) Appropriateness of risk control mechanism, and
  (d) Supporting human resources and organizational back-up.

IV. FEATURES OF RBS APPROACH

1. Risk Profiling of Banks

(a) It entails identification of financial activities in which a Bank has chosen to engage and determination of types and quantities of risks to which these activities expose the Bank. CAMELS rating would continue to be the core of risk profile compilation.

(b) The risk profiling of each Bank will draw upon a wide range of information besides CAMEL rating such as:
- Off site surveillance and monitoring data (OSMOS),

- Market Intelligence reports,
- Ad hoc data from external and internal auditors,
- Onsite findings, and
- Sanctions applied.

(c) The following would be the components of the Risk profile document:
- CAMELS rating with trends,
- Narrative description of key risk features captured under each CAMELS component,
- Summary of key business risks including volatility of trends, key business risk factors,
- Monitorable action plan and Bank's progress to date,
- Strength, Weakness, Opportunities, Threats (SWOT) analysis, and
- Sensitivity analysis.

2. Supervisory Cycle

(a) It commences with the preparation of bank's risk profile,
(b) It varies according to the risk profile of each bank, the principle being, higher the risk shorter will be the cycle of supervision, and
(c) The supervisory cycle will remain at 12 months in the short-term and will be extended beyond 12 months for low risk banks at a suitable stage.

3. Supervisory Programme

(a) The supervisory programme would be prepared at the beginning of the supervisory cycle,
(b) Onsite inspection would be targeted to specific areas, and
(c) A monitorable Action Plan (MAP) would be drawn up for follow-up to mitigate risks to supervisory objectives posed by individual Banks.

Thus variable supervisory cycles and variable frequency of inspections will characterize RBS.

4. Supervisory Organisation

(a) There will be a focal point for all contacts by banks both at the central office of RBI and its Regional offices, and

(b) The focal point would be the main conduit for information and communication between the Banks and RBI.

5. Enforcement Process and Incentive Framework

(a) Banks which a better compliance record and a good risk management and control system would be entitled to an incentive package like a longer supervisory cycle and lesser supervisory intervention,
(b) Banks whether fail to show improvement in response to Monitorable Action Plan (MAP) may be subject to frequent supervisory examination and higher supervisory intervention including directions, sanctions and penalties, and
(c) An independent enforcement cell will be set-up at BSD (Banking Supervisory Division) to ensure consistency of treatment, maintain objectivity and neutrality of enforcement action.

V. BANK LEVEL PREPARATIONS SUGGESTED

1. Setting up of Risk Management Architecture

(a) Involves setting up proper orgnisational structure, policies, procedures and limits for credit market and operational risk management, and
(b) Covering 100 per cent of the Bank's Assets and Liabilities under Asset Liability Management (ALM).

2. Adoption of Risk Focused Internal Audit

(a) In addition to traditional transaction testing the scope of internal audit is widened to carry out a critical evaluation of the adequacy and effectiveness of internal control systems,
(b) It would not only assess the Branch's risks but also offer remedies for the identified trouble areas, and
(c) It would act as an aid to the ongoing risk management by banks as it would provide checks and balances in the system.

3. Strengthening Management Information System (MIS) and IT

(a) Availability of detailed accurate data is the foundation for RBS,
(b) Having a robust MIS is a must for ensuring accuracy, completeness and timeliness of data, and
(c) Banks should review present status of MIS and IT systems and initiate necessary measures to ensure that RBI data needs as well as supervisory reporting systems are streamlined.

4. Addressing HRD Issues

(a) Main issue will be skill formation of staff and placement in appropriate positions,
(b) Creation of a dedicated Risk Management team at HO and re-orientation of internal audit department to undertake risk-based audit, and
(c) For meeting the above objectives the HRD aspects that need to be addressed are manpower planning, selection and deployment of staff and extensive training in risk management including ALM and risk-based audit.

5. Setting up Compliance Unit

(a) RBI will issue Bank specific Monitorable Action Plan (MAP) which will include directions to Banks on actions to be taken,
(b) Hence banks have to have in place a dedicated compliance unit to coordinate various actions of the bank for compliance and for periodical reporting to RBI. They have to also ensure completion of compliance action within the time period indicated in the Monitorable Action Plan, and
(c) The compliance unit should be headed by a Chief Compliance Officer of the rank of not less than a General Manager who will be responsible for the timeliness and accuracy of the compliance.

VI. IMPLEMENTATION SCHEDULE

(a) RBI will be implementing RBS in phases beginning from the last quarter of the Financial year 2002-03,

(b) On experimental basis it has asked 8 banks to submit the risk profile templates, and

(c) As the CAMELS rating is an important input in bank risk profiling, on-site inspection through CAMELS approach will concurrently be followed along with the RBS approach in the short-term.

VII. ISSUES INVOLVED IN RBS

1. Strengthening of MIS and IT

This is the basic requirement to be met and efforts are on to procure software which is compatible across the various platforms on which our systems work (ALPM, IBBS and BANCS, 2000).

2. Addressing HRD Issues

The major task on hand is re-orientation of the staff towards meeting the RBS objectives. Our bank has taken steps in this direction by:

- Training the executives involved in RBS exercise at NIBM, Pune.
- Training as many as 418 inspecting staff at our Staff Training College.

3. Inspection Gradation *vs.* Awarding Risk Ratings

The criteria applied for grading a branch altogether differ from those applied for risk rating a branch. Hence, the auditing officials should be able to recognise this and give an unbiased assessment.

4. Standardising the Method of Awarding Scores

In certain assessment areas the inspecting official may award scores purely based on his personal perception. However, our Inspection Wing is fine-tuning the evaluation methodology to ensure fair scoring/rating. The formation of Quality Assurance teams at the circle level will certainly help in lending further credibility to the risk audit process.

VIII. INITIATIVES TAKEN BY OUR BANK

1. Preparation of Risk Profile templates

(a) RBI had sent Risk-based templates to our Bank in July 2002,
(b) We submitted the first template to RBI in September 2002 taking the position as at 31-03-2002,
(c) Thereafter we have been updating the risk profiles on a quarterly basis and submitting to RBI, and
(d) The risk profile templates are duly vetted by the Quality Assurance Committee consisting of General Managers of Corporate Credit Wing, Risk Management Wing, Inspection Wing, Computer Wing, Treasury and International Operations Wing and Personnel Wing before submission to RBI.

2. Introduction of Risk-based Internal Audit

(a) Risk-based Internal Audit has been introduced in our Bank with effect from 1-03-2003 and 242 VLBs/ELBS have been targeted for the said audit by 31-03-2004.
(b) The risk profiles prepared by Inspecting officials are reviewed by the Zonal Inspectorates. A scoring matrix has been developed by Inspection Wing and the ratings are awarded for the individual assessment areas (Credit, Liabilities, Earnings, Operational risk and control risks based on the scorings achieved.
(c) At circle offices compliance units have been set-up who act as the first contacts of supervision. They ensure that the key concern areas listed in the risk profiles are addressed by the branches through prompt and proper corrective action.
(d) At the Head office the Inspection Wing and Risk Management Wing review the risk profiles and the progress made in mitigating the concern areas. The significant shortcomings will be intimated to top management for necessary action.

3. Setting up Risk Management Architecture

(a) Risk Management Wing came into being in April 2000 to give focused direction to various Risk Management initiatives in tune with RBI's guidelines.

(b) IBM-BCS [erstwhile PWC (Price Waterhouse Coopers)] was engaged by the Bank in September 2001 to provide Bank with an integrated Risk Management Framework.

(c) The design deliverables submitted by IBM-BCS in December 2001 have been accepted and adopted by the Board. The recommendations of IBM-BCS are being implemented in phases.

(d) Following policies have been drawn and adopted by the Bank:
   - Credit Policy,
   - Operational Risk Management Policy,
   - Country Risk Policy,
   - Investment Policy, and
   - ALM Policy.

(e) Software procurement/Model development for the following Risk Management initiatives are on the anvil:
   - For integration of domestic and Forex treasury (i-flex/Reuters),
   - For extending credit rating to all credit exposures (CRISIL/In-house manual model), and
   - Asset-Liability Management (ICICI INFOTECH).

Handbooks on Risk Management and Risk-based Internal Audit have been brought out by our Risk Management Wing and Inspection Wing to familiarise our workforce and Inspectors with the various aspects of risk management and risk audit.

23

Changing Horizon of Insurance Sector

SAM GHOSH

Ensconced in a monopoly run from the nationalization days beginning in 1956, the insurance industry has indeed awakened: to a deregulated environment in which several private players have partnered with multinational insurance giants.

However, despite its teeming one billion population, India still has a low insurance penetration of 1.95 per cent, 51st in the world. Despite the fact that India boasts a saving rate of around 25 per cent, less than 5 per cent is spent on insurance. But there is indeed a great potential for the sector in India as well as those looking for brighter professional opportunities.

LOOKING AHEAD

Today, a combination of the upsurge in consumer awareness and other developments has put the insurance sector under pressure. The lifting of the bar on composite insurance, where companies are allowed to do only life or non-life business today, can also be expected. And thus, instead of categorizing insurance by class, the focus may shift more to the period for which the cover was offered and the risk underwritten. Already, there is a demand for permitting the industry to underwrite pure risk and leaving investment decisions to policy-holders.

The increasingly tough competition has actually changed the

rules of the game. The market is flooded with an array of products. In such a scenario, the differentiators among different players are the products, pricing, and service. Meanwhile, the profile of the Indian consumer is also evolving. Consumers are increasingly more aware and are actively managing their financial affairs. Today, while boundaries between various financial products are blurring, people are increasingly looking not just at products, but also at integrated financial solutions that can offer stability of returns along with total protection.

To cater to these myriad needs of customers, insurance products need to be further customized. Insurance today has emerged as an attractive and stable investment alternative that offers total protection—Life, Health and Wealth. In terms of returns, insurance products today offer competitive returns ranging between 7 per cent and 9 per cent. Besides returns, what really increases the appeal of insurance is the benefit of life protection from insurance products along with health cover benefits.

Consumers today also seek products that offer flexible options. The customers now prefer products with benefits unbundled and customisable to suit their diverse needs.

Further, the trends of the developed economies where people not only live longer but also retire earlier are now catching up in India too. Earlier, the fear of an early death primarily necessitated Insurance today the fear is also of outliving one's assets in the wake of living too long. With the breakdown of traditional forms of social security like joint family system, consumers are now focusing on the needs of a comfortable retired life. The long-term decline in interest rates has further pushed this trend.

This all adds up to major change in demand for insurance products. While sale of traditional life insurance products like individual, whole life and term will remain popular, the new products like single premium, investment linked, retirement products, variable life and annuity products will also rise in the times to come. Firms will need to constantly innovate in terms of product development to meet ever-changing consumer needs. However, product innovations are quickly and easily cloned and pricing will also not vary significantly, with most product premiums hovering around a narrow band.

In this backdrop, a key difference will be the customer experience that each life insurance player can offer, in terms of quality of advice on product choice, policy servicing as well as settlement of claims. Long-term growth in business will depend greatly on distribution network where the emphasis must not only be just on selling insurance but also on acting as financial advisors. This calls for a strong focus on training of the distribution force to act as financial consultants and build a long lasting relationship with customer.

THE INTERMEDIARIES

The intermediaries in insurance business and the distribution channels used by carriers will perhaps be the strongest drivers of growth in the sector. Multi-channel distribution and marketing of insurance products will be the smart strategy for the Indian market. While tied agents will continue to play an important role in distribution, alternative channels like corporate agents, brokers, and bancassurance will play a greater role in distribution. Firms will need to forge relationships with the partners for strategic advantage. They need to have strong partner relationship management. For example, local partners may have strong distribution channel in their line of business. That can be used to sell insurance also in a cost-effective manner.

The time has come for the industry to gradually move from traditional individual agents towards new distribution channels. There are 850,000 insurance agents in India and the qualitative selection of agents by companies is imperative to gain the cutting edge.

WORK-SITE MARKETING

Relatively inexpensive and easy to launch, the work-site marketing is one potential distribution channel. In this scenario, sale of financial products and other services to employees is done through workplace-participation and is entirely on a voluntary basis where the employee pays for the products generally through a payroll deduction. Companies must constantly explore avenues to increase the number of distribution channels through a variety of distribution patterns, particularly given the rapidly changing customer profile. Traditional intermediaries have played a very important role as a distribution outlet for insurance services and products. The Internet and telemarketing will play an increasingly critical role in customer relationship.

Bancassurance is an effective and upcoming distribution

channel for Insurance products and companies. In countries like Italy, France and Spain, insurance companies have taken advantage of customers' typical loyalty to single banks and pattern of long-term banking relationships by successfully selling their products through these banks. Here banks can leverage their existing resources and earn supplementary fees while widening their range of available services.

At present, 12 per cent of the world's insurance products are sold through the Internet, a figure likely to grow exponentially with a likely increase in customer usage of the Internet. Rural and semi-urban sectors are the ones that could be serviced by the banc-assurance model. However, there are some reservations against the efficacy of insurance distribution through public sector banks as these banks do not have deep relationships with their customers.

Other approaches, like call-centre, direct marketing, and the Internet will grow dramatically in importance over the next several years and will enable firms to acquire, retain and build loyalty among customers while lowering transaction costs.

A customer accessing any channel should be recognized as a client and not required to provide information again. What's more, a client should be able to move easily from one mode of service to another (for example, from on-line to face-to-face to on-line) without disruption in service.

THE CHALLENGES

The four main challenges facing the industry are product innovation, distribution, customer service, and investments. Unit-linked personal insurance products might find greater acceptability with rising customer awareness about customized, personalized and flexible products. Flexible products and new technology will play a crucial role in reducing the cost and, therefore, the price of insurance products. Finding the niche markets, having the right product mix through add-on benefits and riders, effective branding of products and services and product differentiation from competitors' offering will be the key challenges for the new companies.

IT IN INSURANCE

In today's highly competitive financial services environment, effective organizations employ technology in a strategic role to achieve competitive edge. Technology plays an increasing role in aiding design and administering of products, as well in efforts to build life-long customer relationships.

At the same time, technology investment will only help as long as firms find the right people: people with the right attitude, values, and ethics, commitment to excellence, and focus on customer service. The critical success factor is a top-down emphasis on exceeding customer expectations with quality people, excellent products, and legendary service.

RURAL-URBAN MIX

It must be borne in mind that India is a predominantly rural country and will continue to be so in near future. New players tend to favour the "creamy" layer of the urban population. But, in doing so, they are missing a large chunk of the insurable population. A strong case in point is the current business composition of predominant market leader—the Life Insurance Corporation of India. The lion's share of its new business comes from the rural and semi-rural markets. In a country of 1 billion people, mass marketing is always a profitable and cost-effective option for gaining market share. The rural sector is a perfect case for mass marketing.

Competition in rural areas tends to be "kinder and gentler" than that in urban areas, which can easily be termed cut-throat.

Rural insurance should be looked upon as an opportunity and not an obligation. A smaller bundle of innovative products in sync with rural needs and perception and an efficient delivery system are the two aspects that have to be developed in order to penetrate the rural markets.

IMPENDING REFORMS

Pension Reforms

The two issues that urgently need to be addressed are the escalating burden of the unfunded government pension and the coverage for building retirement income for the non-salaried workforce. The Insurance Regulatory Development Authority—the regulatory authority in Insurance, has already submitted a road map for pension reforms to the government. The new pension authority would fix the minimum capital requirement for new entrants including mutual funds and banks. Players would need to convince potential of their long-term commitment and responsibility and make known all components of options they intend to offer in pension products.

Some feel that in order to maximize pension fund efficacy, management should be given over to insurance carriers, banks, and mutual funds. They also recommend against auctioning the management of Pension Funds, proposing instead that entities with impeccable reputations, experience, and financial strengths should be entrusted with this important task.

Health Insurance

This is one area where India does not have much progress to date.

CONCLUSION

Competition will surely cause the market to grow beyond current rates, create a bigger "pie" and offer additional consumer choices through the introduction of new products, services, and price options. Yet, at the same time, public and private sector companies have to work together to ensure healthy growth and development of the sector. Challenges such as developing a common industry code of conduct, contributing to a common catastrophe reserve fund, and chalking out agreements between insurers to settle claims to the benefit of the consumer will require concerted effort from both sectors.

24

Insuring Life

H. SADHAK

Life insurance business is significantly influenced by the state of economy of a country and major impacting factors are rate of growth of GDP, domestic savings, household financial savings, disposable income, etc. The size of the life insurance market is also influenced by the rate of growth of population, social security system, health care system, changes in customs and social practices, changes in the attitude, risks, etc. It has been observed that societies where the standard of living has been steadily improving experience a higher insurance penetration. Market competition exerts a very positive influence on market expansion, higher life insurance penetration as well as higher life insurance density. Recent upsurge in Indian economy, particularly since the liberalization and market reforms leading to competition, has created tremendous opportunities for growth of life insurance industry.

During recent times, the momentum of growth of Indian economy has picked up particularly since liberalization initiated in 1980s. Though the overall growth rate during the last decade has fluctuated, it remained well above many countries of the world.

Overall GDP growth rate which was 6.1 per cent during 1995-96 to 2000-01, declined to 4.4 per cent in 2000-01, then moved up to 5.8 per cent in 2001-02 only to decline to 4 per cent in 2002-03. However, there was an improvement in 2003-04, and GDP registered a growth rate of 8.1 per cent. The fluctuation in growth rate of GDP was marked by the sharp fluctuation in growth rate of agriculture and industry. However, growth in services sector was more or less steady since 2000-01 onwards. Services sector growth rate reached its peak at 10 per cent in 1999-00 but declined to 5.5 per cent in 2000-01. Thereafter gradually moved up and registered a 8.4 per cent growth rate in 2003-04.

The high growth rates in GDP have been reflected in absolute growth of GDP, personal disposable income and per capita income. There has been a significant overall increase in GDP and by the end of March, 2004, GDP at the current market prices stood at Rs. 2516912 crore. The per capita income has also moved upward, and it was Rs. 11684 by the end of March 2004.

Like other well-developed economies the services sector has emerged as the leading contributor to the GDP. During the year 2002-03, the share of services sector in real GDP stood at 56.1 per cent. Among the services sector industries, financial services has registered a steady growth. Life insurance, which is an important component of financial services sector also witnessed a significant growth during the last few years.

India is one of the countries in the world which has achieved higher growth rate in domestic savings, and the higher propensity to save by the household sector has been maintained over the period. However, this growth rate has slowed down during the last few years, particularly since economic liberalization and basically due to growth in consumer expenditure and reduced rate of return on investment. Moreover, during the last few years, some of the incentives for the household savings were withdrawn, which adversely affected the domestic savings rate. During 2002-03, GDS at 24.2 per cent increased marginally over the previous year which was 25.5 per cent.

Inspite of marginal fall in household savings from 22.7 per cent in 2001-02 to 22.6 per cent in 2002-03, it remained the major contributor to the GDS. The share of household savings in GDP increased significantly from 17 per cent in 1996-97 to 22.6 per cent in 2001-02. Positive growth in economy, expansion of services sector and increase in household savings contributed significantly to the expansion of insurance market in India.

The share of bank deposits, PF and PPF has fluctuated and declined in the household financial assets, while the share of insurance funds has increased steadily from 8.7 per cent in 1993-94 to 14.4 per cent in 2001-02, while Life Fund in terms of GDP went up from 1.1 per cent to 1.9 per cent during the same period.

LIFE INSURANCE

Indian life insurance industry, since nationalization, has registered a significant growth and gradually increased its share in household financial savings and premium income has done reasonably well. The share of insurance funds has increased from 8.7 per cent in 1993-94 to 14.4 per cent in 2001-02, while the share of life insurance funds increased from 8 per cent to 13.9 per cent during the same period and in terms of GDP it has increased from 1.1 per cent to 1.9 per cent. This is a significant achievement of life insurance industry.

Growth in Life Fund is considered to be an important indicator of growth of life insurance industry and LIC, after nationalization of 256 Life Insurance Companies, started with a Life Fund of Rs. 410.40 crore, which in course of time increased rapidly and stood at Rs. 280887.73 lakhs in 2003.

Similarly, the total assets of LIC, keeping pace with the Life Fund, has increased from Rs. 463 crore in 1958 to Rs. 289895.52 crore and has emerged as the largest financial institution in India.

In the Indian life insurance market the total number of policies underwritten in 2004 increased by 12.78 per cent from 25382690 in 2002-03 to 28626915 in 2003-04, while the premium under these policies increased by 51.80 per cent, from Rs. 1232483.37 lakh to 1871016.02 lakh during the same period. Liberalisation of Indian insurance market has provided further push to the insurance industry. By the end of March, 2004, there were 13 life insurance companies including LIC in the market, which has not only generated competition but also provided a wide range of product choice to the customers.

GLOBAL CONTEXT

Though the share of Life Fund in household financial assets has gone up during the last decade and Indian life insurance industry registered better growth rate compared with global growth rate, total premium volume and global market share remained quite low. Total premium volume of life insurance industry in the world at 9 per cent growth rate increased from US $ 1534061 in 2002 to US $ 1672514 in 2003 (Table 24.1), whereas in India growth rate was much higher at 18 per cent and total premium volume increased from US $ 11515 to US $ 13590 during the same period (Table 24.2).

TABLE 24.1

Top Five Countries in the World in Terms of Life Insurance Premium

Country	*Premium in million (US $)*		*Share in World Market (%)*
	2003	2002	28.75
United States	480919	480452	22.80
Japan	381335	353909	9.26
United Kingdom	154842	159758	4.59
France	105436	80310	4.59
Germany	76436	60860	–
WORLD	1672514	1534061	–

Source: Sigma (No. 3/004), Swiss Re.

TABLE 24.2

Top Five Countries in Asia

Country	*Premium in million US $*		*Share in World Market %*
	2003	2002	
Japan	381335	353909	22.80
South Korea	41998	40190	2.51
PR China	32442	25202	1.94
Taiwan	23739	20765	1.42
India	13590	11515	0.81

Insurance density (premium per capita) and insurance penetration (premium in percentage of GDP) which are important growth indicators are quite low in India. In the year 2003, life insurance density in India was only US $ 12.9 as against the world density of US $ 267.1. Similarly, life insurance penetration in India was only 2.2 per cent as against world penetration level of 4.59. Many of the smaller countries (either in terms of population or in terms of GDP volume) achieved better growth rate in life insurance density and penetration, like Bahamas, Hongkong and South Africa, etc. Bahamas, a country with 0.3 million population and US $ 56 billion GDP registered a density of US $ 699.5 and penetration of 4.38 per cent. Further Australia and Switzerland both are small countries in terms of GDP but achieved high level of density and penetration. Insurance Density in Switzerland was US $ 3431.8 which was highest in the world. It was even better than USA (US $ 1657.5) with highest level of GDP in the world followed by Japan (US $ 3002.9) and UK (US $ 2617.7). Similarly, life insurance penetration in Australia at 12.96 per cent was the highest in the world followed by UK (8.62 per cent), Japan (8.28 per cent) and Taiwan (8.28 per cent).

LOW COVERAGE

Low level of density and penetration was due to the low level of coverage of insurable population. A rough estimate of insurable population on the basis of 1991 Census working age population (age between 15-49) shows that there was 492.12 lakh insurable population, which has increased to 1043.52 lakhs in 2003. Though the life insurance industry has made good progress in India, yet a vast potential remains untapped which has been reflected in the low level of density and penetration. However, only 24.46 per cent of such population has been covered by LIC. If we add up the coverage by other private sector insurance companies it may be around 25 per cent.

A further analysis of coverage of insurable population shows that most of the insured population belong to the age group 25-29 (37.31 per cent), 30-34 (41.76 per cent) and 35-39 (35.55 per cent). Coverage was relatively low for the age group 50-59 (7.25 per cent), 60-69 (1.26 per cent) and 15-19 (19.79 per cent). This indicates that retirement market in India has virtually remained untapped. This also indicates that there is tremendous potential for pension and retirement products in India.

It is quite evident that growth of Indian life insurance market is quite slow when compared with China. China is a late starter in life insurance business but already surpassed India in terms of total premium volume, density and penetration. However, there seems to be tremendous potential for life insurance in India. According to one projection made by National Insurance Academy (NIA), Pune total industry premium is likely to increase from Rs. 60181 crore in

2004 to Rs. 171707 crore in 2010 and the total new business premium is likely to go up from Rs. 13503 crore to Rs. 42834 crore, providing enough space for all the companies in the life market to grow.

CHALLENGES

Concerted efforts are required to increase the coverage and penetration level through a wide range of actions in the areas of strategic business planning, product innovation, management accountability, efficiency in investment management, technology management, HR management, service quality management, improvement in disclosures and corporate governance. We need to focus on some marketing-related issues.

- *Market Segmentation:* In order to increase penetration level, an approach is needed, based on rural and urban market, high end and low end market, saving substitute market, health insurance market, pension and retirement market, etc. Till recently insurance products were not fully segment directed. Uniform marketing strategy was adopted for all types of products. However, in recent times segment specific products and marketing strategies are being designed. A more scientific approach is required through development of distinct product and specialized training to sell them.
- Product innovation and Product Diversification are required to reach the various segments of market. During recent times, global life insurance, industry being driven by single premium and Unit Linked Plans.
- Retirement and Health Insurance Market remained out of major attention. Though a number of pension plans have been launched by the life insurance companies, health sector virtually remained untapped. Serious efforts are required to be made to design products for these two segments and promote them.
- *Rural Market:* Special focus and marketing strategy is required for rural marketing because about 74 per cent of India is still rural and a staggering 740 million people live in villages. During the year 2001-02 the share of agricultural and allied activities was 24.3 per cent of total GDP as against 21.5 per cent contributed by industry sector. The vast

potential of rural sector for insurance can also be seen in terms of household members participating in economic activities. A study conducted by NCAER on households in the country shows that there were 295.2 million such earners in 1994-95 of which 77.1 per cent lived in rural areas. The study further shows that about 34.3 per cent of the total family members were found to be earners in rural households compared to 30 per cent in urban households. All these are indications of growing disposable income in rural areas and ability to save and spend, signify scope in expansion of life insurance market in rural areas.

TABLE 24.3

Life Insurance Density and Penetration in Top 10 Countries in terms of GDP in 2003

Country	*GDP (in US $ Billion)*	*Population (Million)*	*Density (in USD)*	*Penetration (in %)*
United States	10988	290.2	1657.5	4.38
Japan	4429	127.0	3002.9	8.28
Germany	2418	82.3	930.4	4.74
UK	1797	59.2	2617.1	8.62
France	1759	59.6	1767.9	5.99
Italy	1476	57.5	1238.3	4.82
PR China	1410	1290.8	25.1	2.30
Canada	867	31.6	722.9	2.63
Spain	843	41.0	488.6	2.38
Mexico	608	102.5	41.3	0.70
INDIA	601	1056.3	12.9	2.26

Source: Sigma (No. 3/2004), Swiss Re.

- ***Distribution Channel:*** Another important challenge before the insurance industry is to promote more effective distribution channels to meet the new generation demand and distribution of products as the emerging market will be characteristically different in future, particularly due to information explosion and technology led delivery system. Emergence of financial conglomerates, universal banking, integration of financial services has changed the geometry of financial products. Effort of insurance companies should be to promote institutional intermediaries like corporate agents, brokers which will provide a new dimension to distribution channel.

- Managing Customers' Choice and Demand would be a critical task before the insurance companies. Insurance companies need to focus on rendering cost effective quality to customer service. In India, real meaning of marketing has been lost, due to excessive focus on short-term goal. Life insurance contract is a long-term one extending even to 30-35 years. Sales is a single transaction, but servicing is a continuous business for an insurance company. It is this service function which is very important and needs to be provided with efficiency. This however calls for a long-term perspective under a well designed long-term planning.
- *Research:* Functioning of an insurance company will be significantly influenced by quality research inputs like data management and interpretation, policy planning, marketing, analysis of customer's satisfaction, human resource development and funds. Working of an insurance company covers a wide area of socio-economic and financial market. To take corporate decisions and for strategic planning a sound database and easy to use analytical tools would be required along with a team of hard-core research professionals. Life insurance industry has moved from staff monopoly to competitive market place, where management must be Market Driven instead of Marketing Driven.

25

Career in Actuarial Science

HENA NAQVI

Risk, uncertainties, dangers, insecurities are all the dark shades of life. In the modern times, human beings have developed various devices to minimise the harms brought about by risks and uncertainties of life. It's true that certain risk like fear of an early death or an accidental death cannot be avoided but the disastrous repercussions associated with that risk, i.e. financial loss to the family of the breadwinner in case of his early death can be minimised to some extent by making some arrangements well in advance. Among such financial arrangements can be mentioned insurance, bank deposits, mutual fund, pension schemes and so on. But these tools require an efficient management system in order to provide long-term monetary benefits to the clients and also to manage the risk and uncertainties of their lives. Here comes the role of an Actuary. The actuaries are considered to be the analytical backbone of a country's financial security programmes.

Actuaries are the professional who, by using the probability theory and mathematical, statistical and financial techniques; analyse the financial consequences of risk to enable businesses to make better informed decisions. They assess the financial impact of uncertain future events by methodically analysing the past, modelling the future and quantifying the likely range of financial outcomes from different future events. Their work involves a combination of strong analytical skills, business knowledge and understanding of human behaviour in order to design and manage the programmes that control risk.

The Expanding Horizon of the Scope of Actuarial Functionaries

Earlier the Actuaries were demanded only in the insurance sector. In India, LIC, GIC were the major employers of the Actuaries but certain factors like liberalisation, privatisation and emergence of some new professions in the Indian economy have given rise to the emergence of the need of Actuaries in other fields as well. These new fields include, viz. commercial banks, investment banks, retirement funds, employees benefit departments of large corporates and all those businesses that need to manage financial risk. In other words, wherever there is uncertainty, there is scope for Actuarial Science. That is why, a career as an Actuary is better described as a "business" career with a mathematical basis than as a "technical" mathematical career.

Strategic Position of the Actuary

Actuaries are the key players in the management team of the financial companies. Their work is directly related to the strategic management decisions. Since their judgement is heavily relied upon; actuaries' career path often leads to upper management and executive positions.

Role of Actuaries in Insurance

Insurance, the most powerful tool of managing risks, is almost unthinkable without actuaries. Under insurance, we reduce our risk of financial loss by transferring it to an insurance company that accepts the risk for a price (the insurance premium). Actuaries play a key role to design insurance plans, determine the premium, monitor the profitability of the insurance companies and recommend corrective actions. They also ensure that the companies have set aside enough funds to pay claims.

Pre-requisites for being an Actuary

A strong ability and liking for numbers is a must for the aspirants of Actuarial career. Equally essential is a firm determination towards a prolonged study period, five to seven years on an average. Acquaintance with the business environment, economics, finance and accounts are also needed. Good communication skills, computer knowledge and decision-making ability are some other requisites for this career. Actuarial course is considered as a tough course, that's why; the dropout rate is very high. But crossing the barriers of the path successfully would mean reaching out to the soaring heights of name, fame and money.

A Highly Paid Profession

This is a well-known fact that Actuaries are the one of the highest paid professionals. In the beginning of the career itself, an Actuary can earn up to Rs. 8 lakhs per annum in India. Stipend for an Actuarial trainee is approximately Rs. 25,000 per month. The career opportunity begins as soon as the student completes the first five papers.

ESSENTIAL QUALIFICATIONS FOR DOING ACTUARIAL STUDIES

One can opt for this career, if one has any of the following qualifications:

- Graduate in Maths/Statistics/Econometrics/Computer Science with a minimum 55 per cent marks.
- MBA (Finance)/CA/CWA/MCA.

The Actuarial Course

In India, a fellow member of the Actuarial Society of India (ASI), Mumbai is referred to as an Actuary. The Actuarial course (offered by ASI) consisting of 16 papers can be completed between 4-5 years depending upon the time devoted by the student for the preparation of the examinations.

The examinations are divided into four parts—100 series, 200 series, 300 series and 400 series. On passing the 100 series subjects, a student is eligible to get the Certificate in Actuarial Techniques (CAT). On passing all the subjects up to and including 300 series, a student is eligible to be admitted as an Associate member of the Society AASI. After passing the chosen subject from the 400 series, an Associate is awarded Fellowship and can use FASI against his/her name. The examinations are essentially approached through self-study. The course material is provided by the society in all subjects excluding the entrance examination. On occasions, the society organises oral classes and group tuitions. Current cost of the entire course including tuition material can work out to Rs. 50,000. The examinations are conducted twice a year during the months of May and November. Depending upon the efforts put in, one may get through the examinations in four to six years on an average.

Future

The expansion and privatisation of the Indian economy is a boon for the rise of Actuary as one of the most demanding professions of the country in the days to come. Privatisation of the insurance sector has not only created innumerable employment opportunities for the Actuaries but has also led to the popularity of this profession. Actuarial profession, hitherto not a layperson's cup of tea, is now understood and thought over by the commoners as a challenging but highly paid profession. Apart from lucrative jobs in private insurance companies, the opening up of the insurance sector will give rise to many associated opportunities in underwriting marketing, product design, re-insurance and consulting. These factors are suggesting a bright future of the Actuarial profession.

POTENTIAL EMPLOYERS

- Insurance Companies (General and Life),
- Banks,
- Investment Companies,
- Consulting firms,
- Public Accounting firms,
- Big Corporate and business houses, and
- Pension department (Government and private sectors).

INSTITUTES OFFERING COURSES IN ACTUARIAL SCIENCE

(a) Indian

1. Actuarial Society of India, 9, Jeevan Udyog, 3rd Floor, 278, Dr. D.N. Road, Fort, Mumbai-1, Ph. 91 22006794, e-mail: actsoc@vsnl.com.

2. Bharatidasan University, Palkalaipur, Tiruchirapalli-620024.
3. University of Kalyani, P.O. Kalyani-741235, Distt. Nadia, W.B.
4. Kurukshetra University, Kurukshetra-132119.
5. University of Mumbai, M.G. Road, Fort, Mumbai-32.
6. Goa University, Taleigao Plateau, Goa-403002.

(b) Foreign

1. Institute of Actuaries Staple Inn Hall, High Holborn, London, Tel. +44 (O) 20 76322100; web: www.actuaries.org.uk.
2. Society of Actuaries, 475, North Martingale Road, Suit 800, Schaumburg, IL 60173-226, Tel. 847706, Web: www.soa.org.
3. American Academy of Actuaries 1100-17th Street, NW 7th Floor, Washington DC 20036, web: www.actuary.org.
4. City University Northampton Square, London EC 1V OHB, Tel. +44 (O) 20 74778560, web: www.city.ac.uk.

PART IV

RISK IN INSURANCE SECTOR

26

Preserving Capital and Maximising Shareholder Return

MANISH KUMAR JAIN

Entry to life insurance business requires a prospective entity to bring Rs. 100 crores (Rs. 1 billion) as a start up capital in cash besides the stringent test/criteria set by the regulator IRDA (Insurance Regulatory and Development Authority). The regulator has kept such a high requirement of capital so as to create an entry barrier so that only serious players enter this business, who are serious and understand that it is a capital intensive business. It is not only because regulator has imposed a high level of starting capital but estimates of almost all new players also shows that the capital requirement does not just end at this Rs. 100 crores (Rs. 1 billion) but requires additional capital infusion of Rs. 250-350 crores (Rs. 2.5 to 3.5 billion) in the following years. Therefore in a business; which requires such huge amounts of capital, it goes without saying that the management/insurer needs to utilize this money in the most prudent/effective manner, which is available to them upfront.

Ability to demonstrate its capability to utilize the capital in most optimum manner will go a long way in establishing its credibility not only in the eyes of the regulator, academicians, shareholders, people who understand this business today and last but not the least the person who matters the most, the 'man' on the street. This 'man' probably does not understand it today but as he gets educated on the subject going forward and with increasing awareness he will be able to distinguish the insurer he wants to go with among the whole lot available to pick from. Based on my experience I am of the opinion that in this business, insurer's credibility with the regulator and the customer is what matters the most, and it is also the most important ingredient for a successful venture. Any dent to this credibility will require lot of effort, time and money to undo the damage. It is this intangible which will distinguish a company from the competition as mere ability of the shareholders/ promoters to bring cash when required will not be a sustainable distinguishing parameter.

In my opinion, which is based on the limited understanding and experience of working in the insurance sector I have attempted to highlight the issue and possible ways of how byway of doing things differently it can make huge impacts on this requirements of capital by the company.

Shareholders who have decided to infuse Rs. 300-400 crores (Rs. 3-4 billion) in a business and patiently wait for 7-9 years when they see the first profit, are definitely expecting large returns. This expectation is not wrong as nothing comes free in this world. To meet this apparent normal expectation of shareholders also demands on the part of the management to be capital conscious from the beginning. In other words, capital preserved is capital created.

Given to operate within a set of regulations which are more or less fixed, let us explore where is the room for optimizing the use of shareholders' capital and thereby preserving the wealth.

As a starting point let us see what drives or puts strain on capital. The drivers of capital in a life insurance business are namely:

(i) Solvency margin requirements as set by the regulator, which is a combination of a floor limit and a mathematically derived amount, this mathematically derived amount is a function of the volume of business on books, growth rates, product mix (examined later in the article).

(ii) Level of Inadmissible assets.

(iii) Expense overrun or excess of actual expense level *vs.* pricing allowable expenses.

(iv) Actuarial reserves or policyholder reserves actuarial reserving basis (regulator prescribes GPV (Gross Premium Valuation) method to be uniformly adopted by all the companies for easy comparison) etc.

(v) Other drivers which affect capital are product mix, rate of new business growth, etc.

Let us see what each one means and how they affect capital. Allow me to start from the last point of this list as I intend to discuss the top drivers in detail.

Product mix, each product has its own characteristic and effect reserve requirements differently; like Single Premium has reserve day one and has a decreasing pattern but for Endowment it increases with the life of the contract and on the other extreme for Term there is no reserve at all. A combination of the same products in different proportions have a varying impact on the Reserves, Capital requirement, Profits, etc. Here I am only saying that product mix affect the reserves and how reserves affect capital is being examined later.

Now lets take rate of new business growth and how it affects capital, it is worthwhile to mention here that this is a unique business where even fast growths can also bring in closure of business, since it costs more than a Rupee to acquire a new Rupee in the form on new premium (box below), this puts strain on cash and thereby capital. As the volume of business on books grows so does the reserves and thereby solvency (discussed later). See Table 1 below, which shows that the company has to expend more than the new premium itself in the first year and clearly it needs cash to fund the expenses. Therefore, capital is affected both from the cash flow angle and the solvency margins requirements.

TABLE 26.1

	(Rs.)
Say, First Year Premium is (assumed that premium of Rs. 6000 will get a sum insured of Rs. 250,000 at age 30 for a normal make for 25 year Term plan)	6,000
Agent's commission (40 per cent)	2,400
Sales managers overrides (70 per cent of agent's first year commission)	1,680
Other overheads for acquisition (policy document, medical, processing etc.	1,500
Stamp duty (@Rs. 0.40/Rs. 1000 of sum insured)	100
Other overheads for policy owner servicing (change of address, loans, change of nominee, etc.)	500
Total of expenses	6,180
Balance available for recovery all other indirect overheads	(180)

Let us discuss the effect of actuarial reserving basis, there are different methods of reserve determination some give liberal reserves values and some give conservative reserve values, so the choice of a particular method is crucial. No method is wrong but they behave differently, just like depreciation policy straight line method (SLM) or written down method (WDM) both are correct but both impact the profit line differently. In case of India, to keep it uniform for ease of comparison, the regulator (IRDA) has specified Gross Premium Valuation method to be followed for reserve determination.

Expense overrun, simply stated, if the insurer's actual expense is less than what it recovers from the premium income (based on the expense loading that it has put on the net premium while pricing), then the expense over-run is negative thereby a situation of profit in the reverse situation a situation of loss. For an insurer a situation of negative expense overrun, i.e. expense gains is a reflection of a lot of things namely the efficiency of sales force, product pricing capability insurer's market share, matured market situation, etc.

Solvency margin is the excess of assets over liabilities. Statute prescribes what this excess should at least be for an individual life insurer, i.e. prescribes a minimum solvency margins which is to be maintained at all times. Regulations prescribe that solvency margin be higher of;

Rs. 50 crores (Rs. 500 millions),

Or

Mathematically derived number (for an insurer in business of Individual life insurances this number is 4 per cent of Mathematical/ Technical Reserves Plus 0.3 per cent of sums at risk). So reserves affect solvency margins which affect the capital requirement.

As the new insurer starts his business he will take at least 3-4 years, even with most ambitious growth plans, before this mathematically derived amount exceeds Rs. 50 crores (Rs. 500 million).

Which means that in the initial few years itself an insurer has to keep at least Rs. 50 crores (Rs. 500 million) of assets in excess of its liabilities. Since this excess or required solvency margin of Rs. 50 crores (Rs. 500 million) is minimum any shortfall will have to be corrected by way of capital infusion.

In determining the level of excess of assets over liabilities, the regulations also prescribe the manner in which to value these assets and liabilities for the purpose of determining the available solvency margin. This is so to remove any inconsistencies in the methods that may be adopted by different insurers for determining the available solvency margin.

On the liabilities side we have mainly policyholders' liabilities, which are determined actuarially and some other business liabilities like payables, etc. so there is little that can be done on the liability side.

Let us examine what can be done on the asset side.

Regulations talk about if the asset is eligible/admissible fully and/or partly in the first place to be considered for the purpose of valuation or not, then if it passes the eligibility/admissibility test then prescribes what should be its value.

Below is the extract of what the IRDA regulations on Assets, Liabilities and solvency margins say for value of assets.

VALUES OF ASSETS

(1) The following assets should be placed with value zero:
   (a) Agent's balances and outstanding premiums in India, to the extent they are not realised within a period of thirty days;
   (b) Agents' balances and outstanding premiums outside India, to the extent they are not realisable;
   (c) Sundry debts, to the extent, they are not realisable;
   (d) Advances of an unrealisable character;
   (e) Furniture, fixtures, dead stock and stationery;
   (f) Deferred expenses;
   (g) Profit and loss appropriation account balance and any fictitious assets other than pre-paid expenses;
   (h) Re-insurer's balances outstanding for more than three months; and
   (i) Preliminary expenses in the formation of the company.

(2) The value of computer equipment including software shall be computed as under:
   (a) seventy-five per cent of its cost in the year of purchase;
   (b) fifty per cent of its cost in the second year;
   (c) twenty-five per cent of its cost in the third year; and
   (d) zero per cent thereafter."

First impression is that any existence of a fully inadmissible asset or a partly inadmissible asset will hinder the solvency margins to the extent of inadmissible value. What this tells us is that we should not have any fully inadmissible asset or partly non-admissible asset. Since a company need assets to transact business and the need for such assets is not guided by what values regulations attach to it. In my view, this is where there is lot of scope for planning that can be done, specially with regard to the depreciable assets. Since there is a need for such assets by the business, it should try to find alternate channels/modes of using those assets and yet not get them affect your balance sheet.

Let us see the effect of a fully inadmissible asset by way of an illustration with data, by comparison between two companies one going in for purchase and the other for lease/hire.

ASSUMPTIONS

Company A rents a bare shell premises at Rs. 50 per square feet per month and furnishes it on its own at Rs. 2000 per square feet. While Company B enter into a contract with the landlord for similar space but furnished by the land lord at Rs. 94 per square feet per month. This Rs. 94 includes the rent for bare shell of Rs. 50 and a balance Rs. 44 for the furnishing. This Rs. 44 is an equated monthly instalment for Rs. 2000 over 5 years at 14 per cent. Everything is same for the two companies with the only difference being that A has invested their own capital in the furnishings and B has leased them from the landlord. Also Company B invests Rs. 2000 in a government paper yielding 9 per cent annually. Both take one square feet of space. Furniture and fixtures have also been depreciated over 5 year period to keep the parity.

This is how the results of the two companies will look.

The comparison tells us that over a 5 year time period Company A needs higher capital by Rs. 1,740 (Rs. 6,600-Rs. 4,860). Any investments made in inadmissible asset, becomes completely worthless for solvency margin requirements and require additional capital to that extent. Investments in inadmissible assets is advisable after a point when capital becomes indifferent to solvency margin, i.e. solvency no longer puts a strain on the Capital requirement.

Also it should not be concluded that choice of company 'A' is wrong, as long as, it has been consciously chosen so by the shareholders. If shareholders have sufficient capital and they want to put money in the business then it's their choice as long they are

Company A

	Profit and Loss Account				Assets in Balance Sheet (Fixtures and Fittings)	Admissible Value of the asset as per Regulations	Incremental Value to the extent inadmissible	Capital (Additional infusion Required)
	Expense (Lease Rent)	*Expense (Depreciation)*	*Income*	*Net*				
	A	*B*	*C*	*D = C–(A + B)*	*E*	*F*	*G*	*H = D + G*
	(Rs.)	*(Rs.)*	*(Rs.)*	*(Rs.)*	*(Rs.)*	*(Rs.)*	*(Rs.)*	*(Rs.)*
Year 1	(600.00)	(400.00)	–	(1,000)	1,600	–	1,600	2,600
Year 2	(600.00)	(400.00)	–	(1,000)	1,200	–	–	1,000
Year 3	(600.00)	(400.00)	–	(1,000)	800	–	–	1,000
Year 4	(600.00)	(400.00)	–	(1,000)	400	–	–	1,000
Year 5	(600.00)	(400.00)	–	(1,000)	–	–	–	1,000
						Total		6,600

Company B

	Profit and Loss Account				Assets in Balance Sheet (Government Security)	Admissible Value of the asset as per Regulations	Value to the extent inadmissible	Strain on Capital (Additional infusion Required)
	Expense (Lease Rent)	Expense (Depreciation)	Income	Net				
	A	B	C	D = C–(A + B)	E	F	G	H = D + G
	(Rs.)	(Rs.)	(Rs.)	(Rs.)	(Rs.)	(Rs.)	(Rs.)	(Rs.)
Year 1	(1,152)	–	180	(972)	2,000	2,000	–	972
Year 2	(1,152)	–	180	(972)	2,000	2,000	–	972
Year 3	(1,152)	–	180	(972)	2,000	2,000	–	972
Year 4	(1,152)	–	180	(972)	2,000	2,000	–	972
Year 5	(1,152)	–	180	(972)	2,000	2,000	–	972
						Total		4,860

doing so after the above analysis. All I am saying is that the same amount of business can be transacted with a lower capital base.

LET NOW SEE AN ILLUSTRATION FOR PARTLY INADMISSIBLE ASSETS

Company A buys computers, while Company B enter into a contract with a vendor to hire the computers.

To study the comparison let us assume that both need computers worth Rs. 100 which can be hired at Rs. 40 p.a. for 3 years. This rate of Rs. 40 p.a. is a very conservative quote and in the market place it can be closed at a much lower number along with a clause that at the end of 3 years the computers will be transferred to the company at a token amount. Also for the sake of ease of comparison the span for both the companies has been kept at 5 years. Other things have been assumed to be same for both the companies and have been kept out of this illustration.

Now, let us examine how the P&L and the BS of the two companies look, over a five year period. Since company B did not buy computers they have invested Rs. 100 in a government paper earning say, 9 per cent annually.

The foregoing results show that in case of company A the capital requirement over five years period is Rs. 110 as compared to Rs. 93 of company B, which is higher by Rs. 17. However, in practice the hire agreement can easily be staggered over longer periods, say 4 year period, thereby making this point even stronger.

Alternative use shows that capital requirement can be flattened over the years by shifting costs to later years to match them with income of later years after the initial ramp up has taken place in a start up, which again makes a lot of sense.

This analysis has also to be viewed from another financial implication, which cannot be quantified with precision, in light of the fact that since it takes a very long time (7-9 years) to breakeven, i.e. the losses of first few years may actually go waste as they may become time barred for being available for set-off against profits of later years. And even if available for set-off, because of time value of money that loss would have become miniscule or worthless. However, this is a matter of perception and cannot be quantified with precision.

Clearly, some financial planning and analysis can greatly

Company A

	Profit and Loss Account			Assets in Balance Sheet (Computer)	Admissible Value of the asset as per Regulations	Value to the extent inadmissible	Strain on Capital (Additional infusion Required)
	Expense (Depreciation)	Income	Net				
	A	B	C = B–A	D	E	F = D–E	G = C + F
	(Rs.)	(Rs.)	(Rs.)	(Rs.)	(Rs.)	(Rs.)	(Rs.)
Year 1	(20)	–	(20)	80	75	5	25
Year 2	(20)	–	(20)	60	50	10	30
Year 3	(20)	–	(20)	40	25	15	35
Year 4	(20)	–	(20)	20	–	20	20
Year 5	(20)	–	(20)	–	–	–	–
					Total		110

Company B

	Profit and Loss Account			Assets in Balance Sheet (Government Security)	Admissible Value of the asset as per Regulations	Value to the extent inadmissible	Strain on Capital (Additional infusion Required)
	Expense (Hire Charges)	Income	Net				
	A	B	C = B–A	D	E	F = D–E	G = C + F
	(Rs.)	(Rs.)	(Rs.)	(Rs.)	(Rs.)	(Rs.)	(Rs.)
Year 1	(40)	9	(31)	100	100	–	31
Year 2	(40)	9	(31)	100	100	–	31
Year 3	(40)	9	(31)	100	100	–	31
Year 4	–	9	9	100	100	–	–
Year 5	–	9	9	100	100	–	–
					Total		93

impact the requirement of capital and thereby the IRR for the operation by making some decisions after due financial analysis.

Similarly, it can be illustrated to demonstrate savings of capital for other assets/areas. Other assets where this savings is possible are mainly Furniture Fixtures and Fittings Cars, Equipments, employee loans, etc.

CONCLUSION

Any capital expenditure should be considered after evaluating its admissibility for solvency margin purpose. Also, consider the amount of capital shareholder have to infuse in the business.

Identify what are those assets, which are partly or fully inadmissible. Find alternate sources of using them yet not letting it affect infusion of capital. Such alternative means being namely lease, hiring, etc. Surely these alternatives have a built in financing cost but to bear this cost is worth it.

27

New Accounting Framework in Insurance Industry

R.C. GURIA

After opening of the insurance sector in India to the private and the global giants, the entire scenario of the industry has undergone a sea-change. With the following new enactments and regulations, the insurance operations in India are getting more structured and increasingly complex and the expectations from our professionals have also increased manifold.

1. Enactment of The Insurance Regulatory and Development Authority Act, 1999 (IRDA).
2. IRDA (Marketing) Regulations, 2000.
3. IRDA (Life and General Insurance-Re-insurance) Regulations, 2000.
4. IRDA (Insurance Brokers) Regulations 2002 and (Corporate Agents) Regulations, 2002.
5. Introduction of Bancassurance, Third Party Administrator and Ins. Ombudsman.
6. Statutory Status to Institute of Surveyors and Adjusters.
7. IRDA (Investment Regulations), 2000.
8. IRDA (Preparation of Financial Statements and Auditor's Report of Insurance Companies) Regulations, 2002.
9. IRDA (Manner of Receipts of Premium) Regulations, 2002.
10. IRDA (Protection of Policyholder's Interests) (Amendment) Regulations, 2002.

With the last four IRDA regulations, insurance accounting and the audit thereof have witnessed new framework and directions. Now the Financial Statements and Audit Reports of insurance companies are to be prepared strictly in accordance with IRDA (Preparation of Financial Statements and Auditor's Report of Insurance Companies) Regulations, 2002. The said Regulations provide that—

- An insurer carrying on life insurance business shall comply with the requirements of Schedule 'A' to prepare financial statements.
- An insurer carrying on general insurance business shall comply with the requirements of Schedule 'B' to prepare financial statements.
- The Report of the Auditors on the Financial Statements of every insurer/re-insurer shall be in conformity with the requirements of Schedule 'C'.

The Authority may from time to time, issue separate directions/guidelines in the matter of appointment, continuance or removal of Auditors of an insurer or re-insurer as the case may be and these directions/guidelines may include prescriptions regarding qualifications and experience of auditors. This article deals with the requirements of schedule 'B'. Schedule 'B' has been broadly divided into following parts:

- Part I—Accounting Principles for Preparation of Financial Statements.
- Part II—Disclosures forming part of Financial Statements.
- Part III—General Instructions for preparation of Financial Statements.
- Part IV—Contents of Management Report.
- Part V—Preparation of Financial Statements.

As per AAS-28—The Auditor's Report on Financial Statements, Auditors are required to review and report whether the financial statements have been prepared in accordance with an acceptable financial reporting framework applicable to the entity. It is also necessary to review and report whether the financial statements give a true and fair view in accordance with that financial reporting framework. Precisely AAS-28 requires auditors to be thorough with the Financial Statements and Reporting Framework as laid down by Regulatory Authority. AAS-28 provides (para 29) that financial statements comply with relevant statutory requirements and regulations.

PART I
ACCOUNTING PRINCIPLES FOR PREPARING FINANCIAL STATEMENTS

1. Accounting Standard

Financial Statements comprising: (i) Balance Sheet, (ii) Receipts and Payments Account (Cash Flow Statement), Profit & Loss Account (Shareholders' Account) and Revenue Account (Policyholders' Account) shall be in conformity with the Accounting Standards (AS) issued by the Institute of Chartered Accountants of India to the extent applicable to the insurer carrying on general insurance business except that:

- Accounting Standard 3 – Cash-flow Statement shall be only under Direct Method.
- Accounting Standard 13 – Accounting for Investment shall not be applicable.
- Accounting Standard 17 – Segment reporting shall apply to all insurers irrespective of the requirements for listing and turnover mentioned therein.

Note 1: AS-3, Cash Flow Statement is the widely accepted model for preparation of Cash Flow Statements. It classifies Cash Flow in the following categories:

- Cash Flow from Operating activities,
- Cash Flow from Investing activities, and
- Cash Flow from Financing activities.

Cash Flow from Operating activities cover cash flows derived from the principal revenue-producing activities Cash Flows from Investing activities are related to acquisition and disposal of fixed assets and investments and Cash Flows from Financing activities refer to cash flows from and to providers of equity and loan funds to the organization. The method discussed above and shown in the format hereinafter is known as Indirect method of reporting Cash Flow from operating activities as required by SEBI. But AS-3 also stipulates alternative method known as Direct Method of reporting Cash flows where major classes of gross cash receipts and payments from Operation activities are disclosed and reported IRDA stipulates only the direct method of Cash Flow, which has not yet been formatted by IRDA. So Cash flow statement is shown here under Indirect Method for ready reference here.

Note 2: AS-17 *vis-a-vis* IRDA guidelines on Segment Reporting: AS 17-Segment Reporting requires identification of different segments of an enterprise and furnishing information on performance risks and returns of the segments enabling the informed judgments about the enterprise as a whole as well as the segments defined. AS-17 provides guidance on how to identify segments. AS-17 defines a segment as a distinguishable area or component of an enterprise on the basis of particular risks and returns that are different from those of other segments. However as per IRDA requirements segment reporting as specified by AS-17 shall apply to all insurers irrespective of the requirements regarding listing and turnover mentioned therein.

2. Premium Recognition

Premium shall be recognized as income over the Risk Period or Contract Period whichever is appropriate. Hence premium received in advance shall be treated separately in the financial statement. A Reserve for Unexpired Risk shall be created with that part of premium which is attributable to and to be carried forward to the succeeding accounting period and shall not be less than the following limits as specified by Sec. 64V(ii)(b) of the Insurance Act, 1938:

- Fire and Miscellaneous Business 50 per cent of premium
- Marine Cargo Business 50 per cent of premium
- Marine Hull Business 100 per cent of premium

The reserves for Unexpired Risk are also known as Technical reserves. With the creation of Technical Reserve necessary adjustments are made so that premium income included in the Underwriting year's results is the premium actually earned in that year. The adjustments comprise bringing forward an amount for unearned premium from the previous year (previous year's Technical Reserves) and carrying forward an amount for unearned premium (current year's Technical Reserve) into the following year.

3. Premium Deficiency

Premium Deficiency shall be recognized if the sum of claim costs, related expenses and maintenance cost exceeds the related reserves for the unexpired risks.

4. Acquisition Cost

Acquisition costs, if any, shall be expensed in the period in which they are incurred. Acquisition costs are those costs that vary with and primarily related to the acquisition of new and renewal insurance business.

5. Claim Cost

Claim cost comprises the claims under policies and specific claim settlement costs. Claims under policies mean the claim made for losses incurred and those estimated under the policies following a loss occurred. Estimated liability of Outstanding claims which will result in future outgo shall be brought to account in respect of:

- **Claims reported, but not paid on direct business.**
- **Claims reported, but not settled on inward Re-insurance business.**
- **Claims incurred, but not reported (IBNR), and**
- **Claims incurred, but not enough reported (IBNER).**

The change in estimated liability for outstanding claim at the beginning and at the end of the financial period shall be brought into account. The estimated liability for outstanding claims shall be provided net of salvage value if its realization is sufficiently certain.

Actuarial Valuation of Claim Liability

Claims made in respect of contracts where the claim payment period exceeds four years shall be recognized on an actuarial basis subject to regulations that may be prescribed by the Authority.

6. Procedure for Valuation of Investment

An insurer shall determine the values of investments in the following manner:

(a) ***Real Estate/Investment Property***

Investment Property shall be measured at historical costs less accumulated depreciation and impairment loss. If residual value becomes Zero, no revaluation is permissible. The insurer shall asses at each balance sheet date whether any impairment of the investment property has occurred. An impairment loss shall be recognized as an expense in the Revenue/Profit and Loss Account. Fair Value as at the balance sheet date and the basis of its determination shall be disclosed in the Financial Statement as additional information.

(b) ***Debt Securities***

Debt securities including Government securities and redeemable preference shares shall be considered as 'held to maturity security' and, shall be measured at historical cost.

(c) ***Listed/Actively Traded Equity Securities***

(i) Listed equity securities and derivative investments that are traded in the active market shall be valued at fair value as at Balance Sheet date.
(ii) For the purpose of calculation of fair value, the lowest of the last quoted closing price of the stock exchange concerned shall be considered.
(iii) Unrealized gains/losses arising out of changes in the fair value of listed equities and derivatives shall be taken to equity under the Account head 'Fair Value Change Account'.
(iv) The profit or loss on sale of investment shall include accumulated changes in the fair value previously recognized in equity under the head 'Fair Value Changes A/C' in respect of particular security and being recognized to Profit and Loss Account on actual sale of the listed security.
(v) Any balance or any part thereof shall not be available for distribution of dividends while the debit balance in the said account shall be deducted from the profits or free reserves before declaration of dividend.

7. Apportionment of Investment Income

Investment income (net of expenses) is apportioned between Shareholders' Fund and Policyholders' fund in proportion to the Opening balance of these funds. Investment income belonging to policyholders is further apportioned to various departments in proportion to respective Technical Reserves at the beginning of the year.

8. Loans

Loans shall be measured at historical cost subject to impairment provisions which will be provided for in consideration of the quality of loan assets on the basis of guidelines prescribed from time to time by the RBI.

9. Catastrophe Reserve

This reserve is to be created in accordance with the norms prescribed by the Authority. Investment of Funds out of Catastrophe Reserve shall be made in accordance with prescription of the Authority. Catastrophic Reserve means reserve which is meant for meeting losses arising from an entirely unexpected set of events and not for any specific known purpose. This reserve is in the nature of an amount set aside for the potential future liability against the insurance policies. Losses from storms, tornadoes, floods, earthquakes and volcanic eruptions are called catastrophic losses. Reserves against these types of losses are termed as Catastrophe Reserve. IRDA has not yet specified any norms and rules for Catastrophe Reserve though it has been specified in the format. However, creation of catastrophe Reserve is very important in view of a study by the Munich Re-insurance Co. that natural catastrophes caused about $ 13 billion insured losses in 2002.

Note: Application of Accounting Standard 28, Impairment of Assets: IRDA Accounting Principles only prescribe for recognition and provision of impairment loss. The said Accounting Principles do not specify any method for determination assessment of Impairment loss. So the Accounting Standard 28 on Impairment of Assets will apply here for identification measurement, recognition, disclosures and reversal of Impairment Loss of the assets including investments and loans.

PART III
CERTAIN INSTRUCTIONS FOR PREPARATION OF FINANCIAL STATEMENTS

1. The corresponding amounts for the preceding financial year to be shown in all financial statements.
2. Extent of risk retained and re-insured to be disclosed separately.
3. The expression "Reserve" shall not include any amount written off or retained by way of providing for depreciation, renewals or diminution in the value of assets.
4. The expression 'Capital Reserve' shall not include any amount regarded as free for distribution and 'Revenue Reserve' shall mean any reserve other than capital reserve.
5. Any debit balance of Profit and Loss Account shall be shown as deduction from uncommitted reserves and the balance, if any, shall be shown separately.

PART V
PREPARATION OF FINANCIAL STATEMENTS

- Non-life insurer shall prepare Revenue Accounts (policy-holders' Accounts), Profit and Loss Account (Shareholders' Account) and the Balance Sheet in the Form B-RA, Form B-PL and form B-BS respectively.
- Revenue Accounts shall be prepared separately for Fire, Marine and Miscellaneous Departments.
- Separate schedules shall be prepared for Marine Cargo, Marine Hull and following classes of Miscellaneous business departments:
  1. Motor,
  2. Workmen Compensation/Employers' Liability,
  3. Public/Product Liability,
  4. Engineering,
  5. Aviation,
  6. Personal Accidents,
  7. Health Insurance, and
  8. Others.
- Separate Receipts and Payments Accounts shall be prepared

in accordance with the Direct Method as prescribed in AS-3 "Cash Flow Statement".

FORM B—RA

Revenue Account for the Year Ended 31st March . . .

Particulars	*Schedule*	*Current Year (Rs. '000)*	*Previous Year (Rs. '000)*
1. Premium earned (Net)	1		
2. Profit/Loss on sale/redemption of investments			
3. Others (to be specified)			
4. Interest, Dividend and Rent—Gross			
Total (A)			
1. Claims Incurred (Net)	2		
2. Commission	3		
3. Operating Expenses related to Insurance business	4		
Total (B)			
Operating profit/loss from Fire/Marine/Misc. Business C = (A – B)			
Appropriations			
• Transfer to Shareholders' Account			
• Transfer to Catastrophe Reserve			
• Transfer to other Reserves (to be specified)			
Total (C)			

Note to Form B—RA

(a) Premium income received from business concluded in and outside India shall be shown separately.

(b) Re-insurance premium Income whether on business ceded or accepted are to be brought into account for gross (before deduction of commission) under the Re-insurance premium.

(c) Claims incurred shall comprise claims paid, specific claim settlement costs wherever applicable and change in the outstanding provisions for claims at the year end.

(d) Interest, dividends and rentals to be stated as gross and TDS amount to be included under 'Advance Taxes Paid'.

(e) Income from rent shall not include any notional rent.

Profit and Loss Account for the Year Ended 31st March . . .

Particulars	*Sche.*	*Curnt.*	*Prv.*
1. OPERATING PROFITS/LOSS			
(a) Fire Insurance			
(b) Marine Insurance			
(c) Miscellaneous Insurance			
2. INCOME FROM INVESTMENTS			
(a) Interest, Dividends and Rents—Gross			
(b) Profit on Sale of Investments			
3. OTHER INCOME (To be specified)			
TOTAL (A)			
4. PROVISIONS (Other than taxation)			
(a) For diminution in value of investment			
(b) For doubtful debts			
(c) Others (to be specified)			
5. OTHER EXPENSES			
(a) Expenses other than those related to Ins. Business			
(b) Bad Debts written off			
(c) Others (To be specified)			
TOTAL (B)			
Profit Before Tax			
Provisions for Taxation			
APPROPRIATIONS			
(a) Interim Dividend Paid during the year			
(b) Proposed Final Dividend			
(c) Dividend distribution tax			
(d) Transfer to any Reserve or Other Account			
Balance of profit/loss brought forward from last year			
Balance carried forward to Balance Sheet			

Note to B—PL

(a) Items of expenses and income in excess of one per cent of total premium (less re-insurance) or Rs. 5,00,000 whichever is higher shall be shown separately.

(b) Fees/expenses connected with claims shall be included in claims.

(c) Foreign exchange gains/losses shall be shown under head 'Others'.

(d) Interest, Dividends and rental receivable in connection with an investment shall be shown as gross amount, TDS being included under 'Advance tax and tax deducted at source'.

(e) Income from rent shall include only realized rent not notional rent.

Balance Sheet as at 31st March . . .

Particulars	*Schedule*	*Curnt. Yr./Rs. '000)*	*Prv. Yr./Rs. '000)*
Sources of Funds			
Shareholders' Fund			
Share Capital	5		
Reserves and Surplus	6		
Credit/Debit-Fair Value Change A/c			
Sub-Total			
Borrowings	7		
Policyholders' Fund			
Credit/Debit-Fair value Change A/c			
Policy liabilities			
Insurance Reserves			
Provisions for Linked Liabilities			
Sub-Total			
Funds for Future Appropriations			
Total			
Application of Funds			
Investments			
Shareholders	8		
Policyholders	8A		
Assets Held to Coverlinked Liabilities	8B		
Loans	9		
Fixed Assets	10		
Current Assets			
Cash and Bank Balances	11		
Advance and other Assets	12		
Sub-Total (A)			
Current Liabilities			
Provisions	13		
Sub-Total (B)			
Net Current Assets (C) = (A – B)			
Misc. Expenditure (To the extent not written off)	15		
Debit Balance in Profit & Loss Account (Shareholders' Account)			
Total			

Contingent Liabilities:

Particulars	Current Yr.	Prev. Yr.

1. Partly Paid-up Investments.
2. Claims other than against policies not acknowledged as debts.
3. Underwriting Commitments in respect of shares and securities.
4. Guarantees given by or on behalf of the company.
5. Statutory demands/liabilities in dispute, not provided for.
6. Re-insurance Obligations not provided for.
7. Others.

   Total

Cash Flow Statement (Example on Direct Method) for the Period from 01-04-. . . to 31-3-. . .

	Bank Account	*Bank Account*
Balance at the beginning		
Bank Balance		
Cash and Cheque on Hand		
Money in Transit		
Short-term FD		
Petty Cash		
Imprests—Policy Stamps		
Imprests—Postage Stamps		
Imprests—Revenue Stamps		
Imprests—Agency Stamps		
Operating Activities		
Inflow		
Premium Collections		
Advance Premium		
Cash Deposit		
Bank Guarantee		
Environment Fund		
Bhavishya Arogya		
Service Tax		
Transfer and Duplicate Fees		
Coinsurance Premium		
Administrative Expenses		
Coinsurance Commission		
Recover of Expenses		
Claims and Salvage		
Commission		
Brokerage		
Other Collections		

Other Items Including contra items
Premium Accepted Treaty
Premium Accepted Facultative
Claims Ceded Treaty
Claims Ceded Facultative
Commission Ceded Treaty
Commission Ceded Facultative
Service Charges Ceded Facultative
Foreign Group
Other Group

A. Total Inflow

Outflow

Premium Refunds
Excess Refunds
Cash Deposit Refund
Refund of Prem. Adv.
Environment Fund Refund
Bhavishya Arogya Refund
Service Tax Refund
Bank Charges Others
Refund Cheques
Coinsurance Prem.
Coinsurance Claims
Administrative Exp.
Coinsurance Comm.
Exp. & Adv. for Exp.
Claims & Inter Office Claims
Commission
Brokerage
Others
Other items (incld. Contra items)
Adjst. of increase/decrease in
Stamp/petty cash imprests
Premium Ceded Treaty
Premium Ceded Facultative
Claims Accepted Treaty
Claims Accepted Facultative
Comm. Accepted Treaty
Comm. Accepted Facultative
Service Charges Ceded Treaty
Service Charges Ceded Facultative
Foreign Group

Other Group		
B. Total Outflow		
1. Net Funds Generated/ Utilised from Operations (A – B)		
Investing Activities		
Inflows		
Sale of Assets		
Sale/Redemption of Investment		
Recovery of Loans Employees		
Recovery of Loans Others		
Investment Income Interest on FD		
Investment Income		
Others		
C. Total Inflow		
Outflows		
Purchase of Assets incld. Advances for such purchases		
Purchase of investments incld. Adv. for such purchases		
Disbursement of Loans Employees		
Disbursement of Loans to Others		
Investment Expenses		
Others		
D. Total Outflow		
2. Net Funds Generated/ Utilised from Investing Activities (C – D)		
Financing Activities		
Inflows		
Outflows		
3. Net Funds Generated from Financing Activities		
Balances at the End		
Bank Balance		
Cash and Cheques on Hand		
Money in Transit		
Short-term FD		
Petty Cash		
Imprests—Policy Stamps		
Imprests—Postage Stamps		
Imprests—Revenue Stamps		
Imprests—Agency Licence Stamps		

Note: Above Cash Flow Statement has been prepared on direct method as example. This formatted is not prescribed by IRDA while other financial statements have been formatted by IRDA.

SEGMENT REPORTING FOR THE FINANCIAL YEARS

Net Balances of all Revenue Items comprising Net Premium (after adjustment of Reserves for Un-expired Risks), Profit on realization of Investments, Interest, Rent, Dividend, Incurred Claims, Commission, Operating Expenses, Other Foreign Taxes, Revenue A/c results are to be segmented and apportioned in a columnar form among the following departments of insurance business as per IRDA regulations:

1. Fire, 2. Marine Cargo, 3. Marine Hull, 4. Motor, 5. Workmens' Compensation, 6. Personal Accident, 7. Aviation, 8. Engineering, 9. Health Insurance, 10. Public/Product Liability, 11. Others (for current year as well as previous year).

N.B. Above Segment Reporting is little bit different from general guidance of AS-17 as it is specified by IRDA, but the purpose and performance are same as intended in AS.

PART II
DISCLOSURES FORMING PART OF FINANCIAL STATEMENTS

A. Disclosures by Way of Notes to Balance Sheet:

1. Contingent Liabilities as stated earlier.
2. Encumbrances to assets of the company in and outside India.
3. Commitments made and outstanding for loans, investments and fixed assets.
4. Claims less re-insurance paid to claimants in/outside India.
5. Actuarial assumption of claim liabilities in the case of claim payment period exceeding 4 years.
6. Ageing of Outstanding Claims.
7. Premium less re-insurance written from business in/outside India.
8. Extent of Premium Income recognized – Risk-wise, Sector-wise and Jurisdiction-wise.
9. Value of Contracts in relation to investments for:
   (a) Purchases where deliveries are pending.
   (b) Sales where payments are pending.

10. Basis of allocation of operating expenses to various classes of business.
11. Historical cost of those investments valued on fair value basis.
12. Computation of Managerial Remuneration.
13. Basis of amortization of debt securities.
14. (a) Unrealized gains/losses arising out of changes in the fair value of listed equity and derivative instruments taken into equity under the head "Fair Value Change Account".
    (b) Credit Balance in "Fair Value Change Account".
15. Fair Value of Investment Property and the basis thereof.
16. Claim settled and remaining unpaid for more than 6 months on the Balance Sheet date.

B. Accounting Policies and Accounting Standard Followed:

1. All significant accounting policies in terms of the Accounting Standards issued by the ICAI and in terms of Accounting Principles stated in Part I earlier—followed by the insurer shall be stated in the manner required by ASI issued by ICAI.
2. Any departure from accounting policies as stated above shall be disclosed with reasons.

C. The following information shall also be disclosed:

1. Segregation performing and non-performing investments for the purpose of income recognition as per direction, if any, issued by the Authority.
2. Investments, if made, in accordance with any statutory requirements should be disclosed separately together with its amount, nature, security and any special rights.
3. Percentage of business sector-wise.
4. A summary of Financial Statements for last five years in the manner as may be prescribed by the Authority.
5. Accounting Ratios as may be prescribed by Authority.
6. Basis of allocation of Interest, Dividends and Rent between Revenue Accounts and Profit and Loss Account.

Note 1: The schedules as specified by IRDA for respective financial statements could not be explained due to want of space, which may be explained afterwards if required.

References

The Gazette of India, Extraordinary, Part III, Section 4, Notification dt. 30.3.02.
The ICAI Publication of Accounting Standards.

28

Insurance—A Booming Professional Opportunity

N.D. GUPTA

INTRODUCTION

Somebody named "Murphy" has once stated something called "law" which dictates that if something wrong can happen, it will.

The probability of something happening which is not going to have favourable effect on its environment can be termed as risk. More the probability higher the risk. Since the risk itself depends upon the happening of a future event, you cannot assure yourself that risk can be eliminated in entirety. That is why to reduce the impact of that unfavourable event, every enterprise tries to manage the risk so that its impact may be minimised in case of happening of that event.

Risk Management today has become a very complex and demanding profession. Risk managers have greater responsibilities than ever before. Increasingly they are being asked to manage both risks and opportunities with an eye on improving shareholder value.

Risk is a burden not only to the individual but to the society as well. There exist several techniques for meeting the problem of risk, of which insurance is the most practical method for handling major risks.

The Commission on Insurance Terminology of the American Risk and Insurance Association has defined insurance as follows:

"Insurance is the pooling of fortuitous losses by transfer of such risks to insurers, who agree to indemnify insured for such losses, to provide other pecuniary benefits on their occurrence, or to render services connected with the risk."

Insurance is based on the principle of risk pooling. It is the transfer of financial responsibility for the risk at the point of occurrence, and conventionally involves the insurer in a commitment to pay. Provided the terms and conditions of the policy are met, payment of the premium secures a source of funds in the event of loss. The insured is thus exchanging the uncertain cost of losses for the certain and known cost of the premium. The cost arising from pure losses during the period of cover are then fixed for the insured. The stabilisation of loss costs means that earnings are less susceptible to the effects of pure loss than when these are retained.

Insurance however does not always fully compensate the insured for losses suffered. This may be the result of limitation of the liability accepted by the insurer, poor management of instance by the insured leading to gaps in cover or uninsurable losses.

HISTORY OF INSURANCE

The roots of insurance might be traced to Babylonia, where traders were encouraged to assume the risks of the caravan trade through loans that were repaid (with interest) only after the goods had arrived safely – a practice resembling bottomry and given legal force in the Code of Hammurabi (c. 2100 B.C.).

With the growth of towns and trade in Europe, the medieval guilds undertook to protect their members from loss by fire and shipwreck, and to provide decent burial and support in sickness and poverty. By the middle of the 14th century, as evidenced by the earliest known insurance contract (Genoa, 1347), marine insurance was practically universal among the maritime nations of Europe. In London, Lloyd's Coffee House (1688) was a place where merchants, shipowners, and underwriters met to transact business. By the end of the 18th Century, Lloyd's had progressed into one of the first modern insurance companies. In 1693, the astronomer Edmond Halley constructed the first mortality table, based on the statistical laws of mortality and compound interest. The table corrected in the year 1756 by Joseph Dodson, made it possible to scale the premium rate to age; previously the rate had been the same for all ages.

Insurance developed rapidly with the growth of British commerce in the 17th and 18th Century. Prior to the formation of corporations devoted solely to the business of writing insurance, policies were signed by a number of individuals, each of whom wrote his name and the amount of risk he was assuming underneath the insurance proposal, hence the term underwriter. The first stock companies to engage in insurance were chartered in England in 1720, and in 1735, the first insurance company in the American colonies was founded at Charleston, S.C. Fire insurance corporations were formed in New York City (1787) and in Philadelphia (1794). The Presbyterian Synod of Philadelphia sponsored (1759) the first life insurance corporation in America, for the benefit of Presbyterian ministers and their dependents. After 1840, with the decline of religious prejudice against the practice, life insurance entered a boom period. In the 1830s the practice of classifying risks began.

The New York fire of 1835 called attention to the need for adequate reserves to meet unexpectedly large losses; Massachusetts was the first state to require companies by law (1837) to maintain such reserves. The great Chicago fire (1871) emphasized the costly nature of fires in structurally dense modern cities. Re-insurance, whereby losses are distributed among many companies, was devised to meet such situations and is now common in other lines of insurance. The Workmen's Compensation Act of 1897 in Britain required employers to insure their employees against industrial accidents. Public liability insurance, fostered by legislation, made its appearance in the 1880s; it attained major importance with the advent of the automobile.

The business of life insurance in India in its existing form started in the year 1818 with the establishment of the Oriental Life Insurance Company in Calcutta.

HISTORY OF INSURANCE IN INDIA

1818 Europeans started the Oriental Life Insurance Co. in Calcutta.

1870 The first Indian Insurance Company – Bombay Mutual Life Insurance.

1870 The British Government enacted The Insurance Act.

1912 First Indian Insurance Act was passed with an enactment again in 1938.

Some of the important milestones in the life insurance business in India are:

1912 The Indian Life Assurance Companies Act enacted as the first statute to regulate the life insurance business.

1928 The Indian Insurance Companies Act enacted to enable the government to collect statistical information about both life and non-life insurance businesses.

1938 Earlier legislation consolidated and amended to by the Insurance Act with the objective of protecting the interests of the insuring public.

1956 245 Indian and foreign insurers and provident societies taken over by the central government and nationalised. LIC formed by an Act of Parliament, viz. LIC Act, 1956, with a capital contribution of Rs. 5 crore from the Government of India.

The General insurance business in India, on the other hand, can trace its roots to the Triton Insurance Company Ltd., the first general insurance company established in the year 1850 in Calcutta by the British.

1907 The Indian Mercantile Insurance Ltd. set-up, the first company to transact all classes of general insurance business.

1957 General Insurance Council, a wing of the Insurance Association of India, frames a code of conduct for ensuring fair conduct and sound business practices.

1968 The Insurance Act amended to regulate investments and set minimum solvency margins and the Tariff Advisory Committee set-up.

1972 The General Insurance Business (Nationalisation) Act, 1972 nationalised the general insurance business in India with effect from 1st January, 1973.

107 insurers amalgamated and grouped into four companies, viz., the National Insurance Company Ltd., the New India Assurance Company Ltd., the Oriental Insurance Company Ltd. and the United India Insurance Company Ltd. GIC incorporated as a company.

EVOLUTION OF PRESENT INDIAN INSURANCE INDUSTRY

In April 1993, Government set-up a high power committee headed by Mr. R.N. Malhotra to suggest reforms in the insurance sector and make it more efficient and competitive. The committee recommended the establishment of a strong and effective insurance regulatory authority in the form of a statutory autonomous board on the lines of SEBI.

In December 1999, the insurance sector was thrown open to private sector, followed by the establishment of IRDA (Insurance Regulatory and Development Authority) in April 2000. Realising the vast potential in Indian market, companies all over the globe rushed to find a foothold in the lucrative Indian market. Evolution of technology and convergence of services witnessed the insurance products being offered by banks also.

The potential for growth of the Indian Insurance Industry can be gauged by the fact that the Indian Insurance market registered the highest growth in the Asian region even though India's share of global insurance premium is less than 0.5 per cent (1998) compared with the US—24.2 per cent and Japan—21 per cent. The private players are well aware that only 25 per cent of the insurable population have been extended cover which means that market penetration is low and the potential to exploit is high.

LIFE INSURANCE STATISTICS

Indian Population	1 Billion
GDP as in 2000	(Rs.) 20000 Billion
Gross Domestic Savings as per cent of GDP	23 per cent
Estimate of insurable population	(Rs.) 240 Million
Estimated market by 2005	(Rs.) 650 Million

Some of the other factors which make the Indian Insurance Industry highly lucrative are that the Insurance Permia per capita is very low (US $ 4) and there is presence of huge middle class of approx. 300 million. Also the lack of a comprehensive social security system/state benefits and welfare means that demand for pension products is high.

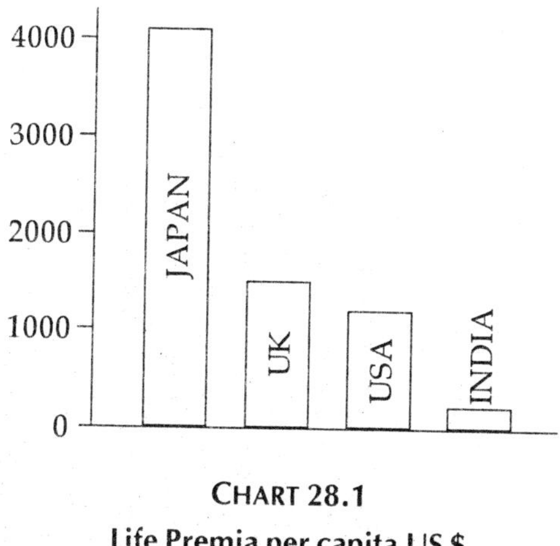

CHART 28.1
Life Premia per capita US $

The Confederation of Indian Industry (CII) has projected growth of life insurance premium from Rs. 350 billion at present to Rs. 1400 billion by 2009 and pension funds from Rs. 10 billion to Rs. 140 billion. The growth in non-life premiums is expected to increase from Rs. 75 billion to Rs. 375 billion.

The Chart shown alongside shows that considerable scope exists to raise the per capita premium.

PROFESSIONAL OPPORTUNITIES IN INSURANCE

Insurance sector has a positive correlation with economic development in an economy. As an economy develops over the years, the insurance sector starts making inroads into the interiors of the economy. During the past several years, the sector of insurance has flourished so much that the insurance business is being considered to be one of the most rapidly developing areas in the financial sector. With this transition in the insurance sector, the horizons for the contribution by Chartered Accountants have broadened. There has emerged a king-size pool of opportunities that the Chartered Accountants can explore and apply their professional wisdom and experience to.

The opportunities available for Chartered Accountants in the Insurance Sector have been summarised in the following paragraphs.

Statutory Audit

Section 12 of the Insurance Act, 1938 provides that the financial statements of every insurer are required to be audited annually by an auditor unless they are subject to audit under the Indian Companies Act.

Among the public sector insurance companies, Section 25 of the Life Insurance Corporation Act, 1956, dealing with 'Audit' is specific about appointment of auditors by the Corporation with the previous approval of the Central Government. The General Insurance Business (Nationalisation) Act has no specific mention and hence Section 619 of the Companies Act, 1956 which prescribes appointment of statutory auditors by CAG becomes applicable.

In the current scenario, with the private insurance companies operating in the market, the appointment of statutory auditors has come within the ambit of the functions of IRDA. Accordingly the IRDA has compiled a panel of Chartered Accountants and has prescribed certain parameters for this purpose.

Internal Audit

Currently, the internal audits of public sector insurance companies are done in-house. Such audits are not done concurrently and hence are not effective. In the changing scenario, private sector insurance companies will be outsourcing these internal audit, requirements. Public sector companies also may follow suit to improve upon the quality of such audits.

Needless to mention that the members of the profession have engaged themselves in the internal audit for long. It has been an area in which Chartered Accountants possess an expertise and can apply it fruitfully.

Tax Audit

The insurance companies are liable to tax audit under section 44AB of the Income Tax Act, 1961. Chartered Accountants being experts in the areas of auditing and with an in-depth knowledge of the provisions of the Income Tax Act, 1961 have ample opportunities in this area.

Surveyor or Loss Assessor

The surveyor is a person whom the insurance company appoints to examine the claims put up by the insured, and to assess and adjust the actual loss suffered, in accordance with the terms and conditions of the policy held by the insured, and submit a report thereon for the consideration of the insurance company.

Section 64UM(2) of the Insurance Act provides that "No claim in respect of a loss which has occurred in India and requiring to be paid or settled in India equal to or exceeding twenty thousand rupees in value on any policy of insurance, arising or intimated to an insurer at any time after the expiry of a period of one year from the commencement of the Insurance (Amendment) Act, 1968, shall, unless otherwise directed by the Authority, be admitted for payment or settled by the insurer unless he has obtained a report, on the loss that has occurred, from a person who holds a licence issued under this section to act as a surveyor or loss assessor." Section 64UM(1) (D) of the Insurance Act, 1938, provides the qualifications which an individual should possess to act as a Surveyor or Loss Assessor. Clause (c) of the said Section includes a fellow or associate member of the Institute of Chartered Accountants of India under its purview. A person intending to act as a Surveyor or Loss Assessor has to apply to the Insurance Regulatory and Development Authority in the appropriate form and with the prescribed fee.

Chartered Accountants can act as qualified surveyors in ascertainment of loss in the following cases:

- Industrial all risk policy,
- Marine transit claims,
- Fire losses involving loss/damage to stocks of inventories,
- Loss of profit insurance claims, and
- Miscellaneous insurance.

Insurance Agent

An insurance agent is a person who takes up agency from the insurance company to sell its policies on a commission basis. He acts as an intermediary between the insurance company and the policyholder.

An insurance agent should be an excellent communicator and must possess a repository of knowledge about insurance policies to market existing policies to individuals, families, businesses, and corporates. They help policyholders choose appropriate policies suitable to their need and assist in the settlement of claims.

The Chartered Accountants can engage themselves in the process by entering into agreement with the insurance companies to function as the Direct Sellers of their products and charge commission in lieu of the services so rendered from them. The area promises attractive scope for the constituents of the profession.

Risk Management and Consultancy

Insurance has traditionally been perceived as the tool for managing risks. With the increasing complexities in business operations and financing structures, the resource exposure of enterprises has been heightened to a large extent.

Risk management thus emerges as a dynamic activity characterized by greater knowledge and technology application in product development and pricing in tandem with emerging requirements. Chartered Accountants can engage themselves in:

- Reserving and pricing studies,
- Full audits of the efficiency and adequacy of risk management programs,
- Risk Management/ Administration reviews,
- Insurance marketing assistance-renewals,
- Actuarial audits of self insured of captive retention, and
- Captive Insurance Company reviews.

The risk-evaluation, segment-wise or client-wise, often requires industry-specific knowledge. The Chartered Accountants possess the knowledge about the operations of the industries or the units with which they deal in their normal course of profession. If the insurers intend to avail out-sourced services for such risk perception and evaluation, the Chartered Accountants may render their services. Chartered Accountants can also take up assignments in managing the risks of their clientele by advising them the right risk management techniques as well as to give them consultancy in areas where they will be needing insurance and such related matters.

Designing of the Insurance Product

Operating department of an Insurance Company is involved in developing products to cover the stipulated risks on the basis of risks perceived. While designing an insurance product, an insurer decides its cost to be charged from the insured in the form of premium, reduction thereof in certain cases like not lodging any claim during the previous covered period(s), suggesting the implementation of risk-mitigating measures, etc.

The Chartered Accountants can play a valuable role in developing the features of an insurance product. They possess adequate knowledge of the financial and technical aspects pertaining to the industry and can apply their skills to yield well-tailored products incorporating the desired features. The Chartered Accountant firms can formulate a model insurance product grounded on the study of an industry and apprise the insurance companies about the development of the same to make them aware of the quality of services, which can be rendered by them to the insurers.

Management of Portfolio

The insurer possesses huge amount of funds, which need proper management. The management of the portfolio of an insurance company requires the identification of investment avenues, evaluation thereof and the selection of the most appropriate mix of alternatives where the funds of the company can be invested. The selection requires the knowledge of finance-related functions and techniques apart from in-depth knowledge of the patterns of requirement of funds in the company, as well as in the industry as a whole, and the regulations of the IRDA in this behalf.

The Chartered Accountants are well versed with the methods and techniques pertaining to the finance-related decision-making including the application of scientific and statistical techniques for the same. There is invariably a large scope for the utilisation of the services of Chartered Accountants in this field.

Insurance Litigation

The Chartered Accountants can render their professional expertise in the quantification of claims, both personal injury and business interruption claims. They may also render their services in determining the consideration of liability involving accountants' negligence and for other professional negligence cases. They may also provide their knowledge in rendering assistance of fidelity insurance disputes and insurance accounting disputes.

Forensic Auditing/Investigative Assignments

The insurance industry is susceptible for fraudulent/inflated claims. The examples of fraudulent claims include auto accidents faked or staged to claim benefits, phony burglaries, thefts, or acts of vandalism reported to insurers. To understand the enormity of these claims on the economy, we consider the following quote from the Fact Book 2001, Insurance Information Institute (New York, NY: Insurance Information Institute, 2001, p. 127) "The Coalition Against Insurance Fraud estimates that insurance fraud is the equivalent of a hidden tax of about $ 900 per family on the cost of goods and services in the United States."

Chartered Accountants with their inherent inquisitive abilities sharpened by their training can provide a lot of value addition to the claim settling techniques. The investigative skills aided by their probing minds and technical assistance can be effectively utilised by insurers by offering investigative assignments to the CAs.

Others

Insurance Brokers

Chartered Accountants can act as Direct, Re-insurance and Composite Insurance Brokers. Here the functions would involve:

- Maintaining proper records,
- Negotiating with insurers/re-insurers, and
- Rendering advice based on technical data of the coverage.

Third Party Administrator Services

Chartered Accountants can render their services in the following areas:

- Negotiation of rates between TPA and Hospitals/Medical Practitioners,

- Verification/audit of pending settlements, and
- Certification for submission of statements to Insurer, etc.

Audit of Claims

The Chartered Accountants can provide services in the following areas:

- A full review of existing arrangements,
- Detailed consultation,
- Recommendations on process improvement,
- Benchmarking reviews,
- Audit of outsource claims service providers,
- Negotiations with suppliers,
- Cost containment in relation to the overall claims, and
- Specialist risk management etc.

Initiatives of the Institute of Chartered Accountants of India

Our Institute has realised that the Insurance Industry is the most happening industry and has set-up an Insurance Committee to leverage the professional skills of Chartered Accountants. The Committee has specially designed a Post Qualification Course on Insurance and Risk Management, which was formally launched on the 19th of April, 2003, in Chennai. It is also proposed to introduce a modular training course for surveyors and loss assessors, exclusive to the members of our profession. The ICAI has initiated dialogues with Department of Banking and Insurance and IRDA for getting audits of risk management practices by insurance companies done by Chartered Accountants.

CONCLUSION

The insurance sector plays a very vital role in the process of economic development of any country. It acts as mobiliser of savings, as financial intermediary, as promoter of investment activities, as stabilizer of financial markets and as a risk manager. Insurance services lead to efficient and productive allocation of capital resources, facilitate growth of trade and commerce, substitute for governments social security programmes, and assist individuals and firms in efficient management of risks. Post 9/11 the CEO's of major companies world over have realised the need for adequate insurance in all perceptible areas affecting their firms. We may safely observe that the insurance market may tremendously improve as India represents huge untapped market. Globalization will certainly increase insurance penetration and all professionals should equip themselves to exploit the opportunities offered by this sector.

29

National Company Law Tribunal and Appellate Tribunal

GOPAL PD. DOKANIA

INTRODUCTION

Before the Companies (Second Amendment) Act, 2002, Corporates were required to apply to High Courts for proceedings such as merger/amalgamation, reduction of capital and winding up of companies. But the High Courts being over burdened with other matters, used to take very long time to dispose-off these matters, and as a result of which the society was not able to derive the intended benefits out of such decision. Even the Winding-up petitions before the various High Courts have been pending for a very long time. Similarly various matters before the Company Law Board (CLB), Board for Industrial and Financial Reconstruction (BIFR) and Appellate Authority for Industrial and Financial Reconstruction (AAIFR) have been pending for a very long period. The detailed data given in tabular form (Appendix A) will give an indication that many of the Companies which were referred to BIFR had their natural death for want of timely help and assistance from BIFR and as such, resulted into wastage of scarce national resources.

Therefore, it was desired that, in place of various bodies presently looking into different matters like merger/amalgamation, acquisition and reconstruction, revival and rehabilitation and winding up of Companies, a body should be constituted to handle all these matters and to dispose of all pending matters as well as fast disposal of new matters which might be referred to it in the future.

Hence the Government constituted a Committee under the Chairmanship of Justice V. Balakrishna Eradi, a retired Supreme Court Judge, to review the law relating to Insolvency and Winding-up of Companies and other laws like The Sick Industrial Companies (Special Provisions) Act, 1985 (SICA), etc. The Committee made various recommendations with the main objective of expediting the revival/rehabilitation of a sick Company and protection of workers' interest, which were incorporated in the Companies (Amendment) Bill, 2001. The said Bill was subsequently passed by both the Houses of the Parliament and finally got the assent of the President of India on 13th January, 2002 and became the Companies (Amendment) Act, 2002.

Consistent with the underlying objectives, as aforesaid, and in the backdrop of the experience of administration of SICA and winding-up process, the Companies (Second Amendment) Act, 2002 provides for setting up of the National Company Law Tribunal (NCLT) and on setting up of NCLT, all the matters relating to companies which were earlier handled by various High Courts, CLB, BIFR and AAIFR will now be handled by the NCLT. Pending matters with the High Courts and CLB will be transferred to NCLT. As the SICA has not yet been repealed, the sick Companies will continue to be under BIFR. Only sick ancillary undertakings will come under the jurisdiction of NCLT, as the newly inserted definition of Industrial Undertaking, seems to be faulty. Further, the definition of Industrial Undertaking is explicitly exempting the Small Scale Industries (SSI) from its ambit and therefore, SSI will remain out of the purview of the BIFR and the NCLT both.

CONSTITUTION OF NCLT

The Central Government shall constitute NCLT on the basis of recommendations of The Selection Committee, which will be consisting of the Chief Justice of India or his nominee as Chairman of the Committee and Secretaries of the Ministry of Finance and Company Affairs, Labour Law and Justice as members of the Committee. The NCLT will be headed by its President who has been a Judge of the High Court or is eligible to be appointed as a Judge of a High Court and such number of judicial and technical members but not exceeding 62.

THE QUALIFICATION FOR THE JUDICIAL MEMBER OF NCLT IS ONE WHO

- has held judicial office for at least 15 years in an Indian territory, or
- has 10 years experience of practising as an Advocate of The High Court or one who has held partly the judicial office and partly practised in High Court, then taking together both should be 15 years experience, or
- 15 years service with the Central/State Government on Group 'A' post [including at least 3 years of service as a member of The Indian Company Law Service (Legal Branch) in a senior administrative grade], and
- has held for at least fifteen years a Group 'A' post or an equivalent post under the Central Government (including at least 3 years of service as a member of the Indian Legal Service in grade I of that service).

THE QUALIFICATION FOR THE TECHNICAL MEMBER OF NCLT IS ONE WHO

- has held for at least 15 years Group 'A' post or an equivalent post under the Central/State Government [including 3 years service as a member of The Company Law Service (Accounts Branch) in a senior administrative grade], or
- is or has been a Joint Secretary to the Government of India which under the Central Staffing Scheme or held any other post under the Central/State Government carrying a scale of pay which is not less than that of a Joint Secretary to the Government of India, for at least 5 years and has adequate knowledge and experience in dealing with the problems relating to the Company Law, or
- is or has been for at least 15 years in practice as a Chartered Accountant/Cost Accountant/Company Secretary under the relevant Act, i.e. CA, ICWA and CS Act, or
- is a person of ability, integrity and standing having special knowledge of and professional experience of not less than 20 years in science, technology, economics, banking, industry, law, matters relating to industrial finance, industrial management, industrial reconstruction, administration, investment,

accountancy, marketing, or any other matter with the special knowledge or professional experience, which would be in the opinion of the Central Government useful to the Tribunal, or

- is or has been a Presiding Officer of a Labour Court, Tribunal or National Tribunal constituted under the Industrial Disputes Act, 1947, or
- is a person having a special knowledge of and experience of not less than 15 years in the matters relating to labour.

The qualification requirement for the Judicial Member focuses on their judicial capacity or as an Advocate of the High Court. One of the criteria namely 15 years of service with the Central/State Government on Group A post (with at least 3 years of service as a member of The Indian Company Law Service) does not appear to be appropriate. Putting at par such an experience with that of 15 years in a judicial capacity or 10 years as a practising High Court Advocate does not appear to be reasonable. Similarly, the eligibility criteria for a Technical Member includes within its realm in a residual category Central/State Government Official with a specified number of years of experience which justify inclusion of everybody and anybody in addition to the professional who deserves more to be a Technical Member.

The tenure of the President and of the Members of the Tribunal is 3 years, subject to reappointment, or removal, before the completion of the term. The retiring age of the President and members of the Tribunal is 67 years and 65 years respectively. By reading together, this should imply that those who have retired would only inspire for a position in the Tribunal. Any other person though otherwise, highly qualified, could not tie his career with a position that has a limited tenure of 3 years.

The President and any Judicial/Technical Member may resign from his Office by notice addressed to the Central Government and on submission of such resignation, the Central Government may allow the Applicant to do so, or he has to wait for a period of 3 months from the date of such notice, or the date of appointment of the successor, whichever is earlier. In case of any vacancy in the office of the NCLTs President it will be filled up by the senior most Member of the Tribunal The Central Government may in consultation, not with the approval, of the Chief Justice of India may remove the President or any member of the Tribunal but no such removal will be done without giving a reasonable opportunity of being heard. One peculiar criteria for not removing the President Member of the Tribunal is that, although one has been convicted of an offence by the Courts of Law but the Central Government finds that such offence does not involve moral turpitude.

The Tribunal will be functioning through its various Benches all over the country comprising of two-Members Bench of a Single-Member Bench as may be warranted and deemed fit by the President of the Tribunal. Such a set-up will enable constituting Benches on geographical or any other appropriate criteria which would expedite the disposal of the cases and at the same time make available the mechanism at the door step of the Companies reducing the cost and efforts involved. The Tribunal will rectify any mistake, within a period of 2 years, from the date of passing of the order and may review its own orders.

POWER TO SEEK ASSISTANCE OF CHIEF METROPOLITAN MAGISTRATE OR THE DISTRICT MAGISTRATE

The Tribunal may seek the help of the Chief Metropolitan Magistrate or the District Magistrate to take possession of any property, books of account or any other document of any sick industrial Company. The Chief Magistrate or the District Magistrate on taking the possession of such property, books of account or other documents, entrust them to the Tribunal or any operating agency duly appointed by the Tribunal. No act of the Chief Metropolitan Magistrate or the District Magistrate shall be called to question in any Court of Law.

NATIONAL COMPANY LAW APPELLATE TRIBUNAL

The Central Government shall by a Notification in the Official Gazette, constitute an Appellate Tribunal which will be called as The National Company Law Appellate Tribunal (NCLAT). The NCLAT will consist of a Chairperson and not more than two Members. The Chairperson shall be a person who has been a Judge of the Supreme Court or Chief Justice of a High Court.

A member of the NCLAT shall be a person of ability, integrity and standing having special knowledge of and professional experience of not less than 25 years in science, technology, economics, banking, industry, law, matters relating to labour, industrial finance, industrial management, industrial reconstruction, administration, investment, accountancy, marketing, or any other matter, the special knowledge of, or professional experience which, would be in the opinion of the Central Government useful to the Appellate Tribunal.

Interestingly, no specific qualification has been prescribed to become a Member of the Appellate Tribunal as in case of a Judicial as well as Technical Member of the NCLT although a Member of the NCLAT will be superior to the member of NCLT to review the orders passed by NCLT.

The procedure for resignation/ removal and filling up of a casual vacancy are more or less the same as in the case of the President/ Members of the NCLT.

Any person aggrieved by an order of the NCLT may prefer an appeal before the NCLAT within a period of 45 days from the date of receiving the order or within such extended time as may be allowed by the NCLAT.

APPEAL TO SUPREME COURT

Any person aggrieved by any decision or order of the Appellate Tribunal may file an Appeal to the Supreme Court within 60 days from the date of communication of the order of the Appellate Tribunal to him, only on any question of law arising out of such decision or order. The Supreme Court may grant an extension of time for filing an Appeal if it is satisfied that the Appellant was prevented by sufficient cause from filing the Appeal within the said period, but the extension period has been limited to a further period of 60 days.

SOME DISTINCTIVE FEATURES OF NCLT IN COMPARISON TO BIFR UNDER SICA

1. SICA provided for a moratorium period of five years for a newly set-up Company and as such no reference was required to be made to BIFR in the first five years of the registration of the Company. This moratorium has been withdrawn by the Amendment Act and now the Company may become sick even in the second or the third year of its registration itself.
2. Section 22(1) of SICA provided for suspension of all legal proceedings when a Company filed its case in BIFR and the

enquiry was pending or the scheme was under preparation or implementation with the BIFR or an appeal was pending with the AAIFR and as such the Sick Industrial Company was protected against any suit for recovery of money, execution against property of the Company or Winding-up proceedings but this provision of SICA was greatly misused by many of the Companies.

This protection has not been provided in The Companies (Second Amendment) Act, 2002 and therefore, pending the proceedings for Revival and Rehabilitation of a Sick Industrial Company before the NCLT the Creditors of the Sick Industrial Company may file a suit for recovery of debts. This provision will create hardship to Companies genuinely interested in revival, because, before the scheme is approved by the NCLT and grant is received if a creditor flies a suit against the Company and takes away the property/assets of the Company, what is left to be revived. However, Winding-up proceedings by any Creditor have been kept pending as the jurisdiction over the same is of that of the NCLT.

3. As per Section 32(1) of SICA the provisions of SICA prevailed over all other laws except FEMA and Urban Land Ceiling Act. In the absence of such overriding powers even if the scheme of revival is approved by the NCLT formalities and procedures as required under the Companies Act and other laws will be required to be completed.
4. The definition of an Industrial Company seems to be faulty because by strict interpretation it covers only an ancillary undertaking, which indeed cannot be the correct intention of the law-makers.
5. The Definition of a Sick Industrial Company has been tightened. A Company having accumulated losses in any financial year equal to 50 per cent or more of its average net worth during four years immediately preceding such financial year and which has failed to pay its creditors for 3 consecutive quarters will be a Sick Industrial Company. The Net worth has now been defined to mean the sum total of the paid-up capital and free reserves, after deducting the provisions or expenses as may be prescribed.

Previously, The Companies Act did not define the net worth and as per Section 3(1)(ga) of SICA which defined the net worth the words after deducting provisions and expenses as may be prescribed, were not there, and as such, companies were not deducting preliminary expenses or development expenses while calculating its net worth.

6. Now the burden of preparing the scheme for revival of a sick company is on the Company itself, which was earlier on the BIFR.
7. The Application for reference to the NCLT by a company should be accompanied with a Certificate by the Auditor from the approved panel as to the reasons for erosion in the net worth of the Company or default in repayment of debt by the company.
8. Previously no cess was payable. Now all companies have to pay cess @ 0.005 per cent to 0.1 per cent of its gross receipts or turnover to the Central Government towards the rehabilitation and revival fund to be used for rehabilitation and revival of sick companies. This may be termed as "robbing Paul to pay Peter".
9. The quantum of dues unpaid has been increased from Rs. 500 to Rs. 1 Lakh in the case of a winding-up.

CIRCUMSTANCES IN WHICH COMPANY MAY BE WOUND-UP BY TRIBUNAL

A company may be wound up by the Tribunal in the following cases:

1. if the Company has, by special resolution, resolved that the Company be wound-up by the Tribunal;
2. if default is made in delivering the Statutory Report to the Registrar or in holding the Statutory Meeting;
3. if the Company does not commence its business within a year from its incorporation, or suspends its business for a whole year;
4. if the number of members is reduced, in the case of a Public Company, below seven, and in the case of a Private Company, below two;
5. if the Company is unable to pay its debts. Presently, a creditor can file a Winding-up petition if the Company is indebted in a sum exceeding Rs. 500. This limit has been increased to Rs. 1 lakh.

6. if the Tribunal is of the opinion that it is just and equitable that the Company should be wound-up;
7. if the Company has made a default in filing with the Registrar its Balance Sheet and Profit and Loss Account or Annual Return for any five consecutive financial years;
8. if the Company has acted against the interests of the sovereignty and integrity of India, the security of the State, friendly relations with foreign States, public order, decency or mortality; and
9. if the Tribunal is of the opinion that the Company should be wound-up under the circumstances specified in section 424G.

The Tribunal shall make an order for winding-up of a Company under clause (h) on an application made by the Central Government or a State Government. Clauses 7, 8 and 9 have been added by the Companies (Second Amendment) Act, 2002.

SOME DISTINCTIVE FEATURES OF WINDING-UP PROCEDURES UNDER NCLT AND BY HIGH COURT

1. A new Section 647A has been inserted which provides that all proceedings pending before the commencement of the Companies (Second Amendment) Act, 2002, before any District Court or High Court, under this Act or the Insurance Act, 1938 or any other law other than the Banking Regulation Act, 1949 shall be transferred to the Tribunal from the date to be notified by the Central Government in the Official Gazette and the Tribunal may proceed with the matter either *de novo* or from the stage it was so transferred. Proviso to this Section provides that where the winding-up of a company has commenced subject to the supervision of the District Court or the High Court, before the commencement of the Companies (Second Amendment) Act, 2002, such winding-up shall continue to be under the supervision of the District Court or the High Court and the Company shall be wound-up in the same manner and in the same incidents as if the Companies (Second Amendment) Act, 2002, had not been passed.
2. Section 439A(2) ordains that the Statement of Affairs is required to be filed by the Company at the beginning itself,

when opposing any winding-up petition. The said statement is very elaborate and if any creditor files any frivolous petition the Company has to incur a lot of time, money and energy.

3. So far only the Government employees can be appointed as the Official Liquidator. Now professionals like CA, CS and ICWA or a body corporate of professionals can also be appointed.
4. Views of the creditors and workmen will be taken into consideration before appointing the Official Liquidator.
5. Practicing CA, CS and ICWA can appear before the Tribunal on behalf of the creditor, contributory or Official Liquidator.
6. New rules regarding winding-up are yet to be framed by the Central Government. Till then the existing rules framed by the Supreme Court will apply, subject to one exception, as to reference to the High Court will be construed as a reference to the NCLT.

In sum and substance the effectiveness of the NCLT and NCLAT would depend in the first place upon the intention of those in the Government who would be entrusted with the constitution of the Bench and appointment of its Members.

APPENDIX A

Board for Industrial and Financial Reconstruction Year-wise Performance

(As on 31.12.2002)

Year	*Total Cases Registered During the Year*	*Cases Disposed-off during the Year*				*Bench Month**
		Cases under Revival	*Cases Revived*	*Winding-up Recom-mended*	*Dis-missed*	
1	*2*	*3a*	*3b*	*3c*	*3d*	*4*
1987	311	0	0	0	8	24
1988	298	0	1	12	29	36
1989	202	0	1	31	78	42
1990	151	3	3	43	44	48
1991	155	4	4	47	28	42
1992	177	8	7	30	42	36
1993	152	9	13	64	59	36
1994	193	10	37	79	48	45
1995	115	22	25	64	29	48
1996	97	29	93	85	25	38
1997	233	13	36	85	22	25
1998	370	13	21	50	36	11
1999	413	13	10	65	70	27
2000	429	10	37	153	158	36
2001	463	50	47	133	118	36
2002	559	74	34	143	252	36
	3759	258	369	1084	1046	566

Notes: 1. Format earlier adopted was indicating cases revival in the year of registration. As a company normally takes 5/7 years to be revived, the new format indicates companies revived in the year in which Net Worth becomes positive and companies were discharged from the purview of SICA.

2. Figures of the Companies revived after the successful implementation of the scheme as well as those where Net Worth becomes positive at the inquiry stage itself have been clubbed together.

3. The above figures are according to the English Gregorian Calendar Year.

*Bench Months is arrived at on the basis of the number of Benches functioning in each year.

PART V

RISK IN BANKING SECTOR

30

Bank Credit—Risk and Profitability

S.B. SINGH

Growth and development of any business organisation depends on its risk management and profit generating capacity. Both risk and profit have time dimension, which leads us to future projections. These future projections have an element of uncertainty because future is not always perfectly predictable. This element of uncertainty gives rise to risk, which, in turn, affects profits. In this backdrop, an analysis has been attempted to know the significance of risk and profitability aspect of bank credit.

Going through the traces of history of the Indian banking industry, it can be observed that it has passed through the following era:

A. Security Oriented Era,
B. Spread Oriented Era, and
C. Risk and Profitability Oriented Era.

A. Security Oriented Era

This era can be classified as the "Pre Nationalisation Period" of the banking industry, which was marked by private ownership of banks. During this period, economic activities and banking products were simple in nature and instances of frauds and forgeries were more of stray instances. The movement of interest rate was mare or less predictable. The major risk was the one in the default of payment, which was, however, secured by primary and/or collateral security.

But, this period witnessed turbulent economic and political conditions emerging as a result of two world wars sandwiching the great depression in between, which led to failures and mergers in various industries including banking industry.

During the post-independence period, Government of India formulated various policies and guidelines for directing the funds of the banking industry towards the socially desirable sectors of the economy for the overall economic development of the country. The experience gained over the years revealed that the policies and guidelines of the government could neither bring the desired changes in the flow of credit nor in the attitude of the management of the private sector banks, as a result of which the decision to nationalise the banks was taken.

B. Spread Oriented Era

This era began with the nationalisation of the banks whereby social objectives of the government became the guiding force of bank policy. This started the regime of controlled and administered products and pricing in the banking industry. The interest rates were determined by the Reserve Bank of India in consultation with Government of India, with the banks not permitted any deviations. Furthermore, banks were forced to channel credits to different sectors of the economy known as priority sector, as per government directives. Thus, the following features dominated this era:

- Need-based finance became the guiding principle of credit decisions instead of security considerations with special emphasis on Priority Sector Credit,
- Credit Guarantee Corporations were set-up to compensate the banks in case of default by the borrowers covered under the priority sector, and
- For ensuring profitability of the banks, the mark-up pricing mechanism was adopted which provided sufficient spread by way of difference in the rate of interest on deposits and advances.

This phase brought banking to the doors of the common people through the branch network in every nook and corner of the country, making banking a habit of the masses of the country. This phase continued till the early nineties.

C. Risk and Profitability Oriented Era

The over-protective policies of the government contributed indirectly to a number of inefficiencies in the banking system, which required significant policy changes for putting the banking industry back on the track. This was in the form of change in the government policies leading to liberalisation and deregulation of the financial sector, for making it internationally competitive, efficient and vibrant. This earmarked the entry of foreign and private sector banks, deregulation of interest rates, introduction of capital adequacy, asset classification, income recognition and provisioning norms based on international standards. Banks were given a lot more freedom in product innovation and their pricing. The liberalisation of economy affected other sectors as well adding to the dynamism and volatility in the economy. These changes made the risk dimension more important in credit decisions, which manifested in the form of operation, credit and market risks. These risk dimensions of credit portfolio, increasing competitiveness and decreasing spreads put the profitability under stress in the initial years of the reforms, with a number of nationalized banks posting losses of a magnitude unheard of in the Indian banking history. Thus, the risk and profit dimensions of the banking sector came to the forefront during this era.

RISK DIMENSION

For ensuring long-term survival of banks, the risk dimension of banking has to be addressed appropriately. Mr. Walter Wriston, ex-CEO, CITI Bank has rightly observed that "... the business of banking is business of risk management, plain and simple, that is business of banking. ..." Banking risks can generally be grouped under three heads:

I. Operational Risk,
II. Credit Risk, and
III. Market Risk.

I. Operational Risk

Operational risks refer to the risks associated with in-house functioning of the organisation, emanating from its internal management and related to the normal activities of the organisation. These risks arise out of system future, human errors, frauds and inadequacies of the system commensurate with the complexities of the business, etc. These risks can be tackled in the following ways:

(i) Establishment of proper Management Information System (MIS).
(ii) Proper manpower planning and continuous upgradation of skills of the staff for handling the complexities of the business through training and in-house information systems.
(iii) Computerisation of banking operations to minimise the element of human errors and frauds.

All these strategies put together can take care of operational risks to a great extent.

II. Credit Risk

Credit risk is the greatest risk because it involves the default in payment of principal itself. Credit risk may arise due to internal functioning of the organisation in the form of inadequate and faulty appraisal mechanism leading to granting of credit to non-viable projects. Credit risk may also arise because of the industry-related changes and government policies rendering some activities unviable such as the introduction of artificial silk and synthetic yarn resulting in phasing out of the traditional silk growers and weavers. The most recent example is the import of battery cells and electronic toys from China. While being very cheap, they pose a major threat to the survival of a number of Indian manufacturers of these articles. With such developments taking place in the economy, some industries are bound to become unviable leading to credit risk for the banks concerned. These risks can be controlled by periodical analysis of the risks associated with the various sectors of the economy and initiation of appropriate steps to restrict the exposure to these sectors. In other words, frequent review of the exposure of a bank to various industries must be undertaken to facilitate early action in cases which are likely to turn weak owing to internal and external factors.

Credit risk may also emanate from wilful default by borrowers who prefer to default on bank dues despite their activities continuing to be profitable. The long drawn-out legal procedure is the main reason for such defaults. The establishment of Debt Recovery Tribunals (DRTs) has partially addressed this issue; however, more stringent policy measures to check such defaults would go a long way in arresting such tendencies. There is a famous saying about Indian industrialists, "There is sickness in Indian industries only, not in industrialists. They are getting richer and richer. This attitude needs to be dealt with firmly in the long-term interest of the economy and the banks."

III. Market Risks

Market risks arise out of the dynamics of market forces, which, for the banking industry, may include interest rate fluctuations, maturity mismatches, exchange rate fluctuations, market competition in terms of services and products, changing customer preferences and requirements resulting in product obsolescence, coupled with changes in national and international politico-economic scenario. These risks are like perils of the sea, which can be caused by any change taking place anywhere in the national and international arena. Market risks affect banks in two ways:

(i) The customer requirements are changing because of the changing economic scenario. Hence, banks have to fine-tune/modify their products to make them customer friendly, otherwise the obsolescence of products will divert the customers to other banks thereby reducing the business and profits of the bank concerned.

(ii) The macro-economic changes in the national and international politico-economic scenario affect the risk element in different business activities differently. This aspect has assumed greater importance in the modern age because of the increasing integration of global markets.

Since both these aspects are dynamic in nature, with change being the only constant factor, market risks need to be monitored on a continuous basis and appropriate strategies evolved to keep these risks within manageable limits. Again, given that one can manage only what one can measure, measurement of risks on a continuous basis deserves immediate attention.

PROFITABILITY DIMENSION

With the introduction of financial sector reforms in the early nineties in the form of capital adequacy, income recognition, assets classification and provisioning norms, profitability of the banking sector came under severe pressure with a large number of nationalised banks incurring heavy losses in the early years of reforms. The liberal entry of private and foreign banks reduced the business share of the existing banks and introduced more competitiveness in the market, thereby further reducing the profit margins. The profitability of banks has further been affected by the recessionary global trend to which India is no exception. All these factors put together have affected profitability. Banks' profitability has also been eroded in the following ways:

(i) Sluggish credit demand due to economic recession has resulted in reduced long-term credit disbursals by the bank, thereby reducing high-income assets with long-term maturity.
(ii) Sluggish credit growth has resulted in easy liquidity in the economy thereby reducing the rates of interest on short-term lending in the money market.
(iii) Easy liquidity in the economy with poor credit off-take has led to reduction in the rates of interest on advances which has made servicing of high cost deposits very difficult, with the rate of interest on deposits already having come down. However, declining rate of interest impacts the income on the credit immediately whereas it takes a long time to derive the benefits of reduced interest expenses because of the existing high cost deposits, thus putting further pressure on the spread.
(iv) Global recessionary conditions have resulted in reduced demand for products and services leading to falling prices and creating a vicious circle of low demand and income. This reduced income has affected the repayment capacity of the corporates leading to non-repayment of principal and interest thus adding to the non-performing assets of the banks leading to higher provisions and consequently, reducing the net profits of the bank.
(v) Big corporate clients are not willing to avail credit even at prime lending rate and are successfully negotiating with the banks for reduction in the rates of interest putting further pressures on the existing sources of revenue.
(vi) Economic recession coupled with increased competition

have forced banks to reduce their charges in the form of appraisal fee, commitment charges, documentation charges, up-front fee and remittance charges, etc. to attract new customers and have an edge over other banks. All these factors are putting the 'other income' of banks also under pressure.

STRATEGIES FOR RISK AND PROFITABILITY MANAGEMENT

In this liberalised economic scenario coupled with global economic recession, risks have increased in depth and dimension whereas profit margins have been squeezed in relative terms. The various strategies, which may be adopted for managing risk and profitability, are:

(i) For managing the operational risk of human errors, frauds and forgeries, massive computerisations is a must, coupled with effective MIS.

(ii) Skill upgradation of the staff should be the continuous endeavour of management for handling complexities of modern business.

(iii) Proper mechanism of checks and balances along with well-defined guidelines on delegation of power and accountability are absolutely essential for managing the business efficiently.

(iv) Credit appraisal mechanism should be strengthened for improving the quality of the credit so as to avoid the evils of over and under financing.

(v) Policy and industry related risks should be managed by in-house research and periodical review of the credit portfolio so as to reduce or limit the exposure to such sensitive sectors. Recourse to in-depth research by rating agencies could also substantially help in this area.

(vi) The risk of wilful default can be checked only to a certain extent by proper pre-sanction inspections and verification of antecedents, which are a must for maintaining the quality of credit. The real remedy to deal with wilful default lies in legislative reforms, some of which have taken place in the form of Securitisation and Reconstruction of Financial Assets and Enforcement of Security Interest Ordinance, 2002.

(vii) Market competition and dynamism have increased risks that should be managed in a pro-active manner, for which a regular risk analysis mechanism should be put in place in the banks, as part of their normal functioning.

(viii) Meaningful post-disbursal monitoring is a must for early identification of signs of incipient sickness so that remedial action can be taken in time.

(ix) An active treasury with proper delegation and well-defined stop-loss limits can also substantially contribute to the profitability of a bank.

CONCLUSION

Deposit and credit constitute the core of banking activity and substantial portion of expenditure and income are associated with them. So far as the deposit is concerned, it is a safe area of business, barring few stray instances of operational risks like human errors, frauds and forgeries. Credit is the real activity that should be managed to generate profitability by keeping the three cardinal principles of banking in mind "Liquidity, Solvency and Profitability". With the thinning of spreads in the deregulated and liberalised economy, risk management has become all the more crucial. So proper mechanism should be put in place for anticipation and identification of risks, together with a suitable mechanism to deal with such risks in an efficient and pro-active manner. Since every credit decision involves risk, one cannot avoid risk altogether. What is important hence is that risks have to be managed effectively. As the adage goes, "Risks and profits have a direct relationship though not proportionate"; hence, concept of "no risk, no gain" applies to banking industry as well. Furthermore, risks are co-related and exposure to one risk may lead to another, so the real mantra for prudent banking lies in successfully managing the risks in a pro-active and integrated manner. Profits, then, will follow automatically.

31

New Approaches to Fraud Deterrence

JOSEPH T. WELLS

Questioning is one of a Chartered Accountant's most valuable talents. The auditing profession's current approach to fraud detection – as well-intended as it is – won't have the impact the public expects until auditors and their firms are willing to invest in improved fraud deterrence and detection skills and resources.

We are still doing much of what we've always done. This article should provoke thought and debate among the professionals on how we might consider different approaches in the way audits are conducted in order to give the public what it really wants: business enterprises with integrity.

DE-PROGRAMMING OURSELVES

In considering new solutions, it becomes necessary for us to critically examine our current thinking. One question that is frequently asked is, "How do we prevent fraud?" The answer: "Internal control". But is it, really?

Under that theory, organisations with adequate controls won't experience fraud. But they do – time and time again. Part of the reason is that no controls exist that provide absolute assurance against fraud. Those who are sufficiently motivated to override or circumvent them usually can find a way. Don't get me wrong: Controls are a vital part of fraud deterrence. However, they need to be considered in a larger context.

Fraud is not an accounting problem; it is social phenomenon. If you strip economic crime of its multitudinous variations, there are three ways a victim can be unlawfully separated from money: by force, stealth or trickery. While the first two are on the wane, the third is not. And the reasons have little to do with accounting controls.

THE CONFUSING ISSUE OF CRIMINAL JUSTICE

But before you jump to the conclusion that increasing penalties for crime is the answer, consider another counter-intuitive fact: The United States has some of the harshest criminal penalties in the modern world—coupled with the highest crime rates. Criminologists almost universally understand why: Punishment-based deterrence simply doesn't work very well. Nearly 75 per cent of incarcerated inmates are re-arrested within three years of their being released, usually for more serious offences.

If you are thoroughly confused, you should be. That's because classic criminological theory says there are three related factors involved in deterrence: the certainty, swiftness and severity of punishment. Of those factors, the first is by far the most important—if punishment is certain and swift, it doesn't need to be severe. As a matter of fact, the longer the prison sentence, the more likely it is the miscreant will offend again.

Regrettably, under the present system of justice, there is nothing certain about being punished. Under Sarbanes-Oxley, the criminal penalties for mail fraud were quadrupled, from five to twenty years per offence in the United States. But there has been no corresponding quadrupling of funds for prosecutors, investigators and prisons.

If the penalties go up and the money devoted to enforcement stays the same, then the certainty of punishment actually goes down. Our prisons are bursting at the seams, so generally the prosecutors and judges across the globe make very unattractive choices of who is prosecuted and who isn't. When it comes to making those decisions, they almost invariably choose to jail those who commit violent crimes—not the people who rip us off.

So when a potential fraud offender thinks he or she can commit a crime and get away with it, that assessment usually is correct. What is society to do, then about the current wave of fraud that seems to have engulfed us?

First, we need to understand that our problems cannot be solved by government intervention. Prosecution of offenders, although necessary in a civilized society is akin—as we might say in Texas—to closing the barn door after the horses are gone.

Second, we must acknowledge the private sector has a responsibility to cure its own ills. Third, we must commit the resources necessary to find solutions that work.

UNDERSTANDING FRAUD PREVENTION

If you accept the postulate that fraud prevention and internal control are not exactly the same—and they aren't—then the accounting profession needs to learn more about preventing fraud. Unfortunately, this issue has not been studied in any great detail, especially when it comes to occupations fraud. We know some of the answers, but not nearly enough.

A DIFFERENT TACTIC

One of the most difficult issues facing the profession is that there are no auditing procedures that can provide absolute assurance in detecting all fraudulent financial reporting. As a result auditors have historically attempted to avoid, albeit unsuccessfully, the responsibility for fraud detection. In the current environment, the public holds expectations of auditors with respect to fraud that simply cannot be fulfilled. The auditing profession could be better served by adopting a more holistic approach to the deterrence of fraud. This concept, called the Model Organisation Fraud Deterrence Programme (the model), employs a "best practices" approach to fraud prevention. Using this model, researchers would identify the factors present in organisations—both accounting and otherwise—that affect occupations fraud (see '*Factors Affecting Occupations Fraud: A Partial List*'). They then would develop a model deterrence programme based on those factors. Thereafter, instead of opining that the entity is essentially free of material fraud, the auditor would disclose the client's degree of compliance to the model.

Although this is a shift in the way audits are conducted, it has three distinct advantages. First, it would move the emphasis away from an unwinnable strategy of detecting fraud to an achievable one—preventing it. Second, it would encourage entities to adopt prevention strategies. Third, it could solve the liability dilemma that plagues the auditing profession.

But we don't have to wait until we have all the answers in order to do something different. Two ideas are worth debating now: the use of anti-fraud specialists on public audits, and financial transparency for executives.

ANTI-FRAUD SPECIALISTS ON PUBLIC AUDITS

Accepting that fraud deterrence and accounting are related but distinctly different disciplines, the auditing profession could utilise the unique skills of anti-fraud specialists on public audits. Virtually all of the major accounting firms currently employ such specialists. However, they are now being used reactively instead of pro-actively.

Rather than using their talents exclusively to investigate allegations of fraud once they have been reported, anti-fraud specialists also should be involved during the audit itself to help identify key risk areas, which then can be furnished to the auditors for further consideration. Moreover, the mere presence of anti-fraud specialists during audits could have a significant impact on increasing the perception that illegal activities will be detected. This is similar to the strategy of reducing crime by putting more cops on the beat. Although punishment after the fact doesn't work very well, criminologists have thoroughly documented that more vigilance to stop crime before it happens is the most effective deterrent.

A number of years ago, I video-taped an interview with legendary fraudster Barry Minkow while he was serving an eight-year sentence in a federal prison in Colorado. (Minkow, a high school dropout with no accounting skills, fooled his independent auditors in a $ 100 million financial statement fraud scheme). When I asked him how auditors could cope with his ilk, Minkow said: "I'll tell you what I would do: I'd send in trained fraud examiners before the auditors arrive. And I'd tell the client, 'You know, I really want your business, but I want to make sure you're not committing fraud, too. So I'm sending the examiners in first. They're going to be looking at everything and asking the tough questions. 'Would that stop a lot of fraud, or what? It certainly would have stopped me".

FINANCIAL TRANSPARENCY WHERE IT COUNTS

From the study of a long list of financial statement frauds, beginning with the classic Equity Funding fraud in the 1970s and continuing through today's multi-billion dollar accounting scandals, a distinct pattern has emerged: Corporate managements—executives, insiders and board members—have lined their pockets at the expense of the shareholders. Their methods vary and are often cloaked behind complex transactions not readily apparent to the entity's auditors.

But the profits from these illegal schemes nearly always find their way into the personal finances and spending habits of those involved. In some situations the same firm that conducted the audit, albeit by different personnel, prepared the individual tax returns of insiders. That was the case in the $ 300 million ESM Government Securities fraud of the 1980s in the US. Although the financial fraud was concealed on the company's books, the insiders had declared huge illegal profits on their own persona tax returns. Had the auditors examined the tax returns of the principals (which they did not) the scheme would have been obvious.

This illustrates a fundamental tenet of fraud examination: Follow the money. There are but two ways that this can be accomplished. Illicit transaction can be traced from an insider to the organisation or *vice-versa*. The former approach is invariably easier than finding funds from the company to the insider, which often are disguised in a variety of ways.

Corporate insiders have a fiduciary duty to act in the best interests of the shareholders. A part of this duty should include their financial transparency. Auditors could be given access to any financial information that bears on this issue. That would include, but not be limited to. Personal tax returns and detailed banking records. By having such access, two important objectives could be accomplished. First, it would make it more difficult for insiders to conceal ill-gotten gain. Second, financial transparency could be a significant and powerful deterrent.

The ideas contained here are not the complete solution. Even if all of them would be adopted in some form, we still would have to recognise that there is no mechanism that could prevent all financial statement fraud. Still, traditional accounting approaches have failed so far to solve these difficult problems. But if we do what we have always done, we'll get what we have always gotten.

32

Forex Market Intervention, Sterilisation and Market Stabilisation Fund

KANCHANA KHANNA

SURGE IN CAPITAL FLOW

India has witnessed a surge in capital inflow since November 2000 when collections amounting to $ 5.520 billion were made under the India Millennium Deposit Scheme for the overseas investors. The net capital inflows has increased from US $ 10 billion during 2000-01 to US $ 12.1 billion in 2002-03. The recent surge in capital flows in India is mainly in the form of non-debt creating investments.

At the same time, the current account deficit declined significantly and turned into a surplus 2001-02 and 2002-03. Foreign exchange reserves have also increased accordingly from US $ 42.3 billion in end-March 2001 to $ 54.1 billion by end-March 2002, $ 74.8 March 2003 and presently about $ 110 billion and that too after prepayment of external debt of $ 2.8 billion to World Bank and Asian Development Bank.

MANAGEMENT OF INTERNATIONAL RESERVE

Reserve management is a process that ensures that adequate official foreign assets are readily available to and controlled by the authorities for meeting a defined range of objectives for a country. As a custodian, the central bank's main objectives are to ensure liquidity, safety and yield on deployment of reserves. Reserve management is a part of exchange rate management.

Policy objectives in regard to forex reserves in India in broader terms are:

(a) to ensure a reasonable level of confidence in the international financial and trading communities about the capacity of the country to honour its obligations,
(b) enhancing capacity to intervene in forex markets, and
(c) limiting external vulnerability.

PROBLEM OF ABSORPTION

Capital inflows are generally welcome in a developing economy. They ease external constraints and help to achieve higher investment and growth. However, sudden and large inflows may have undesirable effects. Major impact could be:

(i) Excessive money supply and consequent pressure on prices,
(ii) Impact on current account balance, and
(iii) Appreciation of nominal and real exchange rates.

Consequences of the increase in foreign exchange would depend on the manner in which the increased supply of forex is used/disposed-off. Theoretically, there are two possibilities:

(i) Central bank (RBI) absorbs the forex by purchasing it and thereby releases the local currency in the market. This will restrain the appreciation of the domestic currency and exert downward pressure on interest rates.

    Further impact would depend to the extent of response of domestic productive activity: If the domestic productive activity gears up then the increased money supply will be absorbed without inflationary pressures in the economy; otherwise inflationary pressures will work in the economy.
(ii) Central bank does not purchase increased supplies of forex. The floating stock of forex increases in the local market is to be purchased by the local players, thereby leading to depreciation of foreign currency (appreciation of the domestic currency).

In reality the response of the central bank may lie between the two extremes. It may absorb a greater part of the forex inflows and may sterilise the increased local currency by Open Market Operations and other measures. The central bank cannot ignore the implications of forex inflows for the conduct of domestic monetary policy and exchange rate management.

IMPACT OF FOREX INFLOWS IN INDIA

The capital inflows in India of such magnitude have created problem of absorption and sterilisation of dollars. It has also affected the money and the bond market.

Appreciation of Rupee

The year 2002 witnessed a trend reversal for the Rupee from depreciation in the previous years to an appreciation. After touching the lowest level at 49.06 by mid-May and remaining depressed around that level through the first half of June 2002, the Rupee started gaining against the dollar throughout 2003. The appreciation has also continued in 2004 so far with Rupee reaching 4-year high with an exchange value of below 44 against the dollar. The appreciation of the Rupee could have been more but for the frequent market intervention by the RBI.

Build-up of Foreign Assets

Net Foreign Assets (NFA) of the RBI increased from Rs. 6,068 crore at end-March 1990 to Rs. 3,58,244 crore at end-March 2003 and over Rs. 4,82,000 crores at present. The share of NFA in reserve money has increased from 7.8 per cent to over 120 per cent during this period.

Easing of Monetary Policy and Forex Policy

In view of the resultant increase in liquidity, the Reserve Bank of India could afford to ease monetary conditions by cut in Bank rate and CRR. Moreover, relaxations were made in foreign trade and other current/capital account transactions.

LIBERALISATION OF FOREX TRANSACTIONS

A number of steps have been taken to manage the excess supply in the foreign exchange market including prepayment of external debt. Some of the measures are:

- Liberalisation of current as well as some of the capital account transactions.
- Minimum maturity prescriptions and Interest rate ceilings on non-resident rupee deposits.
- Expansion of the automatic route abroad.
- Flexibility to corporates to prepay their external commercial borrowings, and
- Flexibility to exporters to hold up to 100 per cent of their proceeds in foreign currency accounts.

Despite various measures by RBI, the overall balance of payments surplus has continued to increase.

FOREX MARKET INTERVENTION

Central bank either buys or sell foreign currency from/to the market so as to establish an equilibrium between temporary mismatches in demand and supply of foreign currency.

The dual objectives of RBI intervention in the foreign exchange markets are:

- To signal the appropriate level for the parity and reduce volatility in the markets, and
- To influence the level of liquidity in the system.

Intervention in forex market would affect money supply. Purchases by the central bank from the market would have expansionary impact and sales of foreign currency would have a squeezing impact on money supply (with consequent implications for price and financial stability). Therefore, the central bank would have to take neutralisation measures in accordance with its policy stance.

In India, '*the concomitant excess supply in foreign exchange market has been absorbed by the Reserve Bank in line with its stance on exchange management and with a view to building-up foreign exchange reserves.* (Report on Currency and Finance, 2002-03). RBI had been a net purchaser of dollar during the last two years—$ 13983 million in the year 2002 and $ 26412 million during 2003.

STERILISATION

To sterilise the increase in money supply, the central bank will mop up the excess supply of money through other measures such as increase in CRR or sale of government bonds/securities. Thus, sterilisation follows forex market intervention. According to the *Report of the RBI Working Group on Instruments of Sterilisation* 'sterilisation keeps base money and money supply unchanged, thereby avoiding the undesirable expansionary effects of capital inflows. Further, forex market intervention accompanied by sterilisation allows the monetary authority to build international reserves that will help to withstand future shocks, and provide comfort and confidence to market participants. On the other hand, prolonged sterilisation may not be possible without upward pressure on interest rates, which could itself attract further forex inflows, thereby neutralising the impact of sterilisation'.

The **sterilisation process** involves: (a) decision of the monetary authority to intervene by substituting foreign currency with domestic currency in case of excess capital inflows, and (b) decision to intervene further in the bond or money market to substitute domestic currency so released out of the intervention in forex market with bonds or other eligible paper.

(a) *RBI purchases dollars → Increase in Rupee liquidity.*
(b) *RBI sells securities/bonds in the market/OMO Sales → Decrease in Rupee liquidity.*

The *sterilised intervention* often involves a trade-off between low return assets and high return assets as far as the central bank is concerned. Earning from the deployment of foreign exchange is lower than the interest loss on account of open market sale of government securities essentially due to interest rate differentials.

COMBINED IMPACT OF FOREX INTERVENTION AND STERILISATION

RBI has adopted a policy of "**managed float**". However, RBI is hard pressed in *'balancing the Trinity of interest rate, exchange rate and inflation'*. According to economic theory, the trinity of stable (low) interest rate, a stable exchange rate and a stable (low) inflation rate is not achievable.

So far RBI has been trying to restrict the appreciating trend of the Rupee *vis-a-vis* the US dollar and at the same time maintaining low inflation and interest rates. However, Rupee is rising and Forward premiums have come down substantially.

Increase in Money Supply and Liquidity

Burgeoning forex inflow is translated into higher money supply in the system. The fact that RBI has been a net buyer of dollars implies that the banking system has received Rupee liquidity. During April 3-6 February 2004, the increase in net foreign exchange assets accounted for 56 per cent of the total increase in money supply (M3).

Increased OMOs and Fall in Yield of Government Securities

In the absence of a strong credit demand there is surplus liquidity in the System which is causing downward pressure on interest rates and thus causing the yield on Rupee securities to fall. Further, call money rate has also been continuously falling.

RBI has been resorting to OMO sales of Rupee securities to mop up the excess liquidity. The OMO sales have been significant, Rs. 52,716 crore during 2002-03. During fiscal year 2003-04, till 20 February 2004, sale of securities under OMO were Rs. 41,780 crore. At the current level of money multiplier of 4.8, total impact on money supply works out to Rs. 2,00,000 crore. Impact of OMO sales is reflected in a higher commercial bank credit to government which has increased substantially. However, such large OMO sales has reduced the stock of government securities available with the Reserve Bank from Rs. 1,46,534 crore at end-March 2001 to less than Rs. 24000 crore by March 2004.

In addition to OMO, RBI has been resorting to Repo auctions to suck the liquidity for a shorter period. Other measures being used are: building up of government balances with the Reserve Bank, particularly through increased issuances of 91-day Treasury Bills and limited forex swaps.

NEED FOR NEW INSTRUMENTS OF STERILISATION OF CAPITAL INFLOWS

The Report of the RBI Working Group on Instruments of Sterilisation has observed that "it is not desirable to use the LAF as an instrument of sterilisation on an enduring basis; however, for limited periods, it can be used in a flexible manner along with other instruments". Further, in view of the finite stock of government securities available with the Reserve Bank for sterilisation, particularly, as the option of issuing central bank securities is neither permissible under the Act nor desirable, the Group recommended setting up a Market Stabilisation Fund (MSF) to be created in the Public Account of the Central Government for issue of Market Stabilisation Bills/Bonds (MSBs) for mopping up enduring surplus liquidity from the system.

MARKET STABILISATION FUND

Monetary Stabilisation Bonds (MSBs) is one of the tools for liquidity absorption. It is meant for structural adjustment of liquidity rather than day-to-day management of liquidity.

Pursuant to the recommendations of the RBI's Report of the Working Group of RBI on Instruments of Sterilisation and Report of the Internal Group on Liquidity Adjustment Facility (LAF), submitted in December 2003, the government has set-up a Market Stabilisation Fund (MSF) in the public account which could issue Market Stabilisation Bills/Bonds (MSBs). Main features of the Scheme, effective from April 2004, are as under:

- The bills/bonds to be issued under MSS would have all the attributes of the existing Treasury Bills and dated securities. It would be eligible for SLR, repo and Liquidity Adjustment Facility.
- The Reserve Bank will decide and notify the amount, tenure and timing of issuance of such treasury bills and dated securities. For the present, the maximum total outstanding obligations of the Government by way of bills/securities thus issued under the MSS from time to time is Rs. 60,000 crore.
- The bills and securities will be issued by way of auctions to be conducted by the Reserve Bank. The RBI would issue a press release to indicate the purpose (market stabilisation and sterilisation) of issue of such securities.
- The bills and securities issued for the purpose of MSS would be matched by an equivalent cash balance held by the Government with the Reserve Bank. The amount would be

held in a separate Market Stabilisation Scheme account. It will be available only for redemption/buyback of T-bills/ securities issued under the MSS. The cost (interest payments) would be shown separately in the Budget.

RBI has indicated that MSS is essentially to differentiate the liquidity absorption of a more enduring nature by way of sterilisation from the day-to-day normal liquidity management operations. The total absorption of liquidity from the system by the Reserve Bank will continue to be in line with the monetary policy stance from time to time and accordingly, the liquidity absorption will get apportioned among the Instruments of LAF, MSS and normal open market operations (OMOs).

The impact of MSBs on various segments of the economy will be as under:

Forex Market

The availability of MSBs will curb short-term volatility in the forex market. Given the fact that USD is still the principal currency, this will ensure that the short-term Re-dollar parity will be controlled. However, the long-term exchange rate will be influenced by economic fundamentals. As the capital inflows are expected to continue, the Rupee is likely to continue its uptrend in the medium-term.

Liquidity

The scheme is expected to fine-tune the structural balance in the money market and enable the RBI to maintain a grip over short-term interest rate. The money from MSBs will be completely sterilised as it will be parked with the- RBI and not available to government for expenditure. The cap on the outstanding bills/securities under MSS (Rs. 60000 crore) is not expected to impact liquidity given the existing scenario of surplus liquidity as reflected by the daily repo auctions attracting about Rs. 40,000 crore.

Costs

To the extent MSBs are used to sterilise the forex inflows 'sterilisation' costs will be quantified and borne by the government. The payments for interest will not be made from the MSS Account. It will be reflected in the budgetary position. This would add transparency to the cost of sterilisation.

Fiscal Deficit

Government will place Cash equivalent to bills/securities issued with the RBI. Thus, here would be no burden of repayment. However, the government will have to bear the interest payments on these bonds. Assuming a coupon rate of 5 per cent this will entail an interest cost of about Rs. 3000 crores. Thus, while repayment is fiscal neutral, the interest outflows will effect the fiscal deficit.

Bond Market

It will increase the holdings of the government paper with RBI to intervene in the market. As a result the size of the government bond market will increase. This is likely to increase the trading of bonds in the secondary market.

33

Minimum Capital Requirement—Pillar 1

P.V. SUBBA RAO

In this paper on minimum capital requirements—Pillar 1, we shall be covering the following areas:

1. The rationale for the revision of the 1988 accord,
2. An overview of the new accord—the pillars, the objectives, etc.,
3. The standardised approach for assessing capital requirements under Pillar 1, and
4. Issues in implementation of the standardised approach.

We would discuss the standardised approach for assessing capital requirements. The paper, however would not go into details of the IRB Approach and capital for operational risk.

1. THE RATIONALE FOR THE REVISION OF THE 1988 ACCORD

If we look back the 1988 Capital accord was one of the most path-breaking supervisory developments of its time. It was the first attempt to prescribe rule-based capital adequacy norms for all the international banks to ensure a level playing field for them. The 1988 accord has been adopted by more than 100 countries and has become a universal benchmark for assessing the adequacy of regulatory capital. There are, however, certain shortcomings in the 1988 accord, some of which are mentioned below:

- The 1988 framework does not make adequate differentiation of credit risk, as there are only four risk weights of 0 per cent, 20 per cent, 50 per cent and 100 per cent. The risk weight applied for AAA company is the same as that for a corner shop although the risk profiles of the two vary substantially. A junior and senior bond held in banking book would receive the same risk weights, although the risk is different as the recovery rates of the two instruments would be different.
- There is no recognition of term structure of credit risk. Capital charges are set at the same level irrespective of the maturity structure of a credit exposure. This approach ignores the fact that there is greater risk of default for the longer exposure.
- The current rules do not recognise the portfolio diversification effects for credit risk while at the same time recognising it for market risk under the internal VAR models of banks. As a result, the current rules can represent a false picture of the riskiness of an institution. For example, two institutions with the same capital adequacy under the present rules can have very different levels of credit risk due to diversification effects that are overlooked under current rules.
- The current rules distort the credit risk pricing, as margins do not reflect the differences between different degrees of default risk, different seniority of instruments or differences in the term of an exposure.
- The current accord does not give due recognition to the credit risk mitigation techniques and does not recognise the role collateral can play in reducing the losses on account of credit risk.
- The 1988 accord does not levy any capital charge for operational risk although that is a very important source of risk and can be more devastating than credit risk.

The process of revision of 1988 accord began in June 1999 when the Basel Committee on Banking Supervision issued a consultative paper in titled "A new capital adequacy framework" on which comments from the industry were invited by 31 March, 2000. Based on the feed-back, the Basel Committee published the second consultative package on January 16, 2001 and invited comments on it by the end of May 2001. It has received more than 250 responses from banks, central banks and supervisors and the academia. The process of consultation is going on and in the third quarter of 2002 the Quantitative impact study (QIS 3) would be launched and based on the feedback the final new accord would be finalized by 2003 with the implementation to be carried out by 2006. (It was earlier proposed to implement the accord by 2004 and then 2005).

2. AN OVERVIEW OF THE NEW ACCORD—THE OBJECTIVES, THE PILLARS, SCOPE OF APPLICATION, ETC.

The Basel Committee points out that there are following differences between the existing and the new accord.

The Existing Accord	*The Proposed New Accord*
Focus on a single risk measure	More emphasis on banks' own internal methodologies, supervisory review, and market discipline
One size fits all	Flexibility, menu of approaches, incentives for better risk management
Broad brush structure	More risk sensitivity

The Objectives of the New Accord

The Basel Committee has the following objectives in developing a comprehensive approach to capital adequacy and in its efforts to refine it:

1. The Accord should continue to promote safety and soundness in the financial system and, as such, the new framework should at least maintain the current overall level of capital in the system;
2. The Accord should continue to enhance competitive equality;
3. The Accord should constitute a more comprehensive approach to addressing risks;
4. The Accord should contain approaches to capital adequacy that are appropriately sensitive to the degree of risk involved in a bank's positions and activities; and
5. The Accord should focus on internationally active banks, although its underlying principles should be suitable for application to banks of varying levels of complexity and sophistication.

The Basel Committee emphasises that safety and soundness objectives cannot be achieved solely through minimum capital requirements and therefore the accord comprises of three mutually reinforcing pillars—

First Pillar - minimum capital requirements,
Second Pillar - supervisory review, and
Third Pillar - market discipline.

The three pillars contribute to a higher level of safety and soundness in the financial system. The three pillars should be seen as a package. The revised Accord can be considered as fully implemented only if all three pillars are in place. Minimum (or partial) implementation of one or two of the pillars will not deliver an adequate level of soundness. Supervisors must at a minimum implement Pillar 1. However, if certain countries are not able to implement all three pillars fully, supervisors should consider more intensive use of the other pillars. For example, the supervisory review process could be used to encourage improvement in transparency in instances where supervisors do not have authority to require certain disclosures.

There are now several approaches to measure credit risk, market risk and operational risk as contrasted with the 1988 accord where there was only one approach for measuring credit risk. These approaches are:

1. *Menu of Approaches to Measure Credit Risk*

(i) Standardised Approach (based on ratings awarded by qualifying external ratings agencies).
(ii) Foundation Internal Rating Based Approach (based on qualifying Internal ratings systems of banks), and
(iii) Advanced internal Rating Based Approach (based on qualifying internal ratings systems).

2. *Menu of Approaches to Measure Market Risk (Unchanged)*

(i) Standardised Approach.
(ii) Internal Models Approach.

3. *Menu of Approaches to Measure Operational Risk*

(i) Basic Indicator Approach,

(ii) Standardised Approach, and

(iii) Internal Measurement Approach—now termed as Advanced Measurement Approach.

The new framework *maintains both the current definition of capital and the minimum requirement of 8 per cent of capital to risk-weighted assets.* The accord modifies the measurement of risks, i.e., the calculation of the denominator of the capital ratio. The *credit risk* measurement methods are more elaborate than those in the current accord. The new framework proposes for the first time a measure for *operational risk,* while the *marker risk* measure remains unchanged. The capital adequacy ratio will be computed as under:

$$\frac{\text{TOTAL CAPITAL (unchanged)}}{\text{Credit Risk + Market Risk + Operational Risk}} = 8 \text{ per cent}$$

As in the 1988 accord the risk-weighted assets account for the credit risk. For market risk and operational risk, the capital charge is calculated using one of the above methods from the menu of approaches available. This capital charge for market risk and operational risk is multiplied by 12.5 (8 per cent capital adequacy ratio = 8/100 = 1/12.5) in the denominator to bring it at par with the risk-weighted assets for credit risk. This can be expressed as under:

$$\frac{\text{TOTAL CAPITAL comprising of Tier 1 + Tier 2 + Tier 3}}{\text{RWA for Credit Risk + 12.5 (capital charge for Market and Operational Risk)}} = 8\%$$

The new accord attempts to capture risks within the entire banking group. The accord has, therefore, been extended to include, on a fully consolidated basis, holding companies that are parents of groups that are predominantly banking groups. The Basel Committee observes that application of capital adequacy requirements on a consolidated basis only at the highest level within a banking group is not sufficient to ensure that capital is immediately available to absorb losses and, thus, protect depositors at each bank within a banking group. Accordingly, the accord will also apply on a sub-consolidated basis to all internationally active banks at every tier below the top banking group level. The combination of the fully consolidated approach at the top level within banking groups and at lower levels on a sub-consolidated and/or stand-alone basis has been prescribed to preserve the integrity of capital and to eliminate double gearing in a banking group.

A bank's investments in insurance subsidiaries would be deducted for measurement of its regulatory capital. The reciprocal cross-holdings of bank capital artificially designed to inflate the capital position of banks will also be deducted for capital adequacy purposes. Significant minority and majority investments in commercial entities which exceed certain materiality levels will be deducted from bank's capital. National accounting and/or regulatory practices will determine materiality levels. The Basel Committee has suggested materiality levels of 15 per cent of the bank's capital for individual significant investments in commercial entities and 60 per cent of the bank's capital for the aggregate of such investments.

3. THE STANDARDISED APPROACH FOR CREDIT RISK

The standardised approach is conceptually the same as the 1988 accord, but is more risk sensitive. As in the 1988 accord, there are three exposure classes, viz., sovereigns, banks and corporates. Unlike in the 1988 accord, there will be no distinction on the sovereign risk weighting depending on whether or not the sovereign is a member of the Organisation for Economic Coordination and Development (OECD). Instead the risk weights for exposures will depend on external credit assessments. The treatment of off-balance sheet exposures will largely remain unchanged, with a few exceptions.

The standardised approach aligns regulatory capital requirements more closely with the key elements of banking risk by introducing a wider differentiation of risk weights and a wider recognition of credit risk mitigation techniques, while avoiding excessive complexity. Accordingly, the standardised approach should produce capital ratios more in line with the actual economic risks that banks are facing, compared to the present accord. This should improve the incentives for banks to enhance the risk measurement and management capabilities and should also reduce the incentives for regulatory capital arbitrage. It is intended that the application of standardised approach should neither produce a net increase nor a net decrease—on average—in minimum regulatory capital, after accounting for operational risk.

Under the standardised approach the risk weights are assigned based on the credit ratings accorded by External Credit Assessment Institutions (ECAIs) as shown in Table 33.1.

TABLE 33.1
Risk Weights for Different Credit Ratings

Exposures	*AAA to AA –*	*A + to A –*	*BBB + to BBB –*	*BB + to B –*	*Below B –*	*Unrated*
Sovereigns	0%	20%	50%	100%	150%	100%
Banks—option 1	20%	50%	100%	100%	150%	100%
Banks—Option 2	20%	50%	50%	100%	150%	50%
Short-term claims	20%	20%	50%	150%	20%	
Corporates	20%	50%	100% (BBB + to RB –)		150% (below BB –)	100%

Risk Weights for Sovereigns

As shown above the risk weights for sovereigns would range from 0 to 150 per cent depending on its credit rating. The above credit rating symbols are used by Standard and Poor's and in case of rating by other agencies such as Moody's and Fitch IBCA comparable ratings should be used. The ratings for claims on sovereigns should generally be in respect of the sovereign's long-term domestic rating for domestic currency obligations and foreign rating for foreign currency obligations. At national discretion, a lower risk weight may be applied to bank's exposures to the sovereign of incorporation denominated in domestic currency and funded in that currency.

Risk Weights for Banks

Under the option 1 for banks, all banks incorporated in a given country will be assigned a risk weight one category less favourable than that assigned to claims on the sovereign of incorporation. However, there will be a cap of a 100 per cent risk weight, except for banks incorporated in countries rated below B–, where the risk weight will be capped at 150 per cent. The option 2 for banks bases the risk weighting on the external credit assessment of the bank itself. Under this option a preferential risk weight that is one category more favourable than the risk weight shown in the Table 33.1 may be applied to claims with an original maturity of three months or less, subject to a floor of 20 per cent. This treatment will be available to both rated and unrated bank claims, but not to banks risk weighted at 150 per cent. Claims on securities firms may be treated as claims on banks provided they are subject to supervisory and regulatory arrangements comparable to those under the new capital adequacy framework (including, in particular, risk-based capital requirements). The inter bank short-term claims are defined as having an original maturity of three months or less and these receive preferential risk weights as shown in Table 33.1.

Risk Weights for Corporates

The risk weights of rated corporate claims, including claims on insurance companies is shown in the last row of Table 33.1. It seems anomalous that the unrated corporates are assigned 100 per cent risk weight as compared to 150 per cent risk weight for corporates rated BB- or below. This may provide an incentive to the corporates to remain unrated. The above risk weights are, however, based on recognition of the fact that the majority of corporates do not need to acquire a rating in order to fund their activities. The fact that a borrower is not rated does not, therefore, necessarily signal low credit quality. The Committee has also emphasised that it does not wish to cause an unwarranted increase in the cost of funding for small and medium-sized businesses, which in most countries are a primary source of job creation and of economic growth. Due to the above reasons a 100 per cent risk weight has been assigned to unrated corporates which is the same risk weight that such corporate exposures received under the 1988 accord.

It should, however, be recognized that the 100 per cent risk weight for unrated corporates is a floor. In countries where corporates have higher default rates, supervisory authorities should increase the standard risk weight for unrated claims where they judge that a higher risk weight is warranted by the overall default experience in their jurisdiction. As part of the supervisory review process, supervisors may also consider whether the credit quality of corporate claims held by individual banks should warrant a standard risk weight higher than 100 per cent.

On July 10, 2002 the Basel Committee announced that the risk weights for residential mortgages under Standardised Approach had been reduced from 50 per cent to 40 per cent. The risk weights for non-mortgage retail exposures [including small and medium enterprise (SME) exposures of less than Euro 1 million] were also reduced from 100 per cent to 75 per cent. The Basel Committee has, therefore, introduced two new risk weights of 40 per cent and 75 per cent under the standardised approach, which was not prescribed in the January 2001 paper.

The External Credit Assessments

As the risk weights under the standardised approach are based on external credit assessments, it is very important to ensure that the institutions carrying out rating are sound and reliable. The supervisors have to determine whether an External Credit Assessment Agency (ECAI) meets the prescribed eligibility criteria. The supervisory process for recognising ECAIs should be made public to avoid unnecessary barriers to entry. The reviewing and recognising of rating agencies in the credit risk area would be a challenge for the supervisors as this would be a totally new activity for them.

Six criteria for the recognition of an ECAI have been prescribed. These are:

(i) ***Objectivity:*** The credit assessment methodology must be rigorous, systematic, and subject to some form of validation based on historical experience. The assessments must be subject to ongoing review. Rigorous back testing of the assessment methodology for each market segment must have been established for at least one year and preferably for three years before the ECAI can be recognised by supervisors.

(ii) ***Independence:*** An ECAI should be independent. It should not be subject to political or economic pressures that may influence the rating.

(iii) ***International Access/Transparency:*** The individual assessments should be available to both domestic and foreign institutions with legitimate interests and at equivalent terms. The methodology used by the ECAI should be publicly available.

(iv) ***Disclosure:*** An ECAI should disclose qualitative and quantitative information. Qualitative disclosures relating to assessment methods enable users to understand the quantitative information in a better fashion. The disclosure should relate to information such as the definition of default, the time horizon, and the largest of the assessment, etc. Quantitative disclosures relate to aspects such as information on the actual default rates experienced in each assessment category and information on rating transitions, i.e. the likelihood of an AAA credit transiting to AA etc. over time, etc.

(v) *Resources:* An ECAI should have sufficient resources to carry out high quality credit assessments.

(vi) *Credibility:* The reliance on an ECAIs external credit assessments by independent parties (investors, insurers, trading partners) is evidence of the credibility of the assessments of an ECAI. The ECAI should have internal procedures to prevent the misuse of confidential information. It is not essential that the ECAI should have rated firms in more than one country for being eligible for recognition.

Supervisors will be responsible for slotting ECAI's assessments into the standardised risk weighting framework. They will have to decide as to which assessment category corresponds to which risk weight. The mapping process should be objective. It should result in a risk weight assignment consistent with that of the level of credit risk reflected in Table 33.1, and should cover the full spectrum of risk weights. The mapping process has to be publicly disclosed.

The banks will not be allowed to cherry-pick the assessments provided by different ECAIs. The banks have to disclose at least annually the credit assessment institutions that they use for the risk weighting of their assets by type of claims, the mapping process determined by supervisors, the *percentage of their risk weighted assets* that are based on the assessments of each eligible institution.

In case there are two assessments by ECAIs chosen by a bank corresponding to different risk weights, the higher risk weight will be applied. If there are multiple assessments (more than two), the two assessments corresponding to the lowest risk weights referred to, and if they are different, the higher risk weight should be used. If the best two assessments are the same, that assessment should be used to determine the risk weight.

Investment by a bank in a particular issue that has an issue-specific rating would be risk weighted on the basis of this rating. In case where the borrower has a specific rating for an issued debt but the bank's claim is not an investment in this particular debt—a high quality credit rating (resulting in a risk weight lower than 100 per cent) on that specific debt may only be applied to the bank's unrated claim if this claim ranks *pari passu* or senior to the claim with a rating in all respects. If not, the credit rating cannot be used and the unrated claim will receive 100 per cent risk weight for the unrated claims.

The issuer rating of a borrower typically applies to senior *unsecured claims* on that issuer. Consequently, only senior claims on that issuer will benefit from a high quality issuer rating. Other unrated claims of a highly rated issuer will be treated as unrated.

Short-term ratings can only be used when the claim is short-term and a long-term rating is not available. If there is a long-term issue of issuer rating, that rating should be used not only for long-term claims but also for short-term claims, regardless of the availability of a short-term assessment, provided that the short-term claim ranks *pari passu* (or better). If the two claims do not rank *pari passu*, then the short-term claim should be treated as unrated. In no event can a short-term rating be used to support a preferential risk weight for a long-term claim. The Basle Committee is, however, carrying out further work in this area.

As a general rule, if short-term claims receive a 150 per cent risk weight, an unrated unsecured long-term claim should also receive a 150 per cent risk weight, unless the bank uses recognised credit risk mitigation techniques on the long-term claim. As a general rule, banks should use solicited ratings from eligible ECAIs. The national supervisory authorities may, however, allow banks to use unsolicited ratings in the same way as solicited ratings. In case it is observed that ECAIs are using unsolicited ratings to put pressure on entities to obtain solicited ratings the supervisors may consider whether to continue recognising such ECAIs as eligible for capital adequacy purposes.

Credit Risk Mitigation

Credit risk mitigation relates to the reduction of credit risks by taking collateral, obtaining credit derivatives or guarantees, or taking an offsetting position subject to a netting agreement. The new accord allows a wider range of credit risk mitigants to be recognised for regulatory capital purposes as compared to the 1988 accord. Under the standardised approach there are two proposed treatments to collateralised transactions:

1. A comprehensive approach, and
2. A smile approach.

The comprehensive approach focuses on the cash value of the collateral taking into consideration its price volatility. The basic principle is to reduce the underlying risk exposure by (a cautious measure of) the value of collateral taken. Partial collateralisation will therefore be recognised. The risk mitigation impact of collateral is measured conservatively, taken into consideration potential changes in the market price of collateral. This approach will also be used in the foundation IRB approach.

The simple approach, developed for banks that engage only to a limited extent in collateralised transactions, maintains the substitution approach of the present accord, whereby the collateral issuer's risk weight is substituted for that of the underlying obligor. Partial collateralisation will also be recognised in the simple approach. Overall, the simple approach will generate higher capital requirements on collateralised transactions than those generated by the comprehensive approach. Furthermore, for collateral to be recognised in the simple approach, it must be pledged for the life of the exposure, i.e., there must be no maturity mismatch—and it must be marked to market with a minimum frequency of six months.

Banks will be permitted to use either the simple or comprehensive alternatives to collateralised transactions, provided they use the chosen alternative consistently for their entire portfolio.

The following collateral instruments are eligible for recognition in both the approaches:

- Cash on deposit with the lending bank;
- Securities rated BB- and above issued by sovereigns/PSEs treated as sovereigns by the national supervisor;
- Bank, securities firm and corporate securities rated BBB and above;
- Equities that are included in a main index; and
- Gold.

The January 2001 proposals introduced "w" factor that provided a floor pegged at 15 per cent to account for the residual risks, i.e., the collateralisation would not lead to 0 per cent capital requirements due to the "w" factor. In November 2001 the Basel Committee proposed that residual risks will be assessed through pillar two and the "w" factor will be eliminated from pillar one of the framework. There is also a possibility of greater recognition of physical collateral and receivables as compared to the January 2001 paper.

4. ISSUES IN IMPLEMENTATION OF THE STANDARDISED APPROACH

There are various important issues in the implementation of the standardised approach of the new accord. We reproduce below the comments made by the Reserve Bank of India on some of the issues relating to minimum capital requirements:

(i) The complexity and sophistication of the proposals restricts its universal application in emerging markets, where the banks continue to be the major segment in financial intermediation and would be facing considerable challenges in adopting all the proposals. The spirit of flexibility, universal applicability and discretion to national supervisors, consistent with the macro-economic conditions specific to emerging markets ought to be preserved while finalizing the New Accord.

(ii) The New Accord should initially be applied to all internationally active banks. Further, a simplified standardised approach may be evolved for other banks and the national supervisors should have discretion to implement the New Accord, in a phased manner.

(iii) To ensure uniform application across all jurisdictions, the Basel Committee should define what constitute internationally active and significant banks. In this regard, the Reserve Bank is of the view that all banks with cross-border business exceeding 15 per cent of their total business may be defined as internationally active banks. Significant banks may be defined as those banks with complex structures and whose market share in the total assets of the domestic banking system exceeds one per cent.

(iv) To moderate the cross-holdings of capital, Basel Committee may consider prescribing a material limit (10 per cent of total capital) up to which cross-holdings of capital and other regulatory investments could be permitted and any excess investments above the limit would be deducted from total capital.

(v) External Credit Assessment Institutions (ECAIs) should not be assigned the direct responsibility for risk assessment of banking book assets. However, such of the Export Credit Agencies (ECAs) that disclose publicly their risk scores, rating process and procedure and subscribe to the publicly disclosed OECD methodology and qualify for use by national supervisors may be used for assigning preferential risk weights.

(vi) Risk weighting of banks should be de-linked from that of the credit rating of sovereigns in which they are incorporated. Instead, preferential risk weights should be assigned on the basis of their underlying strength and creditworthiness.

(vii) On the lines of discretion provided in the case of claims on sovereigns, the national supervisors may be given discretion to assign lower risk weight (one category less favourable than the risk weight to claims on sovereign), subject to a floor of 20 per cent to claims on all banks, which are denominated in domestic currency and funded in that currency. Further, preferential risk weights should not be linked to the maturity of the claims.

(vii) The national supervisors may be given discretion to implement the New Accord, in a phased manner by banks, which are not internationally active and are engaged predominantly in traditional banking.

Many of the above concerns have also been raised by other developing country supervisors in their comments. The Basel Committee has now begun to recognise these issues, and for the first time, in its July 10, 2002 modifications hinted at an extended implementation schedule for such countries— *"the Committee realises that of the more than 100 countries which have implemented the 1988 Basel Accord, some have done so only fairly recently and may need more time beyond 2006 to implement the new framework. The Committee encourages countries to continue laying the groundwork necessary for the effective implementation of the new Accord."*

34

Statutory Audit of Bank Treasury

SHYAM RAMADHYANI

Audit of an Integrated treasury is a complex task requiring high level of skills, knowledge of market practices and the relevant regulatory environment. Treasury income constitutes a significant portion of a bank's income, many a time equal to the entire income received from advances and the extensive branch network of banks. This paper makes an attempt to highlight the products and market practices in vogue which an auditor of an integrated bank treasury operation will have to be aware of, the relevant regulatory standards, the valuation methods applicable, terminologies used that he has to be familiar with and then proceeds with broad guidelines for evaluation of internal controls (including those relating to information systems). A model audit program that can be tailor made to suit individual needs has also been attempted. The paper also deals with certain risk management practices currently in vogue.

Many banks have set-up integrated treasuries, encompassing both rupee and forex denominated transactions. An integrated approach to treasury management involves a common dealer or desk dealing in both domestic and forex financial markets. This enables the bank to optimize its funding and fund deployment and take advantage of arbitrage opportunities between these markets Treasury income constitutes a significant portion of a bank's income, many a time equal to the entire income received from advances and the extensive branch network of banks. Treasury operations are invariably of high value and due to the very nature of its operations, are susceptible to manipulation, fraud or error and consequently to the various types of risks envisaged by Auditing and Assurance Standards (AAS) 6.

KNOWLEDGE OF BUSINESS (AAS 20)

Knowledge of business of a bank treasury is usually low, even in an enlightened community like Chartered Accountants. Consequently, it is important to acquire a thorough knowledge of the products in vogue in the market, market practices, the permissible valuation methods, the regulatory standards prescribed by the Reserve Bank of India (RBI). Foreign Exchange Dealers' Association of India (FEDAI) and Fixed Income Money Market and Derivatives' Association (FIMMDA), the processes followed by the bank, internal controls exercised, information systems used, etc. An idea of the types of trades, settlements, instruments in vogue, certain operational issues relating thereto, principles of valuation, etc. are set out in the ensuing paragraphs for general understanding.

TYPES OF TRADES

Customer Trades

These are deals between the bank and its customers, predominantly in foreign exchange. The profit or loss to the bank is the spread between its inter-bank buying rate and the selling rate to the customer. For example, a customer may place an order to buy USD 100,000. The Bank buys @ Rs. 47.98 in the market and sells @ Rs. 48.00 to the customer, making a profit of Re. 0.02.

Proprietary Trades

These are trades by the bank for its own account. They could be in the domestic or overseas market. Buying G-Sec for trading portfolio, in the expectation that price will go up (i.e., interest rates will fall) is an example of a proprietary trade in the domestic market. Buying US dollars and selling Japanese Yen is a cross-currency trade to profit from US dollar appreciation. Proprietary trades are done in the inter-bank market.

TRADING SYSTEMS

Negotiated Dealing System (NDS)

NDS is an electronic platform for facilitating dealing in government securities and money market instruments. NDS will facilitate electronic submission of bids/application by members and provides a seamless interface to Securities Settlement System (SSS) of Public Debt Office, RBI. All outright and Repo transactions in treasury bills and dated securities are settled through NDS.

Electronic Trading System (ETS)

Bids, offers and quantities are displayed on a screen in descending/ascending order of price to buy/sell. The trader enters his order to buy/sell, quantity and price. If the order is within the live range of buy/sell prices and quantity, it will be executed instantaneously.

Over-the-Counter (OTC)

Deals are struck with counter parties on phone and the same is later confirmed in writing. Forex trading is not centralized on an exchange, as in the case of stocks and futures markets. The forex market is considered an over the counter (OTC) or inter-bank market, since transactions are conducted between two counter parties over the telephone or via an electronic network.

CHANNELS

Transactions could be directly with a counter party or through an intermediary, involving intermediation fees.

SETTLEMENT

Settlement of transactions lakes place by transfers of money between the two parties. The day on which these transfers are effected is called the settlement date.

- Takes place T+X days after trade. X could be 0 or more depending on market practice or regulatory requirements.

- **Negotiated Dealing System (NDS):** Already explained earlier.
- **Delivery *Vs.* Payment:** There is simultaneous exchange of payment and delivery of securities (physical or demat).
- **Electronic Settlement:** Foreign exchange deals are settled electronically with credits/debits to Nostro accounts and take place through SWIFT for transfer of funds.

TYPES OF TRANSACTIONS AND SETTLEMENT DATES (FOREX)

Depending on the time elapsed between the transaction and settlement dates, forex transactions can be categorized into:

Cash Contracts

Settlement date is the same day.

TOM Contracts

Settlement date is the next business day.

Spot Transactions

Settlement date is usually two business days ahead.

Forward Transactions

Settlement date to be fixed by the parties.

Swaps

Simultaneous sale and purchase or purchase and sale of two currencies in the spot and forward markets, i.e., the first leg is spot and the second leg is forward. The transaction may or may not be with the same counter party. Rationale may be arbitrage.

CASH-RESERVE RATIO AND STATUTORY LIQUID RATIO

SLR

Recognising the need to maintain the confidence of the public in the banking system, the Banking Regulation Act stipulates that every bank shall maintain in cash, gold or unencumbered approved securities, an amount which shall not, at the close of business on any business day, be less than 25 per cent of its 'Demand and Time Liabilities' in India as on the last Friday of the second preceding fortnight.

CRR

Cash reserve by way of balance in a current account with RBI or by way of net balance in current accounts a sum equivalent to 5 per cent of its 'Demand and Time Liabilities' in India as on the last Friday of the second preceding fortnight to be maintained by every bank.

CALL/NOTICE/TERM MONEY

Call money is overnight borrowing or lending in the inter-bank money market. Notice money is borrowing or lending in the reporting fortnight. Term money is borrowing or lending for maturities beyond the reporting fortnight. These are resorted to meet SLR and CRR requirements as well deployment of short-term funds.

Money market lending for more than 14 days are not classified under this head, but are classified as 'Deposits' or 'advances' depending on the nature of lending and the parties to whom the money has been lent.

Banks cannot pay any brokerage on call loans and deposits, except to the extent specified in paragraph 8(e) of the RBI's circular dated July 22, 1974.

INTEREST BEARING AND DISCOUNTED INSTRUMENTS

Government securities, which carry an obligation to pay interest at specific dates, are called interest-bearing securities. On the other hand, discounted instruments do not carry any interest but are purchased at a discount to the redemption value. Examples of discounted instruments are zero coupon bonds, certificate of deposits, treasury bills. Treasury bills may be for different tenors (91/181/361 days, etc.)

Repos

Repos involve borrowings from a counter party against pledge of securities to be repurchased at a predetermined date/ rate of interest. They are called reverse repos from the perspective of the lender.

Stock Lending and Borrowings

These involve lending of securities between two counter parties to be returned at a predetermined date/ rate of interest.

DERIVATIVES

Derivatives offer banks the opportunity to hedge financial risks. Its value is determined by the value of the underlying instrument to which it relates.

Different forms of derivative contracts, include:

Forward Contracts

It is an agreement between parties to buy/sell a specified quantity of an asset at a predetermined mutually agreed date/price/quantity.

Options

An option is a derivative transaction where the buyer has an option (and not an obligation) to buy/sell an underlying asset at a specified price on or before a specified future date, by paying a premium. Option may be plain vanilla or exotic (specifically structured) contracts.

Types of Options

An option contract, which can be exercised at any time before expiration date is called as an American Option. A contract, which can be exercised only on the expiration date, is called an European Option. European options are generally traded in India.

Call and Put Options

A call option gives the buyer of option the right (but not the obligation) to buy an underlying asset for a specified price whereas a *put option* gives the buyer of option the right (but not the obligation) to sell an underlying asset for a specified price.

The *specified price* is known as the *strike/exercise price* and the specified date is known as the *exercise/expiration date.*

Cap, Floor and Collar

Limit can be set on the strike price for an option contract. If an upper limit on the strike price is set, it is called a Cap. If a lower limit if fixed, it is called as the *Floor*. If a combination of both Cap and Floor is used, it is called a *Collar*. If the market price on the maturity date is higher than the cap, then cap will be the strike price. Similarly, if the market rate is lower than the floor price, then floor price will be the strike price. Consequently, in case of Collar, the strike price will be between the cap and floor price.

Futures

They are in the nature of forward contracts but are dealt with on stock exchanges.

SWAPS

A swap is a contract whereby parties agree to exchange obligations that each of them have under their respective underlying contracts.

- Major types of Swap,
- Interest Rate Swaps, and
- Currency swaps.

A standard *fixed-to-floating interest rate swap* is an agreement between the two parties in which each party contracts to make payments to the other on particular dates in the future till a specified termination date. The first party (*fixed ratepayer*) makes payments at a fixed rate of interest on a notional mutually agreed amount. The other party (*floating ratepayer*) makes payments, at a rate calculated with reference to a bench marked rate, say a six months LIBOR.

Currency swaps involve exchange of currencies at specified exchange rates.

There could be complex instruments involving a combination of the above two types of swaps.

Summary of Types of Instruments

Money market	Government securities (interest bearing and discounted instruments), call money deposits, Repos and liquidity adjustment facility from RBI, commercial paper, certificate of deposits.
Capital market	Shares, convertible debentures, warrants.
Debt	Corporate debt papers (fixed or floating rate of interest).
Derivatives	Futures, options, swaps.

SOME OPERATIONAL ASPECTS (FOREX)

Banks enter into correspondent relationship with banks in other countries and sign formal agreements (ISDA) with them. Such agreements would broadly specify the kind of transactions they can handle for the correspondent, the monetary ceiling on such transactions, procedures for settlement, the names and designation of authorized signatories and the terms of the relationship.

There is a reporting requirement of transactions at specified intervals, to the RBI by means of 'R' returns.

TERMS USED IN FOREX TRANSACTIONS

Forward Rate Pricing

The exchange rate at which a currency is bought or sold against another currency for delivery and settlement on a future date is called the forward rate. Theoretically, when there is an impediment to capital flows, the forward exchange rate between two currencies differs from the spot rate exactly to the extent of the interest differential between the two countries to which currencies relate.

In general, a currency will be at a premium against another currency in the forward market if the first country's interest rate is lower than that of the second. Conversely, the higher interest rate country's currency will be at a forward discount to that of the lower country's currency.

Nostro and Vostro Accounts

An account maintained by a bank with a foreign bank is called its NOSTRO Account (i.e., Our account with you). Conversely, if a foreign bank were to deal in a local currency of another country, it would maintain a VOSTRO Account (i.e., Your account with us).

Net Open Positions

Forex risk of a bank is basically determined by the net open positions, which refers to the uncovered currency positions or gaps taking into account all relevant assets and liabilities/unmatured spot and forward contracts in a particular currency.

Long or Short Positions

A net position with excess of assets and purchases over liabilities and sales is referred to as long positions. Converse of it, is short position.

Daylight/Overnight Limit

The maximum open position in each currency that may remain uncovered during the course of the day is referred to as day light limit. Net open position at the close of business on each working day is referred to as the Overnight limit.

CATEGORISATION/CLASSIFICATION OF INVESTMENTS

Investments of banks are categorised into SLR and non-SLR securities. SLR securities are securities notified by RBI for reckoning SLR to be maintained by banks.

The investment portfolio of banks should be classified under three categories viz. 'Held to Maturity (HTM)', 'Available for Sale (AFS)' and 'Held for Trading (HFT)'. However, in the balance sheet, the investments will continue to be disclosed as per the Banking Regulations Act.

Banks should decide the category of the investment at the time of acquisition and the decision should be recorded on the investment proposals.

HTM

Securities acquired by banks with an intention to hold them up to maturity will be classified under HTM. They should not exceed 25 per cent of the bank's total investments, subject to an one time exception permitted by circular dated September 2, 2004 referred to below.

Re-capitalization bonds received from Government of India, investment in subsidiaries, joint ventures, debentures/bonds, which are in the nature of advances, would also be classified under HTM category, but will not be counted for the purpose of ceiling specified for this category.

HFT

Securities acquired by the bank with an intention to trade by taking advantage of short-term price/interest rate movements will be classified under HFT category. These securities are to be sold within 90 days.

AFS

Securities not falling in the above two categories are classified under AFS category.

SHIFTING AMONG CATEGORIES

To be in accordance with the RBI guidelines, which are briefly as follows:

- Shifting to/from HTM will normally be allowed once at the beginning of the financial year.
- Shifting from AFS to HFT.
- Shifting from HFT to AFS is not generally allowed. Under exceptional circumstances like not being able to sell a security within 90 days due to tight liquidity or extreme volatility or market becoming unidirectional, transfers are permitted.
- All transfers to be approved by the Board of Directors/ ALCO/Investment Committee.
- Transfer from one category to another, under all circumstances, should be done at the acquisition cost/book value/market value on the date of transfer, whichever is least, and the depreciation, if any, on such transfer should be fully provided for.
- A one time shifting of SLR securities not exceeding 25 per cent of the bank's demand and time liabilities as of the last Friday of the second preceding fortnight to HTM category has been permitted by the RBI (refer circular dated September 2, 2004).

VALUATION OF INVESTMENTS

It may be noted that AS 13 (Accounting for Investments) do not apply to banks.

Cost of Investments

- Incidental charges (example brokerage) not to be included in the cost of AFS and HTM securities;
- Charging of broken period interest (interest accrued up to the time of acquisition on the securities purchased) to the Profit and Loss account; and
- Front-end fees, upfront fees and underwriting commission received in respect of securities devolved are to be generally reduced from the cost of the security.

Recognition of Income

- Debentures/bonds are subject to appropriate provisioning/ de-recognition of unrealized income, in line with the prudential norms.

Profit or Loss on Sale

- To be determined using weighted average or first in first out method.
- Profit on sale of investments in HTM category should be taken to the Profit and Loss Account and thereafter be appropriated to Capital Reserve. Loss on sale will be recognized in the Profit and Loss Account.
- Profit or Loss on sale of investments in HFT and AFS categories will be taken to the Profit and Loss Account.

Valuation

Mode of Valuation	*Security Type*
Acquisition cost, unless it is more than the face value, in which case premium is amortized over the period till maturity.	HTM
Valued at market price, scrip-wise as per quotations received from FIMMDA. Depreciation/appreciation to be aggregated classification-wise, in each category. Net depreciation to be provided and net appreciation to be ignored.	AFS/HFT

Mode of Determination of Market Value or Investments (AFS and HFT Categories)

Security Type	*Mode of Determination*
Central Govt. securities	At market price as per quotations put out by FIMMDA.
State Govt. securities and securities guaranteed by central/state Govt., PSU bonds not being advances.	On appropriate yield to maturity (VIM) as per FIMMDA guidelines.
Treasury bills, Commercial papers, Investments in sponsored Regional Rural banks	At carrying cost.
Equity shares	At market price, if quoted, otherwise at break-up value of the share as per latest balance sheet (not more than 1 year old), otherwise at Re. 1 per company.
Preference shares and Debentures (not in the nature of advances)	At market price, if quoted, or on appropriate YTM not exceeding redemption value as per FIMMDA guidelines.
Mutual funds	As per stock exchange quotation, if quoted, or at repurchase price/NAV.
Investments in subsidiaries, Joint ventures and other Investments	At carrying cost less diminution.
Profit evaluation of foreign currency transactions	At year end rates (Nostro mirror balances, monetary assets and liabilities, outstanding spot exchange contracts) and at forward rates for forward contracts classified tenor-wise—rates and methodology prescribed by FEDAI.
Hedge swaps	Interest rate swaps which hedges Interest bearing asset or liability to be accounted for on accrual basis except the swap designated with an asset or liability that is carried at market value or lower of cost or market value.
Trading swaps	Are marked to market.

INVESTMENT FLUCTUATION RESERVE (IFR)

With a view to building up of adequate reserves, banks have been advised by RBI to build up IFR of a minimum 5 per cent of the investment portfolio within a period of 5 years. IFR should be computed with reference to investments in HFT and AFS category. Banks should transfer maximum amount of the gains realized on sale of investment in securities to IFR.

Risk Management

As per the guidelines issued by RBI, banks encounter three types of major risks – Credit risk, market risk and the operational risk.

Credit Risk

Credit risk is the potential that bank borrowers/counter party fail to meet the obligations on agreed terms. Instruments and tools, through which credit risk management is carried are:

- *Exposure Ceiling:* Prudential limits linked to the capital funds of the counter party.
- *Risk Rating Model:* Set-up a comprehensive risk scoring system. Clearly define rating thresholds and review of the ratings periodically.
- *Portfolio Management:* Quantitative ceiling on aggregate exposure on specific rating categories, distribution in various industries, business group, etc.

Market Risk

Market risk may be defined as the possibility of loss to bank caused by changes in market variables. It is the risk that movements in equity markets, interest rate, currency exchange rates and commodity prices will adversely affect the bank. Market risk management provides a comprehensive and dynamic framework for measuring, monitoring and managing liquidity, interest rates, foreign exchange that needs to be closely integrated with the bank's strategy.

The bank may lay down various ceiling limits borrower-wise, industry-wise, security type-wise in its investment policy. Banks should continuously monitor compliance with the laid down norms.

Evaluation of Internal Control

The existence of an effective system of internal control is a *sine qua non* for efficient treasury operations. It is important that operations of a treasury are effectively segregated among:

- *Front Office*—Dealing in the financial markets for lending and borrowing funds, buying and selling in financial instruments.
- *Back Office*—Settlement, delivery, accounting, custody and reconciliation.
- *Mid Office*—Risk monitoring and control.

An audit of Treasury includes an audit of all the three offices. Amongst other things, the following procedures are to be clearly established:

- Functioning of treasury and the products dealt by it are clearly documented along with policies (risk/market/credit management, investment, asset liability management, etc.).
- Authority to put through deals are clearly specified.
- Dealings powers of each of the dealers are fixed and communicated to all.
- All financial decisions and deviations from laid down procedures are required to be reported to the next higher level for confirmation/information.
- Monitoring and controlling of all treasury activities are on a continuous/online basis.
- A system of concurrent audit is required to be in place in treasury in terms of RBI guidelines.

REGULATORY PROVISIONS

- Section 19 of the Banking Regulations Act, provides overall limits on the holding by banks in shares of companies. This extends to shares held as pledgee, mortgagee or as absolute owner.
- Circulars issued from time to time by RBI, FEDAI and FIMMDA. Frequent reference to their web sites would be helpful. References to some of the extant master. RBI circulars are furnished below:

- Prudential norms on income recognition, asset classification, provisioning and other related matters dated 2.12.2004.
- Prudential norms for classification; valuation and operation of investments portfolio by banks dated 17.7.2004.
- Maintenance of statutory reserves, Cash Reserve Ratio (CRR) and Statutory Liquid Ratio (SLR) dated 26.8.2004.
- Guidelines for issue of Certificate of deposits dated 12.7.2004.
- Risk management and inter-bank dealings dated 1.7.2004.
- Guidelines for issue of Commercial papers dated 1.7.2004.
- Call/Notice money market operations dated 3.7.2004.
- Export Credit in foreign currency dated 1.9.2004.

EDP Controls (AAS 29)

The extent of computerization is usually extensive in treasuries. This calls for strict controls in such an environment. Robust software covering the entire gamut of functionality required for smooth functioning of treasury, a proper security environment, controls in place to prevent unauthorized usage of files, systems, etc., start/end-of-the-day process, business, continuity and disaster recovery plans, well documented user and technical manuals, audit trails in the software, exception reports, complete trail of all back end changes made are a must. Computer assisted audit techniques and a tool, which could extract data to analyze them and identify exceptions, would be invaluable for review of EDP controls.

Audit Programme

A suggested audit program for carrying out the audit is enclosed. This is to be modified or adapted to individual needs.

LONG FORM AUDIT REPORT

These are to broadly cover:

- Existence of investment policy.
- Adherence to investment policy and compliance to RBI guidelines.

- System of purchase and sale of investments, delegation of powers, reporting systems, segregation of back office functions, etc.
- Controls over investments including periodic verification/ reconciliation of investments with book records.
- Valuation mode, changes in valuations compared with previous year, adequacy of provisions.
- System of monitoring income from investments.
- Software/system analysis.
- SLR/CRR requirement-system of ensuring compliance.
- Procedure for revaluation of Nostro accounts and outstanding foreign exchange contracts.
- Review of vostro accounts.
- Reconciliation of FCNR, EEFC and RFC balances and monitoring deployment of funds.
- Claims arising out of delayed settlement of inter-bank funds.
- Borrowings outside India.

Illustrative Checklist for Bank Treasury Audit

Particulars	*Comments*	*Working paper ref.*
(1)	*(2)*	*(3)*
Salient observations of concurrent auditors, RBI, etc. and follow-up action taken.		
Whether there is a functional separation of trading, settlement, monitoring, control and accounting?		
Whether there is a clear bifurcation of transactions of own investments and PMS?		
Whether the limit for the dealer and authority to put through transactions been followed?		
Whether deal slip is prepared for every transaction entered?		
Whether deal tickets are serially numbered and are there adequate controls with regard to unauthorized/ unaccounted use of the deal tickets?		
Do the deal ticket give all the required particulars including the time of the deal and are these checked/ signed/initiated by the dealer.		

(1)	*(2)*	*(3)*
Ensure that alterations and cancellations on deal slips are authorized by the Treasury Manager.		
Check that the copy sent to the counter-party is signed by the client and deals are supported by confirmation letter from the counter-party.		
Does the bank have an approved panel of brokers separately for capital market, wholesale debt segment, forex?		
Whether the deals done through brokers are only with the approved ones?		
To be ensured that the role of the broker is restricted to that of bringing the two parties to the deal together.		
Brokerage paid is at the approved rates and TDS is deducted as per the provisions of the income tax Act, 1961.		
It should be ensured that all transactions made by the bank are in accordance with the approved investment policy and RBI regulation.		
Credit Risk To check whether the counter-party exposure limits have been separately specified for all transactions? To check for the excesses and to be ensured that they are ratified by the competent authority.		
Market Risk Check for various limits specified in the investment policy. To check for the excesses and to be ensured that they are ratified by the competent authority.		
Interface between Front and Back Offices Is there seamless interface between the front and back offices? In other words, how are deals put through by front office captured by back office and what is the system of reconciliation between the two.		
Money Market Are there any over-sold positions?		
To be ensured that rates at which the deals are done are in line with market rates.		

(1)	(2)	(3)
Identify a sample of purchase and sale of investments and vouch them keeping in mind internal procedures, RBI regulations, authorization powers, counter-party contracts, price feeds, etc.		
Whether all investments are appropriate categorized at the time of acquisition?		
Whether capitalization of charges is as per the internal policy? To be ensured that charges to be considered as revenue is not capitalized.		
Whether any shifting of securities is effected? Are they in accordance with the RBI guidelines? Is the loss at the time of shifting provided?		
Ensure that broken period interest paid to seller is not capitalized as a part of cost but treated as expense.		
Check for the accuracy and completeness of: ● Book value of securities in the portfolio; ● Interest accrual in case of dated Govt./debt securities; ● Amortization in case of securities held under HTM category; ● Income/dividends accounted in case of discounted instruments/shares/mutual funds; ● Profit/loss calculation on sale; and ● Valuation as per norms.		
Ensure whether classification of NPA and their accounting is as per statutory regulations.		
Half yearly review of the investment portfolio undertaken by the bank and whether the same is forwarded to RBI within the stipulated time?		
Examination of Reconciliation ● Confirmation to be obtained from the Public Debt Office of RBI for securities (SGL and CSGL), custodian or depository organization (including rights, bonus), and to be cross-checked with bank's books. ● Scrips held in physical form to be physically verified. ● Reconciliation in the balance of securities as per front and back office records.		
Forex Are there separate dealers for inter-bank deals and customer/merchant trade deals?		

(1)	(2)	(3)
Whether any limits are fixed for transactions to be reported by 'B' category (foreign exchange designated) branches and if so, whether they are reported promptly for taking into position? i.e., the bank is not running any uncovered position in respect of transactions undertaken by the branches?		
Is the bank submitting consolidated position sheets to the higher authorities?		
Nostro Accounts Reconciliation and balance confirmation of nostro accounts to be checked. Age-wise analysis of outstanding entries with reasons to be obtained from the bank.		
Forex Suspense/Inter-branch Account Age-wise analysis of outstanding entries in Forex Suspense/ inter-branch account to be done. Has provision for old debit items been made as per extant RBI guidelines?		
Forex Profits/Losses ● Ensure that the bank reckons the Nostro balances as per Mirror Accounts and the outstanding forward transactions as at the date of revaluation for adjustment of the profits/losses? ● Analyze the reasons for increase/decrease in profit Analysis to be separately done for inter-bank and merchant transactions? ● Whether there are any differences between the profit evaluated as per the back office and the front office.		
Merchant-related Contracts Whether the merchant-related contracts (bills, PCFC, forward contracts, etc.) shown as outstanding/overdue in treasury records matched with branch records, particularly overdue items.		
Limits Are the following adhered to? ● Counter-party exposure, daylight, overnight limits. ● Stop loss limit? ● Dealing limits? ● Aggregate Gap Limit (AGL)/Individual Gap Limits (IGL). ● Value at risk. Whether all limits breached been explained and ratified?		

(1)	(2)	(3)
Swap Deals ● Is any swap deal undertaken at level rate (i.e., rate of both the leg of transaction is the same) and if so, whether is it properly explained. ● In case of swap deals, do the spot rate and the swap differences give a realistic reflection of the prevailing conditions in the inter-bank market? ● Whether swap deals were for trading in forward and/ or covering merchant positions?		
Does the bank prepare Daily Rate Scan Report for submission to an official independent of the dealing department?		
Whether there is a proper procedure for hedging against possible exchange losses in respect of foreign exchange transactions?		
Derivatives		
Whether interest rate swaps were undertaken only with scheduled banks (other than RRB), Primary Dealers (PD), All India Financial Institutions (FI) and corporates?		
Has the bank used ISDA documentation for executing IRS/ FRA?		
Whether the transactions for hedging and market making purposes recorded separately?		
Whether the transactions for market making purposes marked to market and accounting entries passed? Whether MTM is in accordance with the RBI guidelines.		
Whether the bank has adhered to the Capital Adequacy Norms applicable?		
Has the bank ensured that the corporate counter-parties are undertaking IRS/FRA only for hedging their own rupee Balance Sheet exposures?		
Whether the exchange of payments made at frequent interval is independently checked by back office?		
Whether accrual entries passed in the books are accurate?		
Whether Option premium received/paid is dealt in accordance with the guidance note issued by ICAI?		

(1)	*(2)*	*(3)*
Maintenance of SLR and CRR.		
Verify position of SLR and CRR on select dates and ensure adherence to the same. ● Correctness of the compilation of DTL positions. ● Maintenance of liquid assets. ● For determining the DTL position, weekly trial balances as on Friday received from different branches are consolidated at the head office. The central auditor should request the branch auditors to verify the correctness of the trial balances and cash balance at the branch on selected dates. As regards weekly returns received from unaudited branches, the return should be broadly reviewed on a sample basis to identify any *prima-facie* errors/inconsistencies.		
Borrowing and Lending ● To identify select transactions and verify them. ● To verify whether rates of interest are in line range of rates specified in RBI website. ● Year-end balances are confirmed. ● Interest payable/receivable if any are provided/taken credit. ● Borrowings and lending in foreign currency are translated at year-end rates. Are in accordance with internal/RBI prudential norms.		
Disclosures Whether all required disclosures made?		

35

Untapped Opportunities in Bancassurance

P.P. PATHROSE

The boundaries de-marking the financial services are fast eroding due to the economic reforms. With the evolution of inter-connected financial services, more and more financial institutions are forced to offer wide range of sophisticated products to their clients. It is no longer possible for any financial institution operating in globalized market to survive without additional sources of revenues. This has prompted two big classes of financial institutions to combine their strengths and create a new means of marketing their products and services. One side is the banking sector, which is traditionally, known to be more competitive, and on the other is insurance sector, which has vast untapped potential of growth. The result is the emergence of Bancassurance, which is having a vast untapped opportunities in India.

BANCASSURANCE OPPORTUNITIES IN THE LIFE INSURANCE AND PENSION MARKETS

Life Insurance is universally acknowledged as a tool to eliminate risk, substitute certainty for uncertainty and ensure timely aid to the family in the unfortunate event of the death of the breadwinner. In other words, it is the civilized world's partial solution to the problems caused by death. In a nutshell, life insurance helps in two ways: premature death, which leaves dependent families to fend for itself and old age without visible means of support.

As one of the non-bank financial intermediaries, insurance

companies have their own special features compared to banks. First, the primary function of an insurance company is the protection against such sudden occurrence as death, not like banks, whose main aim is asset accumulation. Obviously this special function is not replaceable by banks. But with the trend that all institutions involving in one another's business, insurance companies, especially the life insurance companies, are more favourable by the investors who are seeking asset building opportunities due to the special products and services providing by life insurance. And on the other hand, banks are also competing with insurance companies by selling insurance policies (bancassurance).

The second one is that life insurance companies are so called "long-term institutions" which means the way of accumulating asset is aimed for a much longer-term compared to banks. Therefore, they enjoy regulations other than banks and are considered to be more productive in asset building in the long-run.

BENEFITS OF LIFE INSURANCE

Superior to any other Savings Plan

Unlike any other savings plan, a life insurance policy affords full protection against risk of death. In the event of death of a policy-holder, the insurance company makes available the full sum assured to the policyholders' near and dear ones. In comparison, any other savings plan would amount to the total savings accumulated till date. If the death occurs prematurely, such savings can be much lesser than the sum assured. Evidently, the potential financial loss to the family of the policyholder is sizable.

Encourages and Forces Thrift

A savings deposit can easily be withdrawn. The payment of life insurance premiums, however, is considered sacrosanct and is viewed with the same seriousness as the payment of interest on a mortgage. Thus, a life insurance policy in effect, brings about compulsory savings.

Easy Settlement and Protection Against Creditors

A life insurance policy is the only financial instrument the proceeds of which can be protected against the claims of a creditor of the assured by effecting a valid assignment of the policy.

Administering the Legacy for Beneficiaries

Speculative or unwise expenses can quickly cause the proceeds to be squandered. Several policies have foreseen this possibility and provide for payments over a period of years or in a combination of instalments and lump sum amounts.

Ready Marketability and Suitability for Quick Borrowing

A life insurance policy can, after a certain time period (generally three years), be surrendered for a cash value. The policy is also acceptable as a security for a commercial loan, for example, a student loan. It is particularly advisable for housing loans when an acceptable LIC policy may also cause the lending institution to give loan at lower interest rates.

Disability Benefits

Death is not the only hazard that is insured; many policies also include disability benefits. Typically, these provide for waiver of future premiums and payment of monthly instalments spread over certain time period.

Accidental Death Benefits

Many policies can also provide for an extra sum to be paid (typically equal to the sum assured) if death occurs as a result of accident.

Tax Relief

Under the Indian Income Tax Act, the following tax relief is available:

(a) 20 per cent/15 per cent of the premium paid can be deducted from your total income tax liability.
(b) 100 per cent of the premium paid is deductible from your total taxable income for certain policies. When these benefits

are factored in, it is found that most policies offer returns that are comparable/or even better than other saving modes such as PPF, NSC etc. Moreover, the cost of insurance is a very negligible.

Financial services generally and insurance in particular are of primordial importance to economic development. The more developed and efficient a country's insurance market, the greater will be its contribution to economic prosperity. Insurance promotes economic prosperity in seven ways:

- Insurance can promote financial stability.
- Private insurance can substitute for and complement government security programs.
- Insurance can facilitate trade and commerce.
- Insurance can help mobilize national savings.
- Insurers can enable risk to be managed more efficiently.
- Insurers and re-insurers have economic incentives to help insured's reduce losses.
- Insurers foster a more efficient allocation of a country's capital.

UNTAPPED OPPORTUNITIES IN THE LIFE INSURANCE SECTOR

When estimating the potential of the Indian insurance market it is tempting to look at the macro-economic variables such as the premium to GDP etc. Although the growth rate of the economy has been quire impressive in the last decade, the insurance industry still has a low penetration. India is the world's second most populous country and the world's largest democracy. Unfortunately the concept of insurance is not so popular in our country. As per latest estimates, the total premium income generated by life and non-life insurance in India is 1.93 per cent only (1.39 per cent in life and 0.54 per cent in general insurance. In the US it is 8.55 per cent and in UK 13.35 per cent). An international comparison of the insurance penetration and insurance density is given in the following Table 35.1.

Emerging markets will be at the frontier of insurance in the 21st century, according to the latest study from Swiss Re's sigma series. Non-life premiums collected in emerging markets are expected to double from USD 123 billion in 2003 to around USD 250 billion by 2014, at constant prices. Life premiums will increase even faster from

TABLE 35.1

Insurance Penetration and Insurance Density

Countries	*Insurance Penetration (Premiums as % of GDP*			*Insurance Density (Premiums Per Capita (1999) in USD-1999)*		
	Total	*Non-Life*	*Life*	*Total*	*Non-Life*	*Life*
United States	8.55	4.32	4.23	2921.1	1474.4	1446.6
Canada	6.49	3.31	3.19	1375.3	700.6	674.6
Brazil	2.01	1.66	0.35	68.6	56.7	11.8
Mexico	1.68	0.86	0.82	84.6	43.3	41.3
Chile	3.78	1.13	2.65	163.0	48.7	114.3
United Kingdom	13.35	3.05	10.30	3244.3	741.5	2502.8
Germany	6.52	3.55	2.96	1675.7	913.5	762.2
France	8.52	2.82	5.70	2080.9	688.6	1392.3
Japan	11.17	2.30	8.87	3908.9	805.5	3103.4
South Korea	11.28	2.89	8.39	1022.8	262.3	760.5
China	1.63	0.61	1.02	13.3	5.0	8.3
India	1.93	0.54	1.39	8.5	2.4	6.1
Malaysia	3.88	1.72	2.16	140.4	62.3	78.1
Indonesia	1.42	0.76	0.66	9.5	5.1	4.4
South Africa	16.54	2.62	13.92	490.9	77.9	413.0
Australia	9.82	3.39	6.43	2037.4	703.8	1333.6

Source: Swiss Re, SIGMA/9-2000 as reproduced from IRDA Annual Report, 2000-2001.

USD 188 billion to USD 450 billion over the same period. The sigma study identifies China and India as the most promising insurance markets.

Impressive growth prospects for emerging markets are putting them at the frontier of insurance. Among the emerging markets, China and India are very much in the spotlight, on account of their huge populations, growing economic importance and fast liberalising regulatory regimes.

Over the past ten years life and non-life insurance premiums in emerging markets have risen annually by 10.4 per cent and 7.3 per cent respectively in real terms, compared with an average 3.4 per cent and 2.6 per cent for industrialised nations. Premium growth is expected to remain strong at 7.5 per cent per year in the next decade, due to robust economic growth, increased stability, favourable regulatory developments, as well as new product offerings and distribution channels.

China and India are arguably the two most challenging and promising emerging insurance markets. In tandem with robust economic development, their insurance markets have grown spectacularly. Life insurance premiums in China have grown by an annual average of 23.7 per cent over the last decade, while non-life premiums have grown by 10.8 per cent over the same period. Average annual growth rates for insurance in India were 12.7 per cent for life and 6.2 per cent for non-life. In 2003, China and India were respectively the 8th and 18th largest life insurance markets in the world. Their rankings are 13th and 28th in terms of non-life insurance.

Despite the fact that India boasts of a saving rate of around 25 per cent, less than 5 per cent only is spend on insurance. The per capita insurance premium in India is very low as compared to advanced countries. More than three-fourths of India's insurable population has no life insurance or pension cover. Health insurance of any kind is negligible and other forms of non-life insurance are much below the international standards. All these indicate that there is huge untapped potential in the Indian life insurance market.

A recent survey by the Confederation of Indian Industry (CII) had estimated that life insurance premium in India is stated to rise from Rs. 215.81 billion in 1998-99 to Rs. 1449.88 billion in 2009-10. Such growth potential makes Indian life insurance market a very lucrative market.

In untapping the potential the strategy of bancassurers should be not to target the business of existing companies rather than expanding the market. Targeting the business of existing companies only leads to intensive competition. A better approach would be to target specific niches, which are currently under-served or not at all served. Potential buyers for most of the insurance lie in the middle class.

Life insurance is traditionally sold through independent agents. Since this is a very costly way to deliver the product, agents have tended to focus on wealthier individuals who know them, value their advice and tend to buy policies with greater face values. As a result, the majority of Indian households are underinsured. The middle market consumers prefer an institutional relationship with a bank to a personal relationship with an agent.

HIGH LEVEL OF SAVINGS

The accumulation of personal wealth has been instrumental in supporting life insurance business growth. It is true that income inequality and rural poverty are major deterring factors but the emergence of an elite middle class should ensure continued and robust business growth especially in the life insurance segment. It is estimated that there are 200-300 million potential life insurance buyers in India. The savings rate in India is around 23.

Likewise the growth in bank deposits also illustrates the improved savings habit of the Indian public. Deposits, which stood at Rs. 535025 crores in 1996-97, increased to Rs. 9000307 lakhs in 1999-2000.

Traditionally high savings rate will fuel the growth of life insurance business. The savings content in life insurance premium acts as an incentive to save. In Asia, there is relatively a high savings content of life insurance premium as shown in the following Table 35.2.

Against the backdrop of relative social and political stability yield or profitability has replaced liquidity as the major consideration in household investment decisions. While regulatory shirts and competition provide customers with more choice customers preference for products could make life insurance policies the main savings vehicle.

Life Insurance is superior to any other savings plan and encourages and forces thrift. A savings deposits can easily be withdrawn. The

TABLE 35.2

1999

Country	*Share of Savings Premium (Per cent)*	*Gross Domestic Savings as share of GDP (Per cent)*
Japan	84.70	27.70
South Korea	78.10	33.60
Taiwan	87.30	NA
China	89.00	10.10
India	81.30	20.00
Singapore	52.10	61.70

Source: Swiss Re Sigma 9/2000.

payment of life insurance premium however is considered sacrosanct and is viewed with the same seriousness as the payment of interest on a mortgage. Thus, a life insurance policy in effect brings about compulsory savings.

The trend has been further driven by the long-term decline in interest rates, which makes it all the more necessary to start saving early to ensure long-term wealth creation. Today's consumers are increasingly interested in products to help build wealth and provide for retirement income. Although further increase in disposable income (it is assumed that the marginal propensity 10 save will decline along with further increases in disposable income) and an aging population would curb the growth of savings, wealth accumulation will remain a major theme in India giving vast potential to bancassurance to expand.

DEMOGRAPHIC SHIFTS AND PENSIONS

The aging population has become a major issue in the country. Improved nutrition and medical standards have lengthened the life expectancies of most Indians suggesting that retirees will live longer after the retirement. At the same time birth rates have declined. These facts are contributing to the rapid growing of the country's population. As life expectancy increases, the need for retirement provisions becomes a major issue. Where once the fear was one of dying too early, now with increasing longevity the fear also is one of living too long and outliving one's assets. With the breakdown of traditional form of social security like the joint family system, consumers are now concerning themselves with the need to provide for a comfortable retirement. The lack of a proper and adequate social security system in the country, combined with a willingness to save means that Indian demand for pension products will be large. However the current production is poor.

PENSION REFORM

The Old Age Social and Income Security (OASIS) Committee report has pointed out that even from among the gainfully employed, only 11 per cent are covered by a provident fund/pension fund and a large mass of people is left out of any old age security. A road map for a pension scheme for those in the unorganized sector is already drawn by the Government of India. Reforms in the pension sector will open new vistas in the bancassurance opportunity of banks. Pensions or the grant of annuity is part of the life business as laid down by the Insurance Act, 1938. All life companies are therefore eligible to issue pension policies. It seems that the regulator is in favour of permitting all the life insurance players into the pension business without forming separate companies for the purpose.

Beset by budget deficits, the Government needs the insurance industry to help relive it of the burdens of social security and pension provision and to generate funds for investment in infrastructure modernization.

It seems likely that insurers will have a role in each of the three main pillars of pension provision viz.

State Pensions

These are mainly mandatory state-administered schemes invested in state provident funds. Most of the funding comes from companies and employees rather than testate. The OASIS Committee proposed that future contributions be invested in funds managed privately. At least some private insurers may be permitted to act as managers.

Occupational Pensions

Although they currently cover only a very small proportion of the population, occupational pensions will become much more widespread. For the new insurers, good private sector employers represent the best prospects. State enterprises will probably have to continue to use the LIC.

Personal Pensions

The OASIS report proposed introducing individual retirement accounts across the employed and self-employed sectors, with minimum annual contributions as low as Rs. 500 (US$ 10). The report envisages that on retirement, the total individual fund balance will have to be used to buy an inflation-proofed annuity underwritten by an insurer.

Although details have yet to be finalized, insurers are wary of the administrative burden of very small policies and of any requirement to offer life annuity terms, at least until the Government issues more long-term bonds. The more attractive side of the personal pension market is that created by voluntary retirement scheme monies given to those taking early retirement from state-owned industries.

Banks have an important role to play in the pension sector when deregulated. Low cost of collecting pensions contributions is the key element in the sepses of developing the pension sector. Money transfer costs in Indian banking is low by international standards. Portability of pension accounts is a vital requirement, which banks can fulfil, in a credible framework.

Making pension products into attractive savings instruments would require only simple innovations already common in other markets—bancassurers should shift their product focus from traditional event risk (i.e. death and accident) protection to long-term provisions (i.e. pensions and long-term health care).

INCREASING INSURANCE AWARENESS

Closely related to the emergence of the middle-income class but as yet a distinct trend on its own is the public's growing risk awareness. At the same time life insurers have been gearing up efforts to educate the public on the need to protect against event risks and old age poverty. As the Government is withdrawing from previous obligations on welfare provisions individuals are increasingly forced to seek their own protection.

This coincides with a product shift in the market place from simple bank deposits to packaged savings. Introduction of unit linked products and products combining savings with investment via life insurance policies are sure to boost up bancassurance opportunities.

POTENTIAL IN THE RURAL MARKET

India is a predominantly rural country and will continue to be so in the near future. By targeting the creamy layer of the urban population insurers at present miss a large chunk of the insurable population. Rural insurance should be hence looked upon as an opportunity and not an obligation. In a country with a billion people; mass marketing is always a profitable and cost effective option for gaining market share. The rural sector is a perfect case for mass marketing. A smaller bundle of innovative products in synchronization with rural needs and perception and an efficient delivery system are the two aspects that have to be developed in order to tap the potential of the rural markets. Banks enjoy considerable goodwill and access in the rural regions. There are 32600 branches in rural India (about 50 per cent of total), where insurance growth has been most buoyant.

LIFE STYLE CHANGES

The success of bancassurance will be high in life insurance segment mostly, primarily because of the matching of banking products with the personal financial needs of individuals and families. Bancassurance works through a process system that highlights consumer lifestyle changes. Traditionally insurance products have been sold through a process of event-based selling. The process serves to identify individuals or families who require life insurance coverage due to the happening of certain events, which tend to increase future liabilities. Many of these events can be easily matched with banking transactions.

Banks will be in a position to spot existing depositors/borrowers' "life triggers", i.e., milestones in a life that represent insurance opportunities. Although bank staff has always done this in conjunction with bank products, it is new to them to apply this concept to insurance products as well. For example, a younger depositor mentions he is withdrawing part of his savings to purchase his first car. Does such a customer understand the benefits, costs and limits of the various types of car insurance? Does he know which product is best designed to fit current needs? Knowledgeable bank staff functioning now as financial services representatives can provide such sound practical advice, i.e., an insurance product to fit customer current and future needs. A well-trained staff can always count on certain "life triggers" – birth, death, divorce, career change or other catastrophic event – to lead his or her regular bank customers to new insurance products. If the bank's personnel are shown how to capitalize upon these triggers using insurance products, they will automatically provide referrals to the insurance group and insurance sales will follow.

A combination of a bank and an insurance company is seen as being better able to target clients in the early stages of the client's life cycle. For example, young clients are attracted with accounts offering credit cards and other appealing characteristics. By establishing a relationship in the early life stages of a customer, institutions are better able to sell products through all stages of a client's life cycle.

BANCASSURANCE OPPORTUNITIES IN THE NON-LIFE INSURANCE SECTOR

The scope of operations of General Insurance is wider than LIC by definition. In practice, however, general insurance premium has been lower than life insurance. In 1993, total life premium income in India was US $ 3.2 billion while general insurance premium US $ 1.5 billion.

General Insurance premium as a percentage of GDP was a mere 0.5 per cent in 1994. Clearly, there is ample scope for development of general insurance in India. However, its market is smaller in comparison with the huge market for life insurance in this country.

TYPES OF NON-LIFE INSURANCE PRODUCTS

The different types of General Insurance products are listed below. While most policies are optional, i.e. at the behest of the insured, some are mandatory. The mandatory ones are: Motor insurance and public liability (for corporate class).

Motor insurance is mandatory for all types of vehicles in India. There are two types of motor insurance, viz.

(i) Third party, which only insures the party/parties other than the owner in an accident, and
(ii) Comprehensive, which insures the owner as well as the third party involved.

Property Insurance

Property insurance covers land, buildings, and the contents of building. There are several types of property insurance packages, but the most common are the Fire Insurance and Burglary Insurance.

Fire

Fire insurance is a comprehensive policy, which goes beyond only fire accidents. The policy, besides covering loss on account of fire, also covers loss on account of earthquake, riots, strikes, malicious intent and floods. Fire insurance can only be taken by the owner of the premises to be insured. A tenant cannot insure rented premises since he does not have insurable interest. But the tenant has the option of insuring the contents of the premises. The premium is based on 'good faith' and depends on the value of property being insured. It should be noted that though fire insurance is not compulsory, in case of corporates availing of loans, the lending institution may insist on equipment or relevant property to be insured against fire. This trend is now also being followed by housing finance companies, some of which are insisting that the premises be insured against fire.

Burglary

Burglary insurance covers all losses arisen out of burglary committed in one's premises. The only condition for lodging a claim on the insurance party is that there should be "forced entry" into the premises. A forced entry may in the form of physical damage to the entry area, or to a person, or entry gained through coercion. In this case too, the policy has no limitations and it is the prerogative of the insured to decide upon the value of the insurance cover.

Personal Accident Policy

Personal accident policy covers life of an individual in the case of an accident. This policy comprehensively covers death, permanent disability, and loss of limbs and eyesight. In addition to the above, the insured also receives a stipulated amount on the basis of the principal he is insured for in case of inability to perform normal duties.

UNTAPPED POTENTIAL IN THE NON-LIFE INSURANCE SECTOR

In health insurance segment, the existing Indian products are insufficient. By the end of 1988, GIC's mediclaim scheme covered only 2.50 million people. Indian products do not cover disability arising out of illness or disability for over 100 weeks due to accident. Neither do they cover a potential loss of earnings through disability.

In general insurance personal insurance including health, house holders, shop keepers, accident and professional indemnity covers constitute 12 per cent of the general insurance premium. This poor figure is largely due to lack of adequate distribution channels rather than lack of products. The general insurance largely focuses the manufacturing segment. 50 per cent of the current demand for general insurance comes from the corporate segment. Among the classes of business that the general insurers transact, tire and motor portfolios still are the most significant. Whilst the fire policy is around 200 per cent of the total business, the motor portfolio continues to be the most predominant of all the business by around 40 per cent of the total gross premium collected by the non-life insurance industry. Banks can leverage their advance portfolios to expand into these sections of the non-life insurance business.

By tapping the under-served niches the new entrants in bancassurance can expand the market substantially. The services sector is taking a large and growing share of India's GDP (around 42 per cent). This offers expansion opportunities.

There is a growing demand for health care products which banks can distribute and facilitate administration. Though the Insurance Act, 1938 and IRDA Act, 1999 prescribe encouraging standalone health insurance agencies, no one has so far ventured into health insurance business due to the prescription of a too large minimum working capital requirement of Rs. 100 crores. Due to lack of applications in this area the regulators encourage both life and non-life insurance companies to go in for rider policies offering health covers, with an aim that the rider policies would convert themselves into main health policies later. Banks can play a major role in developing a viable health care program. Health insurance, which remained highly underdeveloped and a less significant segment of the product portfolios of the nationalized insurance companies in India, is now poised for a fundamental change in its approach and management. It is estimated that the Indian health care industry is now worth of Rs. 96,000 crore and expected to surge by 10,000 crore annually. The share of insurance market in above figure is insignificant. Out of one billion population of India 315 million people are estimated to be insurable and have capacity to spend Rs. 1,000 as premium per annum. Given the health financing and demand scenario, health insurance has a wider scope in present day situations in India. However, it requires careful and significant effort on the part of bancassurers to tap Indian health insurance market with proper understanding and training.

There remain untapped opportunities in the retail segment too. Housing finance, auto finance, credit cards and consumer loans all offer an opportunity to introduce new products like credit insurance, etc. Banks can successfully integrate insurance products into the existing range of retail banking products. However in doing so, banks will be required to ensure that wrapping the loan product with insurance product does not increase the price of that product significantly as the premium has to be loaded to the loan account This can instead of attracting more borrowers prove as a bottleneck for expanding credit as borrowers today have multiple options available in the market and are conscious of costs.

The first prong of a Bancassurer's strategy could be to stimulate demand in the areas that are currently not served at all. For example, Indian non-life insurers focus mainly on the manufacturing segment. However, the services sector is taking a large and growing share of India's GDP giving immense opportunities. Likewise being an agrarian economy, there exist immense opportunities to provide the liability and risks associated in this sector like weather insurance, rainfall insurance, cyclone insurance, crop insurance, etc.

A recent survey by the Confederation of Indian Industry (CII) had estimated that non-life premium would increase from Rs. 88.54 billion in 1998-99 to Rs. 436.99 billion in 2009-2010. Such growth potential makes Indian non-life insurance market, a very lucrative market.

CONCLUSION

Bancassurance in India is in the very early stages of development, it's new and untried but the potential is undoubtedly large. The initial stumbling blocks for the growth of bancassurance in the country, like clarity of legislation, etc. are expected to be overcome very soon. External pressures on banks and insurance companies to adopt some form of bancassurance strategy are likely to intensify. Whilst many forms of bancassurance can contribute to improving cross selling, only much closer forms of integration are likely to yield benefits in operational efficiency.

36

Treasury Integration—The Process

A.K. Trivedi

"Indian Rupee's sharp fall triggers dollar selling", "Indian call steady in early trade, bonds quiet", "Rupee came under pressure", "With the increase in volatility, bid/offer spreads have also widened, Forward premia have softened."

We read these reports very often in the financial pages and business pages of newspapers without understanding much of it. What is integrated treasury? What is methodology? Who are the players? What is pre-requisite by way of forex markets? How to go about it as a process? An attempt is made to explain such like related issues in this article.

Genesis

Funds manager is to manage the cash flows in various currencies in the most efficient and profitable way with all concern and compliance to the exchange control and business practices/procedures. The management of cash flows involves making sure that payments are made when due and invested at the highest possible returns. Alternately, finding optimal liability mix for a given asset financing is part of role of the funds manager. When dealing in international markets/the funds markets the funds manager do maintain the appropriate positions in various currencies. The desired postings depend on currencies of the cash flows involved as well as manager's views of the currency's future value. It has a linkage to financial indicators fundamental and technical analysis of the economic and political factors.

Methodology

Attempt is made to define an "Integrated Treasury" in the context of modern banking system. From the definition, roles of such a treasury are arrived at. Role clarity throws light or need for integration of Treasury. An organizational structure to fulfil the roles is suggested in Fig. 36.1. This is followed by elaboration on infrastructural needs. The last section puts forth a plan for phased implementation of the integration process, where things are not likely to flow in a single go.

Integrated Treasury—A Definition

The scope of definition is restricted to a banking company engaged in intermediation of investments and credit. It takes into consideration a banking structure that is widely in place and gaining increasing acceptance in the largest credit market the US. The latter is due to the dilution of the Glass-Steagall Act that separated investment banking and commercial banking. The integrated treasury is expected to serve a universal bank that encompasses both.

Integrated Treasury in the new environment is expected to manage all market risks associated with bank liabilities and assets. The market risks of liabilities pertain to floating interest rate risks and asset-liability mismatches. As for assets, market risks is due to increasing levels of securitisation of assets, change in funding pattern of corporates from bank loans to debt issues and recent development of credit derivatives (a proxy of participation certificates). While the credit risk assessment continues to rest with credit function, the cash flow impacts from change in asset prices due to interest rate changes would be monitored by the treasury. Thus, an integrated treasury apart from short-term liquidity management is expected to provide policy inputs to strategic planning group on medium-term basis with respect to the following aspects: funding mix (currency, tenor and cost), yield expected on credit and investment (yield and classes of investment).

WHY INTEGRATION?

Of the three roles identified under an Integrated Treasury, viz. Autonomous Forex, Autonomous Money and Integrated Role, the last one gains pre-eminence in an era of liberalization. Specifically, this refers to freedom to corporates and banks to structure multi-currency

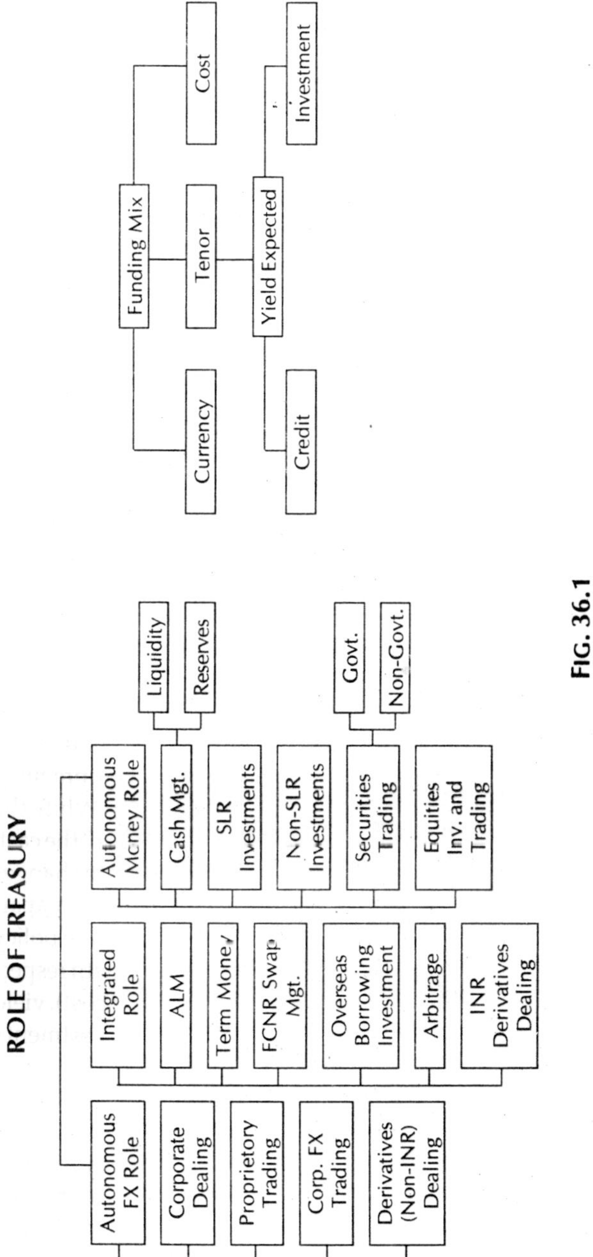
ROLE OF TREASURY
Autonomous FX Role
Corporate Dealing
Proprietary Trading
Corp. FX Trading
Derivatives (Non-INR) Dealing
Integrated Role
ALM
Term Money
FCNR Swap Mgt.
Overseas Borrowing Investment
Arbitrage
INR Derivatives Dealing
Autonomous Money Role
Cash Mgt.
SLR Investments
Non-SLR Investments
Securities Trading
Equities Inv. and Trading
Liquidity
Reserves
Govt.
Non-Govt.
Funding Mix
Currency
Tenor
Cost
Yield Expected
Credit
Investment

FIG. 36.1

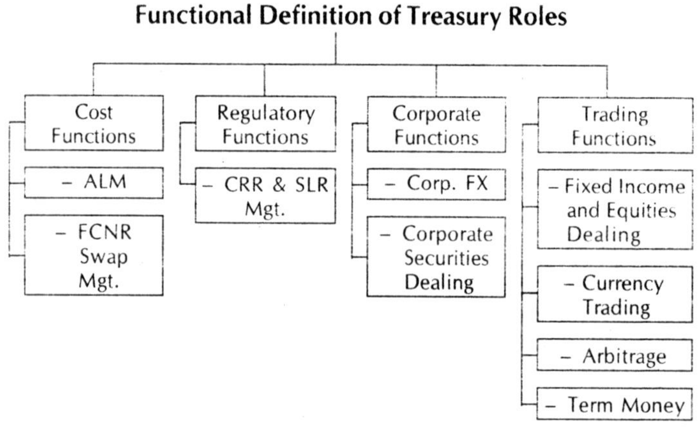

FIG. 36.2

balance sheets and to take advantage of strategic positioning. The expert Committee report on Capital Account Convertibility (CAC) dwells at length on phased liberalization on this count. The report's recommendations goes beyond the corporate sector to retail sector too. The relevance of integrated treasury is dwelt on to capitalize on the freedom envisaged.

Cost of Capital

As per norms by Reserve Bank of India, it is possible for banks to borrow up to 15 per cent of Tier 1 capital of the Bank over and above FCNR funds, at the short end. Thus depending on call rates and swap rates at the short-end, it would be possible for banks to save significantly to meet short-term liquidity needs. These arbitrage opportunities may dwindle in quantum and exist for shorter period of time but would continue to exist even beyond capital account convertibility. At the long-end, bank's choice of currencies in its liabilities can be decided based on demand from customers. As FCNR rates are fully freed by the Central bank, banks will have to hedge themselves against a floating LIBOR in the absence of interest risk-free lending opportunities.

Return on Investment

Banks have also been given freedom to invest up to 15 per cent of

Tier 1 capital of the i.e. Bank in overseas instruments (either Government T-bills or money market instruments of banks rated by Moodys and S&P). As amount investible is enough increased and/or the range of investments widened, this avenue would compete with the current areas for short-term and medium-term (up to 1 year) investment of Indian banks. Further, floating rate dollar liabilities would find a natural hedge in US T-bills (as for other currencies too) and obviate need to go in for costly hedging programmes.

Inter-bank Products

Term money market is likely to gain pace with adoption of Asset Liability, Management (ALM) practices by the Indian Banks as it would increase demand for tenor funds to match duration of assets and liabilities. Two percentage point reduction in Cash Reserve Ratio prompts augmentation in Bank's resources to the tune of Rs. Term market is expected to receive a further boost. Forex forward rates would however be an indispensable index to quote term rates. Experts are of opinion that only an integrated treasury can embark on such a task.

Corporate Products

Interest rate swaps call for counter-parties with USD and INR liabilities. As and when FIIs and DFIs are allowed to operate in Forward markets, more such matches could emerge. Banks could earn fee-based income by intermediating such deals. As money and forex markets integrate, INR yield curve could mature and trigger off a wave of USD/INR forex and debt derivative products. Making a market in these products to banks and customers would be made possible through an integrated treasury in a better way.

Expert Committee on Capital Account Convertibility headed by Dr. S.S. Tarapore recommended towards Risk Management as under:

- The RBI should prescribe prudential norms for mismatches in the rupee book of the banks and FIs and prescribe a reporting system for monitoring mismatches.
- The banks and FIs should be required to move progressively to a 100 per cent market-to-market investment portfolio by the year 2000.

- The best practices of risk management as outlined in the Report of the Expert Group on Forex Markets (Chairman: Shri O.P. Sodhani) may be adopted by all entities including corporates. This will require strong internal control systems to identify, measure, monitor and manage all types of risks.
- Introduction of internationally accepted accounting and disclosure norms for banks, financial institutions as also corporates simultaneously with the introduction of new instruments/products.
- Upgradation of skills: The Committee underscores the need for strong initiatives on the part of market participants to upgrade their human resource skills by appropriate training inputs. In the long-run, only skilled manpower can withstand vigorous competition and add value to the products and services rendered. In order that they attract the best talent and expertise, individuals banks and FIs should have freedom to determine their personnel policies including recruitment and war policies without being constrained by any rigidities. The committee required that without appropriate changes in labour laws it will not be possible to create an environment conducive to operational efficiency which is pre-requisite for enabling Indian financial entities to compete meaningfully with their counterparts abroad.

Most of the measures set out by the committee on CAC are expected to be implemented in a phased manner.

INFORMATION FLOWS

To achieve the objective Organisational Chart is found to be as per Fig. 36.3.

Treasury Head

- from MIS on micro-level branch asset and liability statements representing liquidity position,
- from Credit department on business projections for medium-term,
- from mid-office on Value At Risk and adherence by dealers to internal and external guidelines, and

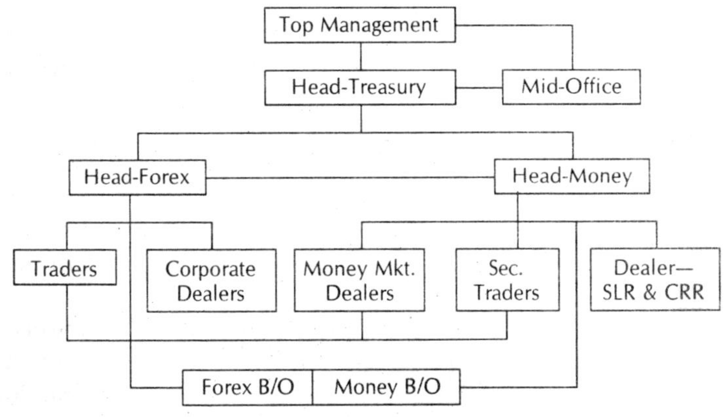

FIG. 36.3

Proposed Integrated Treasury Structure

- to Forex branch heads on currency market and money market developments (weekly).

Dealers

Regular information flow between the dealers on money and forex desk (swap side especially) is envisaged to exploit arbitrage opportunities at the short-end and medium-term too as and when a decision is taken to that effect.

Mid-office

A Mid-office set-up independent of the treasury unit could act as a risk monitoring and control entity reporting directly to top management. Keeping tab on Value At Risk, ensuring adherence to external and internal guidelines and evolving risk monitoring systems would be some responsibilities of such a set-up. Regular information flow from Treasury head to Mid-office chief is expected toward discharge of these responsibilities. To take real time advantage the operation need to be on-line with sophisticated need-based information technology intervention. However, manual intervention will suffice till switch over to sophisticated technology-based control mechanism is feasible.

INFRASTRUCTURE

Location

Considering that banks do have a well-established forex operation at a place different to money operations, there would be a proposal to locate the Integrated Treasury at one place only. In case it is decided to go for integrated treasury in one go, it is suggested that extensive planning go into designing the dealing room inputs. Information vendors like Reuters & Dowjones, MTNL Engineers, Electricians and others also add value in such layout design proposals. It has to be ideal location in view of cost benefit analysis in short- and long-term. This is to ensure futuristic design of the dealing room to be a state of the art operation.

Information Systems

Treasury needs to be equipped with information systems, viz. from Reuters and Dowjones. The former includes the sophisticated RMDS (Reuters Monitor Dealing System) to do deals directly with banks globally. Further, hotlines with brokers need to be established. Utilizing the services of information vendor Knight Ridder (now called Bridge) may also be considered given their reputation in debt markets worldwide. This can be arranged/organised in view of the size of operation *vis-a-vis* cost benefit analysis.

Communication Lines

With integration, hotlines with money brokers need to be put in place. A hotline with corporate office needs to be established. The number of direct telephone lines can also be considered as per requirement, i.e. considering the number of personnel in the dealing room. Money and Forex dealers can be equipped with mobile phones/pagers to facilitate operations even when they are on the move.

Settlement

Rupee settlement for security operation and Forex operations are done as an important event on day-to-day basis as a time bound exercise. Considering the proximity of control place to RBI and other banks, it is suggested that settlement continue to operate from the same or around location in case these are located at two different places due to obvious unavoidable reasons. It is suggested to link the integrated Treasury with settlement office through modem to automatically deliver instructions. This would reduce transmission costs and also speed up the process of settlement of Rupee funds.

Treasury Software

An Integrated Treasury Software that incorporates the compact i.e. current and future requirement is at the heart of the process. Features like Transfer pricing mechanism to price deals involving the money and forex side of treasury would lead to a true reflection of profitability on either sides. Talks with vendors of such software and bankers already using such software could be a starting point towards acquiring it. Since Treasury is considered to be a profit centre of the Bank advantage, Transfer Price Mechanism (TPM) is all the same important and must to assess true bottomline of operations.

Implementation of Integration

Integration process is followed by well thought policy papers and well conceived/drawn action plan giving weightage right from swapping the ideas/concepts of money and forex operations to integrated treasury operations with well defined roles and job expectations by the management policy/goals sharing of market information in the group within and by the team leader is a pre-requisite. It will ensure smooth lending of proposal to launch as an integrated treasury. Nuts and bolts have to be at place. There has to be at place the communication devices to ensure internal and external access easy and pragmatic. The implementation can be phased out by coordinating the present infrastructure, setting-up the additional requirement and finally moving for functions. For it there is a need to have committed workforce with capability of assimilation. Nevertheless the Treasury head and corporate management need to have capacity and capability to absorb the shocks as a result of dilution in the process. Thus need for standby or second line of defence cannot be ruled out to ensure smooth succession and trouble free operation.

Risk Management/Control

The MIS as per Guidelines for Internal Control over Foreign Exchange Business by RBI has to be placed to the satisfactions of RBI and the Bank's directions/ policy framework. It will ensure effective supervision and control over Treasury Operations, viz. over Daylight, Overnight Limits, Stop Loss Limits, Individual Gap Limit, Aggregate Gap Limit, Merchant, Trading positions nostro reconciliation, Cash management, Maturity Gaps, FCNR portfolio, etc.

37

Use of Derivatives to Manage Market Risk

NIALL S.K. BOOKER

INTRODUCTION

Contrary to the perception that financial derivatives are a recent phenomenon, the origin of a financial derivative contract can be traced back to about 600 BC. About that time Thales of Miletus, after having concluded that there would be a bumper crop of olives raised money to put a deposit on the olive presses of Miletus and Chios. So when the bumper crop did happen he was able to let the presses out at a tidy profit. The above transaction captures the essence of a derivative contract, which is defined as a contract that derives its value from the price of an underlying asset (liability). The demand and consequently the rent of an olive press are a function of quantity of olives to be processed. Underlying the contract is the production of olives. In case the production was lower than the forecast, Thales would at most have lost the money he had put up as deposit. But as per Thales's forecast there was a very successful crop and the rest is history. In a nutshell Thales synthesized a Call option on the olive production by putting up a deposit on the olive presses. Of course, as Thales *per se* did not have any interest in the production or the price of olives, his purpose in executing the mentioned transaction was "speculative", that is to assume a certain amount of risk for some reward.

More recently, the first formal interest rate derivative transaction was undertaken by between IBM and the World Bank in 1981, when IBM wanted to convert its CHF and DEM loans into USD and the

World Bank was looking for funding in the same currencies for its customers. The transaction concluded helped achieve the objective for both parties at a significantly lower cost. In India, Rupee interest rate and currency swaps were first permitted in 1999. RBI has also introduced exchange traded interest rate futures and FX options in 2003. Most of these products draw huge interest from banks, financial institutions and corporates alike.

In our discussion we shall focus on the use of derivative instruments to manage financial risk. Before we explore the applications of derivative instruments it is necessary to understand the framework required to identify and quantify financial risk.

TYPES OF RISK

Risk can be defined as the probability of unexpected outcomes. Specifically risk can be unbundled into the following elements:

- Market risk,
- Credit risk,
- Liquidity risk,
- Legal risk,
- Operational risk, and
- System/model risk.

The focus of this paper is on market risk. In India for a bank or a financial institution market risk would primarily constitute currency and interest rate risk. A sound risk management process would involve appropriate board and senior management guidance, adequate risk management policies and procedure, appropriate risk measurement, monitoring and control functions and comprehensive independent audits.

STRATEGIC RISK MANAGEMENT

The process of strategic risk management can be summarised in the following steps:

Exposure Identification and Measurement

All drivers of currency and interest rate risk should be identified and classified. It is imperative to understand their characteristics and business impact. The impact of these potential risk parameters should be measurable both at a transaction as well as on a portfolio basis.

For currency risk the measurement is straightforward and would be in units of foreign currency. In the case of a foreign currency payable or receivable at a future time, the exposure would have to be broken up into currency risk and interest rate risk. The currency exposure would simply be the present value of the foreign currency cash flows.

Computation of interest rate risk is a little more involved than that of currency risk. Some of the popular measures of interest rate risk are duration and PVBP (Present value of 1 basis point) which measures the change in the value of the asset or liability for a basis point change in the underlying interest rate.

Strategy Design and Implementation

Once the interest rate and currency exposures are quantified, the next step is to decide what to hedge and by using which instruments. Hedging further raises issues of covering budget rates, hedge appropriateness and risk limits. Selling up limits for hedging is important, as some hedges are not perfect even though the hedging efficacy might be very high.

Tracking and Performance Measurement

This involves setting up processes and systems required to monitor exposure and hedge values. Hedge valuation should be available on request as this measures the success of the hedging program. Both the hedge and the underlying exposure are to be marked-to-market on an on-going basis and any ineffectiveness is to be recorded in the profit and loss account.

Contingency Planning

There should be a defined process and personnel to handle crisis or problem situation.

Management Buy-in for the Above

Management buy-in is critical for the smooth functioning of any hedge program. It would entail obtaining agreement from senior management on the goals of the risk management process. It also means a clear understanding of the trade-off between risk reduction and return enhancement at all levels of management.

DERIVATIVE BENCHMARK

With a risk management process in place it should be possible to get a snapshot of firm wide risk. Having obtained a risk profile of the enterprise the next step is to identify an appropriate Derivative instrument. All Derivative contracts are settled with respect to a benchmark. The efficacy of a derivative instrument should be tied as closely as possible to the benchmark. Some necessary features of Derivative Benchmarks are:

1. It should be a Market determined,
2. Ample liquidity, that is it should be widely traded,
3. Transparent and easily calculated,
4. Relevant to the user (least basis risk), and
5. Availability for the life time of the derivative transaction.

Some of the benchmarks for Derivative products available locally are given in the following Table 37.1.

DERIVATIVES AND MARKET RISK MANAGEMENT

In this section we illustrate the use of derivatives for practical risk management through a few real life examples.

Example 1: Managing Asset Liability Tenor Mismatches

On 21st June, 2002 Bank X has a simple balance sheet with 5-year liability of INR 100 million. It has an option to acquire a AAA asset for a tenor of 2, 3 or 5 years. Basically the bank would like to lend for 5 years as in this case it does not have a tenor mismatch. In the absence of such an asset it is only able to lend for 2 years at 8.30 per cent. Indicative rates for AAA asset and OIS are given in Table 37.2. When the asset matures on 21st June, 2004 the proceeds can only be redeployed at 6.00 per cent, bringing down the effective return on the asset to 6.92 per cent. This is much lower than initial 5-year AAA yield of 8.44 per cent. Clearly for bank X the decision to borrow for 5 years and lend for 2 years has exposed it to the risk of interest rate

TABLE 37.1

Benchmark	*Instrument*	*Description*	*Market acceptability*	*Swap (option) Tenor*	*Liquidity*	*Published page on Reuters*
Overnight MIBOR	OIS	Overnight deposit	High	5 years	High	MIBR = NS
MIFOR	6-month implied rate from forward premium	Term rate linked to 6 months forward premia	High	10 years	High	MIFOR =
INBMK	GOI Yield	GOI yield linked interest rate	High	10 years	Medium	INBMK =
USD/INR Spot Volatility	FX Option	European option on USD/INR Spot	High	1 year	Medium	INVOLFIX

TABLE 37.2
Market Rates—AAA/OIS

Tenor	21st June, 2002		21st June, 2004	
	AAA	OIS	AAA	OIS
2 years	8.30	7.14	5.80	5.43
3 years	8.35	7.30	6.00	5.73
5 years	8.44	7.56	6.25	6.13

movement. Ideally if bank X does not have an interest rate view it would not like to carry such a risk. Bank X has a gap between year 2 and year 5.

This position can be hedged through a Interest rate swap starting 2 years from now with a tenor of 3 years. From the data in Table 37.2. Fixed rate for such an OIS works out to 7.91 per cent. Bank X now receives Fixed 7.91 per cent and pays daily MIBOR fixing. There would not be any settlement for the first two years as the swap starts two years from 21st June, 2002.

On 21st June, 2004 the OIS can be unwound at a profit of 218 bps per annum (7.91 - 5.73). This improves the yield of 3-year AAA asset to 8.18 per cent. With the swap the effective return for 5 years improves to 8.23 per cent which is closer to the initial 5-year AAA yield of 8.44 per cent. The return is not exactly equal to the initial AAA return which also highlights the fact the hedges are seldom perfect.

Example 2: Conversion of Fixed Rate Issuance into Floating Rate

Banks raise long tenor capital through Tier II bonds. Due to market acceptance, these bonds are typically of a fixed rate nature. The tenor of these bonds is typically in the range of 7-10 years. While rising interest rates would benefit the issuer, a fall in interest rates is likely to have a negative impact. The issuer would like to protect himself against such fluctuations in interest rates. This can be achieved through an interest rate swap which changes the profile of the liability to a floating rate. While quite a few benchmarks are available, the bank needs to choose the one which best replicates the character of its asset book.

Let us take a case wherein the bank believes that the interest rate profile of its asset book is best characterised by the yield on sovereign securities plus a certain spread. The bank has issued fixed rate bonds of maturity of 10 years, paid annually. The bank enters into a swap wherein it pays the 1-year INBMK rate, reset annually and receives the fixed rate. Such a swap protects the issuer against the floating rate nature of its asset book while allowing the bank to raise capital through a fixed rate.

Example 3: Hedging of Housing Loan Asset Book

One of the largest components of the asset book for a bank is housing loans, whose maturity is between 5-20 years. Apart from the mismatch between the relatively short tenor fund raising and the long tenor asset, housing loans also pose a unique problem – that of the pre-payment option available to its customers. In effect, the bank is selling a put option to the borrower for pre-paying the loan before the end of the term. In case the tendency to prepay such loans is high due to unforeseen economic reasons, the bank is saddled with a complex asset liability mismatch. This risk can be addressed through an amortizing interest rate swap with a "puttable" notional principal. Unfortunately, while pre-payment of loans by the borrower is common place, banks are currently not permitted to enter into swaps with such an embedded option. In developed markets, the same would be possible and is illustrated below.

Let us suppose the bank has a housing loan book of INR 200 crores maturing in 10 years. Principal of the loans is repayable in equal instalments annually. In case the borrower wishes to prepay the loan, there would be a penalty as per the following schedule:

Years	*Prepayment penalty*	*Likelihood of prepayment*
Up to 2 years	X_1%	Unlikely
Between 2 and 5 years	X_2%	Low probability
Between year 5 and 7	X_3%	Likely
Between year 7 and 10	X_4%	Highly likely

The bank will enter into a swap in which the principal is equally amortized over the life of the swap. In addition, the bank also has the option to reduce (put) the principal and pays an up front (or deferred) premium for this option-linked to $X_{1\text{-}4}$. In addition, the swap will incorporate other provisions which will align the asset book to the interest rate view of the bank or protect it from adverse changes in interest rates. In effect by entering into this swap, the bank is protecting itself against the prepayment risk which is characteristic of its housing loan portfolio, while also using the swap to hedge against changes in interest rates or crystallizing its interest rates view.

Example 4: Use of Interest Rate Futures to Hedge a Bond Portfolio

A significant component of banks' assets are in sovereign bonds, often far exceeding their mandatory SLR requirements. RBI has permitted the use of exchange traded interest rate futures to allow banks to hedge their exposures arising out of such investments. Futures as a derivative product are similar to forward contracts, except for the following differences:

1. Futures are exchange traded unlike forward contracts which are typically over the counter deals.
2. The mark to market on a futures position is regularly settled (typically daily) as against a forward contract which is settled only on maturity of the contract.
3. Futures involve a clearing house, which maintains and settles margins as and when required.
4. Futures are traded in pre-defined contract sizes and maturity.

Since the banks are long on bonds, they are susceptible to rising interest rates. The bank may effectively hedge the risk of rising interest rates through selling the bond in the futures market. By doing this the bank has effectively created a long position on bonds and a short position on the futures of the same bond. In case the price of the bond in the cash market was to fall, the short position in the futures market would be in the money. Unlike in India, bond futures are extremely popular in most developed markets. There are numerous trading strategies that have been developed by traders, where bond futures are active. FIMMDA is currently, in the process of revamping the regulations governing the futures product in order to enhance its acceptance as a risk management tool.

FUTURE DEVELOPMENTS IN ACCOUNTING AND REPORTING

All companies presenting their books of account under US GAAP adhere to FAS 133 for accounting of derivative contracts, embedded or otherwise. Similarly in response to demands for greater transparency in the accounts of publicly traded companies, the European Commission has proposed that all listed companies in a regulated market prepare accounts to comply with International Accounting Standard (IAS) 39 "Financial Instruments: Recognition and Measurement" by 2005. Going forward we envisage convergence of accounting norms to the essence of IAS39/FAS133 which is the fair value representation of assets and liabilities. Sooner rather than later we expect similar guidance from local accounting standards.

Both IAS 39 and FAS 133 require all derivatives to be measured at fair value on the balance sheet, with changes in fair value being accounted through the profit and loss statement, except for derivatives that qualify as effective hedging instruments. The criteria for hedge-accounting of derivatives is rather stringent.

Compliance to the above standards would produce fundamental changes to the way firms are required to account for a wide range of transactions. Whilst the business operations and decisions to apply particular risk management and business strategies should not be dictated by accounting treatments, it is important to assess how existing practices could be affected by the standard. The new requirements on hedge accounting, classification and measurement of financial assets and liabilities could all have serious implications on the magnitude and nature of derivative usage.

SUMMARY

In this article we have explained the concept of derivatives and their uses in market risk management. We have developed a framework for the implementation of a market risk management strategy. Further we have elaborated through examples, certain means by which banks can use derivative structures to effectively manage market risks arising out of their regular business operations.

In summary, as the markets mature, banks are increasingly using derivative structure, to manage their market risk. Overtime, a number of liquid benchmarks have gained popularity, offering a variety of solutions to banks. However, derivatives must be used only after senior management has reviewed the risks and rewards that stem from these products, and after a thorough analysis of the accountancy involved.

38

Audit of Forex Transactions

K. PARAMESWARAN

In terms of the 'Triennial Central Bank Survey of Foreign Exchange and Derivatives Market Activity for April 2004', published by Bank for International Settlements (BIS) in September 2004, the average daily turnover in traditional forex markets is USD 1.880 trillion. Out of the total turnover, 1.5 per cent represents trade related transactions, 0.5 per cent represents miscellaneous transfers and 8 per cent represents Capital transfers. Remaining 90 per cent transactions represent trading. Considering the volume of turnover under trading, any country's foreign exchange reserve can be traded in the foreign exchange market within few minutes. This is the only market, which never sleeps, shifting to different centres through out.

Under such situations, the responsibility of any Central Bank will be to regulate the inflows and outflows of foreign exchange through proper legislations. FEMA 1999 was introduced in our country for the purpose of 'facilitating external trade and payment and for promoting the orderly development and management of foreign exchange market in India.' Features of FEMA 1999 are: Freeing of current account transactions, permitting identified capital account transactions and delegating more powers to Authorised Dealers (ADs) for independently handling transactions on verifying proper documents. Under such liberalised environment an efficient audit system will help the Central Bank and the Authorised Dealers to ascertain the impact of liberalisation and also to monitor compliance of prescribed regulations.

Role of an Auditor in Forex Audit will be to—

- Ensure that regulatory provisions are complied with.
- Detect revenue leakages wherever credit facilities are extended.
- Ensure compliance of bank specific policies/guidelines.
- Prevent recurrence of frauds by checking the existing systems so that the top management is able to capture the details of frauds in time and will be in a position to review their corporate policy for introducing appropriate preventive measures.

REGULATIONS/GUIDELINES RELATED TO FOREX TRANSACTIONS

- FEMA 1999 – Notifications issued by Reserve Bank and Rules framed by Government of India.
- Guidelines issued by IECD/DBOD/DBOS/FED of the Reserve Bank.
- Foreign Trade (Development and Regulation) Act, 1992.
- Foreign Trade Policy, 2004-09.
- Foreign Contribution Regulation Act, 1976.
- The Conservation of Foreign Exchange and Prevention of Smuggling Activities Act, 1974.
- Uniform Customs and Practice for Documentary Credits (UCPDC ICC 500).
- FEDAI Rules.
- SEBI guidelines.

Forex audit will cover the following areas:

- Trade Services.
- Export transactions.
  - (1) Fund-based facilities.
  - (2) Pre- and Post-shipment Finance.
  - (3) Non-Fund-based facilities.
  - (4) Export Guarantees.
- Import transactions:
  - (1) Non-Fund-based facilities.
  - (2) Issuing Letters of Credit, Guarantees and Standby Credits – arranging for trade credits and external commercial borrowings.
  - (3) Handling Import collections.
- Remittances.
- Inward remittances.

- Outward remittances.
- Dealing/Treasury operations.

REGULATORY ISSUES

FEMA 1999 on Export of Goods and Services

Section 7 of FEMA 1999 and Notification No. 23 prescribe that exporter should realise full payment for his exports within the prescribed time limit in the prescribed manner. Delay in realisation, realising reduced value or 'write off' of export receivables can now be permitted/ approved by the authorised dealer under their delegated powers. In case of overdue export bills beyond the prescribed time limit, AD is advised to report such transactions to Reserve Bank Audit will ensure whether AD properly monitors the export realisations and/or exercising the delegated authority with due diligence and reports the overdue export bills in time to Reserve Bank.

The audit, therefore, has to cover cases where the appraisal, sanction, documentation, disbursement and the operations in the Export Credit/ non-fund-based transactions to ensure the objectives of audit referred to earlier are fully complied with. The auditor, in particular, has to evaluate the system and procedure prescribed by the bank and whether they are updated and are fully applied to each case. Deviations are to be highlighted in the Audit report with necessary sample of irregularities for an effective follow-up and rectification by the controlling office.

FEMA 1999 on Import of Goods and Services

Value of forex outflow for import of goods and services should be covered equally with matching physical import of goods or services. The time limit within which import payments should be remitted is also prescribed by Reserve Bank. To enable the importers for availing cheaper credit facilities at international market rates, importers are allowed to raise trade credits or external commercial borrowings from recognised overseas sources. Importers are also allowed to remit advance payments. While simplifying the procedures and relaxing most of the regulations, Reserve Bank has prescribed certain conditions to ensure end use. Audit will ensure whether the conditions specified by Reserve Bank for undertaking such transactions are properly complied with by the importers and the ADs. For example, trade credits from overseas source can be availed for import of capital goods, provided the maturity of the loan is less than three years and the rate of interest should not exceed LIBOR plus 1.25 per cent subject to a monetary ceiling of USD 20 mn. equivalent per transaction. Audit will ensure compliance of the prescribed conditions by the importer and the ADs in handling such transactions.

There is a possibility of illegal money transfers routed through trade transactions. Further customers can use the trade route to effect capital transfer. In order to avoid such misutilisation of trade transactions Reserve Bank has advised ADs to implement 'Know Your Customer' (KYC) norms and also due diligence on the overseas seller.

Role of audit will ensure whether AD has complied with the guidelines issued by Reserve Bank while undertaking such import transactions so that genuine transactions are alone carried out.

FEMA on Remittances

Remittances can be for:

- Resident Individuals,
- Resident organizations,
- Resident corporate, and
- Transfer of funds under various schemes meant for FDI/FII/NRIs.

While handling inward remittances, Reserve Bank wants to ensure that such remittances are for genuine purposes only.

For instance, foreign inward remittances for organizations if not monitored properly may be diverted for purposes other than for what it is meant for AD is advised to ensure that the organisation, which receives foreign inward remittance is registered under FCRA, 1976 with Ministry of Home Affairs and such remittances should be handled only by the identified branch of a bank. AD has also fixed with the responsibility of reporting operations in such accounts to Government of India. Audit can check whether organizations, which are receiving foreign inward remittances are properly registered with Government of India and the AD is regular in reporting to Government of India.

In case of remittances by FIIs for investments in securities and stocks it will be of short-term in nature and the flow may have a direct impact on the forex market. Audit can examine whether only registered FIIs are routing their investments and repatriations through the branch authorized to handle such transactions and the reporting is done by the bank to Reserve Bank promptly on daily basis.

Since Non-Resident Indians (NRI) are enjoying full convertibility in certain schemes there are possibilities for ineligible funds getting repatriated out of India through such schemes. NRIs are also enjoying the facilities of repatriating current income, sale proceeds of immovable assets subject to compliance of tax liabilities and certain conditions. Audit may bring out whether the prescribed conditions are fulfilled before handling such remittances since such unauthorized remittances not only are ineligible but also will have an impact on our country's balance of payment.

Regarding outward remittances relating to Travel, Higher Studies, Medical Treatment, Emigration, etc., Reserve Bank has simplified the procedures. Audit can bring out whether such relaxations and simplification of procedures are extended to residents by the ADs.

REVENUE LEAKAGES

With the deregulation of interest rates and free pricing of products, banks are having their own guidelines on such issues. Most of the banks are following their own rating system on their borrowers and such ratings are used as the base for fixing the interest rates and pricing of their products. Audit may check whether the parameters fixed for rating of the borrower is properly arrived at. To enable the exporters to quote their price more competitively in the International market, Reserve Bank has allowed more flexibility for the banks to offer export credit facilities at comparatively cheaper interest rates. Export finance is a purpose-oriented advance and ultimately export should take place to enable the exporter to avail credit facilities at concessional rate of interest. If the exporter could not complete his export obligation the entire credit facility losses concessional rate of interest and will be treated as commercial advance.

If the advance becomes overdue, such overdue advances are not eligible for concessional rate of interest for the overdue period. All such guidelines are for promoting exports and also to fulfil the export obligations by the exporter in time.

AUDIT SHOULD CHECK THE FOLLOWING

- The credit rating system and the relevant parameters fixed by the bank for rating a customer;
- The maximum period of advance eligible for concessional rate of interest;
- The mode of liquidation of such advances either with export documents or with local funds;
- Recovery of overdue interest/commercial interest wherever the advance becomes overdue/liquidated with local funds;
- In case of export bills purchased/discounted/negotiated by the bank, if the payment is not realized on the notional due date, AD should crystallize exporters foreign exchange liability on the 30th day after the expiry of Normal Transit Period in case of unpaid DP bills and 30th day after notional due date in case of DA bills at market TT Selling Rate ruling on the day of crystallization or the original bills buying rate whichever is higher;
- Scrutiny of such transaction may enable the Auditor to identify any diversification of funds for local commercial operations;
- In case of import bills drawn under letter of credit transactions, AD should recover interest from the importer from the date of debit in their nostro account; and
- In case of import bills drawn at sight under letter of credit, if not paid by the importer within 10 days from date of receipt of the bill (DP bills) the forex exposure to be crystallised. And in case of usance bills if not paid on due date the forex exposure should be crystallised on the due date.

BANK SPECIFIC ISSUES

Each bank will have their own corporate credit and forex policy approved by their board. This policy will specify the thrust areas for credit deployment and guidelines for risk management. For example, certain banks will be more cautious in extending credit facilities to diamond exports, software exports, etc. Some of the issues that will be addressed in the policy are:

(i) Organization chart and line of command.

(ii) Limits fixed at different levels for faster credit decisions.
(iii) Pricing.
(iv) Reporting system.
(v) Review process.
(vi) Exceptions.

To quote certain illustrations, bank at its own discretion may cover the default of the exporter at pre and post-shipment stage with ECGC through a guarantee scheme. If a bank has not opted for such guarantee scheme with ECGC, bank may advise their exporters to cover themselves with ECGC under appropriate specific buyer-wise policy.

Dealing room operations are exposed to highly volatile, vibrant forex market movements. Reported incident of a dealer who has taken a huge exposure resulting in liquidation of an established 125 years old bank is on record. In this referred case, it was pointed out that the bank was not having a proper 'Risk Management Policy'. Auditing of dealing room and treasury operations are of different nature. In this regard Reserve Bank has issued an 'Internal Control Guidelines' specifying certain general check points. On the basis of broad guidelines issued by Reserve Bank and also with the present changes, bank's 'Risk Management Policy' should cover the following areas:

- Market Risk,
- Credit Risk,
- Liquidity Risk, and
- Operations Risk.

Some of the issues that should be looked into while auditing such transactions are:

- Limit fixed for 'intra day' trading and 'over night' exposures—currency-wise for the dealer.
- Fixing review standards, indicating methodology for calculation and validating market risk models.
- Exceptions.
- Fixing limits for counter party exposures.
- Monitoring the gaps and funding plans.
- Operations risk consisting of procedures, reporting system, capturing transactions, reconciliation, valuation, payment of brokerage and disaster recovery system.

- Compliance of Accounting Standards (AS 11, IAS 39, FASB, GAAP norms).

PREVENTIVE VIGILANCE

Audit can bring out the deficiencies, if any, in the systems, the time interval in capturing the occurrence of a fraud and the time taken for the reviewing authority/board in getting the report and examining the fraud and the remedial measures to avoid such recurrence in future.

CONCLUSION

To conclude, the impact of irregularities in forex transactions can have greater consequences affecting initially the bank's financial position and later on country's reserve and destabilize the economic growth. With the help of an efficient audit system Bank will be in a position to take corrective measures at the appropriate time and also will be able to contribute to establish a robust economy.

Index